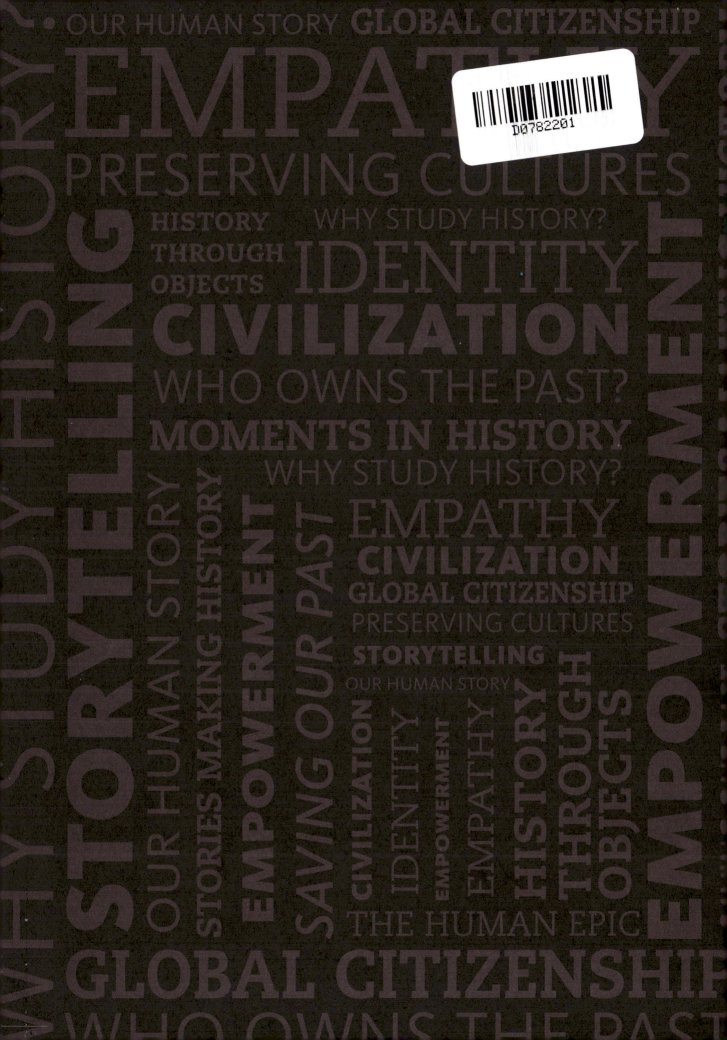

WHY? · OUR HUMAN STORY GLOBAL CITIZENSHIP
EMPATHY
PRESERVING CULTURES
HISTORY   WHY STUDY HISTORY?
THROUGH   IDENTITY
OBJECTS
CIVILIZATION
WHO OWNS THE PAST?
MOMENTS IN HISTORY
WHY STUDY HISTORY?
EMPATHY
CIVILIZATION
GLOBAL CITIZENSHIP
PRESERVING CULTURES
STORYTELLING
OUR HUMAN STORY
THE HUMAN EPIC
GLOBAL CITIZENSHIP
WHO OWNS THE PAST

THE HUMAN EPIC GLOBAL CITIZENSHIP

STORYTELLING

WHY STUDY HISTORY? EMPATHY

IDENTITY CIVILIZATION

STORIES MAKING HISTORY

EMPOWERMENT

SAVING OUR PAST

EMPATHY

HISTORY THROUGH OBJECTS

EMPOWERMENT
PRESERVING CULTURES
SAVING OUR PAST
WHY STUDY HISTORY?
GLOBAL CITIZENSHIP
IDENTITY
THE HUMAN EPIC
STORYTELLING
OUR HUMAN STORY

CIVILIZATION

PRESERVING CULTURES

GLOBAL CITIZENSHIP

PRESERVING CULTURES

EMPATHY

OUR HUMAN STORY

CIVILIZATION THE HUMAN EPIC

WHO OWNS THE PAST?

STORIES MAKING HISTORY

EMPOWERMENT

GLOBAL CITIZENSHIP

SAVING OUR PAST

EMPOWERMENT

MOMENTS IN HISTORY

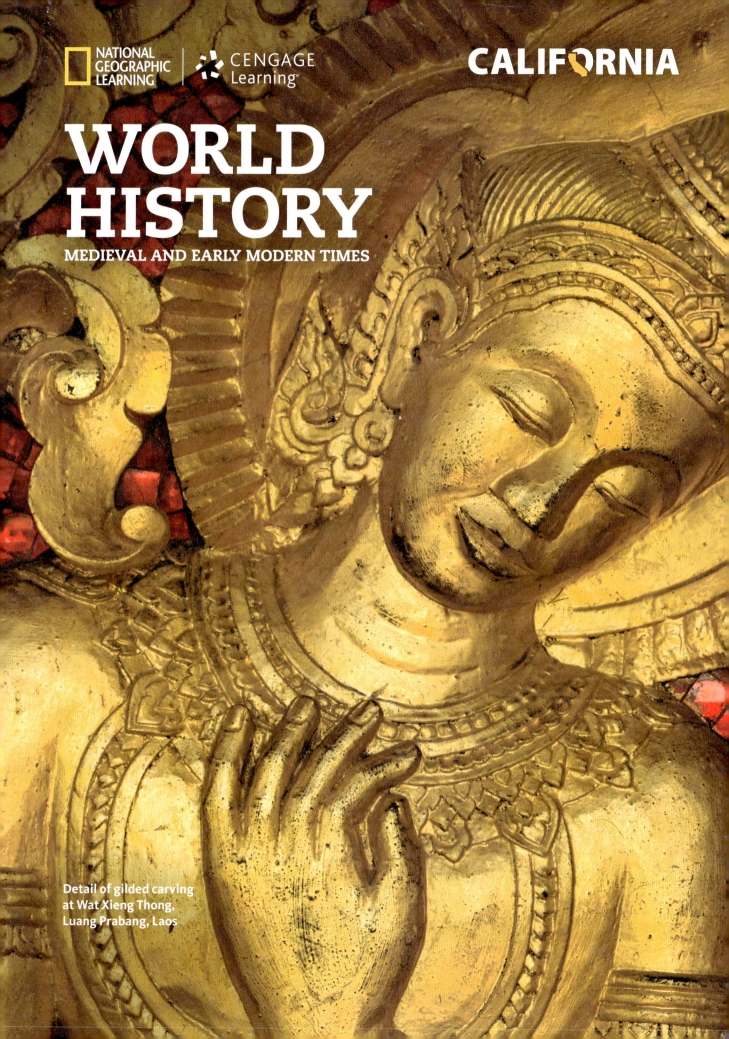

NATIONAL GEOGRAPHIC LEARNING | CENGAGE Learning

CALIFORNIA

WORLD HISTORY

MEDIEVAL AND EARLY MODERN TIMES

Detail of gilded carving
at Wat Xieng Thong,
Luang Prabang, Laos

Acknowledgments

Grateful acknowledgment is given to the authors, artists, photographers, museums, publishers, and agents for permission to reprint copyrighted material. Every effort has been made to secure the appropriate permission. If any omissions have been made or if corrections are required, please contact the Publisher.

Photographic Credits
Front Cover: ©Michael Melford /National Geographic Creative

Acknowledgments and credits continue on page R23.

"National Geographic", "National Geographic Society" and the Yellow Border Design are registered trademarks of the National Geographic Society ® Marcas Registradas

For product information and technology assistance, contact us at Customer & Sales Support, 888-915-3276

For permission to use material from this text or product, submit all requests online at **www.cengage.com/permissions**

Further permissions questions can be emailed to **permissionrequest@cengage.com**

National Geographic Learning | Cengage Learning
1 N. State Street, Suite 900
Chicago, IL 60602

Cengage Learning is a leading provider of customized learning solutions with office locations around the globe, including Singapore, the United Kingdom, Australia, Mexico, Brazil, and Japan. Locate your local office at **www.cengage.com/global.**

Visit National Geographic Learning online at **NGL.Cengage.com**

Visit our corporate website at **www.cengage.com**

ISBN: 978-13371-10808

Printed in the United States of America

Print Number: 04
Print Year: 2018

PROGRAM CONSULTANTS

Fredrik Hiebert

Dr. Fred Hiebert is a National Geographic Explorer and Archaeology Fellow. He has led archaeological expeditions at ancient Silk Roads sites across Asia and underwater in the Black Sea. Hiebert rediscovered the lost Bactrian gold in Afghanistan in 2004 and was curator of National Geographic's exhibition *Afghanistan: Hidden Treasures from the National Museum, Kabul*, which toured museums throughout the world. Hiebert curated National Geographic's exhibition *Peruvian Gold: Ancient Treasures Unearthed* and, most recently, the exhibition *The Greeks: Agamemnon to Alexander the Great*.

Christopher P. Thornton

Dr. Chris Thornton is the Lead Program Officer of Research, Conservation, and Exploration at the National Geographic Society, and Director of the UNESCO World Heritage Site of Bat in the Sultanate of Oman. Thornton works closely with NGS media to promote grantees and other scientists, overseeing research grants in anthropology, archaeology, astronomy, geography, geology, and paleontology. He also manages the Society's relationship with academic conferences around the world.

Jeremy McInerney

Dr. Jeremy McInerney is chairman of the Department of Classical Studies at the University of Pennsylvania. McInerney recently spent a year as Whitehead Professor in the American School of Classical Studies in Athens, Greece. He has excavated at Corinth, on Crete, and in Israel. Author of *The Cattle of the Sun: Cows and Culture in the World of the Ancient Greeks* (2010), McInerney has received top teaching awards, including the Lindback Award for Distinguished Teaching.

PROGRAM CONSULTANTS

Michael W. Smith

Dr. Michael Smith is the Associate Dean for Faculty Development and Academic Affairs in the College of Education at Temple University. He became a college teacher after 11 years of teaching high school English. His research focuses on how experienced readers read and talk about texts, as well as what motivates adolescents' reading and writing. Smith has written many books and monographs, including the award-winning *"Reading Don't Fix No Chevys": Literacy in the Lives of Young Men*.

Peggy Altoff

Peggy Altoff's long career includes teaching middle school and high school students, supervising teachers, and serving as adjunct university faculty. Peggy served as a state social studies specialist in Maryland and as a K–12 coordinator in Colorado Springs. She was president of the National Council for the Social Studies (NCSS) in 2006–2007 and was on the task force for the 2012 NCSS National Curriculum Standards.

David W. Moore

Dr. David Moore is a Professor Emeritus of Education at Arizona State University. He taught high school social studies and reading before entering college teaching. His noteworthy co-authored publications include the *Handbook of Reading Research* chapter on secondary school reading, the first International Reading Association position statement on adolescent literacy, and *Developing Readers and Writers in the Content Areas (6e)*.

PROGRAM WRITER

Special thanks to Jon Heggie for his extensive contributions to *National Geographic World History: Medieval and Early Modern Times*. Heggie became fascinated with history as a small child, a passion nurtured by his parents and educators. He studied history at Oxford University and received his Post Graduate Certificate in Education from Bristol University. Heggie has taught English and History at a number of schools in the UK and has written for *National Geographic* magazine for the past ten years. He is currently working on a number of history projects and serving as the editor of the recently launched National Geographic *History* magazine.

REVIEWERS OF RELIGIOUS CONTENT

The following individuals reviewed the treatment of religious content in selected pages of the text.

Dr. Charles C. Haynes
Director, Religious Freedom
Center of the Newseum Institute
Washington, D.C.

Munir Shaikh
Institute on Religion and
Civic Values
Fountain Valley, California

NATIONAL GEOGRAPHIC SOCIETY

The National Geographic Society contributed significantly to *National Geographic World History: Medieval and Early Modern Times*. Our collaboration with each of the following has been a pleasure and a privilege: National Geographic Maps, National Geographic Education and Children's Media, National Geographic Missions programs, and National Geographic Studios. We thank the Society for its guidance and support.

We BELIEVE in the power of science, exploration, and storytelling to change the world.

UNIT EXPLORERS

Each unit in this book opens and closes with a National Geographic Explorer discussing the content presented in the unit and explaining his or her own related work in the field. Within the Student eEdition, you can watch video footage of each Unit Explorer "on location" to expand and enhance your world history learning experience.

Christopher DeCorse
Archaeologist
National Geographic
Grantee

Francisco Estrada-Belli
Archaeologist
National Geographic
Grantee

Fredrik Hiebert
Archaeologist
National Geographic
Fellow

Albert Lin
Research Scientist/Engineer
National Geographic
Emerging Explorer

Jodi Magness
Archaeologist
National Geographic
Grantee

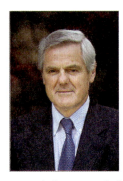

Maurizio Seracini
Cultural Heritage
Engineer
National Geographic
Fellow

CHAPTER AND FEATURED EXPLORERS

In the chapters of this book and throughout the Student eEdition, National Geographic Explorers tell the story of their work as it relates to the time in history you're learning about. Archaeologists, photographers, and writers explain their historical and cultural findings and the process involved in making the important discoveries that help us understand more about the past—and the future.

Caroline Alexander
National Geographic
Writer/Journalist

Nicole Boivin
Archaeologist
National Geographic
Grantee

Steve Boyes
Conservation Biologist
National Geographic
Emerging Explorer

Christine Lee
Bio-Archaeologist
National Geographic
Emerging Explorer

Thomas Parker
Archaeologist
National Geographic
Grantee

Matt Piscitelli
Archaeologist
National Geographic
Grantee

Max Salomon
National Geographic
Producer

William Saturno
Archaeologist
National Geographic
Grantee

Anna Secor
Political Geographer
National Geographic
Grantee

Shah Selbe
Conservation Technologist
National Geographic
Emerging Explorer

Simon Worrall
National Geographic
Writer

Xiaobai Angela Yao
Geographer
National Geographic
Grantee

Dave Yoder
Photojournalist
National Geographic
Grantee

UNIT 1

ROMAN, BYZANTINE AND ISLAMIC CIVILIZATIONS

(31 B.C.—A.D. 1858)

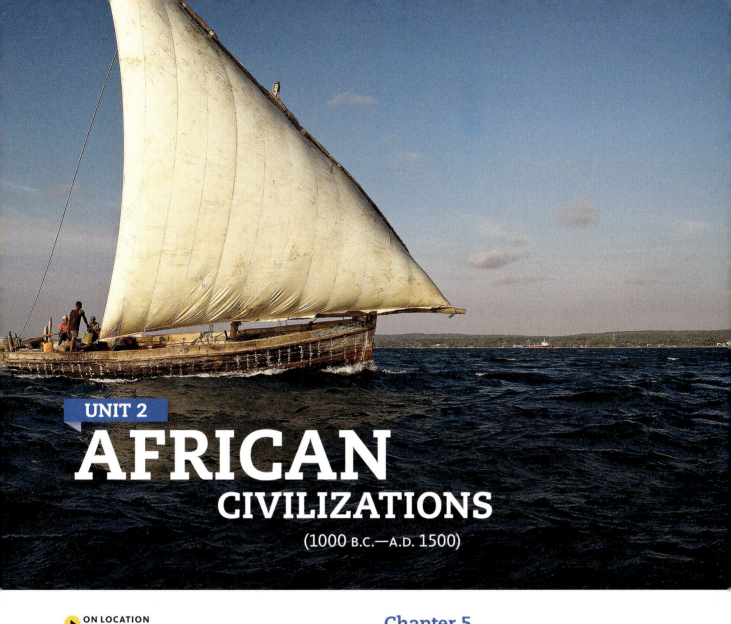

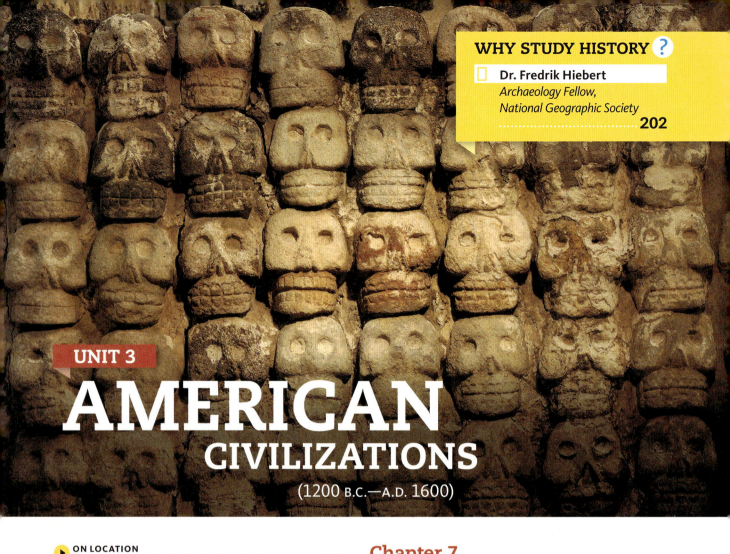

WHY STUDY HISTORY ❓

▢ **Dr. Fredrik Hiebert**
Archaeology Fellow,
National Geographic Society
.... **202**

UNIT 3

AMERICAN
CIVILIZATIONS

(1200 B.C.—A.D. 1600)

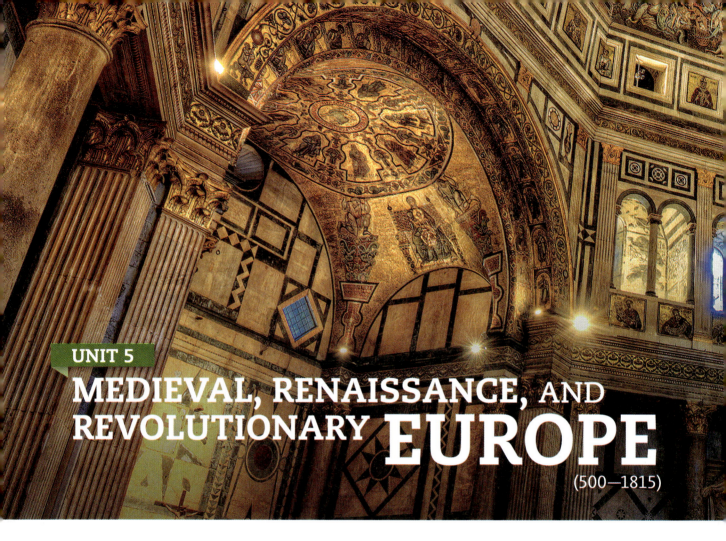

UNIT 5
MEDIEVAL, RENAISSANCE, AND REVOLUTIONARY EUROPE
(500—1815)

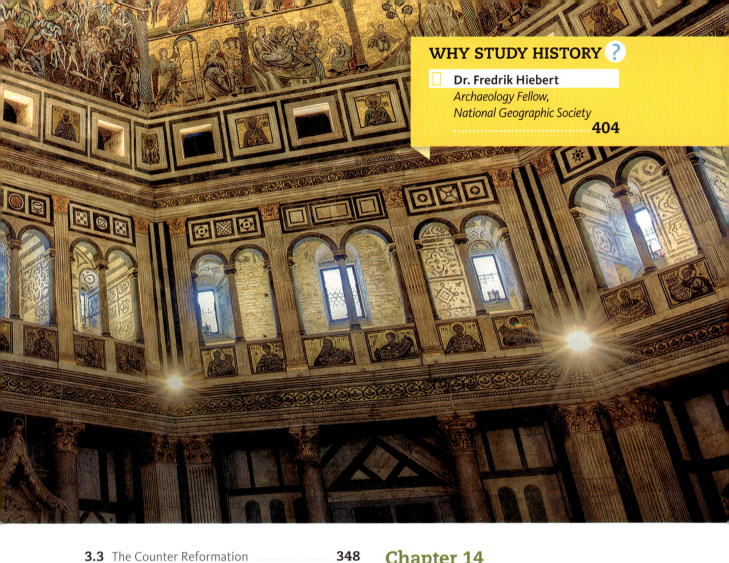

The world changes on a daily basis, and National Geographic is there. Join three National Geographic voices as they tell the stories of three current global events. Learn about these newsworthy topics, discuss what might come next, and think about how these events impact you, the place you live, and the people you know—your global citizenship.

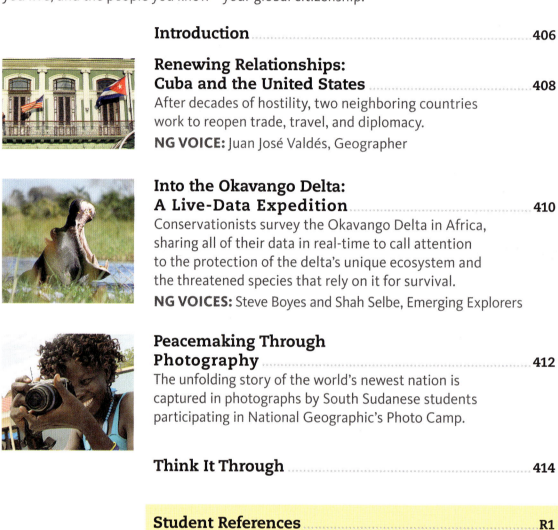

SPECIAL FEATURES

DOCUMENT-BASED QUESTIONS

TIME LINES, CHARTS, MODELS, GRAPHS, INFOGRAPHICS

MOMENTS IN HISTORY

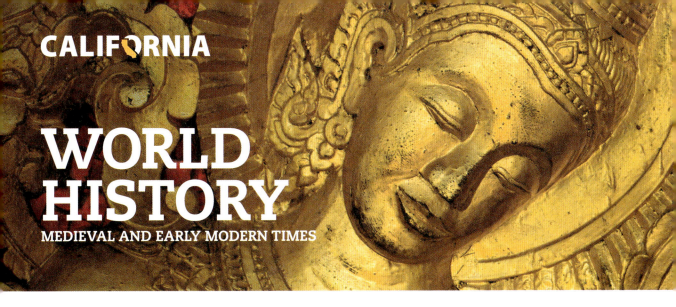

WORLD HISTORY
MEDIEVAL AND EARLY MODERN TIMES

History–Social Science Content Standards and California Common Core State Standards
Grade 7

HSS Correlations

CA CCSS Correlations

History-Social Science
Content Standards

GRADE 7 CONTENT STANDARDS

STANDARD	STUDENT EDITION
7.1 Students analyze the causes and effects of the vast expansion and ultimate disintegration of the Roman Empire.	
7.1.1 Study the early strengths and lasting contributions of Rome (e.g., significance of Roman citizenship; rights under Roman law; Roman art, architecture, engineering, and philosophy; preservation and transmission of Christianity) and its ultimate internal weaknesses (e.g., rise of autonomous military powers within the empire, undermining of citizenship by the growth of corruption and slavery, lack of education, and distribution of news).	14–15, 16–17, 18–19, 20–21, 22–23, 24–25, 26–27, 30–31, 32–33, 38, 39
7.1.2 Discuss the geographic borders of the empire at its height and the factors that threatened its territorial cohesion.	16–17, 32–33, 38, 39
7.1.3 Describe the establishment by Constantine of the new capital in Constantinople and the development of the Byzantine Empire, with an emphasis on the consequences of the development of two distinct European civilizations, Eastern Orthodox and Roman Catholic, and their two distinct views on church-state relations.	34–35, 38, 42–43, 44–45, 48–49, 50–51, 54–55, 56, 57
7.2 Students analyze the geographic, political, economic, religious, and social structures of the civilizations of Islam in the Middle Ages.	
7.2.1 Identify the physical features and describe the climate of the Arabian peninsula, its relationship to surrounding bodies of land and water, and nomadic and sedentary ways of life.	60–61
7.2.2 Trace the origins of Islam and the life and teachings of Muhammad, including Islamic teachings on the connection with Judaism and Christianity.	62–63, 64–65, 88, 89
7.2.3 Explain the significance of the Qur'an and the Sunnah as the primary sources of Islamic beliefs, practice, and law, and their influence in Muslims' daily life.	64–65, 66–67
7.2.4 Discuss the expansion of Muslim rule through military conquests and treaties, emphasizing the cultural blending within Muslim civilization and the spread and acceptance of Islam and the Arabic language.	68–69, 70–71, 72–73, 76–77, 78–79, 88, 271
7.2.5 Describe the growth of cities and the establishment of trade routes among Asia, Africa, and Europe, the products and inventions that traveled along these routes (e.g., spices, textiles, paper, steel, new crops), and the role of merchants in Arab society.	60–61, 104–105, 108–109, 114–115, 126–127, 128–129, 136
7.2.6 Understand the intellectual exchanges among Muslim scholars of Eurasia and Africa and the contributions Muslim scholars made to later civilizations in the areas of science, geography, mathematics, philosophy, medicine, art, and literature.	74–75, 80–81, 82–83, 84–85, 86–87, 88, 89, 114–115
7.3 Students analyze the geographic, political, economic, religious, and social structures of the civilizations of China in the Middle Ages.	
7.3.1 Describe the reunification of China under the Tang Dynasty and reasons for the spread of Buddhism in Tang China, Korea, and Japan.	212–213, 214–215, 216, 250
7.3.2 Describe agricultural, technological, and commercial developments during the Tang and Sung periods.	216–217, 218–219
7.3.3 Analyze the influences of Confucianism and changes in Confucian thought during the Sung and Mongol periods.	222, 234

STANDARD	STUDENT EDITION
7.3.4 Understand the importance of both overland trade and maritime expeditions between China and other civilizations in the Mongol Ascendancy and Ming Dynasty.	224–225, 228–229, 234
7.3.5 Trace the historic influence of such discoveries as tea, the manufacture of paper, wood-block printing, the compass, and gunpowder.	218–219, 234
7.3.6 Describe the development of the imperial state and the scholar-official class.	216, 226–227
7.4 Students analyze the geographic, political, economic, religious, and social structures of the sub-Saharan civilizations of Ghana and Mali in Medieval Africa.	
7.4.1 Study the Niger River and the relationship of vegetation zones of forest, savannah, and desert to trade in gold, salt, food, and slaves; and the growth of the Ghana and Mali empires.	102–103, 104–105, 106–107, 112–113, 114–115, 120
7.4.2 Analyze the importance of family, labor specialization, and regional commerce in the development of states and cities in West Africa.	112–113
7.4.3 Describe the role of the trans-Saharan caravan trade in the changing religious and cultural characteristics of West Africa and the influence of Islamic beliefs, ethics, and law.	104–105, 106–107, 108–109, 112–113, 120
7.4.4 Trace the growth of the Arabic language in government, trade, and Islamic scholarship in West Africa.	108–109, 112–113, 114–115
7.4.5 Describe the importance of written and oral traditions in the transmission of African history and culture.	116–117, 118–119, 120
7.5 Students analyze the geographic, political, economic, religious, and social structures of the civilizations of Medieval Japan.	
7.5.1 Describe the significance of Japan's proximity to China and Korea and the intellectual, linguistic, religious, and philosophical influence of those countries on Japan.	238, 243, 244–245, 258
7.5.2 Discuss the reign of Prince Shotoku of Japan and the characteristics of Japanese society and family life during his reign.	242–243, 259
7.5.3 Describe the values, social customs, and traditions prescribed by the lord-vassal system consisting of shogun, daimyo, and samurai and the lasting influence of the warrior code in the twentieth century.	252–253, 254–255, 258, 259
7.5.4 Trace the development of distinctive forms of Japanese Buddhism.	250–251
7.5.5 Study the ninth and tenth centuries' golden age of literature, art, and drama and its lasting effects on culture today, including Murasaki Shikibu's Tale of Genji.	246–247, 248–249, 258, 259
7.5.6 Analyze the rise of a military society in the late twelfth century and the role of the samurai in that society.	253, 256
7.6 Students analyze the geographic, political, economic, religious, and social structures of the civilizations of Medieval Europe.	
7.6.1 Study the geography of the Europe and the Eurasian land mass, including its location, topography, waterways, vegetation, and climate and their relationship to ways of life in Medieval Europe.	294–295
7.6.2 Describe the spread of Christianity north of the Alps and the roles played by the early church and by monasteries in its diffusion after the fall of the western half of the Roman Empire.	294–295, 297, 299

STANDARD	STUDENT EDITION
7.6.3 Understand the development of feudalism, its role in the medieval European economy, the way in which it was influenced by physical geography (the role of the manor and the growth of towns), and how feudal relationships provided the foundation of political order.	300–301, 304–305, 318–319, 320, 321
7.6.4 Demonstrate an understanding of the conflict and cooperation between the Papacy and European monarchs (e.g., Charlemagne, Gregory VII, Emperor Henry IV).	296–297, 306–307, 320, 321
7.6.5 Know the significance of developments in medieval English legal and constitutional practices and their importance in the rise of modern democratic thought and representative institutions (e.g., Magna Carta, parliament, development of habeas corpus, an independent judiciary in England).	308–309, 310–311, 320
7.6.6 Discuss the causes and course of the religious Crusades and their effects on the Christian, Muslim, and Jewish populations in Europe, with emphasis on the increasing contact by Europeans with cultures of the Eastern Mediterranean world.	312–313, 320
7.6.7 Map the spread of the bubonic plague from Central Asia to China, the Middle East, and Europe and describe its impact on global population.	314–315, 316–317, 320
7.6.8 Understand the importance of the Catholic church as a political, intellectual, and aesthetic institution (e.g., founding of universities, political and spiritual roles of the clergy, creation of monastic and mendicant religious orders, preservation of the Latin language and religious texts. St. Thomas Aquinas's synthesis of classical philosophy with Christian theology, and the concept of "natural law").	306–307
7.6.9 Know the history of the decline of Muslim rule in the Iberian Peninsula that culminated in the Reconquista and the rise of Spanish and Portuguese kingdoms.	73, 312–313
7.7 Students compare and contrast the geographic, political, economic, religious, and social structures of the Meso-American and Andean civilizations.	
7.7.1 Study the locations, landforms, and climates of Mexico, Central America, and South America and their effects on Mayan, Aztec, and Incan economies, trade, and development of urban societies.	150–151, 154–155, 156–157, 166–167, 176–177, 180–181, 196
7.7.2 Study the roles of people in each society, including class structures, family life, warfare, religious beliefs and practices, and slavery.	152–153, 154–155, 156–157, 158–159, 168–169, 172, 180
7.7.3 Explain how and where each empire arose and how the Aztec and Incan empires were defeated by the Spanish.	156–157, 166–167, 170–171, 180, 184–185, 196, 372–373
7.7.4 Describe the artistic and oral traditions and architecture in the three civilizations.	158, 160–161, 164–165, 168–169, 172, 173, 178–179, 182–183, 196, 197
7.7.5 Describe the Meso-American achievements in astronomy and mathematics, including the development of the calendar and the Meso-American knowledge of seasonal changes to the civilizations' agricultural systems.	162–163, 172
7.8 Students analyze the origins, accomplishments, and geographic diffusion of the Renaissance.	
7.8.1 Describe the way in which the revival of classical learning and the arts fostered a new interest in humanism (i.e., a balance between intellect and religious faith).	324–325, 352
7.8.2 Explain the importance of Florence in the early stages of the Renaissance and the growth of independent trading cities (e.g., Venice), with emphasis on the cities' importance in the spread of Renaissance ideas.	324–325, 330–331, 336–337, 352

STANDARD	STUDENT EDITION
7.8.3 Understand the effects of the reopining of the ancient "Silk Road" between Europe and China, including Marco Polo's travels and the location of his routes.	224–225, 324
7.8.4 Describe the growth and effects of new ways of disseminating information (e.g., the ability to manufacture paper, translation of the Bible into the vernacular, printing).	326–327, 340–341
7.8.5 Detail advances made in literature, the arts, science, mathematics, cartography, engineering, and the understanding of human anatomy and astronomy (e.g., by Dante Alighieri, Leonardo da Vinci, Michelangelo di Buonarroti Simoni, Johann Gutenberg, William Shakespeare).	324–325, 326–327, 328–329, 332–333, 336–337, 338–339, 342–343, 352, 353
7.9 Students analyze the historical developments of the Reformation.	
7.9.1 List the causes for the internal turmoil in and weakening of the Catholic church (e.g., tax policies, selling of indulgences).	344–345, 346–347
7.9.2 Describe the theological, political, and economic ideas of the major figures during the Reformation (e.g., Desiderius Erasmus, Martin Luther, John Calvin, William Tyndale).	336–337, 344–345, 346–347
7.9.3 Explain Protestants' new practices of church self-government and the influence of those practices on the development of democratic practices and ideas of federalism.	350–351
7.9.4 Identify and locate the European regions that remained Catholic and those that became Protestant and explain how the division affected the distribution of religions in the New World.	290–291
7.9.5 Analyze how the Counter-Reformation revitalized the Catholic church and the forces that fostered the movement (e.g., St. Ignatius of Loyola and the Jesuits, the Council of Trent).	348–349, 352
7.9.6 Understand the institution and impact of missionaries on Christianity and the diffusion of Christianity from Europe to other parts of the world in the medieval and early modern periods; locate missions on a world map.	349
7.9.7 Describe the Golden Age of cooperation between Jews and Muslims in medieval Spain that promoted creativity in art, literature, and science, including how that cooperation was terminated by the religious persecution of individuals and groups (e.g., the Spanish Inquisition and the expulsion of Jews and Muslims from Spain in 1492).	73, 312
7.10 Students analyze the historical developments of the Scientific Revolution and its lasting effect on religious, political, and cultural institutions.	
7.10.1 Discuss the roots of the Scientific Revolution (e.g., Greek rationalism; Jewish, Christian, and Muslim science; Renaissance humanism; new knowledge from global exploration).	356–357, 378
7.10.2 Understand the significance of the new scientific theories (e.g., those of Copernicus, Galileo, Kepler, Newton) and the significance of new inventions (e.t., the telescope, microscope, thermometer, barometer).	358–359, 378, 379
7.10.3 Understand the scientific method advanced by Bacon and Descartes, the influence of new scientific rationalism on the growth of democratic ideas, and the coexistence of science with traditional religious beliefs.	360–361, 378

STANDARD	STUDENT EDITION
7.11 Students analyze political and economic change in the sixteenth, seventeenth, and eighteenth centuries (the Age of Exploration, the Enlightenment, and the Age of Reason).	
7.11.1 Know the great voyages of discovery, the locations of the routes, and the influence of cartography in the development of a new European worldview.	362–363, 364–365, 366–367, 369, 378
7.11.2 Discuss the exchanges of plants, animals, technology, culture, and ideas among Europe, Africa, Asia, and the Americas in the fifteenth and sixteenth centuries and the major economic and social effects on each continent.	370–371, 378
7.11.3 Examine the origins of modern capitalism; the influence of mercantilism and cottage industry; the elements and importance of a market economy in a seventeenth-century Europe; the changing international trading and marketing patterns, including their locations on a world map; and the influence of explorers and map makers.	374–375, 376–377, 378, 379, 384
7.11.4 Explain how the main ideas of the Enlightenment can be traced back to such movements as the Renaissance, the Reformation, and the Scientific Revolution and to the Greeks, Romans, and Christianity.	382–383
7.11.5 Describe how democratic thought and institutions were influenced by Enlightenment thinkers (e.g., John Locke, Charles-Louis Montesquieu, American founders).	384–385, 388–389, 396–397, 398, 399
7.11.6 Discuss how the principles in the Magna Carta were embodied in such documents as the English Bill of Rights and the American Declaration of Independence.	310–311, 386, 388–389

HISTORICAL AND SOCIAL SCIENCES ANALYSIS SKILLS

STANDARD	STUDENT EDITION
Chronological and Spatial Thinking	
CST 1 Students explain how major events are related to one another in time.	6–7, 10–11, 12, 25, 38, 96–97, 115, 135, 144–145, 174, 196, 206–207, 215, 231, 234, 288–289, 297, 352
CST 2 Students construct various time lines of key events, people, and periods of the historical era they are studying.	10–11, 12, 38, 174, 196
CST 3 Students use a variety of maps and documents to identify physical and cultural features of neighborhoods, cities, states, and countries and to explain the historical migration of people, expansion and disintegration of empires, and the growth of economic systems.	8–9, 12, 17, 27, 35, 43, 51, 61, 77, 89, 98–99, 105, 113, 121, 125, 127, 131, 137, 146–147, 151, 157, 167, 181, 208–209, 213, 221, 239, 263, 271, 275, 281, 290–291, 295, 313, 345, 362, 371, 379, 399
Research, Evidence, and Point of View	
REP 1 Students frame questions that can be answered by historical study and research.	12, 13, 163, 414
REP 2 Students distinguish fact from opinion in historical narratives and stories.	12, 83, 347, 399
REP 3 Students distinguish relevant from irrelevant information, essential from incidental information, and verifiable from unverifiable information in historical narratives and stories.	12

STANDARD	STUDENT EDITION
REP 4 Students assess the credibility of primary and secondary sources and draw sound conclusions from them.	12, 13, 28–29, 39, 57, 66–67, 89, 118–119, 121, 164–165, 197, 224–225, 235, 248–249, 259, 281, 310–311, 321, 346–347, 353, 368–369, 379, 396–397, 399
REP 5 Students detect the different historical points of view on historical events and determine the context in which the historical statements were made (the questions asked, sources used, author's perspectives).	12, 347
Historical Interpretation	
HI 1 Students explain the central issues and problems from the past, placing people and events in a matrix of time and place.	13, 38, 39, 56, 129, 136, 197, 320, 353, 361, 378, 398
HI 2 Students understand and distinguish cause, effect, sequence, and correlation in historical events, including the long- and short-term causal relations.	13, 23, 33, 37, 40, 43, 55, 56, 61, 63, 69, 81, 88, 103, 107, 111, 115, 120, 122, 135, 136, 172, 191, 217, 219, 227, 234, 239, 241, 257, 267, 280, 309, 315, 319, 341, 351, 365, 375, 378, 383, 387, 395
HI 3 Students explain the sources of historical continuity and how the combination of ideas and events explains the emergence of new patterns.	13, 23, 38, 49, 56, 81, 88, 343, 371, 389, 398
HI 4 Students recognize the role of chance, oversight, and error in history.	13, 369, 377
HI 5 Students recognize that interpretations of history are subject to change as new information is uncovered.	1, 13, 161
HI 6 Students interpret basic indicators of economic performance and conduct cost-benefit analyses of economic and political issues.	13, 16–17, 107, 113, 125, 127, 129, 133, 135, 213, 217, 263, 277, 375, 377

California Common Core
State Standards

READING STANDARDS FOR LITERACY IN HISTORY/SOCIAL STUDIES	
STANDARD	STUDENT EDITION
Key Ideas and Details	
RH.7.1 Cite specific textual evidence to support analysis of primary and secondary sources.	29, 39, 57, 67, 89, 119, 121, 165, 197, 210, 225, 234, 235, 236, 249, 258, 259, 281, 292, 311, 320, 321, 347, 353, 354, 369, 378, 379, 397, 399
RH.7.2 Determine the central ideas or information of a primary or secondary source; provide an accurate summary of the source distinct from prior knowledge or opinions.	29, 39, 57, 58, 67, 89, 119, 121, 148, 165, 197, 225, 235, 249, 259, 281, 311, 321, 347, 369, 379, 397, 399
RH.7.3 Identify key steps in a text's description of a process related to history/social studies (e.g., how a bill becomes law, how interest rates are raised or lowered).	151, 341, 361

STANDARD	STUDENT EDITION
Craft and Structure	
RH.7.4 Determine the meaning of words and phrases as they are used in a text, including vocabulary specific to domains related to history/social studies.	28, 51, 56, 88, 109, 117, 120, 129, 136, 155, 161, 172, 196, 234, 258, 260, 269, 280, 307, 320, 322, 339, 352, 357, 378, 380, 398
RH.7.5 Describe how a text presents information (e.g., sequentially, comparatively, causally).	174, 196
RH.7.6 Identify aspects of a text that reveal an author's point of view or purpose (e.g., loaded language, inclusion or avoidance of particular facts).	100, 109, 117, 120, 129, 161, 249, 307, 322, 352
Integration of Knowledge and Ideas	
RH.7.7 Integrate visual information (e.g., in charts, graphs, photographs, videos, or maps) with other information in print and digital texts.	46–47, 49, 52–53, 74–75, 86–87, 159, 178–179, 184–185, 193, 231, 254–255, 264–265, 302–303, 316–317, 341, 366–367, 392–393
RH.7.8 Distinguish among fact, opinion, and reasoned judgment in a text.	12, 83, 347, 399
RH.7.9 Analyze the relationship between a primary and secondary source on the same topic.	225
Reading and Level of Text Complexity	
RH.7.10 By the end of grade 8, read and comprehend history/social studies texts in the grades 6-8 complexity band independently and proficiently.	The Lexile measure for the Student Edition falls within the stretch band for the California Common Core State Standards.

WRITING STANDARDS FOR LITERACY IN HISTORY/SOCIAL STUDIES, SCIENCE, AND TECHNICAL SUBJECTS

STANDARD	STUDENT EDITION
Text Types and Purposes	

WHST.7.1 Write arguments focused on discipline-specific content.
   a. Introduce claim(s) about a topic or issue, acknowledge and distinguish the claim(s) from alternate or opposing claims, and organize the reasons and evidence logically.
   b. Support claim(s) with logical reasoning and relevant, accurate data and evidence that demonstrate an understanding of the topic or text, using credible sources.
   c. Use words, phrases, and clauses to create cohesion and clarify the relationships among claim(s), counterclaims, reasons, and evidence.
   d. Establish and maintain a formal style.
   e. Provide a concluding statement or section that follows from and supports the argument provided.
	119, 249

STANDARD	STUDENT EDITION

WHST.7.2 Write informative/explanatory texts, including the narration of historical events, scientific procedures/experiments, or technical processes.
  a. Introduce a topic clearly, previewing what is to follow; organize ideas, concepts, and information into broader categories as appropriate to achieving purpose; include formatting (e.g., headings), graphics (e.g., charts, tables), and multimedia when useful to aiding comprehension.
  b. Develop the topic with relevant, well-chosen facts, definitions, concrete details, quotations, or other information and examples.
  c. Use appropriate and varied transitions to create cohesion and clarify the relationships among ideas and concepts.
  d. Use precise language and domain-specific vocabulary to inform about or explain the topic.
  e. Establish and maintain a formal style and objective tone.
  f. Provide a concluding statement or section that follows from and supports the information or explanation presented.
	29, 39, 57, 67, 89, 121, 137, 165, 173, 197, 225, 235, 259, 281, 311, 321, 347, 353, 369, 379, 397, 399

Production and Distribution of Writing

WHST.7.4 Produce clear and coherent writing in which the development, organization, and style are appropriate to task, purpose, and audience.	39, 57, 89, 121, 137, 173, 197, 235, 259, 281, 321, 353, 379, 399
WHST.7.5 With some guidance and support from peers and adults, develop and strengthen writing as needed by planning, revising, editing, rewriting, or trying a new approach, focusing on how well purpose and audience have been addressed.	121, 197, 281, 353
WHST.7.6 Use technology, including the Internet, to produce and publish writing and present the relationships between information and ideas clearly and efficiently.	121, 197, 281, 353

Research to Build and Present Knowledge

WHST.7.7 Conduct short research projects to answer a question (including a self-generated question), drawing on several sources and generating additional related, focused questions that allow for multiple avenues of exploration.	414
WHST.7.8 Gather relevant information from multiple print and digital sources, using search terms effectively; assess the credibility and accuracy of each source; and quote or paraphrase the data and conclusions of others while avoiding plagiarism and following a standard format for citation.	414
WHST.7.9 Draw evidence from informational texts to support analysis, reflection, and research.	39, 57, 89, 121, 137, 173, 197, 235, 259, 281, 321, 353, 379, 399, 414

Range of Writing

WHST.7.10 Write routinely over extended time frames (time for reflection and revision) and shorter time frames (a single sitting or a day or two) for a range of discipline-specific tasks, purposes, and audiences.	29, 39, 57, 67, 89, 119, 121, 137, 165, 173, 197, 225, 235, 249, 259, 281, 311, 321, 347, 353, 369, 379, 397, 399

THE GEOGRAPHER'S TOOLBOX

Geographic Thinking

SPATIAL THINKING

Geography is about more than the names of places on a map. It involves spatial thinking, or thinking about the space on Earth's surface. Geographers use spatial thinking to ask questions, such as:

- Where is a place located?
- Why is this location significant, or important?
- How does this place influence the people who live there?
- How do the people influence the location?

By asking and answering these questions and many others, geographers can find patterns. Geographic patterns are similarities among places. The location of large cities near water is one example of a geographic pattern. Many geographers use computer-based Geographic Information Systems (GIS) to study patterns, such as those that affect population distribution, economic development, the spread of diseases, and water resources. They create maps and analyze their patterns using many layers of data.

The photo below shows the fertile land alongside the Nile River in Egypt. Thousands of years ago, many people settled along this river. They farmed along its shores and traveled and traded on its waters. In time, a great civilization grew in the Nile River Valley: the civilization of ancient Egypt.

Other ancient settlements and civilizations rose in river valleys in many parts of the world. Geographers note this pattern and others when they think spatially.

The Nile River is still a vital resource for present-day Egypt.

THINK LIKE A GEOGRAPHER

Summarize What are geographic patterns, and how do geographers find them?

Geographic Thinking THEMES AND ELEMENTS

Geographers ask questions about how people, places, and environments are arranged and connected on Earth's surface. The five themes and six elements will help you categorize, or group, information.

THE FIVE THEMES OF GEOGRAPHY

Geographers use five themes to categorize similar geographic information.

1. **Location** provides a way of locating places. Absolute location is the exact point where a place is located. Geographers use a satellite system called the Global Positioning System (GPS) to find absolute location. Relative location is where a place is in relation to other places. For example, the Great Wall of China is located near Beijing in northern China.

2. **Place** includes the characteristics of a location. A famous place in the western United States is the Grand Canyon. It has steep rock walls that were carved over centuries by the Colorado River.

3. **Human-Environment Interaction** explains how people affect the environment and how the environment affects people. For example, people throughout much of history have built dams to change the flow of rivers.

4. **Movement** explains how people, ideas, and animals move from one place to another. The spread of different religions around the world is an example of movement.

5. **Region** involves a group of places that have common characteristics. A region can be as big as a continent such as North America, which includes the United States, Canada, and Mexico. A region can also be as small as a neighborhood.

THE SIX ESSENTIAL ELEMENTS

In addition to the five themes, some geographers also identify essential elements, or key ideas, to study physical processes and human systems.

1. **The World in Spatial Terms** Geographers use tools such as maps to study places on Earth's surface.

2. **Places and Regions** Geographers study the characteristics of places and regions.

3. **Physical Systems** Geographers examine Earth's physical processes, such as earthquakes and volcanoes.

4. **Human Systems** Geographers study how humans live and what systems they create, such as economic systems.

5. **Environment and Society** Geographers explore how humans change the environment and use resources.

6. **The Uses of Geography** Geographers interpret the past, analyze the present, and plan for the future.

THINK LIKE A GEOGRAPHER

Make Inferences How do geographers use the themes and elements to better understand the world?

Critical Viewing Tourists climb the Great Wall of China. What physical land features can you see in the photo?

Critical Viewing The Great Wall runs through the Chinese countryside. Which themes and elements does this photo represent?

Geographic Thinking CONTINENTS

In 1413, a Chinese admiral and explorer, Zheng He, sailed from China to Arabia. When he arrived in Arabia, he saw people dressed in ways he had never seen. Yet, like him, these people wanted to trade.

Zheng He came to understand that regions of Earth have similarities and differences. The places within a region are linked by trade, culture, and other human activities. They also share similar physical processes and characteristics, such as climate.

As you've read, a region often contains an entire continent. A continent is a large landmass on Earth's surface. Geographers have identified seven continents: Africa, Asia, Australia, Europe, North America, South America, and Antarctica.

Geographers study the world's continents, but they also take a global perspective when they investigate Earth. They might, for instance, study ocean currents around the globe or how one region affects another. Both ways of looking at the world add to our understanding of it.

THINK LIKE A GEOGRAPHER

Draw Conclusions Why do geographers study the world by dividing it into continents?

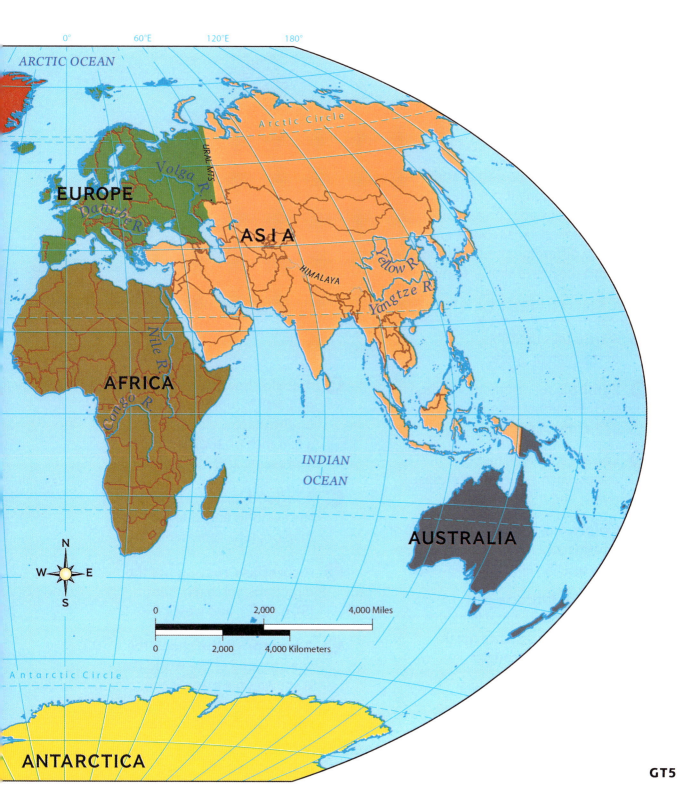

ARCTIC OCEAN

EUROPE

ASIA

AFRICA

AUSTRALIA

ANTARCTICA

INDIAN OCEAN

0°   60°E   120°E   180°

Arctic Circle

URAL MTS.

Volga R.

Danube R.

Nile R.

Congo R.

HIMALAYA

Yellow R.

Yangtze R.

N
W   E
S

0   2,000   4,000 Miles

0   2,000   4,000 Kilometers

Antarctic Circle

Maps ELEMENTS OF A MAP

Have you ever needed to figure out how to get to a friend's house? Maybe you usually use the GPS on your phone to navigate such distances, but imagine that the only resource you had was a globe. In order to see enough detail to find your friend's house, the globe would have to be enormous—much too big to carry around in your pocket!

GLOBES AND MAPS

A three-dimensional, or spherical, representation of Earth is called a globe. It is useful when you need to see Earth as a whole, but it is not helpful if you need to see a small section of Earth.

Now imagine taking a part of the globe and flattening it out. This two-dimensional, or flat, representation of Earth is called a map. Maps and globes are different representations of Earth, but they have similar features.

MAP AND GLOBE FEATURES

A A **title** tells the subject of the map or globe.

B **Symbols** represent information such as natural resources and economic activities.

C **Labels** are the names of places, such as cities, countries, rivers, and mountains.

D **Colors** represent different kinds of information. For example, the color blue usually represents water.

E **Lines of latitude** are imaginary horizontal lines that measure the distance north or south of the equator.

F **Lines of longitude** are imaginary vertical lines that measure the distance east or west of the prime meridian.

A GERMANY'S ECONOMIC ACTIVITY

G A **scale** shows how much distance on Earth is represented by distance on the map or globe. For example, a half inch on the map above represents 100 miles on Earth.

H A **legend,** or key, explains what the symbols and colors on the map or globe represent.

I A **compass rose** shows the directions north (N), south (S), east (E), and west (W).

J A **locator globe** shows the specific area of the world that is shown on a map. The locator globe on the map above shows where Germany is located.

LATITUDE

Lines of latitude are imaginary lines that run east to west, parallel to the equator. The equator is the center line of latitude. Distances north and south of the equator are measured in degrees (°). There are 90 degrees north of the equator and 90 degrees south. The equator is 0°. The latitude of Berlin, Germany, is 52° N, meaning that it is 52 degrees north of the equator.

LONGITUDE

Lines of longitude are imaginary lines that run north to south from the North Pole to the South Pole. They measure distance east or west of the prime meridian. The prime meridian runs through Greenwich, England. It is 0°. There are 180 degrees east of the prime meridian and 180 degrees west. The longitude of Berlin, Germany, is 13° E, meaning that it is 13 degrees east of the prime meridian.

Remember that absolute location is the exact point where a place is located. This point includes a place's latitude and longitude. For example, the absolute location of Berlin, Germany, is 52° N, 13° E. You say this aloud as "fifty-two degrees North, thirteen degrees East."

HEMISPHERES

A hemisphere is half of Earth. The equator divides Earth into the Northern Hemisphere and the Southern Hemisphere. North America is entirely in the Northern Hemisphere. Most of South America is in the Southern Hemisphere.

The Western Hemisphere is west of the prime meridian. The Eastern Hemisphere is east of the prime meridian. South America is in the Western Hemisphere. Most of Africa is in the Eastern Hemisphere.

THINK LIKE A GEOGRAPHER

Monitor Comprehension How are maps and globes different? How is each one used?

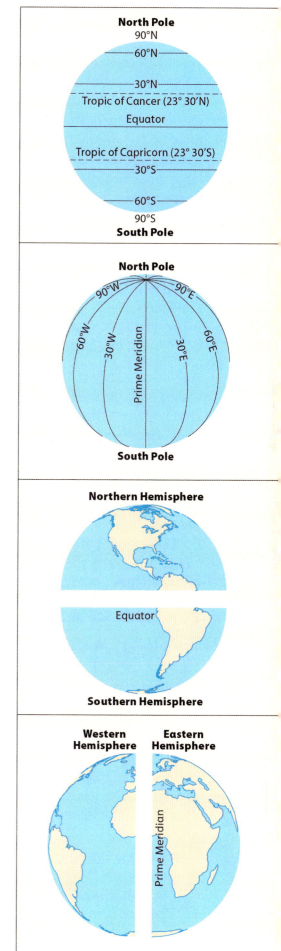

Maps MAP SCALE

On a walk through a city, such as Charlotte, North Carolina, you might use a highly detailed map that shows only the downtown area. To drive up the Atlantic coast, however, you would use a map that covers a large area, including several states. These maps have different scales.

INTERPRETING A SCALE

A map's scale shows how much distance on Earth is shown on the map. A large-scale map covers a small area but shows many details. A small-scale map covers a large area but includes few details.

A scale is usually shown in both inches and centimeters. One inch or centimeter on the map represents a much larger distance on Earth, such as a number of miles or kilometers.

To use a map scale, mark off the length of the scale several times on the edge of a sheet of paper. Then hold the paper between two points to see how many times the scale falls between them. Add up the distance.

PURPOSES OF A SCALE

The scale of a map should be appropriate for its purpose. For example, a tourist map of Washington, D.C., should be large-scale, showing every street name, monument, and museum.

Maps of any scale show geographic patterns. The map of Washington, D.C., for instance, would show that many government buildings are in one area.

THINK LIKE A GEOGRAPHER

Summarize What are the purposes of a small-scale map and a large-scale map?

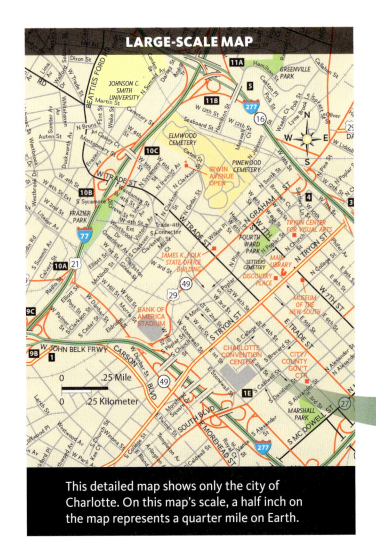

LARGE-SCALE MAP

This detailed map shows only the city of Charlotte. On this map's scale, a half inch on the map represents a quarter mile on Earth.

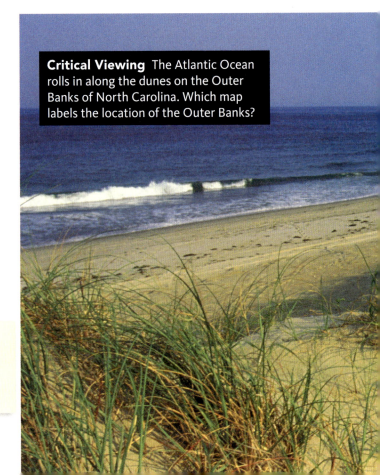

Critical Viewing The Atlantic Ocean rolls in along the dunes on the Outer Banks of North Carolina. Which map labels the location of the Outer Banks?

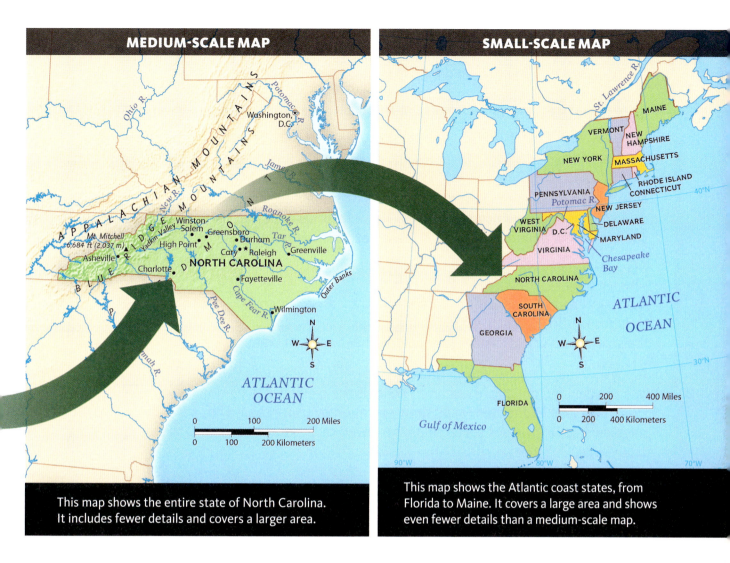

MEDIUM-SCALE MAP

This map shows the entire state of North Carolina. It includes fewer details and covers a larger area.

SMALL-SCALE MAP

This map shows the Atlantic coast states, from Florida to Maine. It covers a large area and shows even fewer details than a medium-scale map.

Maps POLITICAL AND PHYSICAL

The governor of a state needs a map that shows counties and cities. A mountain climber needs a map that shows cliffs, canyons, and ice fields. Cartographers, or mapmakers, create different kinds of maps for these different purposes.

POLITICAL MAPS

A political map shows features that humans have created, such as countries, states, provinces, and cities. These features are labeled, and lines show boundaries, such as those between countries.

PHYSICAL MAPS

A physical map shows natural features of physical geography. It includes landforms, such as mountains, plains, valleys, and deserts. It also includes oceans, lakes, rivers, and other bodies of water.

A physical map can also show elevation and relief. Elevation is the height of a physical feature above sea level. Relief is the change in elevation from one place to another. Maps show elevation by using color. The physical map below uses seven colors for seven ranges of elevation.

THINK LIKE A GEOGRAPHER

Monitor Comprehension How is a political map different from a physical map?

Critical Viewing The Sobaek Mountains cut diagonally across South Korea. Which map best indicates the location of these mountains?

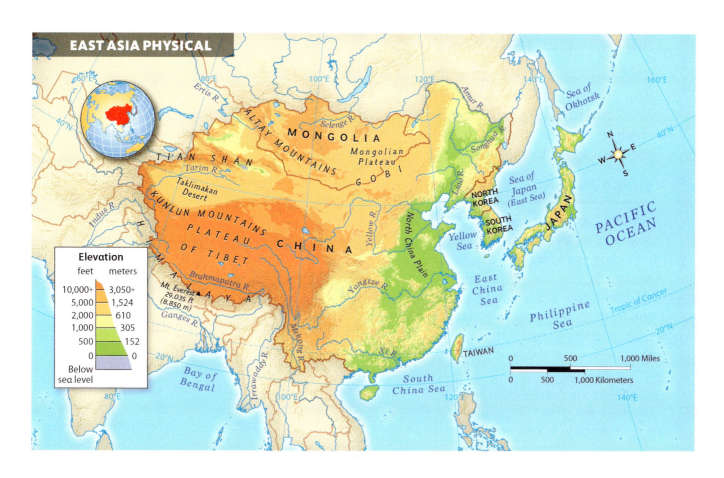

60°E 80°E 100°E 120°E 140°E 160°E

Ertis R.

40°N

MONGOLIA

ALTAY MOUNTAINS

Selenge R.

Mongolian Plateau

G O B I

Amur R.

Songhua R.

Sea of Okhotsk

TIAN SHAN

Tarim R.

Taklimakan Desert

KUNLUN MOUNTAINS

Liao R.

NORTH KOREA

SOUTH KOREA

Sea of Japan (East Sea)

JAPAN

40°N

PLATEAU OF TIBET

C H I N A

Yellow R.

North China Plain

Yellow Sea

PACIFIC OCEAN

H I M A L A Y A

Brahmaputra R.

Mt. Everest 29,035 ft (8,850 m)

Yangtze R.

East China Sea

Elevation

feet	meters
10,000+	3,050+
5,000	1,524
2,000	610
1,000	305
500	152
0	0

Below sea level

Ganges R.

Mekong R.

Xi R.

TAIWAN

Philippine Sea

Tropic of Cancer

20°N

20°N

Bay of Bengal

Irrawaddy R.

South China Sea

0   500   1,000 Miles
0   500   1,000 Kilometers

80°E 100°E 120°E 140°E

60°E 80°E 100°E 120°E 140°E 160°E

Ertis R.

40°N

Selenge R.

Amur R.

Songhua R.

Sea of Okhotsk

Tarim R.

MONGOLIA

★ Ulaanbaatar

Liao R.

NORTH KOREA

Sea of Japan (East Sea)

40°N

Beijing ●

P'yongyang ★

★ Seoul

SOUTH KOREA

JAPAN

Tokyo ★

PACIFIC OCEAN

C H I N A

Yellow R.

Yellow Sea

Brahmaputra R.

Mt. Everest 29,035 ft (8,850 m)

Chengdu ●

Chongqing ●

Yangtze R.

Shanghai ●

East China Sea

Ganges R.

Mekong R.

Kunming ●

Xi R.

Taipei ●

TAIWAN

Hong Kong ●

Philippine Sea

Tropic of Cancer

20°N

20°N

Bay of Bengal

Irrawaddy R.

South China Sea

0   500   1,000 Miles
0   500   1,000 Kilometers

80°E 100°E 120°E 140°E

Maps THEMATIC MAPS

Suppose you wanted to create a map showing the location of sports fields in your community. You would create a thematic map, which is a map about a specific theme, or topic.

TYPES OF THEMATIC MAPS

Thematic maps are useful for showing a variety of geographic information, including economic activity, natural resources, and population density. Common types of thematic maps are the point symbol map, the dot density map, and the proportional symbol map.

THINK LIKE A GEOGRAPHER

Identify Look through your world history textbook and identify an example of a thematic map. What geographic information does the map show?

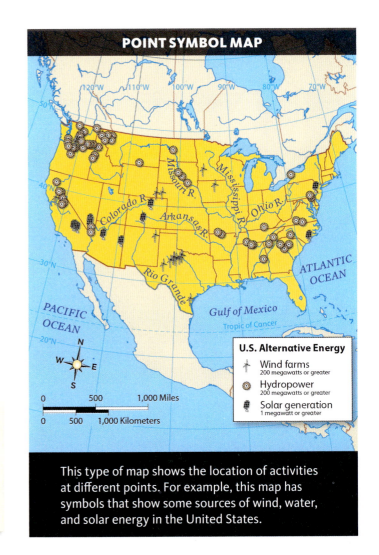

POINT SYMBOL MAP

U.S. Alternative Energy

- ✈ Wind farms
  200 megawatts or greater
- ⚙ Hydropower
  200 megawatts or greater
- ▥ Solar generation
  1 megawatt or greater

0   500   1,000 Miles

0   500   1,000 Kilometers

This type of map shows the location of activities at different points. For example, this map has symbols that show some sources of wind, water, and solar energy in the United States.

DOT DENSITY MAP

Population Density

· One dot represents 50,000 people

This type of map uses dots to show how something is distributed in a country or region. Each dot represents an amount. For example, each dot on this map represents 50,000 people living in Thailand.

PROPORTIONAL SYMBOL MAP

Earthquake Magnitude

- 7.3–7.6
- 6.8–7.2
- 6.3–6.7
- 5.5–6.2

This type of map uses symbols of different sizes to show the size of an event. For example, the size of the circles on this map shows the severity of earthquakes in the Philippines.

Solar panels in the Nevada desert absorb light from the sun and turn it into energy.

Maps MAP PROJECTIONS

The world is a sphere, but maps are flat. As a result, maps distort, or change, shapes, areas, distances, and directions found in the real world. To reduce distortion, mapmakers use projections, or ways of showing Earth's curved surface on a flat map. Five common map projections are the azimuthal, Robinson, Mercator, Winkel Tripel, and homolosine. Each projection has strengths and weaknesses—each distorts in a different way.

When cartographers make maps, they need to choose a map projection. The type of projection depends on the map's purpose. Which elements are acceptable to distort? Which are not acceptable to distort? For example, if a cartographer is creating a navigation map, it is important that direction should not be distorted. It may not matter, however, if some areas or shapes are distorted.

THINK LIKE A GEOGRAPHER

Make Inferences How do cartographers decide which projection to use?

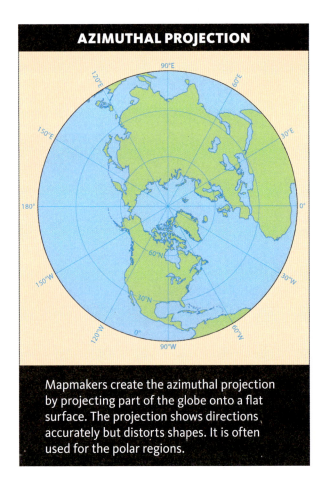

Mapmakers create the azimuthal projection by projecting part of the globe onto a flat surface. The projection shows directions accurately but distorts shapes. It is often used for the polar regions.

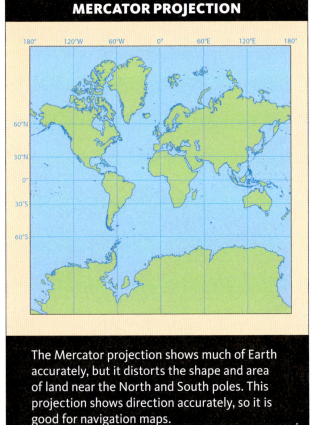

The Mercator projection shows much of Earth accurately, but it distorts the shape and area of land near the North and South poles. This projection shows direction accurately, so it is good for navigation maps.

HOMOLOSINE PROJECTION

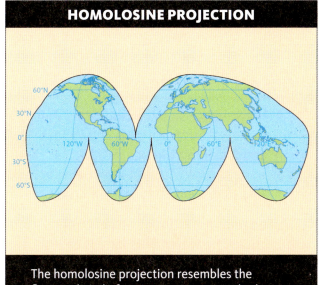

The homolosine projection resembles the flattened peel of an orange. It accurately shows the shape and area of landmasses by cutting up the oceans. However, it does not show distance accurately.

ROBINSON PROJECTION

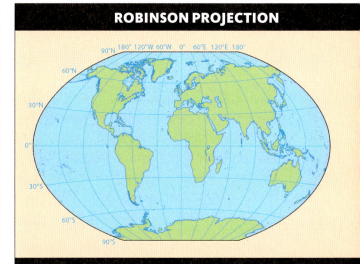

The Robinson projection combines the strengths of other projections. It shows the shape and area of the continents and oceans with reasonable accuracy. However, the North and South poles are distorted.

WINKEL TRIPEL PROJECTION

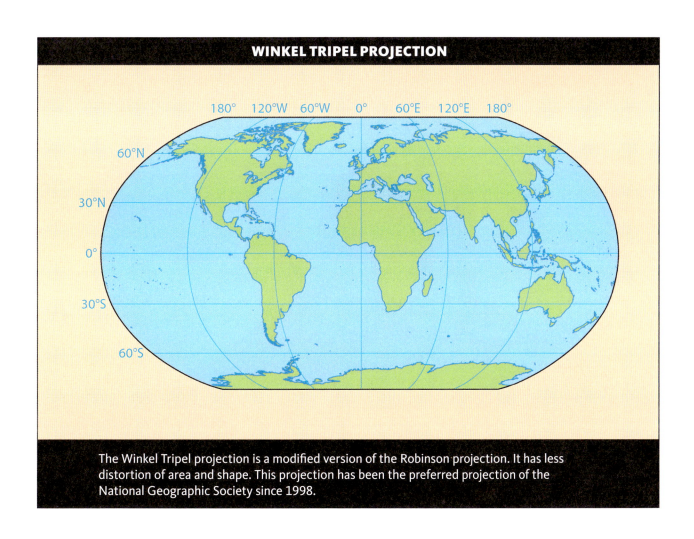

The Winkel Tripel projection is a modified version of the Robinson projection. It has less distortion of area and shape. This projection has been the preferred projection of the National Geographic Society since 1998.

Physical Geography   EARTH'S LANDFORMS

The Rocky Mountains rise more than 14,000 feet above sea level. The Grand Canyon is more than 5,000 feet deep. Both are landforms, or physical features on Earth's surface.

SURFACE LANDFORMS

Landforms such as the Rocky Mountains in western North America and the Grand Canyon in Arizona provide a variety of physical environments. These environments support millions of plants and animals.

Several landforms are commonly found on Earth's surface. A mountain is a high, steep elevation. A hill also slopes upward but is less steep and rugged. In contrast, a plain is a level area. The Great Plains, for example, are flat landforms stretching from the Mississippi River to the Rocky Mountains. A plateau is a plain that sits high above sea level and usually has a cliff on all sides. A valley is a low-lying area that is surrounded by mountains.

OCEAN LANDFORMS

Earth's oceans also have landforms that are underwater. Mountains and valleys rise and fall along the ocean floor. Volcanoes erupt with hot magma, which hardens as it cools to form new crust.

The edge of a continent often extends out under the water. This land is called the continental shelf. Most of Earth's marine life lives at this level of the ocean. Beyond the continental shelf, the land develops a steep slope. Beyond the slope, before the ocean floor, the land slopes slightly upward. This landform is called the continental rise. It is formed by rocks and sediment carried by ocean currents. Together, these landforms are known as the continental margin.

A butte is a hill or mountain with steep sides and a flat top. These buttes in Monument Valley, Arizona, are called "the Mittens."

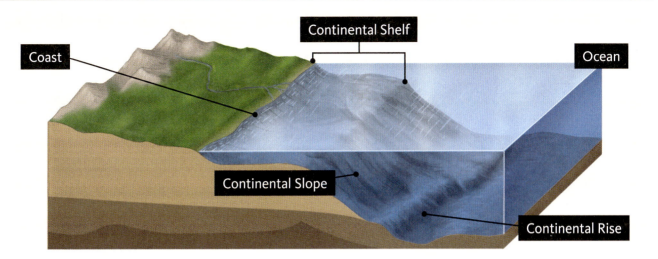

Coast

Continental Shelf

Ocean

Continental Slope

Continental Rise

THE CHANGING EARTH

Earth is always changing, and the changes affect plant and animal life. For example, a flood can cause severe erosion, which can ruin farmers' fields. Erosion is the process by which rocks and soil slowly break apart and are swept away.

THINK LIKE A GEOGRAPHER

Draw Conclusions How do physical processes reshape Earth's landforms?

Physical Geography NATURAL RESOURCES

What materials make up a pencil? Wood comes from trees. The material that you write with is a mineral called graphite. The pencil is made from natural resources, which are materials on Earth that people use to live and to meet their needs.

EARTH'S RESOURCES

There are two kinds of resources. Biological resources are living things, such as livestock, plants, and trees. These resources are important to humans because they provide us with food, shelter, and clothing.

Mineral resources are nonliving resources buried within Earth, such as oil and coal. Some mineral resources are raw materials, or materials used to make products. Iron ore, for example, is a raw material used in making steel. The steel, in turn, is used to make skyscrapers and automobiles.

CATEGORIES OF RESOURCES

Geographers classify resources in two categories. Nonrenewable resources are resources that are limited and cannot be replaced. For example, oil comes from wells that are drilled into Earth's crust. Once a well runs dry, the oil is gone. Coal and natural gas are other examples of nonrenewable resources.

Renewable resources never run out, or a new supply develops over time. Wind, water, and solar power are all renewable. So are trees because a new supply can grow to replace those that have been cut down.

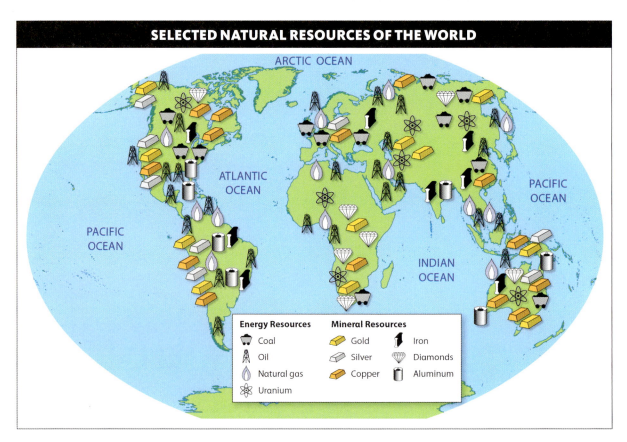

SELECTED NATURAL RESOURCES OF THE WORLD

Natural resources are an important part of everyday life, yet countries with a large supply are not always wealthy. Nigeria, for example, is a major supplier of oil, but seven out of every ten Nigerians live in poverty. Japan is one of the wealthiest countries in the world—yet it must import oil from other countries.

Pumpjacks pump oil at a field in California.

THINK LIKE A GEOGRAPHER

Monitor Comprehension
Why are natural resources important?

Physical Geography CLIMATE AND WEATHER

People who live in Sacramento, California, have mild winters. When they go skiing in the nearby Sierra Nevada Mountains, they wear parkas to protect themselves from the colder temperatures. They have adapted to a different climate.

CLIMATE ELEMENTS

Climate is the average condition of the atmosphere over a long period of time. It includes average temperature, average precipitation, and the amount of change from one season to another. For example, Fairbanks, Alaska, has a cold climate. In the winter, the temperature can reach -8°F. Yet the temperature can rise to 90°F in the summer. The city goes through changes from one season to another.

Four factors that affect a region's climate are latitude, elevation, prevailing winds, and ocean currents. Places at high latitudes, such as Fairbanks, experience more change between winter and summer. Places close to the equator have nearly the same temperature throughout the year. Places at higher elevations have generally colder temperatures than places closer to sea level.

Prevailing winds are winds coming from one direction that blow most of the time. In Florida in the summer, the prevailing winds come from the south, making a warm climate even hotter.

Ocean currents also affect climate. The Gulf Stream is a current that carries warm water from the Caribbean Sea toward Europe. Air passing over the water becomes warm and helps create a mild winter climate in England and Ireland.

WEATHER CONDITIONS

Weather is the condition of the atmosphere at a particular time. It includes the temperature, precipitation, and humidity for a particular day or week. Humidity is the amount of water vapor in the air. If a weather forecaster says the humidity is at 95 percent, he or she means that the air is holding a large amount of water vapor.

Weather changes because of air masses. An air mass is a large area of air that has the same temperature and humidity. The boundary between two air masses is called a front. If a forecaster talks about a warm, humid front, he or she usually means that thunderstorms are headed toward the area.

WESTERN UNITED STATES: CLIMATE MAP

CANADA

PACIFIC OCEAN

UNITED STATES

Climate Regions
- Humid Temperate– No dry season
- Humid Temperate– Dry summer
- Unclassified highlands
- Dry–Semiarid
- Dry–Arid
- Humid Cold– No dry season

MEXICO

Critical Viewing Skiers head to the top of Clouds Rest in Yosemite National Park, California. What does the photo suggest about the weather at this location?

WESTERN UNITED STATES: WEATHER MAP

Wet, stormy weather
Sunny, dry weather
Cold front
Warm front

CANADA

PACIFIC OCEAN

UNITED STATES

MEXICO

N
W   E
S

THINK LIKE A GEOGRAPHER

Make Inferences What is the difference between climate and weather?

Physical Geography   CLIMATE REGIONS AND VEGETATION

A climate region is a group of places that have similar temperatures, precipitation levels, and changes in weather. Geographers have identified 5 climate regions that are broken down into 12 subcategories. Places that are located in the same subcategory often have similar vegetation, or plant life.

Saguaro Cactus, Sonora Desert, Arizona

Mixed Forest, Great Smoky Mountains, North Carolina

B **Humid Temperate Climates** have cool winters, warm summers, and ample rainfall. Plant life includes mixed forests with evergreens and leafy trees.

A **Dry Climates** have little to no rain or snow and both hot and cold temperatures. Plant life includes shrubs and cacti.

Bromeliads, Amazon rain forest, Peru

C **Humid Equatorial Climates** are found near the equator. They have high temperatures and rainfall all or most of the year. Plant life includes tropical plants and rain forests or grasslands with trees.

NORTH AMERICA

PACIFIC OCEAN

ATLANTIC OCEAN

SOUTH AMERICA

Mosses, Disko Bay, Greenland

D **Tundra** or **Ice Climates** are north of the Arctic Circle and south of the Antarctic Circle. They have long, cold winters and short summers. Plant life includes mosses or no vegetation.

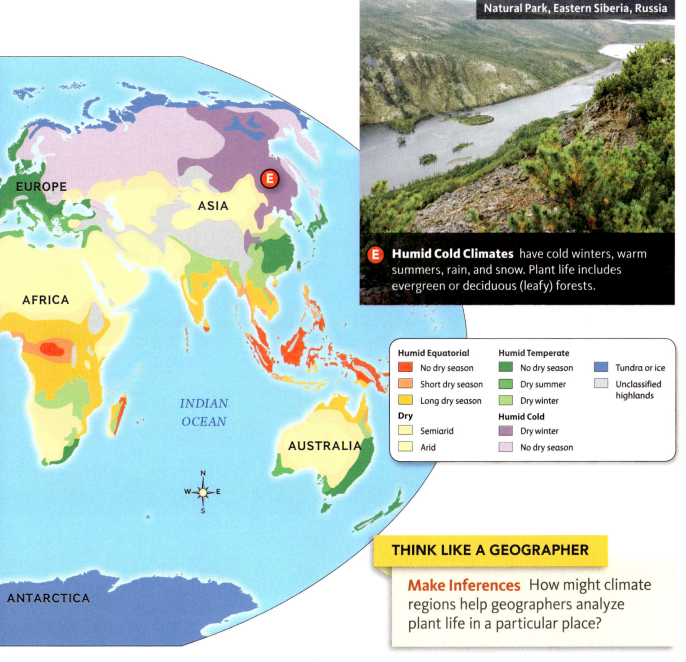

Natural Park, Eastern Siberia, Russia

E **Humid Cold Climates** have cold winters, warm summers, rain, and snow. Plant life includes evergreen or deciduous (leafy) forests.

EUROPE

ASIA

E

AFRICA

INDIAN OCEAN

AUSTRALIA

ANTARCTICA

N
W · E
S

Humid Equatorial
No dry season
Short dry season
Long dry season

Dry
Semiarid
Arid

Humid Temperate
No dry season
Dry summer
Dry winter

Humid Cold
Dry winter
No dry season

Tundra or ice
Unclassified highlands

THINK LIKE A GEOGRAPHER

Make Inferences How might climate regions help geographers analyze plant life in a particular place?

Human Geography ADAPTING TO THE ENVIRONMENT

Human geography explores the relationship between people and their surroundings. An important aspect of this relationship is the way in which people adapt to their environment.

Throughout history, people have had to adapt to their surroundings. Early humans did this simply to survive. They learned how to build a fire to warm themselves in cold weather and find plants and animals when food was scarce. In modern times, people have developed sophisticated technologies, including heating and cooling systems, to help them live in environments with challenging weather.

People have also learned to build structures to adapt to their environment. They build houses to protect them from the elements. They build dams to hold water back, bridges to span bodies of water, and tunnels to more easily travel over mountainous areas. In many cases, the materials people use to build these structures are obtained from the surrounding environment.

THINK LIKE A GEOGRAPHER

Make Connections What kinds of adaptations do you make in different types of weather?

China built the Three Gorges Dam on the Chang Jiang River, in part, to prevent flooding along the eastern part of the river.

In the city of Noril'sk in the Russian region of Siberia, people deal with the snow and ice that covers the ground throughout much of the city's long winter.

Human Geography HUMAN IMPACT ON THE ENVIRONMENT

When people adapt to their surroundings, their actions sometimes have a lasting impact on the environment. Some adaptations have a positive impact on the environment, but some can be harmful.

NEGATIVE IMPACT

As people moved to cities over the last few centuries, they needed housing and ever-increasing supplies of energy to fuel their homes, businesses, and cars. As a result, entire forests were cut down, new mines were carved into the earth, and oil and natural gas were pumped from the ground and from underwater sources.

When forests and other natural environments are cleared, an entire ecosystem can be destroyed. An ecosystem is a community of plants and animals and their natural environment. The destruction of one ecosystem can affect another. For example, many scientists believe the destruction of rain forest habitats has led to global climate change.

The use of fossil fuels—including, coal, oil, and natural gas—has had a largely negative impact on the environment. Burning these energy sources has polluted the air and contributed to global warming. Even mining and transporting the sources has affected the environment. Oil spills from tankers and underwater oil rigs have damaged our waters, shorelines, and wildlife.

POSITIVE IMPACT

As understanding of human impact on the environment has grown, people around the world have taken steps to save ecosystems, preserve natural habitats, and protect our air and water. In 1973, for example, the United States passed the Endangered Species Act, which protects the habitats of endangered species. People have also restored, or brought back, habitats such as forests by planting trees. In addition, laws and regulations have been passed to limit the amounts of pollutants released into the air, land, and bodies of water by vehicles and industrial plants.

Scientists have worked to educate the public on pollution's impact on the environment. For example, some scientists have formed Mission Blue, a program that seeks to heal and protect Earth's oceans. One of the program's goals is to establish marine-protected areas in endangered hot spots, or "hope spots." These spots are ocean habitats that can recover and grow if human impact is limited.

Critical Viewing This satellite map of the world shows the location of 17 "hope spots," places that are important to the overall health of Earth's oceans. What patterns, if any, do you notice about the location of these spots?

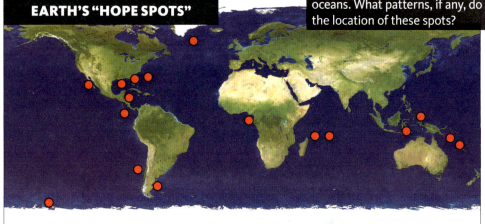

EARTH'S "HOPE SPOTS"

In 2010, the Deepwater Horizon oil rig exploded in the Gulf of Mexico. The explosion killed 11 people and dumped more than 200 million gallons of oil in the Gulf. Thousands of birds, fish, and marine mammals were injured or killed in the disaster.

Elephants roam the Samburu National Reserve in Kenya.

THINK LIKE A GEOGRAPHER

Evaluate What can you do to have a positive impact on the environment?

Human Geography MOVEMENT AND SPREAD OF IDEAS

People have been on the move since early *Homo sapiens* first began moving within Africa about 100,000 years ago. The movement of people to a new location is called migration.

HUMAN MOVEMENT

Since our beginnings in Africa, we have migrated to new locations and populated the globe. Early humans moved because their survival depended on it. The climate changed, making food and water scarce. So people moved to find more hospitable homes and to follow the herds of animals they liked to hunt.

People have continued to migrate throughout history. The map on this page shows the Bantu migrations, which began about 2,000 years ago and continued for about 1,500 years. Historians say that this massive migration is the most important since our human ancestors first left Africa.

Historians don't really know why the Bantu people decided to leave their homes in West Africa and head south. Today, however, many immigrants are motivated to move by what are called push-pull factors. Push factors are those that drive people away from an area, such as war, political or religious persecution, and lack of job opportunities. Pull factors are those that attract people to a new place, such as higher wages, educational opportunities, and a more tolerant government. And of course, people are still drawn to a more favorable climate.

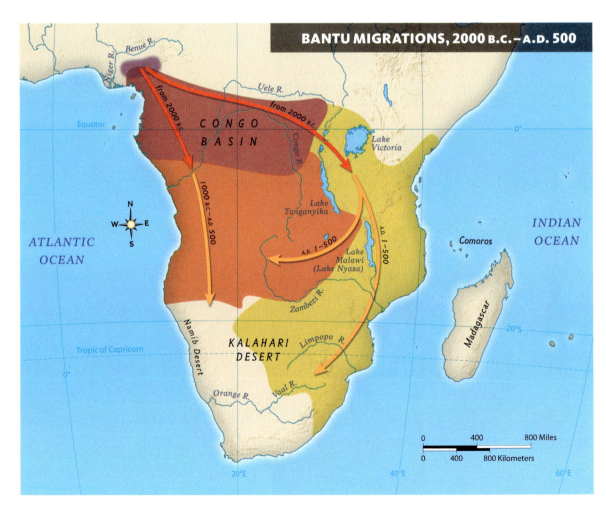

SPREAD OF IDEAS

As people migrate, they bring their ideas, culture, skills, and language to their new homes. This spread of ideas results in great change. For example, the exchange of skills and ideas that occurred as a result of the Bantu migrations had an enormous impact on Africa's culture, economy, and government practices. You can see the impact of migration today in any large city. Restaurants, shops, and places of worship reflect the culture of the people who have moved to the city.

Trade has also spread ideas. The Silk Roads, a network of trade routes that began in China around 100 B.C., carried ideas as well as goods to Asia, Africa, and Europe. Over time, Chinese inventions and ideas reached Europe, and Indian traders brought Buddhism to China.

Movement isn't the only means by which ideas spread. Technological innovations can have the same impact. For instance, the invention of the printing press around 1450 resulted in an information explosion throughout Europe. The press produced books rapidly and cheaply and spread ideas quickly. Today, computers, the Internet, and social media carry ideas around the world at the touch of a button. These technologies—and those yet to come—are part of human geography and will continue to bring people together.

THINK LIKE A GEOGRAPHER

Evaluate What technologies and other means do you use to spread ideas?

The development of cell phones has connected people and their ideas in places where landline phone systems would be too expensive to install.

WHY STUDY HISTORY ?

Hi! I'm Fred Hiebert, National Geographic's Archaeology Fellow. We're about to embark on a journey all over the world and back through time—the history of the world as we know it today.

So why do we study past civilizations? The basis of civilization is identity—who we are and what we stand for. We express identity by creating unique ways to be housed and fed and to thrive. The basic building blocks of civilization are the same around the world: what kinds of plants and animals to tend and consume, how to find enough water, and how to survive the changes of the seasons. All core civilizations— from China, India, and Mesopotamia, to Europe and Mesoamerica— struggled with these issues.

Look at the sculptures shown below. These prehistoric "selfies" reveal a universal need to think about ourselves—in relation to the environment, the future, our religious beliefs—that dates from the earliest civilizations.

THE HUMAN EPIC

Historians, archaeologists, and anthropologists constantly update the story of human civilizations as new data surfaces from the latest dig site or the most recent scholarship. The Framework of World History at right is only one way to think about how human identity developed—there are many pathways from the past to the present.

I've lived and worked all over the world in lots of different cultures, and I know first-hand that you and others your age are more alike than you are different. You share the same need to understand yourself, your family, and your community and the same urge to hope and plan for your future. Your generation may be one of the first to truly be considered global citizens.

ARTEMIS
This Greek marble sculpture dating back to the 4th century B.C. is known as *Artemis Hunting*.

NEFERTITI
The bust of this famous Egyptian queen and wife of Pharaoh Akhenaten was sculpted more than 3,300 years ago.

FRAMEWORK OF WORLD HISTORY

Fred Hiebert
▶ **Watch the Why Study History video**

The ancient cave painting in the background is located in Snake Cave in Australia. An Aboriginal artist created it by blowing pigment over his or her hand, leaving a blank hand shape.

◀ **TERRA COTTA BUDDHA**
This 5-foot tall statue was discovered at the site of Hadda in Afghanistan.

The model below is one way to view the development of civilizations. For all cultures, it's not just the famous leaders who make history—it's all of us, through small actions that grow into world-changing events and ideas.

1 CORE CIVILIZATIONS
Humans begin to think about where they live, what they eat, and what they believe in—and plan for the future. Across the centuries and in all world cultures, humans use these building blocks to think about who they are and where they come from—the beginning of identity.

2 PRIMARY CIVILIZATIONS
Humans develop more effective responses to their environment, creating irrigation and other farming methods that make agriculture more predictable and more productive. People are able to form groups and move together, and eventually cities develop.

3 SECONDARY CIVILIZATIONS
Human understanding of identity comes into focus, and writing develops partly as an expression of identity. Codes of law and better rulers come to the forefront as cultures take on characteristics that embody those identities.

4 WORLD SYSTEMS
Civilizations reach out to each other, and trade develops along what would eventually be called the Silk Roads. The urge to move results in new road systems, new country borders with border guards, and new systems of taxation.

HI 5 Students recognize that interpretations of history are subject to change as new information is uncovered.

1

TO BECOME A GLOBAL CITIZEN

As you study world history, you're going to meet some National Geographic Explorers along the way—men and women who are making incredible contributions to our lives through their work. Studying world history is part of what they do because they believe they can add to our understanding of the human story. Here are just a few.

NICOLE BOIVIN ▶
Boivin is investigating the development of early seafaring activity in the Indian Ocean and the beginning of a connection between India and Africa.

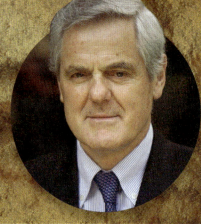

ALBERT LIN ▲
Lin combines technology and citizen science to conduct noninvasive investigations of potential archaeological sites.

◀ MAURIZIO SERACINI
Seracini uses multispectral imaging and other technology to study works of art and historic buildings.

BECOME PART OF THE GLOBAL CONVERSATION!

Think About It

1. In what ways are you a global citizen?

2. Describe a situation or problem in which you think people should strive for global citizenship. What actions do you think should be taken to solve the problem?

3. Pick one action you named above and explain how you would go about accomplishing it. Develop a detailed action plan that could be put in place to make this happen.

WILLIAM SATURNO ▶
Saturno supervises excavations in the jungles of Guatemala and determines the architectural history of a site by studying the little pieces that remain.

◀ **JODI MAGNESS**
Magness specializes in the archaeology of ancient Palestine (present-day Israel, Jordan, and the Palestinian territories) during the Roman, Byzantine, and Islamic periods.

FUTURE EXPLORER ▶
WILL THIS BE YOU?

Write About It

SYNTHESIZE What does **identity** mean to you? Answer this question in two or three paragraphs in your notebook. Be sure to include your definition of identity, explain the various parts that make up your identity, and describe how you express your identity. Then designate a spot in your notebook where you can record how your understanding of identity changes as you read each chapter.

MAKE CONNECTIONS What different types of identities do you notice in your school and community? Create a chart that represents these identities and write your description of each.

ASK AND ANSWER QUESTIONS Imagine that you are at a panel discussion that includes the Explorers shown above. Write three questions you would like to ask the panel, including specific questions for individual Explorers.

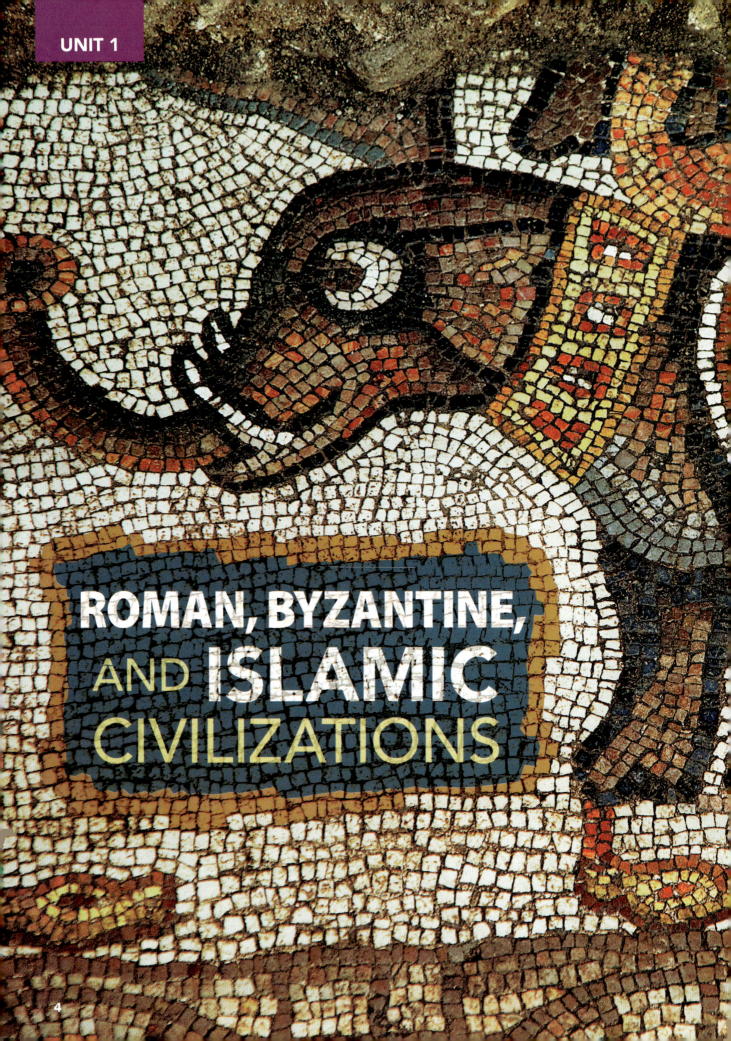

ROMAN, BYZANTINE, AND ISLAMIC CIVILIZATIONS

NATIONAL GEOGRAPHIC

ON **LOCATION** WITH

Jodi Magness
Archaeologist

People say that the Roman Empire fell in 476, and a part of it did. But the empire lived on in the East. This part became known as the Byzantine Empire, but its citizens called themselves Romans. In the 600s, Muslim Arabs invaded Southwest Asia and conquered some of the territory held by the Byzantines, including Palestine. I'm Jodi Magness, and I excavate archaeological sites in Israel. Join me as we dig through the history of the Roman, Byzantine, and Islamic civilizations!

‹ **CRITICAL VIEWING** Magness discovered a 5th-century synagogue and this Byzantine-inspired mosaic of an elephant at a site in Israel. What does the mosaic suggest about the skill of its artist?

UNIT 1

TIME LINE OF WORLD EVENTS

Roman, Byzantine, and Islamic Civilizations

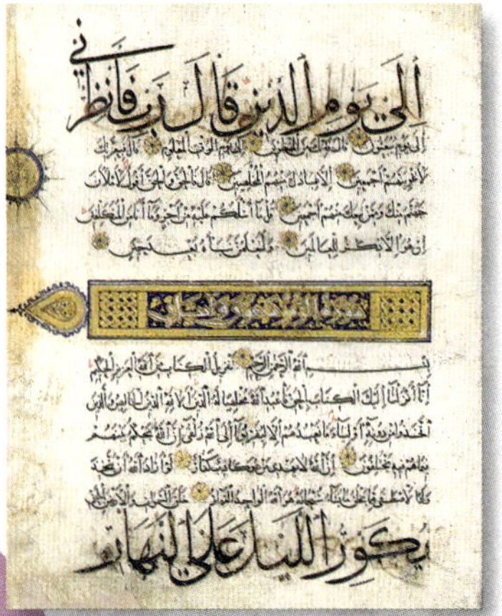

476
Invasions bring about the fall of the Western Roman Empire.

500

630
Muhammad unites much of Arabia under Islam.

750
Muslim rule spreads Islam over parts of Asia, Africa, and Europe.
(page from the Qur'an)

800

1054
Christianity splits, and the Eastern Orthodox Church forms in Byzantium.

The World

800
EUROPE
Charlemagne unites and rules much of Western Europe.

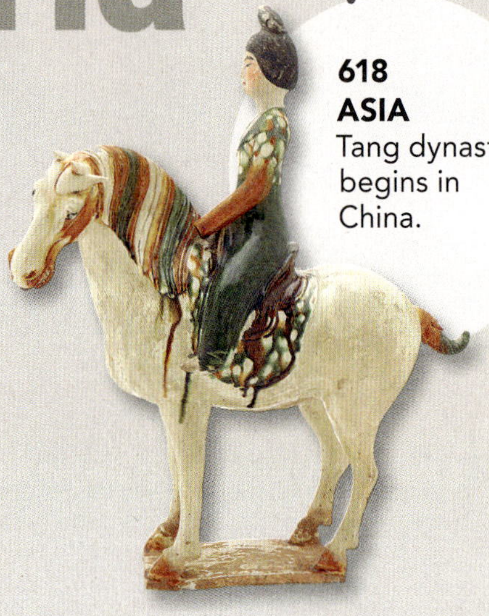

618
ASIA
Tang dynasty begins in China.

c. 1000
AMERICAS
Inca civilization arises in South America.
(gold Inca figurine)

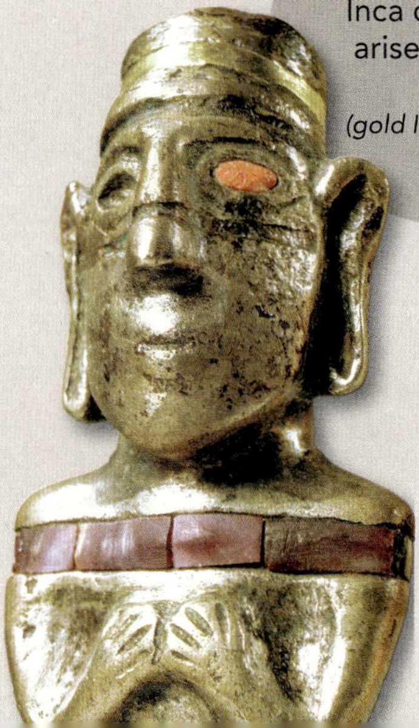

What world event occurred soon after the Byzantine Empire came to an end?

1453
Ottoman Turks capture Constantinople, and the Byzantine Empire comes to an end.
(Suleyman I, Ottoman ruler)

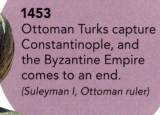

1556
Akbar the Great leads Muslim India to a golden age.

mid-1600s
Mughal emperor Shah Jahan builds the Taj Mahal in India.

1501
The Safavid Empire arises in Persia.

1400

1200

1600

1492
AMERICAS
Christopher Columbus sails to the Americas.

1312
AFRICA
Mansa Musa begins rule of Mali.

1215
EUROPE
England's Magna Carta lays the groundwork for later democratic developments.

CST 1 Students explain how major events are related to one another in time.

7

BYZANTINE AND EARLY MUSLIM EMPIRES, 565–750

EUROPE

France

Alps

Spain
ABBASSID
EMPIRE

• Córdoba
• Granada

Rome •

BYZANTINE
EMPIRE

Mediterranean Sea

Black Sea

Constantinople
(Istanbul) •

Caucasus Mts.

Caspian Sea

Aral
Sea

ASIA

A B B A S S I D

Damascus •

Alexandria •

Cairo •

Egypt

AFRICA

Jerusalem •

UMAYYAD

EMPIRE

Persia

Baghdad •

U M A Y Y A D   E M P I R E

Persian Gulf

Medina •

Mecca •

Red Sea

Arabian
Peninsula

Himalaya

Agra •

India

Arabian
Sea

Bay
of
Bengal

INDIAN
OCEAN

Legend:
- Byzantine Empire, 565
- Umayyad Empire, 661
- Abbassid Empire, 750

BYZANTINE & MUSLIM EMPIRES 565–1683

After the Western Roman Empire fell in 476, invaders overran its lands. But the eastern part of the empire, which came to be known as the Byzantine Empire, survived. The empire reached its height in 565.

The Byzantine Empire's power was soon overshadowed by a Muslim state that arose in Arabia. Over many centuries, Muslim armies conquered lands in Europe, Asia, and Africa. Muslim leaders established empires there and spread their Islamic faith.

Byzantine mosaic of a lion from the 5th or 6th century

On which continent were the later Muslim empires mostly located?

CST 3 Students use a variety of maps and documents to identify physical and cultural features of neighborhoods, cities, states, and countries and to explain the historical migration of people, expansion and disintegration of empires, and the growth of economic systems.

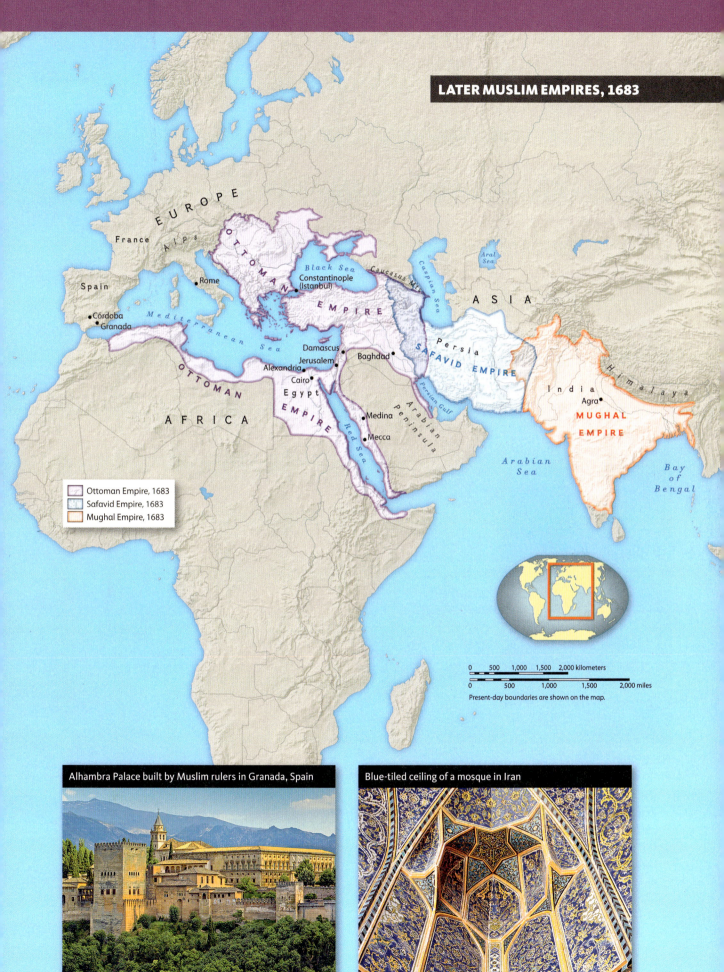

EUROPE

France

Alps

Spain

Rome

Córdoba
Granada

Mediterranean Sea

OTTOMAN EMPIRE

Constantinople
(Istanbul)

Black Sea

Caucasus Mts.

Caspian Sea

Aral Sea

ASIA

Persia

SAFAVID EMPIRE

Damascus
Jerusalem
Alexandria
Cairo
Baghdad

Persian Gulf

Red Sea

Egypt

AFRICA

Medina
Mecca

Arabian Peninsula

Himalaya

India
Agra

MUGHAL EMPIRE

Arabian Sea

Bay of Bengal

Ottoman Empire, 1683
Safavid Empire, 1683
Mughal Empire, 1683

| 0 | 500 | 1,000 | 1,500 | 2,000 kilometers |
| 0 | 500 | 1,000 | 1,500 | 2,000 miles |

Present-day boundaries are shown on the map.

Alhambra Palace built by Muslim rulers in Granada, Spain

Blue-tiled ceiling of a mosque in Iran

9

1

THE ROMAN EMPIRE AND CHRISTIANITY

31 B.C. – A.D. 476

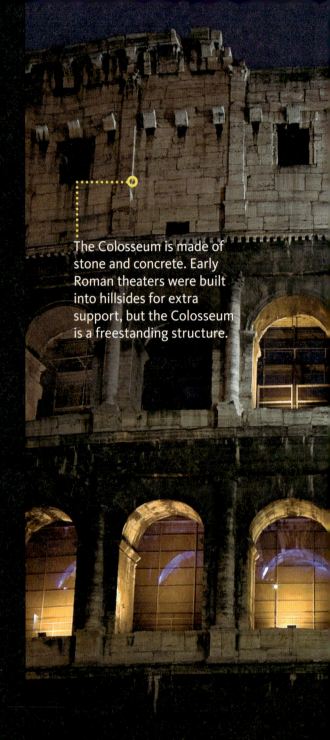

ESSENTIAL QUESTION What made the Roman Empire so powerful and long lasting?

SECTION 1 THE EMPIRE AT ITS HEIGHT

KEY VOCABULARY	NAMES & PLACES
aqueduct	Augustus
arch	Latin
bas-relief	Pax Romana
emperor	Virgil
fresco	
mosaic	
oral history	
oratory	
primary source	
secondary source	

The Colosseum is made of stone and concrete. Early Roman theaters were built into hillsides for extra support, but the Colosseum is a freestanding structure.

SECTION 2 CHRISTIANITY

KEY VOCABULARY	NAMES & PLACES
catacomb	Christianity
epistle	Constantine
missionary	Gospels
parable	Jesus
pope	New Testament
	Paul
	Roman Catholic Church
	Twelve Apostles

SECTION 3 DECLINE AND FALL

KEY VOCABULARY	NAMES & PLACES
barbarian	Attila
tetrarchy	Diocletian

READING STRATEGY

ORGANIZE IDEAS: SEQUENCE EVENTS

When you sequence events, you place them in the order in which they occurred. As you read the chapter, use a time line like this one to keep track of key people and events in the Roman Empire.

People and Events of the Roman Empire

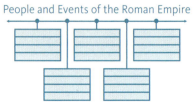

CST 1 Students explain how major events are related to one another in time; CST 2 Students construct various time lines of key events, people, and periods of the historical era they are studying.

Spectators entered and exited through 76 gates that sat just inside the 80 arches surrounding the ground floor.

The Roman Colosseum was opened in A.D. 80 and is still standing today.

Studying the **Past**

Historians are detectives. They ask questions about the past that begin with *Who, What, Where, When, Why,* and *How*. They then search for and examine evidence, seeking answers to their questions. As you study the past, you'll become a detective too. You'll learn to think like a historian and use the same skills. You'll develop a historian's mind-set.

MAIN IDEA

Historians—and students of history—apply distinct thinking and research skills to learn the story of human life on Earth.

THINKING ABOUT TIME AND PLACE

Historians ask questions that are rooted in a particular time and place. The most basic information that historians must establish is *when* and *where* a person lived or an event occurred.

Because time and place are so basic to the study of history, time lines and maps are crucial tools of historians. Time lines indicate how major events, people, and periods are related to one another in time. Maps show the physical and cultural features of neighborhoods, cities, states, and countries. Maps can help explain such events as the historical migration of a group of people and the growth of an empire or economic system. If you skim through this book, you'll find time lines and maps that show this kind of information.

RESEARCHING AND EVALUATING EVIDENCE

As you've learned, historians begin their research by asking questions about a particular time and place. They then conduct research by examining evidence from both primary and secondary sources. **Primary sources** are writings or recordings that were created by someone who witnessed or lived through a historical event. These sources include letters, diaries, autobiographies, photographs, and oral histories. An **oral history** is a recorded interview with a person whose experiences and memories have historical significance. **Secondary sources** are writings, recordings, or objects created after an event by someone who did not see it or live during the time when it occurred. Secondary sources are often based on primary sources. History books and many biographies are secondary sources.

As historians examine primary and secondary sources, they apply reasoning skills to evaluate information. For example, to evaluate a piece of writing, a historian asks such questions as:

- Is the author stating a fact or an opinion?

- Is this information relevant—that is, does it apply to the issue being studied?

- Is this information essential or important?

- Can the information be verified, or proven by another reliable source?

- What is the context, or setting, for this information?

- What is the author's point of view?

 CST 1 Students explain how major events are related to one another in time; CST 2 Students construct various time lines of key events, people, and periods of the historical era they are studying; CST 3 Students use a variety of maps and documents to identify physical and cultural features of neighborhoods, cities, states, and countries and to explain the historical migration of people, expansion and disintegration of empires, and the growth of economic systems; REP 1 Students frame questions

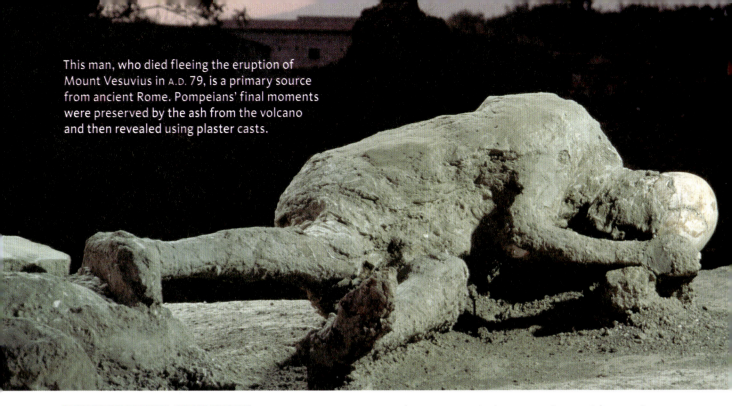

This man, who died fleeing the eruption of Mount Vesuvius in A.D. 79, is a primary source from ancient Rome. Pompeians' final moments were preserved by the ash from the volcano and then revealed using plaster casts.

INTERPRETING EVIDENCE

After historians examine and evaluate evidence, they try to put together a whole picture or story. They explain the central issues, placing people and events in a particular setting. They identify causes, effects, and sequence of events. They look for patterns that continue across time and place as well as the emergence of new patterns. For example, in many eras, nations have formed armies and fought wars against other nations for political, economic, or religious reasons. Global terrorism, however, is a relatively new pattern of warfare.

All historians do not tell the same story. Different historians may interpret the same evidence in different ways. A historian may accidently overlook certain evidence or make an error in interpreting evidence. In addition, new evidence is continually being discovered. That means that interpretations of history differ and often change.

A historian's focus depends partly on the time period and the place being studied. For example, a historian examining the 1900s in Italy might choose to focus on basic indicators of economic performance— statistics that tell how strong an economy is—and analyze the costs and benefits of economic and political decisions. But a historian studying an ancient state would not choose such a focus because such statistics are not available.

As you continue to study history, be prepared to apply the intellectual reasoning, reflection, and research skills of a historian.

REVIEW & ASSESS

1. **READING CHECK** Why do interpretations of history differ and often change?

2. **ASK QUESTIONS** Frame two questions that can be answered by historical study and research.

3. **COMPARE AND CONTRAST** What is the difference between a primary source and a secondary source?

that can be answered by historical study and research; REP 2 Students distinguish fact from opinion in historical narratives and stories; REP 3 Students distinguish relevant from irrelevant information, essential from incidental information, and verifiable from unverifiable information in historical narratives and stories; REP 4 Students assess the credibility of primary and secondary sources and draw sound conclusions from them; REP 5 Students detect the different historical points of view on historical events and determine the context in which the historical statements were made (the questions asked, sources used, author's perspectives); HI 1 Students explain the central issues and problems from the past, placing people and events in a matrix of time and place; HI 2 Students understand and distinguish cause, effect, sequence, and correlation in historical events, including the long- and short-term causal relations; HI 3 Students explain the sources of historical continuity and how the combination of ideas and events explains the emergence of new patterns; HI 4 Students recognize the role of chance, oversight, and error in history; HI 5 Students recognize that interpretations of history are subject to change as new information is uncovered; HI 5 Students recognize that interpretations of history are subject to change as new information is uncovered.

Augustus and the Pax Romana

When Julius Caesar was assassinated, Romans rolled their eyes and thought, "Here we go again." After decades of dictatorships and civil wars, they hoped for stability in the empire. They got it, but the republic was dead. A new type of leader was about to rule Rome for the next 500 years.

MAIN IDEA

Augustus transformed Rome from a violent republic into a peaceful empire.

A NEW EMPIRE

After Caesar's death, his heir, Octavian, found himself at the center of a deadly power struggle. At 18 years old, he had to kill or be killed. He survived and thrived. Octavian defeated his rivals, killed Caesar's assassins, and crushed revolts. He emerged victorious, immensely rich, and all-powerful. In 31 B.C., he became Rome's sole ruler. Four years later, the Senate gave him the name **Augustus**, or "exalted one."

Augustus was smarter than Caesar had been. He used his wealth and political skill to take control of the army and secure the people's support. He also won over the Senate, which awarded him dictator-like powers. He did all this while working within the law and appearing to uphold republican ideals. The Senate, among other institutions, continued, but Augustus controlled its decisions. He was the supreme ruler in Rome, or its **emperor**. His powers were granted for life and could be passed to a successor, which was something that made the Romans uneasy. They didn't want to return to the harsh rule of kings. However, the people accepted Augustus because he moved slowly, carefully, and legally. Above all, he finally brought peace to Rome.

PEACE UNDER AUGUSTUS

Augustus' reign began the **Pax Romana**, or "Roman Peace"—200 years of peace and prosperity enjoyed across the empire. The Pax Romana was possible because Augustus tackled some long-standing problems. The poor thanked Augustus for guaranteeing free handouts of grain. Most of the people might not have noticed that Augustus' newly paid officials were improving government. However, everyone took immense pride in his transformation of Rome into an impressive capital with magnificent marble monuments. Meanwhile, Augustus' new laws were restoring order, and he actively encouraged art, literature, and education.

Augustus also cleverly prevented any threat that might have been posed by the army. He cut its size in half but kept out-of-work veterans happy with grants of land. Soldiers still serving were kept constantly busy defending and expanding the empire's frontiers. The army also now had standardized pay and conditions and a new oath of loyalty to the emperor himself.

The elite Praetorian (pree-TAWR-ee-uhn) Guard were the only soldiers stationed in Rome, and they were committed to upholding the emperor's authority. In addition, to protect the empire's coasts and shipping trade, Augustus created Rome's first permanent navy. All of these changes helped ensure long-term stability for the empire and for many Roman emperors to come.

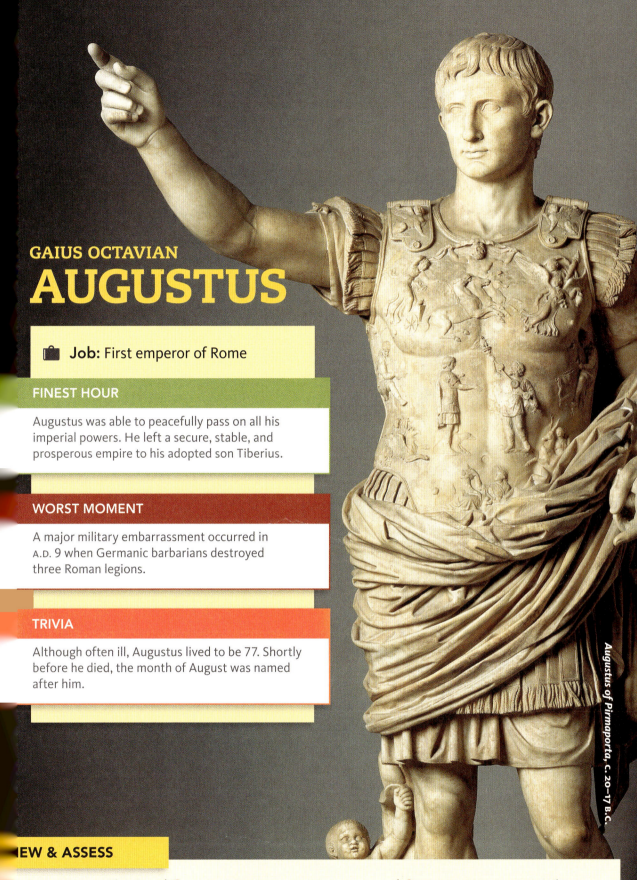

GAIUS OCTAVIAN
AUGUSTUS

Job: First emperor of Rome

FINEST HOUR

Augustus was able to peacefully pass on all his imperial powers. He left a secure, stable, and prosperous empire to his adopted son Tiberius.

WORST MOMENT

A major military embarrassment occurred in A.D. 9 when Germanic barbarians destroyed three Roman legions.

TRIVIA

Although often ill, Augustus lived to be 77. Shortly before he died, the month of August was named after him.

Augustus of Pirimaporta, c. 20–17 B.C.

EW & ASSESS

ADING CHECK What is Pax Romana?

2. IDENTIFY MAIN IDEAS AND DETAILS What are three things Augustus did to secure people's support?

3. MAKE INFERENCES Why do you think Augustus was careful to reward soldiers and reduce the size of the army?

dy the early strengths and lasting contributions of Rome (e.g., significance of Roman citizenship; rights under Roman law; Roman art, ture, engineering, and philosophy; preservation and transmission of Christianity) and its ultimate internal weaknesses (e.g., rise of autonomous nwers within the empire, undermining of citizenship by the growth of corruption and slavery, lack of education, and distribution of news).

1.3 Growth and Trade

During the Pax Romana, you could travel easily and safely across the entire Roman Empire. By A.D. 117, that meant you could cross most of the known western world. It was a merchant's dream, and the economy boomed as Romans enjoyed goods imported from almost everywhere.

MAIN IDEA

As the Roman Empire expanded, trade became easier and the economy boomed.

IMPERIAL EXPANSION

Under Augustus, the Roman army became the mightiest in the world. Its relentless march expanded the empire's frontiers and cultural influence farther than ever before. Soldiers in forts on three continents—Europe, Asia, and Africa—protected the empire's frontiers from attacks by numerous enemies. The soldiers could be soaking in the rains of northern Britain, sweltering in the deserts of southern Egypt, battered by Atlantic winds in western Spain, or swimming in the waters of the Red Sea.

Some of the frontier military camps became permanent settlements. Soldiers stationed at these settlements often stayed in the community when they retired. This practice helped expand Roman culture and influence in the region.

The Roman Empire did not always rely on military conquest to expand its borders. If an area looked like it would be difficult or costly to conquer outright, Augustus would support a local ruler. In return, the territory would be required to provide the empire with military aid if needed. In this way, Augustus was able to expand the empire while saving the expense of an all-out war. This arrangement also made it easier for Augustus to invade the territory in the future if he felt that it was necessary.

A network of roads, bridges, and tunnels built by soldiers connected these far-flung frontiers. It allowed the army to march swiftly across great distances and quickly crush trouble wherever it arose. The roads helped the army keep order, but they also benefited everyone in the empire. The official mail service used the roads to keep information flowing across the empire. Rest areas and inns for overnight stays were built at regular intervals. Everyone in the empire could travel farther, faster, more easily, and more safely than ever before.

A BOOMING ECONOMY

These excellent roads also stimulated the economy by making it easy to transport and sell goods throughout the empire—basic goods as well as luxuries. Even citizens with limited incomes could afford African olive oil and Spanish salted fish. This flow of goods around the empire created a thriving economy as well as a sense of community. Roman merchants gained great benefits from all of this trade.

Rome's craftspeople produced beautiful objects that archaeologists have found as far away as Vietnam, but what flowed out of the empire most was money. The city of Rome itself was the main consumer of imports, or goods brought from other places. Rome especially needed food to feed its huge population. Agriculture, though still Rome's largest industry, was focused on luxuries such as fruit.

7.1.1 Study the early strengths and lasting contributions of Rome (e.g., significance of Roman citizenship; rights under Roman law; Roman art, architecture, engineering, and philosophy; preservation and transmission of Christianity) and its ultimate internal weaknesses (e.g., rise of autonomous military powers within the empire, undermining of citizenship by the growth of corruption and slavery, lack of education, and distribution of news); 7.1.2 Discuss the geographic borders of the

ROMAN TRADE, C. A.D. 117

EUROPE

BRITAIN

ATLANTIC OCEAN

GAUL

Black Sea

Rome

SPAIN

Mediterranean Sea

To China

AFRICA

EGYPT

Red Sea

Tropic of Cancer

To India

Roman Empire at its height, c. A.D. 117
Trade routes
Slave trade
Goods traded

Gems	Spices
Grain	Textiles
Marble	Timber
Metals	Wild animals
Olive oil	Wine

0   300   600 Miles
0   300   600 Kilometers

The most important Roman goods in terms of the quantity traded were wine, olive oil, and grain. Traders moved these bulky goods by ship before transferring them to slower ox-drawn carts. Adventurous traders looked far beyond the empire's borders. These merchants would sail east to India or travel the Silk Roads to China. There they sought to trade wool, gold, and silver for luxuries such as silks, spices, and gems.

The introduction of a standard currency, or money, throughout the empire made it easier to conduct trade as well as collect taxes and pay soldiers. The empire made coins called *denarii* (dih-NAIR-ee) out of silver and *sesterces* (SEHS-tuhrs) out of brass. Roman coins were accepted not only in the empire but also beyond. The expanded empire and the Pax Romana were certainly good for business.

REVIEW & ASSESS

1. **READING CHECK** What innovation helped expand the empire and increase trade?

2. **INTERPRET MAPS** From which locations in the empire did Rome import grain to feed its citizens?

3. **ANALYZE CAUSE AND EFFECT** How did the introduction of a standard currency affect the Roman economy?

Roman Engineering

Step outside your door and you'll see a road. Follow the road and you'll reach a city. In the city, you'll find large concrete buildings. Two thousand years ago, Roman engineers were perfecting the techniques that enabled the building of these "modern" constructions.

MAIN IDEA

The Romans were skilled engineers who helped transform how things were built.

ROMAN INVENTIONS

Arch
A curved structure over an opening

Vault
An extended series of arches

Dome
A rotated series of arches

ROADS

Before the Romans began building their network of roads, travel generally meant following dirt tracks. Rome's first great road was the Appian Way built in 312 B.C. It connected Rome with southern Italy. As the empire expanded, its armies built new roads back to the capital—which is where the saying "All roads lead to Rome" comes from.

The army used specialized tools and lots of human power to build roads. Soldiers marked the route, dug foundations, and built up the road with several layers of material. The center of the road was slightly higher than the edges, which helped rain run into drainage ditches.

Where possible, the soldiers built the road wide and straight, making marches shorter and easier. Engineers developed special techniques to overcome obstacles. Roads sometimes included bridges over rivers or tunnels through hills. Every mile a milestone marked the distance to major cities. By A.D. 300, the Romans had built about 53,000 miles of roads.

ARCHES AND AQUEDUCTS

Concrete is not usually very interesting, but at the time of Augustus it transformed construction. The Romans developed a new, stronger type of concrete and used it to build huge freestanding structures, like the Colosseum. This large amphitheater was designed to seat 50,000 spectators and was the site of violent entertainment, such as animal fights and gladiator battles.

Roman architecture was modeled on Greek architecture, but the use of arches, vaults, and domes created a distinctive Roman style. An **arch**, or curved structure over an opening, is strong and inexpensive to build. Lengthening an arch creates a vault, and joining a circle of arches at their highest point creates a dome.

Long stone channels called **aqueducts** (AK-wih-duhkts) carried clean water from hilltops into cities and towns. The engineers' precise calculations over long distances ensured a steady flow of water. Rome received 35 million cubic feet of water every day. While most of an aqueduct ran underground, sometimes huge arched bridges were built to carry the water across valleys. Many of these magnificent structures still stand as reminders of Roman engineering ability: building big and building to last.

Critical Viewing The Claudian Aqueduct carried fresh water to Rome from surrounding rivers and lakes. What elements of Roman architecture appear in this structure?

REVIEW & ASSESS

1. **READING CHECK** What techniques and constructions did Roman engineers develop?

2. **SUMMARIZE** What was the process Roman soldiers used to build roads?

3. **MAKE INFERENCES** How did aqueducts help unify the empire?

7.1.1 Study the early strengths and lasting contributions of Rome (e.g., significance of Roman citizenship; rights under Roman law; Roman art, architecture, engineering, and philosophy; preservation and transmission of Christianity) and its ultimate internal weaknesses (e.g., rise of autonomous military powers within the empire, undermining of citizenship by the growth of corruption and slavery, lack of education, and distribution of news).

Latin and Literature

Students learning Latin have a rhyme: "Latin is a language as dead as dead can be. First it killed the Romans, and now it's killing me." But Latin is not dead. Latin is still used—especially by scientists and doctors. In fact, you use Latin words every day. It's one of Rome's lasting contributions.

MAIN IDEA

The Latin language spread across the empire and influences the way we speak and write today.

AN INFLUENTIAL LANGUAGE

As you've learned, the Romans conquered people who spoke hundreds of other languages, but the language spoken in Rome was **Latin**. Although Greek was also commonly used, Latin was established as the official language for international communication, government, law, and trade. It was used for official business from Britain to Egypt.

The Romans brought writing to northern Europe, and we still use the Latin alphabet today. However, back then the alphabet had only 22 letters. The letters *i* and *j* were interchangeable, as were *u* and *v*. The letters *w* and *y* did not exist at all.

Over time, new languages, called Romance languages, developed from Latin. These languages include French, Italian, Spanish, and Portuguese. Each language is distinctive but shares a common root in Latin, the "Roman" in *Romance*. The English language was greatly influenced by the Romance languages and uses many Latin words, including *campus, census, curriculum, index, item, sponsor,* and *stadium*.

ORATORY, POETRY, AND PHILOSOPHY

Roman writers and thinkers used the Latin language to create great works of literature, including speeches, poetry, and philosophical works. **Oratory**, or public speaking, was especially prized, and promising young men were trained in the art of argument and persuasion. Speeches by ancient Roman orators are still studied by serious students of public speaking.

The Romans also loved poetry, which was based on Greek traditions. The ultimate poem was the epic, a long story describing a hero's adventures. The most celebrated Roman epic was **Virgil's** *Aeneid* (uh-NEE-uhd), which fills 12 volumes. Written between 30 and 19 B.C., it tells the story of Aeneas, the legendary founder of Rome.

Roman philosophy was another extension of Greek ideas. Philosophy is the study of reality, knowledge, and beliefs. Ethical and religious arguments interested Romans more than theory and speculation. The Greek Stoic (STOH-ihk) philosophy was especially influential in Roman life. It stressed a practical approach to life in which people performed their civic duty and accepted their circumstances—good or bad.

The Roman Catholic Church, which you will learn about in Lesson 2.4, became the keeper of Roman literature and preserved works that could be used to educate young men in morality, government, and law. A 15th-century fascination with the ancient world revived the popularity of Roman literature and has ensured its widespread circulation ever since.

LATIN AND ENGLISH

Many English words have Latin roots, or origins. Examine the prefixes and suffixes listed. What words can you add?

-ty, -ity
FORMS NOUNS FROM ADJECTIVES

Similarity
Technicality

Sub-
UNDER

Submarine ›
Subway

Re-
AGAIN

Rebuild
Remake

-ation
FORMS NOUNS FROM VERBS

Celebration
Formation

Pre-
BEFORE

Preview
Prepay

Dis-
NOT ANY

Disbelief
Disrespect

-ment
FORMS NOUNS FROM VERBS

Entertainment
Statement

-ible, -able
FORMS ADJECTIVES FROM VERBS

^ *Flexible*
Likable

Post-
AFTER

Postgame
Postwar

-fy, -ify
FORMS VERBS AND MEANS "TO MAKE"

‹ *Purify*
Humidify

LEGEND

● Prefix ● Prefix Definition ● Suffix ● Suffix Explanation ● Example Words

REVIEW & ASSESS

1. READING CHECK How has the English language been influenced by Latin?

2. MAKE CONNECTIONS What additional words can you think of that include the Latin prefixes and suffixes listed above?

3. MAKE INFERENCES How did Roman ideas about philosophy support the ancient Roman approach to life?

 7.1.1 Study the early strengths and lasting contributions of Rome (e.g., significance of Roman citizenship; rights under Roman law; Roman art, architecture, engineering, and philosophy; preservation and transmission of Christianity) and its ultimate internal weaknesses (e.g., rise of autonomous military powers within the empire, undermining of citizenship by the growth of corruption and slavery, lack of education, and distribution of news).

1.6 Art, Architecture, and Law

The Romans shaped the ancient world for a thousand years. But what have they ever done for us? Well, quite a lot actually. If you know what to look for, you can spot Rome's legacy in modern-day art, architecture, and law.

MAIN IDEA

The Romans developed many ideas that continue to influence our lives today.

ART AND ARCHITECTURE

As with their philosophy, Romans preferred a realistic approach to art. The paintings and statues that decorated their homes showed people and things as they really looked. Like the Romans, people today often display realistic family portraits, although photos have generally replaced statues.

The Romans also enjoyed forms of decorative art that are still popular today. An expensive design feature in Roman villas was mosaic floors. A **mosaic** contains tiny colored stone cubes set in mortar to create a picture or a design. Wealthy Romans also covered their walls in **frescoes**, or pictures painted directly onto the wall while the plaster is still wet. The Roman **bas-relief** (bah-ruh-LEEF) is a realistic sculpture with figures raised against a flat background. These sculptures appear today on monuments such as the National World War II Memorial in Washington, D.C.

Rome's architectural influence is everywhere. Starting from the ground up, the Romans showed the world the benefit of an extensive, well-built, and well-maintained all-weather road network. European roads still follow Roman routes and sometimes cross original Roman bridges.

When a new Roman town was created, city planners took into account the city's climate and geography. The Romans always tried to establish a grid pattern for the streets. That means that the streets formed a network of intersecting horizontal and vertical lines. Many towns and cities use this pattern today.

Like the Romans, modern builders rely on concrete to build strong, tall, and unusual buildings. Roman architectural styles such as columns, arches, and domes can be seen in the U.S. Capitol and other buildings. Many modern stadiums follow the design perfected in the Colosseum.

This panel from a Roman sarcophagus, or stone coffin, is an example of bas-relief.

LAW AND GOVERNMENT

Rome even influences the way people today live. Roman ideas of civic duty are encouraged in the United States and elsewhere. The structure of the U.S. government reflects elements of the Roman Republic, including representative assemblies and the system of checks and balances. Roman laws are the basis of law codes around the world, including that of the United States. The ideas of a fair judge, presumption of innocence, and equality under the law also come from the Romans.

The Latin language is still very much a part of modern law and other fields and professions. Legal documents, science papers, and memorial inscriptions are rich with Latin text. As you learned earlier, many everyday English words have their roots in Latin. Studying Latin can also make it easier to learn other modern languages that have Latin roots.

So don't just think about the legacy of Rome, search it out. It's in our language, laws, government, art, and architecture. The Romans are everywhere.

REVIEW & ASSESS

1. **READING CHECK** What Roman achievements in art and architecture influence our lives today?

2. **MAKE CONNECTIONS** How has the government of the Roman Republic influenced the structure of the U.S. government?

3. **COMPARE AND CONTRAST** How are the layouts of many towns and cities today similar to those in ancient Rome?

 7.1.1 Study the early strengths and lasting contributions of Rome (e.g., significance of Roman citizenship; rights under Roman law; Roman art, architecture, engineering, and philosophy; preservation and transmission of Christianity) and its ultimate internal weaknesses (e.g., rise of autonomous military powers within the empire, undermining of citizenship by the growth of corruption and slavery, lack of education, and distribution of news); HI 2 Students understand and distinguish cause, effect, sequence, and correlation in historical events, including the long- and short-term causal relations; HI 3 Students explain the sources of historical continuity and how the combination of ideas and events explains the emergence of new patterns.

The Origins of Christianity

A man named Jesus who lived in Nazareth was a Jew whose beliefs became a threat to Jewish and Roman leaders. His teachings formed the foundation of a religion that has powerfully shaped the world for over 2,000 years.

MAIN IDEA

Christianity developed in Jewish communities and was based on the teachings of Jesus.

JEWISH ROOTS

As the empire expanded, the Romans were usually tolerant of the many different religions practiced throughout the empire. As long as people worshipped their emperor as a god, they could follow whatever faith they liked. This was not a problem for most religions. The exception was Judaism, the religion of the Jewish people.

The Romans captured the Jewish city of Jerusalem in 63 B.C., which brought the Jewish people under Roman control. At first the Romans allowed the Jews to worship one God. Over time, tensions grew. Rome began to enforce emperor worship, and the tensions exploded into conflict. In A.D. 70, Rome defeated the Jews, who then scattered throughout the empire. This helped spread a new religion that was developing in the Jewish community: Christianity.

JESUS OF NAZARETH

Christianity is based on the teachings of **Jesus**, a man born into a poor family in Judea around 6 B.C. Most of what we know about Jesus' teachings comes from the four **Gospels**. These books were written after Jesus' death by four of his followers—Matthew, Mark, Luke, and John. The Gospels are part of the **New Testament**, which presents the history, teachings, and beliefs of Christianity. According to historical record, Jesus was a practicing Jew and worked as a carpenter. When he was about 30 years old, he began to teach ideas that differed from Jewish practices. Biblical accounts claim that Jesus could perform miracles, such as healing the sick.

In time, Jesus traveled around Judea preaching and gathering disciples, or followers. He chose his closest followers, known as the **Twelve Apostles**, to help spread his teachings. He often used **parables** (short stories about everyday life) to make his religious or moral points. In his Sermon on the Mount, Jesus declared that love for God and charity toward all people were more important than following Jewish law. He also promised that those who sought God's forgiveness for their sins would go to heaven after death. To his followers, Jesus became Christ, "the anointed one." They believed he was the promised Messiah—the one who would free them.

According to Christian writings, Jesus criticized Jewish practices while visiting Jerusalem during the Jewish observance of Passover. Jesus was arrested and turned over to Roman authorities. Pontius Pilate, the Roman governor of Judea, sentenced Jesus to death by crucifixion—being nailed to a cross and left to die. Jesus' body was buried, and then, according to the Gospel accounts, he was resurrected, or rose from the dead, and ascended into heaven. For Christians, the resurrection signals victory over sin and death. The man called Jesus was gone, but Christianity was just beginning.

The Last Supper, Leonardo da Vinci, 1498

THE LAST SUPPER

Leonardo da Vinci completed this painting in 1498. It was painted directly on the wall of a church in Milan, Italy.

Jesus and his Twelve Apostles have gathered for a final Passover supper. The painting depicts the moment when Jesus tells his Apostles that one of them will betray him. Da Vinci captures a range of emotions among the Apostles and a sense of calm in Jesus. According to Christian belief, the Apostle Judas would betray Jesus after the meal. The next day Jesus was put to death.

LEGEND

1. Bartholomew
2. James Minor
3. Andrew
4. Judas
5. Peter
6. John

7. Jesus
8. Thomas
9. James Major
10. Philip
11. Matthew
12. Thaddeus
13. Simon

REVIEW & ASSESS

1. READING CHECK What were some of Jesus' teachings?

2. SEQUENCE EVENTS What were the key events in the life of Jesus?

3. MAKE INFERENCES What do you think makes parables an effective way to teach Christian ideas?

 7.1.1 Study the early strengths and lasting contributions of Rome (e.g., significance of Roman citizenship; rights under Roman law; Roman art, architecture, engineering, and philosophy; preservation and transmission of Christianity) and its ultimate internal weaknesses (e.g., rise of autonomous military powers within the empire, undermining of citizenship by the growth of corruption and slavery, lack of education, and distribution of news); CST 1 Students explain how major events are related to one another in time.

Christianity **Spreads**

Faith is very personal. We follow a particular religion (or no religion) for different reasons. Early Christians were the same way. Christianity had broad appeal and attracted a wide mix of people. They all believed that Jesus was the Messiah.

MAIN IDEA

Christianity attracted many followers and spread throughout the Roman Empire.

CHRISTIANITY'S APPEAL

At first all Christians were practicing Jews who still met in synagogues, places for Jewish worship. However, soon Christianity placed less emphasis on the laws of Judaism and welcomed Gentiles (GEHN-tylz), or non-Jews. As a result of the split from Judaism, Christianity grew and developed its own identity.

Christianity appealed to a lot of people. The religion's main appeal was the promise of salvation made possible by the sacrifice of Jesus. Many followers were also attracted by Christianity's rejection of the Roman focus on wealth and image. They preferred Jesus' focus on living simply and peacefully, sharing property, and providing charity to help the less fortunate. The poor liked the way Christian communities shared their wealth and established hospitals, schools, and other public services to improve their lives. Women and slaves liked Christianity because it treated them more like equals than other religions and Roman society did. Finally, many people embraced the idea of a personal relationship with God.

SPREADING THE WORD

In spite of Christianity's broad appeal, the religion's survival was far from certain, and it could easily have faded away. Instead it thrived because Jesus' followers spread his teachings fast and far. Through the Roman road network, Christianity spread rapidly in Jewish communities across the empire. Another big break was that the Romans confused Christianity with Judaism, and so they ignored the new religion, which allowed it to grow.

Even so, life as a Christian wasn't easy. The Romans often persecuted, or

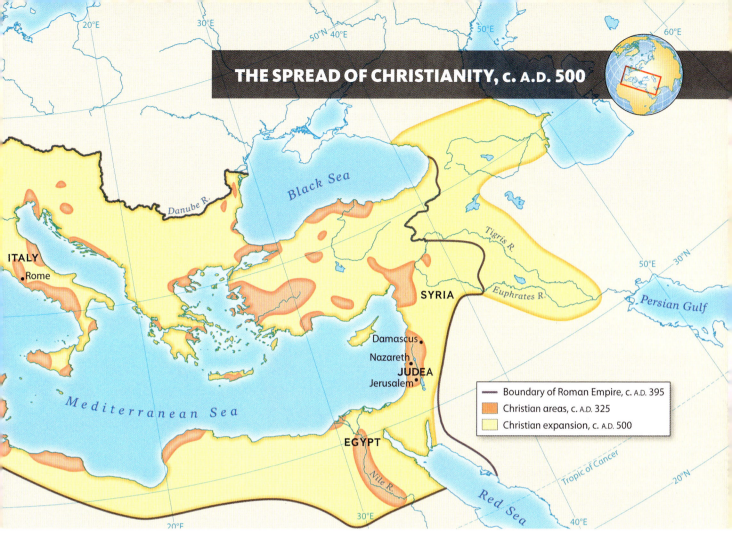

Map labels: ITALY, Rome, Danube R., Black Sea, Tigris R., Euphrates R., Persian Gulf, SYRIA, Damascus, Nazareth, JUDEA, Jerusalem, Mediterranean Sea, EGYPT, Nile R., Red Sea, Tropic of Cancer

Legend:
— Boundary of Roman Empire, c. A.D. 395
■ Christian areas, c. A.D. 325
■ Christian expansion, c. A.D. 500

punished, Christians for their beliefs. However, one of Christianity's fiercest persecutors, a man named **Paul**, eventually became its biggest champion.

Paul was most responsible for spreading early Christianity. He was a well-educated Jew and a Roman citizen. He converted to Christianity while traveling on the road to Damascus. According to Paul's own account, he had a vision in which Jesus was revealed to him as the Son of God. As a result, Paul became a <mark>missionary</mark>, a person who travels to another country to do religious work. He began spreading Jesus' teachings. Paul was often arrested, but he always escaped to preach again. He wrote many letters, or <mark>epistles</mark> (ih-PIH-suhls), explaining Jesus' teachings by answering specific questions. According to tradition, Paul was killed in a Roman massacre of Christians in A.D. 64. By then, Roman leaders realized that Christianity was a separate religion from Judaism and a popular religion—too popular. Fearful that Christianity might threaten the stability of the empire, Roman rulers made the religion's practice illegal.

REVIEW & ASSESS

1. **READING CHECK** How did Christianity spread throughout the Roman Empire?

2. **INTERPRET MAPS** What natural features served as the northern border for Christian expansion by A.D. 500?

3. **MAKE INFERENCES** Why was Paul so successful at spreading the teachings of Christianity?

7.1.1 Study the early strengths and lasting contributions of Rome (e.g., significance of Roman citizenship; rights under Roman law; Roman art, architecture, engineering, and philosophy; preservation and transmission of Christianity) and its ultimate internal weaknesses (e.g., rise of autonomous military powers within the empire, undermining of citizenship by the growth of corruption and slavery, lack of education, and distribution of news); CST 3 Students use a variety of maps and documents to identify physical and cultural features of neighborhoods, cities, states, and countries and to explain the historical migration of people, expansion and disintegration of empires, and the growth of economic systems.

2.3 DOCUMENT-BASED QUESTION

Writings from the New Testament

The Christian Bible is made up of two parts: the Old Testament (or Hebrew Bible) and the New Testament. The New Testament includes the Gospel of Luke and Paul's Epistles. At the core of the New Testament teaching is the death and resurrection of Jesus, giving the world a "new covenant" (new testament) that would enable all who repented of their sins to enter the kingdom of heaven.

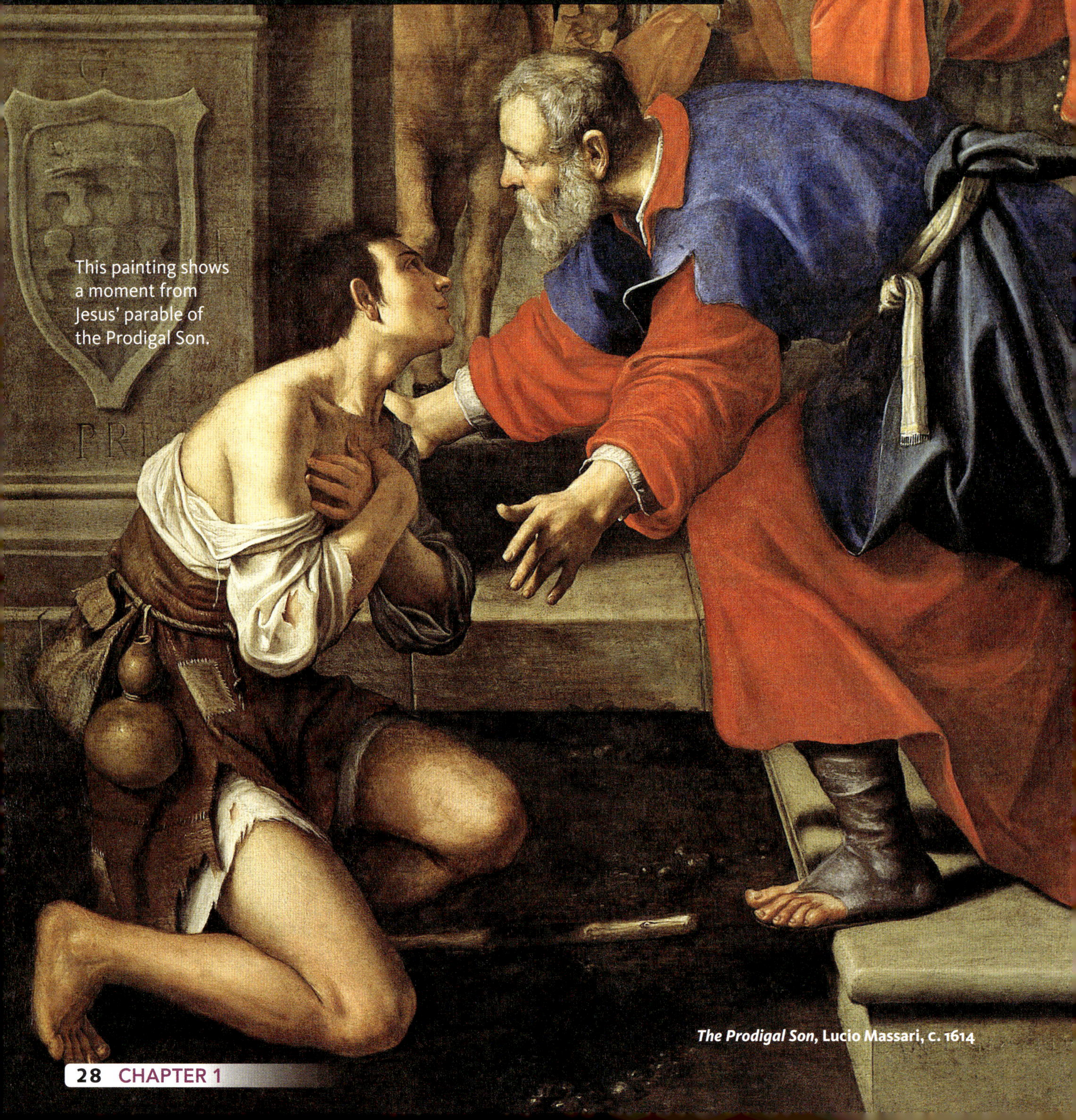

This painting shows a moment from Jesus' parable of the Prodigal Son.

The Prodigal Son, Lucio Massari, c. 1614

The Parable of the Good Samaritan

This parable was recorded in the Gospel of Luke in the first century A.D. The Samaritans (suh-MEHR-uh-tuhns) were a community of people who were generally distrusted by the Jews, the audience of the parable. According to the Gospel of Luke, Jesus tells this parable to answer the question "Who is my neighbor?"

CONSTRUCTED RESPONSE How does the Samaritan's response to the beaten man differ from the responses of the priest and Levite?

Good Samaritan, Julius Schnorr von Carolsfeld, 1860

A man was going down from Jerusalem to Jericho, when he fell into the hands of robbers. They stripped him of his clothes, beat him, and went away, leaving him half dead. A priest happened to be going down the same road, and when he saw the man, he passed by on the other side. So too, a Levite [a Jew], when he came to the place and saw him, passed by on the other side. But a Samaritan, as he traveled, came where the man was; and when he saw him, he took pity on him. He went to him and bandaged his wounds, pouring on oil and wine. Then he put the man on his own donkey, took him to an inn, and took care of him. The next day he took out two silver coins and gave them to the innkeeper. "Look after him," he said, "and when I return, I will reimburse you for any extra expense you may have."

Luke 10:30–35

from Paul's Epistle to the Galatians

Paul wrote his letter to the Galatians (guh-LAY-shuhnz) in the first century A.D. The Roman province of Galatia contained a number of early Christian communities. In his letter, Paul stresses some important ideas of the Christian faith.

CONSTRUCTED RESPONSE What important Christian ideas is Paul stating in this epistle?

You all are sons of God through faith in Christ Jesus, for all of you who were baptized . . . have clothed yourselves with Christ. There is neither Jew nor Greek, slave nor free, male nor female, for you are all one in Christ Jesus.

Galatians 3:26–28

SYNTHESIZE & WRITE

1. **REVIEW** Review the ideas expressed in the parable of the Good Samaritan and Paul's Epistle to the Galatians.

2. **RECALL** On your own paper, write down the main idea expressed in each document.

3. **CONSTRUCT** Write a topic sentence that answers this question: What are some fundamental Christian ideas about how people should treat one another?

4. **WRITE** Using evidence from the documents and from the chapter, write a paragraph that supports your answer to the question in Step 3.

The Early Christian Church

Being different can make you a target for attacks. Early Christians were violently attacked, but their courage and determination ensured Christianity's survival.

MAIN IDEA

In time, Christianity became the official religion of the Roman Empire.

CONSTANTINE

Constantine was very generous to his supporters. Historians have suggested that he could afford to be so generous only because he robbed temples and used tax money for his own purposes. It is also clear that some of his supporters gained favor by faking conversions to Christianity.

CONSTANTINE'S CONVERSION

As you have learned, Christians were often persecuted by their Roman rulers. In A.D. 35, a Christian named Stephen became the first of thousands of Christian victims. He was killed for his religious beliefs. Roman leaders punished Christians for refusing to worship the emperors.

This persecution only got worse. In A.D. 64, the emperor Nero blamed Christians for a great fire that swept through Rome. He had thousands of Christians put to death. Just being a Christian became punishable by death. As a result, worshippers were forced to meet in secret. They buried their dead in hidden underground chambers called **catacombs** (KA-tuh-kohms).

In A.D. 312, Christian persecution had reached its highest point when an amazing change began. On the eve of a battle for control of the empire, a young Roman leader named **Constantine** prayed for help. He believed his prayers were answered with a vision of the Christian cross. The vision led him to paint a symbol on his soldiers' shields. Constantine went on to win the battle. As a result, he immediately put an end to Christian persecution.

Constantine made many other changes after he became emperor. He built churches in Roman lands and declared Sunday the Christian day of rest. He even had Christian symbols placed on coins. Constantine ruled for a long time. However, it was only after Constantine's rule that the emperor Theodosius officially closed all the temples to the Roman gods and made Christianity the official religion of Rome.

FORMATION OF THE EARLY CHURCH

With the legalization of Christianity, Christian communities could openly share their beliefs. Church leaders from across the empire held councils, or meetings, to discuss Christianity and the writings of religious scholars. Their discussions helped them define Christian beliefs and practices.

Christian practices were then communicated to Christian churches throughout the empire and beyond. Each church was led by a priest, and groups of churches were overseen by a bishop. The first bishop of Rome, according to Christian tradition, was the apostle Peter, who died for his beliefs in A.D. 64. Constantine had a church, St. Peter's Basilica, built

St. Peter's Basilica represents modern Catholicism. The splendid art and architecture convey the power of the Catholic Church.

over the apostle's tomb. The photo above shows the basilica, which was rebuilt in the 1600s. In time the bishop of Rome became the most important bishop, or **pope**. He was seen as the leader of the unified church, known as the **Roman Catholic Church**.

Church leaders standardized Christian beliefs into a common creed, or statement of beliefs. One such statement was the definition of God as a Holy Trinity, or the union of Father, Son (Jesus), and Holy Spirit. The Christian Bible contained the foundations of the faith in two books: the Jewish Old Testament and a New Testament of approved writings. Worship in the Christian church focused on some common sacraments, or religious ceremonies, such as baptism, an individual's acceptance by the church. As Christianity grew more structured and became more organized, it became a powerful religion.

REVIEW & ASSESS

1. **READING CHECK** How did Christianity become the official religion of the Roman Empire?

2. **DESCRIBE** How was the leadership of the early church organized?

3. **DRAW CONCLUSIONS** In what way did their persecution help unite the Christians?

7.1.1 Study the early strengths and lasting contributions of Rome (e.g., significance of Roman citizenship; rights under Roman law; Roman art, architecture, engineering, and philosophy; preservation and transmission of Christianity) and its ultimate internal weaknesses (e.g., rise of autonomous military powers within the empire, undermining of citizenship by the growth of corruption and slavery, lack of education, and distribution of news).

3.1 Internal Weaknesses

Despite the occasional unbalanced emperor, the Roman Empire ran smoothly for 200 years. Then things began to fall apart. Disputes over who should be emperor caused the return of political violence and civil war. In some years, four or even six emperors were on the throne. By A.D. 235, the Roman world had plunged into a crisis.

MAIN IDEA

Military problems led to a crisis in the Roman Empire.

MILITARY PROBLEMS

So what went wrong? Arguably the empire had physically outgrown the emperor's ability to govern it. At its height, the Roman Empire stretched from Scotland to the Sahara, an area about half the size of the United States. This vast expanse, with huge geographic and cultural differences, was very difficult to govern effectively.

Defending such a large area also proved difficult. Rome faced attacks on two fronts at the same time, which drained money and resources all across the empire. In the east, Rome fought the powerful Parthian Empire from Persia, while Germanic tribes raided Rome's northern borders.

Meanwhile, warring groups within the empire once again fought to decide who would be emperor. Civil wars bled the empire of desperately needed food, money, and soldiers. With so many Roman soldiers engaged in warfare, invaders from outside the empire invaded and plundered, or stole riches from, the unguarded interior. It was a sure sign of trouble when cities, including Rome, rebuilt their long-neglected defensive walls. These military problems provoked further political and social problems.

POLITICAL, ECONOMIC, AND SOCIAL PROBLEMS

War was not only dangerous for soldiers; it was disruptive for everyone. Emperors were blamed for not protecting the empire, and they were regularly replaced or murdered. Fifty different emperors ruled between A.D. 235 and 285. People living in what would become Spain, France, and Britain preferred to trust local rulers. They broke from Rome to form a separate Gallic Empire. These events weakened imperial authority and prevented the strong, decisive, and long-term action needed to restore order.

This constant warfare also ruined the economy. Trade was interrupted, and the empire had to rely on its inadequate agricultural resources. The people suffered food shortages and higher taxes. Wars are expensive, and the emperors expected the people to pay for them. Even heavier taxes were enforced when the imperial currency lost value. This affected rich and poor but mostly the poor.

Ordinary people grew angry, criminal organizations grew, and outbursts of mob anger increased. It even became difficult to recruit local officials. Nobody wanted these jobs because people risked a beating for doing them. In these unstable times, good citizenship took second place to looking after oneself.

7.1.1 Study the early strengths and lasting contributions of Rome (e.g., significance of Roman citizenship; rights under Roman law; Roman art, architecture, engineering, and philosophy; preservation and transmission of Christianity) and its ultimate internal weaknesses (e.g., rise of autonomous military powers within the empire, undermining of citizenship by the growth of corruption and slavery, lack of education, and distribution of news); 7.1.2 Discuss the geographic borders of the

Illustration of a parade honoring victories of Emperor Augustus

Military Reasons

- Fighting the Parthian Empire in the east
- Fighting Germanic tribes in the west
- Fighting civil wars at home

Stone relief showing a government bureaucrat at work

Political Reasons

- Difficult to govern huge empire
- Frequently changing emperors
- Power gained by local leaders

Relief depicting a tax payment

Economic Reasons

- Trade interrupted
- People heavily taxed
- Lower value of currency

Illustration of a Roman party with the poor waiting on the rich

Social Reasons

- Unrest from gap between rich and poor
- More criminal organizations
- Civic responsibility no longer important

REVIEW & ASSESS

1. **READING CHECK** Why did the size of the Roman Empire cause military problems?

2. **ANALYZE CAUSE AND EFFECT** What was the result of the emperors' expensive wars?

3. **DRAW CONCLUSIONS** How did Rome's military problems lead to political, social, and economic problems?

empire at its height and the factors that threatened its territorial cohesion; HI.2 Students understand and distinguish cause, effect, sequence, and

Eastern and **Western** Roman Empires

The Roman Empire was too big for one person to manage. Unfortunately that didn't stop ambitious men from trying and failing. Then Rome's luck changed. In A.D. 284, the throne was seized by an emperor who had the sense and strength to make the big changes that could keep the empire alive.

MAIN IDEA

In A.D. 285, the Roman Empire was divided into the Western Roman Empire and the Eastern Roman Empire.

DIOCLETIAN DIVIDES THE EMPIRE

The new emperor was named **Diocletian** (dy-uh-KLEE-shuhn), and he had a lot on his plate. He faced endangered frontiers, overstretched armies, economic collapse, weak imperial authority, and widespread unrest. However, Diocletian had a radical plan: In A.D. 285, he divided the empire in two. Diocletian ruled the Eastern Roman Empire, and his trusted friend Maximian ruled the Western Roman Empire. Each man appointed a junior emperor to rule with him. This rule by four emperors, called a **tetrarchy** (TEH-trahr-kee), worked really well at first.

Each emperor focused on his specific region while cooperating to introduce reforms.

Together they increased the army to 400,000 men and reorganized and strengthened the frontier forces. They also created a mobile field army ready to tackle trouble wherever it broke out. On the political front, Diocletian and Maximian reformed government administration and divided the provinces into more manageable units. To promote unity, they enforced emperor worship and the Latin language everywhere. They encouraged economic recovery by reforming tax laws, controlling inflation, and stabilizing the currency. The empire was on the road to recovery, and after 20 years, Diocletian and Maximian retired, letting the junior emperors take over. However, this was as good as the tetrarchy got.

CONSTANTINE MOVES THE CAPITAL

You've learned that the emperor Constantine made the practice of Christianity legal in the empire. Before he did that, he had to fight to become emperor. Constantine's father was emperor of the Western Roman Empire. When Constantine's father died in A.D. 306, however, the tetrarchy refused his claim to be western emperor, sparking a civil war. Constantine won the war and became emperor of east and west. However, Constantine was more interested in the eastern half of his empire.

ATLANTIC OCEAN

Western Roman Empire
Eastern Roman Empire

Rome's importance had long been decreasing. Emperors no longer lived in Rome, and Italy had lost its privileged status.

The differences between east and west were increasing. The east produced more people, more food, more taxes, and more soldiers, while the west just grew weaker. So Constantine moved the capital from Rome to the ancient Greek city of Byzantium, which he renamed Constantinople. (Today the city is called Istanbul.) He built his new capital on the strategically important Bosporus, a narrow stretch of water separating Europe and Asia.

Constantine also continued the reforms begun by earlier emperors, earning the title "the Great." However, his sons plunged the empire into another civil war. The emperor Theodosius later reunited the empire, but the division of east and west became permanent after his death in A.D. 395. From then on, the fortunes and futures of the two empires were very different.

ROMAN EMPIRE: EAST AND WEST, c. A.D. 395

NATURAL BORDERS The Rhine and Danube rivers on the northern border of the Roman Empire were difficult to cross, which made it easier for the Roman army to defend the empire.

CONSTANTINOPLE Constantine's new capital on the Bosporus provided easy access to many resources and allowed the empire to control trade.

ROME Diocletian's decision to rule the Eastern Roman Empire made it clear that Rome was no longer the center of political power.

EUROPE

Rhine R.

Danube R.

Black Sea

Bosporus

Rome

Constantinople

ASIA

AFRICA

Mediterranean Sea

REVIEW & ASSESS

1. **READING CHECK** Why did Diocletian divide the Roman Empire in half?

2. **INTERPRET MAPS** In what ways was Rome's location similar to that of Constantinople?

3. **IDENTIFY PROBLEMS AND SOLUTIONS** What was Diocletian's plan for ruling the vast empire more efficiently?

7.1.3 Describe the establishment by Constantine of the new capital in Constantinople and the development of the Byzantine Empire, with an emphasis on the consequences of the development of two distinct European civilizations, Eastern Orthodox and Roman Catholic, and their two distinct views on church-state relations; CST 3 Students use a variety of maps and documents to identify physical and cultural features of neighborhoods, cities, states, and countries and to explain the historical migration of people, expansion and disintegration of empires and the

Critical Viewing This painting shows Attila the Hun attacking a Roman city. In what ways has the artist made Attila seem very fierce?

End of the Western Roman Empire

If you lived in the Western Roman Empire in A.D. 375, you'd be unhappy with the way things were going. While the west struggled to rule itself, feed itself, pay its bills, and defend its borders, you would enviously watch the Eastern Roman Empire grow richer, stronger, and more stable. However bad things got, you could never imagine a world without the Roman Empire—but that reality was just 101 years away.

MAIN IDEA

Invaders attacked the Western Roman Empire and caused its downfall.

FOREIGN INVADERS

Diocletian and Constantine only delayed the end of the Western Roman Empire. The end came in the form of **barbarians**, a Greek word Romans used to describe all people outside of the empire. Three main tribes of barbarians would finally tear the Western Roman Empire apart. The Visigoths (VIH-zuh-gahths) and Vandals were Germanic tribes from northern Europe. Looking for better farmland, both groups migrated south toward the Roman frontier.

The Huns formed the third tribe of barbarians. Migrating from Asia, they were nomads, or wandering cattle herders. Their skill with horses and bows made them a ferocious fighting force. Beginning in A.D. 445, a man named **Attila** was their sole ruler.

THE WESTERN ROMAN EMPIRE FALLS

Attila and his army swept into Europe. Forced into the Western Roman Empire by the Huns, the Visigoths soon invaded Italy. Around the same time, the Vandals invaded Gaul and then Spain. By now the emperor, who had few Roman soldiers to call on, had to enlist barbarian fighters to defend the empire.

On August 24, 410, the Visigoths shocked the world by sacking, or destroying, Rome. They then conquered Gaul and Spain, driving the Vandals into North Africa. Then came Attila. The Huns attacked Gaul in A.D. 451, and the emperor relied on barbarian armies to fight them. Rome had lost control. In A.D. 476, the last emperor quietly left the throne.

The Western Roman Empire was broken up into many Germanic kingdoms, and the Eastern Roman Empire became known as the Byzantine Empire. The Roman Empire was over. Historians argue about why the Western Roman Empire fell. Did it end naturally because of internal failings? Was it brought down by external forces? Or was it simply transformed into something new?

REVIEW & ASSESS

1. **READING CHECK** What three barbarian tribes invaded Roman territory, leading to Rome's downfall?

2. **SEQUENCE EVENTS** What events led to the fall of the Western Roman Empire?

3. **DRAW CONCLUSIONS** Why were so many tribes able to invade the Western Roman Empire?

HI 2 Students understand and distinguish cause, effect, sequence, and correlation in historical events, including the long- and short-term causal relations.

VOCABULARY

Match each word in the first column with its definition in the second column.

WORD	DEFINITION
1. aqueduct (HSS 7.1.1)	a. the practice and skill of public speaking
2. primary source (HSS REP 4)	b. the leader of the Roman Catholic Church
3. parable (HSS 7.1.1)	c. a writing or recording created by someone who witnessed or lived through a historical event
4. oratory (HSS 7.1.1)	d. a system of government in which there are four rulers
5. bas-relief (HSS 7.1.1)	e. a simple story told to make a moral point
6. tetrarchy (HSS 7.1.2)	f. a stone channel that carries water
7. pope (HSS 7.1.1)	g. a sculpture with figures raised against a flat background

READING SKILL

8. **ORGANIZE IDEAS: SEQUENCE EVENTS** If you haven't already, complete your time line of key people and events in the Roman Empire. Then answer the question.

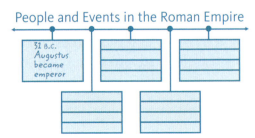

People and Events in the Roman Empire

31 B.C. Augustus became emperor

Which person or event do you think had the greatest impact on the Roman Empire? Why?
(HSS CST 2)

MAIN IDEAS

Answer the following questions. Support your answers with evidence from the chapter.

9. What was accomplished during the Pax Romana? **LESSON 1.2** (HSS HI 1)

10. What effect did safe seas and a network of excellent roads have on the Roman Empire's economy? **LESSON 1.3** (HSS HI 6)

11. How did Roman ideas about government and law influence the government of the United States? **LESSON 1.6** (HSS HI 3)

12. What role did Constantine play in the growth of Christianity? **LESSON 2.4** (HSS 7.1.1)

13. What political problems contributed to the decline of the Roman Empire? **LESSON 3.1** (HSS 7.1.1)

CRITICAL THINKING

Answer the following questions. Support your answers with evidence from the chapter.

14. **ESSENTIAL QUESTION** What was the main reason the Roman Empire became so powerful and long lasting? (HSS 7.1.1)

15. **SYNTHESIZE** How did Christianity grow and develop into a powerful religion? (HSS 7.1.1)

16. **EVALUATE** What role did technology play in Roman architecture? (HSS 7.1.1)

17. **ANALYZE CAUSE AND EFFECT** How did the Roman Empire's vast geographic expanse become a serious disadvantage in the third century? What was the effect of this disadvantage? (HSS 7.1.2)

18. **MAKE CONNECTIONS** How did the Latin language influence the Romance languages and English? (HSS HI 3)

19. **YOU DECIDE** Which emperor had a more lasting impact, Augustus or Constantine? Support your opinion with evidence from the chapter. (HSS REP 1)

INTERPRET MAPS

Study the map and answer the questions that follow.

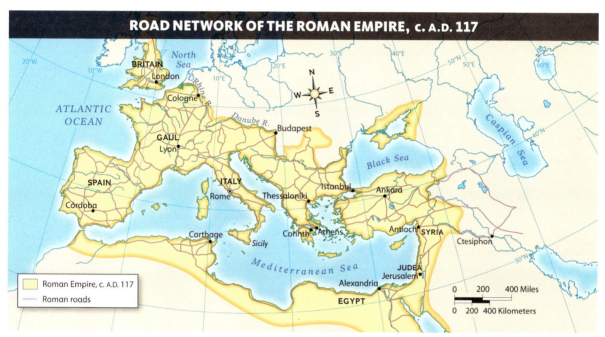

ROAD NETWORK OF THE ROMAN EMPIRE, c. A.D. 117

Roman Empire, c. A.D. 117
Roman roads

20. Where is Rome located in relation to the rest of the Roman Empire? (HSS CST 3)

21. In A.D. 117 how far north and how far south did the Roman Empire extend? (HSS CST 3)

ANALYZE SOURCES

Read the selection from Jesus' Sermon on the Mount. Then answer the question.

> Blessed are the poor in spirit, for theirs is the kingdom of heaven.
>
> Blessed are the meek, for they will inherit the Earth.
>
> Blessed are the merciful, for they will be shown mercy.
>
> Blessed are the pure in heart, for they will see God.
>
> —Matthew 5:3–8

22. SYNTHESIZE How might these teachings have helped guide people to lead their lives during the Roman Empire? (HSS REP 4)

WRITE ABOUT HISTORY

23. EXPLANATORY Many social, political, and economic problems contributed to the decline and fall of the Roman Empire. Put yourself in the position of a senator at that time. Write a speech explaining three of these problems. (HSS 7.1.1)

TIPS

- Take notes as you review the portion of the chapter about the decline and fall of the Roman Empire.

- State your main idea and supporting details in a clear, well-organized way.

- Present evidence to support your explanation.

- Use vocabulary from the chapter to explain the problems.

- Make a concluding statement based on your explanation of and evidence about the decline and fall of the Roman Empire.

2

THE BYZANTINE EMPIRE

330 – 1453

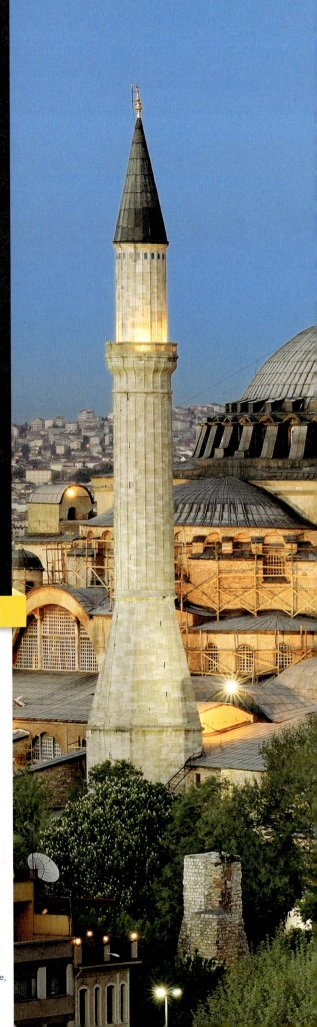

ESSENTIAL QUESTION How did the Byzantine Empire carry on the culture and traditions of the old Roman Empire?

SECTION 1 THE EARLY EMPIRE

KEY VOCABULARY

crossroads
diversity
divine
heresy

NAMES & PLACES

Bosporus
Constantinople
Hagia Sophia
Justinian
Justinian Code
Theodora

SECTION 2 THE LATER EMPIRE

KEY VOCABULARY

creed
excommunicate
icon
patriarch
schism

NAMES & PLACES

Eastern Orthodox
  Church

READING STRATEGY

ORGANIZE IDEAS: ANALYZE CAUSE AND EFFECT
Analyzing cause and effect means figuring out why things happen. Often, an effect will have several contributing causes. As you read the chapter, use a diagram like this one to take notes and to think about what people and events caused the Byzantine Empire to grow and thrive.

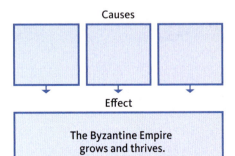

Causes

Effect

The Byzantine Empire
grows and thrives.

 HI 2 Students understand and distinguish cause, effect, sequence, and correlation in historical events, including the long- and short-term causal relations.

The Hagia Sophia dominates the skyline of Istanbul in present-day Turkey. Originally built as a church by a Byzantine emperor, it later became a mosque and is now a museum.

The Geography of the Byzantine Empire

The Western Roman Empire fell in A.D. 476, but that's not the end of its story. For a thousand years after that date, the glory of Rome lived on in the Byzantine Empire.

MAIN IDEA

The Byzantine Empire was well located for trade but open to attack.

CONNECTING EAST AND WEST

From law to architecture, the Byzantine (BIHZ-uhn-teen) Empire's achievements were extraordinary. One reason for those achievements was the empire's location at the **crossroads** of Europe and Asia, the place where the trade routes from each continent met. As a result of the empire's geography, many influences came together to create the Byzantine civilization.

As you may recall from the previous chapter, the emperor Diocletian divided the Roman Empire in A.D. 293. The Eastern Roman Empire became known as the Byzantine Empire because its capital was built on the old Greek town of Byzantium (buh-ZAN-tee-uhm). In fact, the Byzantine Empire is often referred to as Byzantium. By A.D. 330, the emperor Constantine had transformed Byzantium into a grand "New Rome." He named the city **Constantinople**, or city of Constantine. Today it is called Istanbul.

While the Western Roman Empire was ripped apart by invading barbarians, the Byzantine Empire managed to survive similar attacks. A series of strong emperors fought off Byzantium's enemies and strengthened the empire. Thus, the Byzantine Empire continued the traditions of Roman civilization for another thousand years after the collapse of the Western Roman Empire. The people we now call Byzantines proudly called themselves Romans.

Constantinople occupied one of the ancient world's most important geographic locations. At the heart of the empire was the small but important land link between Asia and Europe that permitted trade between east and west. The empire itself reached into both continents. Its heartland was in what are now Greece and Turkey.

Constantinople was also located on the **Bosporus**, a strait that links the Black Sea with the Mediterranean. The city was a major trade center for goods traveling by land and sea from all over the world. Constantinople and the Byzantine Empire grew rich on this trade. The city also attracted people from many parts of the world. They came to trade goods from their homelands and wound up living in the bustling city. These immigrants gave Constantinople the cultural **diversity**, or variety, for which it was famous.

EXPANDING THE EMPIRE

The Byzantine Empire's location brought problems as well as advantages. Although Constantinople itself was well protected, the rest of the empire was surrounded by enemies. To the north and west were many barbarian kingdoms forcefully pressing on Byzantium's borders. To the east was an age-old enemy, the powerful and hostile Persian Empire.

The rich resources and great wealth of Byzantium made it a tempting target for raids and invasions. With no strong geographic barriers to prevent invasion by enemies, the empire was dangerously

7.1.3 Describe the establishment by Constantine of the new capital in Constantinople and the development of the Byzantine Empire, with an emphasis on the consequences of the development of two distinct European civilizations, Eastern Orthodox and Roman Catholic, and their two distinct views on church-state relations; CST 3 Students use a variety of maps and

SLAVS

FRANKS

EUROPE

GOTHS

HUNS

GOTHS

Ravenna•

DALMATIA

ITALY

MACEDONIA

Black Sea

Bosporus

Corsica

•Rome

Constantinople•

•Nicaea

Sardinia

ANATOLIA

PERSIAN EMPIRE

•Cartagena

Sicily

Athens•

SYRIA

NUMIDIA

Carthage•

Cyprus

Crete

Damascus•

AFRICA

Mediterranean Sea

Jerusalem•

TRIPOLITANIA

Alexandria•

CYRENAICA

EGYPT

Red Sea

Legend:
- The Byzantine Empire before Justinian
- Expansion under Justinian

0   250   500 Miles
0 250 500 Kilometers

exposed. Its long borders were constantly under attack by invading neighbors.

The Byzantine Empire needed strong leadership to hold it together in the face of so many threats. Over a thousand years, its borders grew and shrank, depending on the ability of its rulers and the eagerness of its enemies to wage war. At its greatest extent, the empire completely encircled the Mediterranean Sea.

Probably the greatest Byzantine ruler was one of its earliest—**Justinian**, the emperor from A.D. 527 until his death in 565. He not only recaptured lost Byzantine lands but also reconquered large areas of the old Western Roman Empire. His armies defeated the Persians and reconquered North Africa, Italy, and parts of Spain. For a brief time, Justinian reunited the Eastern and Western Roman Empires. He built up the strength of the Byzantine Empire, even while Rome was being overrun by invaders. Justinian's legacy of leadership remained influential throughout the time of the Byzantine Empire and beyond.

REVIEW & ASSESS

1. **READING CHECK** Why was Constantinople's geographic location an advantage for trade?

2. **ANALYZE CAUSE AND EFFECT** What caused the Persian Empire and other enemies to attack and invade Byzantium?

3. **INTERPRET MAPS** How far west did the borders of the Byzantine Empire expand after Justinian's conquests?

documents to identify physical and cultural features of neighborhoods, cities, states, and countries and to explain the historical migration of people, expansion and disintegration of empires, and the growth of economic systems; HI 2 Students understand and distinguish cause, effect, sequence, and correlation in historical events, including the long- and short-term causal relations.

43

Justinian and Theodora

There's a popular saying that two heads are better than one. This was certainly true of Justinian's reign. Justinian became Byzantium's greatest emperor thanks in part to the support and intelligence of his wife, Theodora.

MAIN IDEA

Justinian and Theodora ruled over a golden age for Byzantium.

A POWERFUL RULER

Justinian was born in A.D. 482 or 483 to a peasant farmer. It was a humble beginning, but Justinian's uncle rose to become a great general and then emperor. The uncle educated Justinian, gave him important jobs, and appointed him as his successor. It was a smart choice. Justinian was intelligent, talented, and ambitious. He modeled himself on the old Roman Caesars. After he became emperor in 527, Justinian worked to bring a golden age to Byzantium.

In many ways, Justinian proved to be a powerful and effective leader. As you have read, he greatly expanded the empire's borders. Within those borders, he made major improvements in the areas of government, construction, and law. He reformed Byzantine government to improve efficiency and get rid of corruption. Justinian also started an ambitious construction program. He ordered the building of the **Hagia Sophia** (HY-uh soh-FEE-uh), a church in Constantinople that today is considered a masterpiece of Byzantine architecture. He also sponsored many other civic projects in the city, including a magnificent new building for the Senate.

Justinian was a dedicated Christian actively involved in issues of faith. He punished those he found guilty of **heresy** (HAIR-uh-see)—beliefs contrary to church teachings—including Jews. For example, he prohibited Jews from building synagogues and reading the Bible in Hebrew.

Justinian also worked hard to settle the differences of opinion that divided the early church. For example, groups within the church had different beliefs about whether Jesus Christ was fully **divine** (having the nature of a god) and should be worshipped as an equal to God. This disagreement continued long after Justinian's death.

Justinian's reform of the law was far more successful. He reorganized and standardized confusing Roman laws and had the surviving laws written down clearly and logically in a single work called the **Justinian Code**. This remarkable work has formed the basis of European law until modern times.

A COURAGEOUS EMPRESS

Of all Justinian's advisors, the most influential was his wife, **Theodora**. An actress when she was young, Theodora was part of a lower social class, so Justinian had to have the law changed to marry her. Together, they formed an unstoppable team who shared power as nearly equal co-rulers.

Theodora was extremely bright and energetic. Justinian admired her intelligence and deeply respected her opinions. As a result, she had a huge influence on imperial policy. Theodora was probably behind the laws passed to protect women, children, and some Christian minority groups.

This sixth-century mosaic shows Justinian in the center with religious leaders on his right and government officials on his left.

Theodora even saved Justinian's crown. In 532, some of Justinian's opponents turned a riot between rival sports fans into a widespread rebellion against his policies. As Justinian prepared to flee the city, Theodora refused to leave. Her courageous determination to stay and fight the rebels inspired Justinian. He ordered the army to crush the rebellion, which led to the deaths of 30,000 protesters. Order was restored, along with the emperor's authority. Following these events, Justinian decided to rule more carefully in the future.

SPORTS, POLITICS, AND PASSIONS

The people of Byzantium passionately followed the sport of chariot racing. More than just entertainment, the races were a focus of life and politics in the city. The people were bitterly divided in their support of the two main chariot teams—the Blues and the Greens. Races were an emotional standoff between supporters who often became violent. Justinian and Theodora both supported the Blues.

REVIEW & ASSESS

1. **READING CHECK** In what areas did Justinian make major improvements during his reign?

2. **IDENTIFY MAIN IDEAS AND DETAILS** What evidence from the text shows that Justinian's law reforms were successful?

3. **ANALYZE VISUALS** What can you infer about Justinian's reign from the people portrayed in the mosaic?

 7.1.3 Describe the establishment by Constantine of the new capital in Constantinople and the development of the Byzantine Empire, with an emphasis on the consequences of the development of two distinct European civilizations, Eastern Orthodox and Roman Catholic, and their two distinct views on church-state relations.

DECEMBER 27, 537

The newly completed Hagia Sophia, which means "Holy Wisdom," was officially blessed on this date. The church, which still stands, is considered a remarkable achievement in architecture. The centerpiece of the vast building is its extraordinary brick dome, which is 180 feet high and 100 feet across. After the fall of the Byzantine Empire, the Hagia Sophia was converted to a mosque—an Islamic place of worship. Today, it is a museum. In Justinian's time, the church symbolized Byzantine power and wealth.

CONSTANTINOPLE: THE HEART OF THE EMPIRE

Constantinople was the vibrant center of the Byzantine Empire. Beginning with Constantine, the emperors adorned the city with numerous churches, monuments, and civic buildings. Every day, thousands of people from all around the ancient world thronged the streets, buying, selling, and socializing.

Emperor Constantine built the first strong wall around Constantinople. As the city expanded, later emperors built walls farther out.

The Mese was the main street of Constantinople. Lined with shops, it led from the Hagia Sophia through the city's forums.

Like Rome, Constantinople had forums where people met to do business. The oval Forum of Constantine was one of these.

The Hagia Sophia overlooked the Bosporus and commanded a view of the entire city as well.

Emperor Constantine built the Hippodrome, the largest stadium of its time. It could seat some 60,000 people.

1.4 Life in Constantinople

You had to like people to enjoy living in Constantinople. It was the world's largest city, with its 500,000 inhabitants packed tightly together. The people of the city considered it the new Rome.

MAIN IDEA

Constantinople was a lively capital city modeled on ancient Rome.

THE CAPITAL CITY

Like Rome, Constantinople relied on resources from outside the city for its survival. The people consumed grain imported from Egypt and water piped in from more than 70 miles away.

Surrounded by the sea on three sides, Constantinople expanded to the west as it constantly attracted new people. Its strategic location on the Bosporus made it the richest and most influential city of its time. Merchants and traders from many parts of Europe and Asia brought in a constant flow of business and goods.

Like the residents of Rome, many of Constantinople's residents lived in poor conditions. They relied on government handouts of bread. Just a short walk away, though, spectacular public buildings and magnificent monuments inspired civic pride. As in Rome, a Senate house, public baths, triumphal arches, columns, and statues reflected the wealth and glory of the empire.

The city's people would frequently cram into the huge Hippodrome, a massive arena almost 1,500 feet long, to watch chariot races. The track was decorated with treasures from ancient Greece and Egypt. The emperor supervised the games from the imperial box, just as in Rome.

ROMAN CULTURAL INFLUENCE

Constantinople reflected everything that was glorious about ancient Rome. Its design, architecture, and monuments all reinforced the fact that the Byzantines considered themselves Roman. They saw themselves as the true inheritors of Roman cultural traditions—far more than Rome itself. Indeed, the Byzantine emperors brought many great monuments from Roman Italy, Africa, and Greece to adorn the capital.

Constantinople was also a center of cultural diversity because it was a center of trade. People who came from abroad to trade sometimes settled in the city. Greece was a strong influence as well. Greek, not Latin, was the people's language and the official language of the state. However, the Justinian Code, based on Roman law, continued as the basis for the Byzantine legal system. In this way, Byzantium helped preserve Greek and Roman learning for later generations.

REVIEW & ASSESS

1. **READING CHECK** What was one way in which Constantinople modeled itself on ancient Rome?

2. **MAKE INFERENCES** Why was trade with other regions necessary for Constantinople?

3. **INTERPRET VISUALS** What details in the drawing illustrate the idea that Constantinople was a busy, wealthy city?

7.1.3 Describe the establishment by Constantine of the new capital in Constantinople and the development of the Byzantine Empire, with an emphasis on the consequences of the development of two distinct European civilizations, Eastern Orthodox and Roman Catholic, and their two distinct views on church-state relations; HI 3 Students explain the sources of historical continuity and how the combination of ideas and events explains the emergence of new patterns.

2.1

The Church Divides

It's Saturday afternoon in the Hagia Sophia. Just before the service, three men burst in, march up to the altar, slam down a piece of paper, shout in a foreign language, and storm out. You've just witnessed the Christian church being split in two—forever.

MAIN IDEA

Christianity in the East and the West developed differently, causing arguments and finally a split.

EAST VERSUS WEST

When the old Roman Empire divided, the cultures of its eastern and western empires developed very differently. Arguments arose over Christian religious practices. In the East, the emperor was seen as God's representative on Earth. The emperor had a great deal of influence over the church and its leader, the **patriarch**. The first patriarchs of Constantinople were bishops under the governance of the pope. Over time, however, they became more independent of Rome.

The West did not have an emperor after 476, when the Roman Empire fell. As you may recall, the pope in Rome grew extremely powerful and claimed absolute authority over all western Christians, even kings. He then claimed authority over the eastern Christians, which led to a long power struggle with the Byzantine emperors.

With different leaders and with very little contact, eastern and western Christians drifted apart in their beliefs and practices.

One key conflict was a disagreement about the Holy Trinity—the Father, the Son, and the Holy Spirit. The western church adopted a **creed**, or statement of belief, that claimed the Holy Spirit comes from the Father and the Son—God and Jesus. The eastern church maintained the belief that the Holy Spirit comes only from the Father.

Another major clash was over **icons**, images of Jesus and the saints. Many Christians had icons, and some began to pray to them. In the East, the emperor banned icons and ordered that they be destroyed. In the West, the pope rebuked the emperor and condemned the destruction of the icons. Religion was an extremely important topic to the Byzantine people. They believed their eternal salvation depended on proper understanding of God and the Bible. As a result, these religious disagreements brought about strong feelings.

THE SCHISM OF 1054

Growing disagreements created suspicion and hostility between eastern and western Christians. Finally, the pope's representatives in Constantinople announced that the Byzantine patriarch was **excommunicated**—no longer part of the church. They made this announcement by placing the letter of excommunication on the altar of the Hagia Sophia. The furious patriarch then excommunicated the pope. In 1054, the church split in what is called the East-West Schism (SKIH-zuhm) or the Schism of 1054. A **schism** is a separation. The Roman Catholic Church remained in the West, and the **Eastern Orthodox Church** developed in Byzantium.

Followers of each religion shared some important common ground. They both based their beliefs on Jesus and the Bible, and they both worshipped in churches with services led by priests and bishops. However, in

Eastern Orthodox Church
Roman Catholic Church

NORWAY
SWEDEN
SCOTLAND
DENMARK
ENGLAND
EASTERN SLAVIC PRINCIPALITIES
POLAND
HOLY ROMAN EMPIRE
FRANCE
KINGDOM OF NAVARRE
KINGDOM OF LEÓN
KINGDOM OF ARAGON
BURGUNDY
HUNGARY
KINGDOM OF CASTILLE
CATALONIA
CROATIA
Corsica
PAPAL STATES • Rome
Black Sea
Constantinople
Nicaea
Sardinia
BYZANTINE EMPIRE
Sicily
Crete
Cyprus
Mediterranean Sea
Jerusalem

0 250 500 Miles
0 250 500 Kilometers

the Roman Catholic Church, the pope had authority over all the clergy and even kings. Priests could not marry, and services were conducted in Latin. In the Eastern Orthodox Church, the emperor had spiritual authority over the clergy, priests could marry, and services were conducted in Greek.

ICONS

The word *icon* comes from the Greek word for "image." Many icons were painted on wood, but some were made from mosaic tiles, ivory, and other materials. Although Byzantine emperors banned icons more than once, people kept them in their homes and businesses and placed them in churches.

REVIEW & ASSESS

1. **READING CHECK** What was one principal difference between the eastern and western churches?

2. **DETERMINE WORD MEANINGS** How does knowing that *ortho* refers to "correct" and *dox* refers to "opinion" clarify the meaning of the word *orthodox*?

3. **INTERPRET MAPS** What does the map add to the text's description of the Schism of 1054?

 7.1.3 Describe the establishment by Constantine of the new capital in Constantinople and the development of the Byzantine Empire, with an emphasis on the consequences of the development of two distinct European civilizations, Eastern Orthodox and Roman Catholic, and their two distinct views on church-state relations; CST 3 Students use a variety of maps and documents to identify physical and cultural features of neighborhoods, cities, states, and countries and to explain the historical migration of people, expansion and disintegration of empires, and the growth of economic systems.

2.2 HISTORY THROUGH OBJECTS
BYZANTINE MOSAICS

The Byzantine Empire developed an influential artistic culture. Its distinctive style is well represented by the remarkable mosaics found in churches such as the Hagia Sophia. Covering entire walls and ceilings, Byzantine mosaics stood out for their exceptional quality and craftsmanship. Large expanses of gold-backed glass created a rich glow. Natural stone cubes helped create vibrant, detailed scenes. The breathtaking results still awe viewers today.

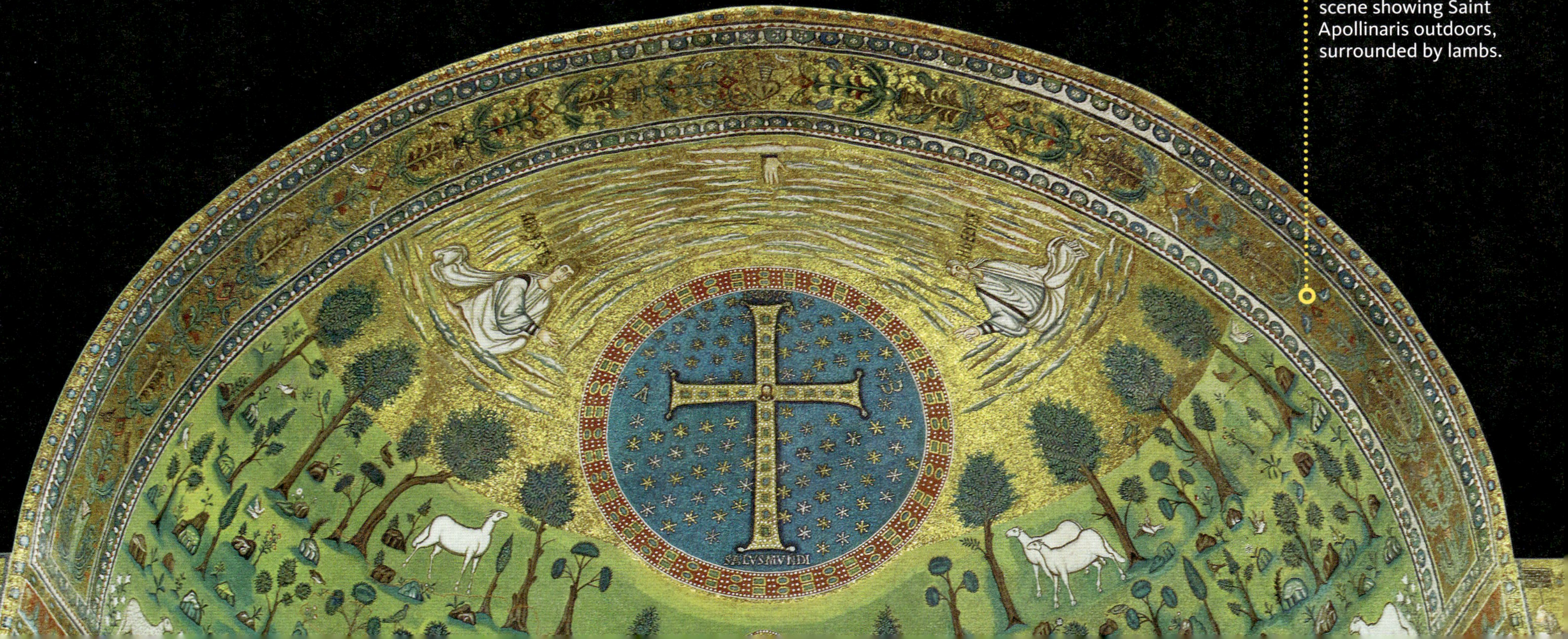

Sant'Apollinare The Basilica of Sant'Apollinare in Classe in Ravenna, Italy, is an excellent example of Byzantine mosaic art. The church was built in the sixth century. The area around its altar is covered with an elaborate mosaic scene showing Saint Apollinaris outdoors, surrounded by lambs.

Realistic Animals
The artists used naturally white stone cubes to depict the snowy white sheep in the scene.

Dazzling Gold
The pieces in this mosaic from another church in Ravenna are made of gold leaf sandwiched in clear glass. They are precisely angled to reflect light in different directions and create a sparkling effect.

Natural Coloring
Byzantine mosaic artists were able to create highly detailed and realistic pictures of people and animals. In this image of Saint Apollinaris, stone tesserae create natural tones and shadows on the face.

Mosaic Technique
To make a mosaic, the artist spreads a layer of plaster onto a surface and sets the cubes into the plaster before it dries.

Cubes Up Close
These present-day mosaic cubes, or tesserae, give an idea of the shapes the Byzantines used in their mosaics. Like the Byzantine tesserae, modern cubes also come in many colors.

The End of an Empire

On May 29, 1453, the last Byzantine emperor died fighting as his enemies swarmed through his capital's shattered walls. That day, the Byzantine Empire ended. It was a heroic finale for an empire that had survived against the odds for a thousand years.

MAIN IDEA

After Justinian, the empire experienced invasions and another golden age before it finally collapsed.

GREEK FIRE

The Byzantine army had a secret weapon: Greek fire. It was liquid fire soldiers could propel at enemy troops. It burned with an incredible intensity, and not even water could extinguish it.

The formula for making Greek fire was a closely guarded secret that died with the empire.

DEBTS AND INVASIONS

After Justinian died in 565, the debts the emperor had taken out to pay for his many wars nearly bankrupted the empire. In addition, the plague, which had already attacked during Justinian's time, made a return. Rats arriving aboard grain ships from Egypt carried the deadly disease, and it spread quickly through the overcrowded city. At the height of the plague, perhaps 10,000 people died every day.

As if that weren't enough, Byzantium's old enemies, including the Persians, renewed their attacks on the empire's borders. And then, in 634, the Byzantine Empire confronted a new rival. The religion of Islam had united Arab tribes, who formed a mighty Muslim army. This army conquered Egypt—a disaster for Constantinople's grain supply. By 711, the Arabs had conquered Syria, Egypt, parts of Southwest Asia, North Africa, and the Persian Empire.

NEW GOLDEN AGE AND FALL

Still, the Byzantine Empire was not yet down or out. By the early 1000s, the empire had entered a new golden age. Under the leadership of Basil II, Byzantium regained more control over trade, restored many of Constantinople's buildings and institutions, and spread Christianity among Slavic peoples to the north.

The empire's prosperity was short-lived, however. In 1096, an army of Christian Europeans launched a series of wars called the Crusades to fight the spread of Islam. The Crusaders soon came into conflict with Byzantine leaders. In 1204, they sacked Constantinople and occupied the city until 1261.

In time, the Byzantine Empire became a shadow of its former power—and then came the Turks, a people who had migrated into the region. By 1450, the Turks, who were Muslims, controlled all the lands around Constantinople. The city stood alone and surrounded.

In 1453, Mehmed II, the Turkish ruler, launched an army of 100,000 men against Constantinople's walls. The city's defenders, in contrast, numbered 7,000. On May 29, 1453, the Turks launched a final assault. They broke through the city's walls and killed the last Byzantine emperor, Constantine XI, as he charged into the invading army. By nightfall, Constantinople was under Turkish control.

The Capture of Constantinople in 1204, Jacopo Robusti Tintoretto, 16th century

Critical Viewing This painting shows the invasion of Constantinople by the Crusaders. Based on this painting, how would you describe the battle?

REVIEW & ASSESS

1. **READING CHECK** What was one factor that led to the decline and collapse of the Byzantine Empire?

2. **ANALYZE CAUSE AND EFFECT** Why was the plague able to spread so quickly throughout Constantinople?

3. **SEQUENCE EVENTS** What events took place in Byzantium during the 1000s?

7.1.3 Describe the establishment by Constantine of the new capital in Constantinople and the development of the Byzantine Empire, with an emphasis on the consequences of the development of two distinct European civilizations, Eastern Orthodox and Roman Catholic, and their two distinct views on church-state relations; HI.2 Students understand and distinguish cause, effect, sequence, and correlation in historical events

VOCABULARY

Match each word in the first column with its meaning in the second column.

WORD	DEFINITION
1. divine (HSS 7.1.3)	**a.** an image of Jesus or another holy figure
2. patriarch (HSS 7.1.3)	**b.** a belief that goes against church teachings
3. heresy (HSS 7.1.3)	**c.** having the nature of a god
4. icon (HSS 7.1.3)	**d.** variety
5. diversity (HSS 7.1.3)	**e.** a leader of the Eastern Orthodox Church

READING SKILL

6. ORGANIZE IDEAS: ANALYZE CAUSE AND EFFECT If you haven't already, complete your diagram to identify the factors that caused the Byzantine Empire to grow and thrive. Then answer the question.

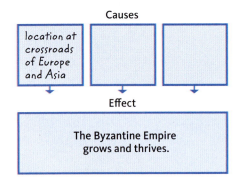

Causes

| location at crossroads of Europe and Asia | | |

Effect

The Byzantine Empire grows and thrives.

What conditions made it possible for the Byzantine Empire to grow, thrive, and enter a golden age? (HSS HI 2)

MAIN IDEAS

Answer the following questions. Support your answers with evidence from the chapter.

7. In what ways was the location of Constantinople important to the growth of the Byzantine Empire? **LESSON 1.1** (HSS 7.1.3)

8. In what ways did the Justinian Code improve on the Roman laws that it replaced? **LESSON 1.2** (HSS HI 3)

9. What actions did Justinian take to bring a golden age to Byzantium? **LESSON 1.2** (HSS 7.1.3)

10. Why did the Byzantines use ancient Rome as the model for their capital city, Constantinople? **LESSON 1.4** (HSS HI 3)

11. How did the Byzantine emperor affect the religious life of the empire? **LESSON 2.1** (HSS 7.1.3)

12. What effect did the plague have on the Byzantine Empire? **LESSON 2.3** (HSS HI 2)

CRITICAL THINKING

Answer the following questions. Support your answers with evidence from the chapter.

13. **ESSENTIAL QUESTION** How did the Byzantine Empire carry on the culture and traditions of the old Roman Empire? (HSS HI 3)

14. **DRAW CONCLUSIONS** How do events that took place during the Byzantine Empire still affect the present-day world? (HSS HI 3)

15. **ANALYZE CAUSE AND EFFECT** Why was the Byzantine Empire a target for invaders throughout its long history? (HSS HI 2)

16. **MAKE GENERALIZATIONS** How does geographic location help determine whether a city will become wealthy and powerful? (HSS CST 3)

17. **YOU DECIDE** What was Justinian's greatest accomplishment? Support your opinion with evidence from the chapter. (HSS REP 1)

Study the diagram below to compare and contrast the two branches of Christianity that developed after the East-West Schism. Then answer the questions that follow.

The East-West Schism

Roman Catholic Church
- Led by the pope
- Pope had authority over all Christians, including kings and emperors
- Priests could not marry
- Services conducted in Latin
- Worship and use of icons promoted by the pope

Similarities
- Faith based on belief in Jesus and the Bible
- Services held in churches led by priests and bishops

Eastern Orthodox Church
- Led by the patriarch
- Emperor had authority over all church officials
- Priests could marry
- Services conducted in Greek
- Some believed the worship of icons should be forbidden

18. In what way did the pope have greater influence in the West than patriarchs did in the East? **HSS 7.1.3**

19. How were the faiths of both branches of Christianity similar? **HSS 7.1.3**

The historian Procopius was present at and recorded the events of a rebellion in 532. Read his account of Theodora's speech to Justinian as the emperor prepared to flee Constantinople. Then answer the question that follows.

> I believe that flight, now more than ever, is not in our interest even if it should bring us to safety. . . . For one who has reigned it is intolerable to become a fugitive. May I *never* be parted from the purple [the imperial color]! May I *never* live to see the day when I will not be addressed as Mistress by all in my presence! Emperor, if you wish to save yourself, that is easily arranged. . . . But consider whether, after you have saved yourself, you would then gladly exchange safety for death.

20. What does this this speech suggest about Theodora's character and influence?

HSS REP 4

21. INFORMATIVE Suppose you are in the court of the emperor Justinian. Write an explanation for your fellow citizens of how Theodora influences Justinian's rule of the Byzantine Empire. **HSS HI 1**

TIPS

- Take notes from the lessons about Justinian and Theodora.
- Write a topic sentence that clearly introduces your main idea about Theodora and Justinian.
- Choose relevant facts, concrete details, and examples for your explanation.
- Use vocabulary from the chapter where appropriate.
- Organize your details, facts, and examples clearly and logically.
- Provide a concluding statement that summarizes the information presented.

ESSENTIAL QUESTION What major contributions did Muslim leaders and scholars make to world civilization?

SECTION 1 THE ROOTS OF ISLAM

KEY VOCABULARY	NAMES & PLACES
caliph	Bedouin
clan	Islam
imam	Mecca
mosque	Muhammad
oasis	Muslim
pilgrimage	Qur'an
prophet	Sunna
shari'a	

SECTION 2 MUSLIM EMPIRES

KEY VOCABULARY	NAMES & PLACES
bureaucracy	Abbasids
janissary	Mughals
mercenary	Ottomans
shah	Safavids
sultan	Shi'ite
tolerance	Suleyman I
	Sunni
	Umayyads

SECTION 3 ISLAMIC CULTURAL LEGACY

KEY VOCABULARY	NAMES & PLACES
arabesque	al-Zahrawi
calligraphy	Ibn Rushd
medieval	Omar Khayyám
minaret	

READING STRATEGY

IDENTIFY MAIN IDEAS AND DETAILS

When you identify a text's main idea, you must support it with evidence from the text. As you read the chapter, use a web like this one to note evidence that supports the following idea: Islamic culture has had a lasting influence on the world.

The Great Mosque of Córdoba in Spain is a magnificent example of Muslim architecture. Its prayer hall is noted for its many double arches and columns.

Trading Crossroads

People living on the Arabian Peninsula in the 600s had to be tough. Their homeland was mostly a sea of sun-scorched sand that offered little shelter, shade, or water. But its location—at a spot where three continents meet—proved to be an advantage.

MAIN IDEA

The Arabian Peninsula became an important crossroads for trade among the continents of Asia, Africa, and Europe by the early 600s.

DESERT LIFE

The huge rectangle of the Arabian Peninsula, also known as Arabia, is one of the hottest and driest places on Earth. Almost the entire 1.2 million square miles is scorching desert and dry, flat land. Rain falls in few places, making water scarce and precious. Much of the peninsula gets only three to five inches of rain a year.

The region's harsh climate has long placed limits on farming. Many of Arabia's early inhabitants made their living as nomadic herders called **Bedouin** (BEH-duh-wuhn). They constantly moved their sheep, goats, and cattle among sources of water and grazing land. *Bedouin* is an Arabic word meaning "desert dweller."

In the 600s, the Bedouin were organized into tribes based on **clans**, or groups of related families who believed they shared a common ancestor. Each tribe formed an extended family to which members were fiercely loyal. Tribe members owned land and most property together, and each tribe had an elected leader called a sheikh (SHAYK). The tribes often fought one another to maintain or gain control of areas of the desert. As a result, the tribesmen became strong and skilled warriors.

GROWTH OF CITIES

The only place life could flourish in Arabia was at an **oasis**. An oasis is an isolated, reliable source of water in a desert where plants can grow. The oases were like stepping stones across the vast desert. They naturally attracted people, who then built permanent settlements. Anyone crossing the desert had to visit the oases, which became useful places to trade.

Because of its central location, Arabia became an important crossroads connecting routes from Asia, Africa, and Europe. Merchants led camels carrying silks, spices, metals, and other products along these trade routes. As a result, some oases grew into rich market towns and then into cities.

Arabia's most important city was **Mecca**, which became a center for both trade and religion. The various Arab tribes worshipped different nature gods. These beliefs were polytheistic, or based on the existence of multiple gods. Most Arabs also recognized the existence of a supreme God, called Allah (AL-luh) in Arabic. According to ancient Islamic tradition, the religious leader known in the Hebrew Bible as Abraham had stopped at Mecca and built a shrine called the Ka'aba (KAH-buh). Although Abraham dedicated the Ka'aba to the one supreme God, the shrine came to include representations of many Arabian tribal gods. Mecca became an important site for polytheistic Arabs. People from all over the peninsula made a **pilgrimage**, or journey, to worship there.

TRADE IN SOUTHWEST ASIA, c. 570

Critical Viewing Sand dunes like these cover much of the Arabian Peninsula. What dangers might traders have faced as they crossed the vast desert?

REVIEW & ASSESS

1. **READING CHECK** How did Arabia's location contribute to its development as an important trading crossroads?

2. **ANALYZE CAUSE AND EFFECT** How did Arabia's physical geography influence the Bedouin's way of life?

3. **INTERPRET MAPS** Find Mecca on the map. Why is Mecca's location good for trade?

7.2.1 Identify the physical features and describe the climate of the Arabian peninsula, its relationship to surrounding bodies of land and water, and nomadic and sedentary ways of life; 7.2.5 Describe the growth of cities and the establishment of trade routes among Asia, Africa, and Europe, the products and inventions that traveled along these routes (e.g., spices, textiles, paper, steel, new crops), and the role of merchants in Arab society; CST 3 Students use a variety of maps and documents to identify physical and cultural features of neighborhoods, cities, states, and countries and to explain the historical migration of people, expansion and disintegration of empires, and the growth of economic systems; HI 2 Students understand and distinguish cause, effect, sequence, and correlation in historical events, including the long- and short-term causal relations

1.2

The **Prophet** of **Islam**

An oasis city in Arabia became the birthplace of a major world religion in the 600s. In a cave near Mecca, a middle-aged merchant heard messages that he reported came from an angel named Gabriel. The merchant began preaching those messages and united Arabia under a new religion.

MAIN IDEA

Muhammad was a great religious, political, and military leader who preached the religion of Islam and unified much of Arabia.

THE LIFE OF MUHAMMAD

Today the religion of **Islam** has about 1.5 billion followers worldwide. Its prophet, **Muhammad**, was born into a family of Mecca's ruling tribe about 570. A **prophet** is a teacher believed to be inspired by God. As a young man, Muhammad gained a reputation for intelligence, honesty, and kindness. He worked as a trader for a wealthy widow and merchant named Khadijah (kah-DEE-juh). She was so impressed by Muhammad's virtues that she married him.

Muhammad had a deep interest in religion. He periodically retreated to a cave outside of Mecca to pray. When he was about 40 years old, he had the first of many religious experiences. As he prayed in his cave, he heard a voice that he identified as the angel Gabriel. The main message was that people could achieve salvation, or go to heaven, in the afterlife only by worshipping and obeying the one true God. Muhammad thereafter rejected the polytheism that was common in Mecca. Instead, he followed the teaching attributed to Abraham, who said that there is only one God.

In 613, Muhammad began to preach that only the God of Abraham should be worshipped and obeyed, not the traditional tribal gods. In Arabic, *Islam* means "submission to the will of God." The name for a follower of Islam, **Muslim**, means "one who has submitted to God."

THE LEADERSHIP OF MUHAMMAD

Muhammad's teachings about the one true God threatened Mecca's political leaders. They supported traditional religion and benefitted from the city's position as a pilgrimage center for polytheistic Arabs. The leaders made life difficult for Muhammad and his followers, who then fled to the Arabian city of Yathrib. This event became known as the Hijrah (HEEJ-rah). The year of Muhammad's flight, 622, marks the beginning of the Muslim calendar. Yathrib was later renamed Medina (muh-DEE-nuh).

Muhammad and his followers were given leadership of Medina, where they established an Islamic community called the umma (OO-muh). Muhammad made loyalty to the umma more important than that to a tribe. He began uniting Arabia's many quarrelling tribes under Islam.

The ruling tribes of Mecca tried to crush this movement. However, in 630, Muhammad conquered Mecca, removed all idols at the Ka'aba, and dedicated the shrine to the God of Abraham. This victory and others helped spread Islam. By 632, when Muhammad died, most Arab tribes had joined the umma. Muhammad had proved himself a great religious, political, and military leader.

Muslims from all over the world journey to pray at the Ka'aba. This shrine takes the form of a stone cube and contains a holy rock called the Black Stone.

REVIEW & ASSESS

1. **READING CHECK** On what main belief did Muhammad base the religion of Islam?

2. **ANALYZE CAUSE AND EFFECT** Why did Muhammad and his followers move from Mecca to Medina?

3. **IDENTIFY DETAILS** The text states that Muhammad was a great religious, political, and military leader. What details in the text support this claim?

Beliefs and Laws

Could you point toward the direction of your home no matter where you were, even if you were in a faraway city? Muslims must be able to point toward the holy city of Mecca wherever they happen to be. It's an important aspect of a Muslim's daily life, which revolves around faithfully following Islamic religious practices.

MAIN IDEA

Islamic religious practices are based on Islam's holy book and the life of Muhammad.

THE QUR'AN AND THE SUNNA

The holy book of Islam is called the **Qur'an** (kuh-RAN). Muslims believe that the Qur'an contains the flawless words of Allah as revealed to Muhammad by the angel Gabriel. The Qur'an teaches that there is only one God, whom all Muslims should worship. According to the Qur'an, God is the creator and is merciful and compassionate. Islam teaches that God will judge individuals for their good and bad actions and send them to heaven or hell on a final judgment day. The Qur'an states how Muslims should behave. For example, the Qur'an promotes charity and forbids gambling and drinking alcohol.

Muslims believe that Muhammad demonstrated perfectly how to apply the Qur'an in daily life. The words and actions attributed to Muhammad, called the **Sunna** (SOON-uh), were written down by his followers. Muslims rely on both the Qur'an and the Sunna as guides. For example, the Qur'an instructs Muslims to wash before prayer but does not explain how. However, accounts of the Sunna claim to describe how Muhammad washed for prayer, so Muslims carefully follow this description.

Together, the Qur'an and the Sunna form the basis of Islamic law, which is called **shari'a** (shah-REE-ah). This system of law is comprehensive. It covers all aspects of human behavior, including family life, community life, moral conduct, worship, and business.

Early Muslims recognized Islam's link to the other monotheistic religions of Judaism and Christianity. They regarded Jews and Christians as "people of the book" because they consider Abraham a prophet and had a holy book with teachings similar to those of the Qur'an. Muslims believed the Qur'an was the final book of revelations from the same God that Jews and Christians worshipped. They regarded Muhammad as the final prophet of God.

EVERYDAY PRACTICES

Muslims apply their religious beliefs to their daily lives by following a set of duties called the Five Pillars of Islam. Additional Islamic customs guide their daily lives. For example, Muslims avoid eating certain meats and eat meat only from animals that are killed in a humane way.

Each Islamic community centers on a **mosque**, a Muslim place of worship. The main weekly service is on Friday afternoon. Worshippers wash themselves before entering a mosque and kneel on special prayer mats facing Mecca. A religious teacher called an **imam** leads the weekly service, which includes prayer and a sermon. Mosques also serve as centers of education and social work.

Critical Viewing A group of Bedouin in Saudi Arabia stop for evening prayer. According to the Five Pillars of Islam, in what direction should these Muslims be facing as they pray?

THE FIVE PILLARS OF ISLAM

All believers of Islam are called upon to carry out the following duties.

1 Faith Testify to this statement of faith: "There is no god but God, and Muhammad is His Prophet."

2 Prayer Pray five times a day, facing toward Mecca.

3 Alms Donate a portion of one's wealth to help people in need.

4 Fasting Eat and drink nothing between dawn and sunset during the Islamic holy month of Ramadan.

5 Pilgrimage Perform the hajj (haj), or pilgrimage to Mecca, at least once in a lifetime if able.

REVIEW & ASSESS

1. **READING CHECK** What is one practice that Muslims follow based on the Qur'an?

2. **SYNTHESIZE** How are the Qur'an and the Sunna related?

3. **MAKE GENERALIZATIONS** What are some links among Judaism, Christianity, and Islam?

7.2.2 Trace the origins of Islam and the life and teachings of Muhammad, including Islamic teachings on the connection with Judaism and Christianity; 7.2.3 Explain the significance of the Qur'an and the Sunnah as the primary sources of Islamic beliefs, practice, and law, and their influence in Muslims'

The Qur'an and Hadith

The Qur'an, Islam's holy book, provides religious guidance to Muslims on all aspects of life, from saying prayers to conducting business. Muslims also look to the Sunna, or Muhammad's example, to guide their behavior. Accounts of what Muhammad reportedly said, did, or approved were recorded by his followers after his death and are called hadith (huh-DEETH). The word *hadith* can refer either to a specific account of Muhammad's words and actions or to all the accounts in general.

This Persian painting shows the angel Gabriel. Muslims believe that Gabriel revealed the words of the Qur'an to Muhammad.

from the Qur'an

Muslims consider the Qur'an to be the words of God revealed in human language. In this excerpt, God speaks using the pronoun *We*, even though God is a single being. This use of *We* serves to emphasize the majesty and authority of God. This excerpt and the following one focus on why God created diversity among people.

CONSTRUCTED RESPONSE According to the Qur'an, who are the noblest human beings?

> O mankind, We have created you male and female, and appointed you groups and tribes, that you may know one another. Surely the noblest among you in the sight of God is the most godfearing of you. God is All-knowing, All-aware.
>
> Qur'an 49:13

from the Qur'an

As this excerpt suggests, tolerance of diversity is an important value in the Qur'an. In this excerpt, the pronoun *He* is used to refer to God. Muslims believe that God has no gender. The use of *He* is simply a custom.

CONSTRUCTED RESPONSE According to the Qur'an, why did Allah create a world of diversity?

> If God had willed, He could have made you one nation; but [He willed otherwise] that He may try [test] you in what has come to you. So be you forward [active] in good works; unto God shall you return, all together.
>
> Qur'an 5:54

Hadith

The Qur'an strongly warns Muslims to prepare for a day of judgment, when the worthy will go to paradise and the unworthy will suffer in hell. This hadith offers guidance on how to behave on Earth in order to attain paradise.

CONSTRUCTED RESPONSE According to this hadith, what should Muslims do to be worthy of entering paradise on the Last Day?

> Anyone who believes in God and the Last Day [of Judgment] should not harm his neighbor. Anyone who believes in God and the Last Day should entertain his guest generously. And anyone who believes in God and the Last Day should say what is good or keep quiet.
>
> Sahih Al-Bukhari, 6018

SYNTHESIZE & WRITE

1. **REVIEW** Review what you have learned about the Qur'an and hadith.

2. **RECALL** On your own paper, write down the main idea expressed in each of the three documents.

3. **CONSTRUCT** Write a topic sentence that answers this question: According to sacred Islamic writings, how should people behave?

4. **WRITE** Using evidence from the documents, write an informative paragraph that supports your topic sentence.

7.2.3 Explain the significance of the Qur'an and the Sunnah as the primary sources of Islamic beliefs, practice, and law, and their influence in Muslims' daily life; REP 4 Students assess the credibility of primary and secondary sources and draw sound conclusions from them.

67

The Prophet's Mosque in Medina, Saudi Arabia, contains the tomb of Muhammad and is a holy site for Muslims.

1.5 After Muhammad

If your classroom teacher were suddenly called away, is there a student in your class who could take control and keep everyone focused on the lesson? After Muhammad died, Muslims needed a leader to keep the community focused. After a period of uncertainty, the Muslim state met the challenge.

MAIN IDEA

The Muslim state recovered from a period of disorder after Muhammad's death and soon expanded to form a powerful empire.

NEW LEADERS

In 632, the Muslim state in Arabia almost collapsed when Muhammad died without naming a successor. His followers disagreed over how to choose a leader. Then a few leading Muslims acted decisively. They appointed Muhammad's father-in-law, Abu Bakr (uh-boo BA-kuhr), as **caliph** (KAY-lihf), which means "successor." He promised to follow Muhammad's example.

As the first of many caliphs, Abu Bakr served as the supreme religious, political, and military leader of a growing Muslim empire. Though he ruled for just two years, he was critical to the survival of Islam. He crushed rebellions that could have destroyed the young state. His strong leadership kept all of Arabia united under Islam.

ISLAM SPREADS

The early caliphs succeeded in establishing a large Muslim empire that stretched thousands of miles from the Mediterranean region into Central Asia. The Muslims faced two great superpowers in the region. The Byzantine Empire ruled Syria and Egypt, while the Persian Empire ruled Iran and Iraq. However, these two rival empires had become exhausted by fighting long and bitter wars. Meanwhile, the Muslim empire had developed a skilled, disciplined, and enthusiastic army. By 652, just 20 years after Muhammad's death, the Muslims had conquered Syria, Palestine, Iraq, Iran, Egypt, and various parts of North Africa. (A map of Muslim conquests appears in the Chapter Review.)

The Qur'an forbade the conquering caliphs from forcing their new non-Muslim subjects to convert to Islam. Instead of being persecuted, or mistreated, as they had been under Byzantine and Persian rule, Jews, Christians, and those of other faiths were allowed to follow their own religious customs with some restrictions. Even so, many people chose to convert to Islam. Some people were genuinely attracted by Islamic ideas and customs. Other people converted for practical reasons of social, political, and economic gain.

REVIEW & ASSESS

1. **READING CHECK** How did Muhammad's death in 632 affect the Muslim state he had established?

2. **ANALYZE CAUSE AND EFFECT** Why were the Muslims able to conquer the powerful Byzantine and Persian Empires in just 20 years?

3. **MAKE GENERALIZATIONS** Why did many Jews, Christians, and other non-Muslims convert to Islam in the growing Muslim empire?

7.2.4 Discuss the expansion of Muslim rule through military conquests and treaties, emphasizing the cultural blending within Muslim civilization and the spread and acceptance of Islam and the Arabic language; HI 2 Students understand and distinguish cause, effect, sequence, and correlation in historical events, including the long- and short-term causal relations.

69

The **Umayyads** and the **Abbasids**

Running an empire is hard work. There are complicated issues to understand, mountains of paperwork to complete, and tough decisions to make. The caliphs lost interest and let others govern while they enjoyed luxurious lifestyles. Their actions lost them both respect and control of their empire.

MAIN IDEA

Opposing groups competed for power in the Muslim empire, and a major split developed in Islam in the late 600s.

UMAYYAD EXPANSION

Despite its military successes, the Muslim community could not maintain unity as various groups struggled for power. The last three of the first four caliphs were assassinated. After the last one, Ali, was murdered in 661, a family known as the **Umayyads** (oo-MY-yadz) gained power.

The Umayyads established a hereditary system of succession, with the title of caliph automatically passing within the clan, usually from father to son. They also moved the capital of the Muslim empire to Damascus in Syria, which made it easier to control conquered lands. However, many Muslims felt the new capital was too far from Islam's heartland near Medina.

These unpopular actions helped split Islam into two branches. The majority group, the **Sunni** (SU-nee), accepted Umayyad rule. They believed that any Muslim could be caliph. The other group, the **Shi'ite** (SHEE-yt), believed that only members of Muhammad's family, especially Ali and his descendants, could rule as caliph. This major division in Islam remains today.

Despite this split, the Umayyads expanded the Muslim empire, which spread Islam into new areas. To govern their growing territory, the Umayyads set up an efficient **bureaucracy**, a system of government with specialized departments. They also divided the empire into provinces governed by Muslim rulers. A postal service connected the provinces, and a strong army kept order. These actions helped unite the diverse empire. However, many Muslims believed that the Umayyads put too much emphasis on gaining wealth and power.

ABBASID RULE

Opposition to the Umayyads grew until rebel groups overthrew them in 750. A rival clan called the **Abbasids** (AB-uh-sihdz), who were descendants of Muhammad's uncle, took control of the empire. Non-Arab converts and Shi'ites lent support to the Abbasids, who moved the capital to Baghdad in central Iraq.

The Abbasids ruled during a prosperous golden age in Muslim history, but the caliphs were isolated from the people. Government was left to trusted advisers who held the empire together through force. They built a huge army that relied on mainly Turkish **mercenaries**, or hired soldiers.

Eventually, a group called the Seljuk (SEHL-jook) Turks converted to Islam and came to control the government of the Muslim empire. Then, in 1258, an invading group from Central Asia called the Mongols stormed Baghdad and killed the last Abbasid caliph.

This painting shows philosophers working in the House of Wisdom, a great library and academy built by the Abbasids in Baghdad about 830.

REVIEW & ASSESS

1. **READING CHECK** What major division in Islam developed after the Umayyads came to power?

2. **IDENTIFY MAIN IDEAS AND DETAILS** How did the Umayyads strengthen the Muslim empire?

3. **EVALUATE** What flaws of the Abbasid caliphs contributed to their downfall?

7.2.4 Discuss the expansion of Muslim rule through military conquests and treaties, emphasizing the cultural blending within Muslim civilization and the spread and acceptance of Islam and the Arabic language.

Muslim Spain

When they overthrew the Umayyads in 750, the Abbasids ruthlessly hunted down and killed members of the Umayyad family. But they missed one important person. An Umayyad prince escaped to Spain and soon founded a rival Muslim dynasty that was destined for fame.

MAIN IDEA

The Umayyads transformed Muslim Spain into a center of power, learning, and culture between 756 and 1031.

THE UMAYYADS RETURN

Muslims had first conquered Spain in 711, and much of the region came under Umayyad control by 750. The last surviving Umayyad prince, Abd al-Rahman, fled to this region in 755 and founded an Umayyad dynasty in 756. From the city of Córdoba, he established a powerful, independent state called al-Andalus (al-an-duh-LUS) and refused to acknowledge Abbasid authority in Baghdad.

Al-Andalus flourished under the Umayyad dynasty, developing a thriving economy. The state reached its peak under the leadership of Abd al-Rahman III. At the time he assumed power in 912, rebel Arab leaders had been challenging the authority of the Umayyad dynasty. However, Abd al-Rahman III vigorously fought the rebels and proclaimed himself caliph in 929, directly competing with the Abbasids. His strong leadership preserved Umayyad power, and all of Muslim Spain was united under his rule by 933.

A GREAT CAPITAL

Abd al-Rahman III transformed Córdoba into one of the largest and greatest cities in the world. He built a series of lavish palaces and extended the Great Mosque, one of the most beautiful buildings ever created. Its vast prayer hall could hold over 50,000 worshippers and is famous for its hundreds of soaring arches. (A picture of the prayer hall appears at the beginning of the chapter.)

7.2.4 Discuss the expansion of Muslim rule through military conquests and treaties, emphasizing the cultural blending within Muslim civilization and the spread and acceptance of Islam and the Arabic language; 7.6.9 Know the history of the

The Great Mosque of Córdoba, shown in the background, is today a Catholic cathedral.

Córdoba became most celebrated as a center of learning. Its huge library was said to contain about 400,000 books. In Córdoba, Christians, Jews, and Muslims lived together under a government that practiced religious **tolerance**, or sympathy for the beliefs and practices of others. In this rich intellectual environment, many advances in science, philosophy, medicine, and the arts were made.

Muslim rulers of al-Andalus faced many challenges, however. After the death of Abd al-Rahman III in 961, civil war erupted. Al-Andalus split into many small Muslim kingdoms after 1031. The increasingly powerful Christian kings of northern Spain steadily took over more of al-Andalus. In 1492, the Christians captured Granada, Spain's last Muslim city, ending almost 800 years of Muslim rule in western Europe.

REVIEW & ASSESS

1. **READING CHECK** How did the Umayyad dynasty transform Muslim Spain?

2. **DRAW CONCLUSIONS** Why did Córdoba become an international center of learning in the 900s?

3. **SEQUENCE EVENTS** What series of events ended almost 800 years of Muslim rule in Europe?

decline of Muslim rule in the Iberian Peninsula that culminated in the Reconquista and the rise of Spanish and Portuguese kingdoms; 7.9.7 Describe the Golden Age of cooperation between Jews and Muslims in medieval Spain that promoted creativity in art, literature, and science, including how that cooperation was terminated by the religious persecution of individuals and groups (e.g., the Spanish Inquisition and the expulsion of Jews and Muslims from Spain in 1492); CST 1 Students explain how major events are related to one another in time; HI 2 Students understand and distinguish cause, effect, sequence, and correlation in historical events, including the long- and short-term causal relations.

73

JANUARY 2, 1492

Paradise on Earth—that's what Muslim rulers intended the Alhambra to represent. This fortified palace dominates the Spanish city of Granada. Begun around 860, the palace was expanded and perfected by Muslim rulers over the course of many years. The Alhambra is considered one of the greatest surviving examples of Islamic architecture. On January 2, 1492, Muslim rulers surrendered Granada to forces of the Spanish rulers Ferdinand and Isabella. Thereafter, Christian kings used the Alhambra as a royal palace for centuries. Based on this photograph, how would you describe Islamic architecture?

The Ottoman Empire

In the 1500s, one Muslim leader became the most powerful monarch in the world. A devout Muslim, Suleyman I oversaw one of the largest empires in history—and one of the longest lasting. This empire included the lands of Persia, Byzantium, and Egypt as well as parts of eastern Europe.

MAIN IDEA

A Muslim state known as the Ottoman Empire became the largest empire in the world in the 1500s.

SULEYMAN THE LAWGIVER

Suleyman I reformed the legal system in the Ottoman Empire. He cracked down on corruption and passed laws to protect non-Muslims. His commitment to justice earned him the title Suleyman the Lawgiver.

A VAST EMPIRE

While al-Andalus was in decline, a new Muslim power was arising to the east. A dynasty of Turkish Muslims, known as the **Ottomans**, emerged as frontier warriors against the Byzantines in Anatolia, or what is now Turkey, around the 1290s. These warriors and their leader, Osman, captured many Byzantine cities, fueling the Ottomans' expansion into the Balkans in southeastern Europe. In 1453, the Ottomans ended the Byzantine Empire by capturing Constantinople. This city, renamed Istanbul, became the Ottomans' capital and the center of their highly efficient government. The Ottomans continued to build an empire as they challenged the Safavid Empire, a rival Muslim power, and then captured Syria, Palestine, and Egypt from other Muslim rulers.

The Ottoman rulers were called **sultans**. The greatest of them was **Suleyman I**, known as Suleyman the Magnificent. He ruled the Ottoman Empire at the height of its power and grandeur, from 1520 to 1566. He led a powerful navy and a large army well-equipped with guns and cannons, which helped him conquer vast portions of northern Africa and eastern Europe. Only bad weather made him turn back from besieging the Austrian capital of Vienna.

However, military conquest wasn't Suleyman's only interest. He was also a celebrated poet, a talented goldsmith, and a generous patron of the arts. His rule inspired a cultural era that made Istanbul the artistic center of the Muslim lands. Suleyman commissioned work on restoration of the Grand Mosque in Mecca. He built magnificent mosques and palaces, transforming Istanbul's skyline with many buildings still seen there today.

DAILY LIFE

The Ottoman Empire steadily declined after the reign of Suleyman I, but it lasted into the early 1900s. One reason for its long life was its religious tolerance, which helped reduce internal conflict. Jews and Christians enjoyed religious and cultural freedom in return for paying a tax and being loyal to the state. They were organized into large self-governing communities, whose leaders worked with the Ottoman government to ensure positive relations. These communities prospered.

Many "people of the book," or Jews and Christians, played important roles in the Ottoman Empire. Like other civilizations, the empire had different social classes. The Ottomans relied heavily on special slaves to staff the government and army. These slaves attained elite status and became rich and powerful. Many senior government officials were technically slaves. Slaves also made up the **janissaries**, a group of highly trained and disciplined soldiers in the Ottoman army who received the best equipment and benefits. To form the janissary corps, the government took young boys from non-Muslim villages, educated them, and trained them to fight for the sultan.

As elsewhere in the world, women in the Ottoman Empire led more restricted lives than men did. Lower-class women had more access to public areas than did upper-class women, who were often kept isolated from the outside world. Upper-class women influenced elite culture and royal policies, and they used their wealth to promote the arts, architecture, and charitable causes.

REVIEW & ASSESS

1. **READING CHECK** What were some of the major achievements of Suleyman I?

2. **MAKE INFERENCES** How did the Ottoman Empire benefit from practicing religious tolerance?

3. **INTERPRET MAPS** Along what major seas did the Ottoman Empire extend?

 7.2.4 Discuss the expansion of Muslim rule through military conquests and treaties, emphasizing the cultural blending within Muslim civilization and the spread and acceptance of Islam and the Arabic language; CST 3 Students use a variety of maps and documents to identify physical and cultural features of neighborhoods, cities, states, and countries and to explain the historical migration of people, expansion and disintegration of empires, and the growth of economic systems.

The Safavid and Mughal Empires

As Islam spread over parts of three continents—Asia, Africa, and Europe—rival dynasties arose that challenged one another. The Ottoman Empire was the largest empire of its time, but it faced strong rivals in Persia and India.

MAIN IDEA

Rival Muslim empires arose in Persia and India during the time of the Ottoman Empire.

THE SAFAVID EMPIRE

The Ottomans formed the largest Muslim empire of the time. However, it was not the only one. The **Safavids** (suh-FAH-vihdz), a Shi'ite dynasty, became rivals of the Sunni Ottomans.

The Safavid Empire arose when a youthful leader named Ismail united the Persian kingdoms into an independent state in 1501. He took the Persian title for king, shah. Ismail rapidly expanded Persia's borders north and west by boldly invading Ottoman lands. The Safavids and Ottomans went on to fight a long war that lasted more than 100 years. They battled mainly over control of Mesopotamia's fertile plains. Over and over again, the Safavids gained and lost possession of this land.

Located at the center of international trade routes, the Safavid Empire developed a strong economy. The Safavids used their wealth to build fabulous palaces and mosques and schools, hospitals, roads, and bridges. They made their new capital of Esfahan into one of the most magnificent cities in the world. It had more than 160 mosques and more than 270 public baths.

The Safavids also made Persia into a cultural center by encouraging the immigration of Shi'ite scholars and attracting craftspeople, artists, and traders of many nationalities. The government actively supported both art and industry, resulting in a rich mix of beautiful textiles, carpets, and other products. Europeans eagerly imported these products from Safavid merchants.

The Safavids actively spread Shi'ite Islam. They established it as the dominant Islamic faith in the Caucasus (a region between the Black and Caspian Seas) and in western Asia.

The Safavid Empire reached its peak between 1588 and 1629, during the reign of Shah Abbas I. It then declined steadily under the leadership of weak shahs. In 1722, a group of Afghan warriors invaded the Safavid Empire, which resulted in its downfall.

THE MUGHAL EMPIRE

The Safavid Empire was wedged between two other Muslim empires—the Ottoman Empire to the west and the Mughal Empire to the east. The **Mughals** (MOO-guhlz) were nomads from Central Asia who invaded India. In 1526, troops headed by a Mughal leader named Babur swept out of Central Asia and conquered north and central India. Babur laid the foundation of the Mughal Empire, which eventually stretched across almost the entire subcontinent.

In 1556, the Mughal leader Akbar the Great came to the throne at the age of 13 and led Muslim India to a brilliant golden age. Akbar doubled Babur's conquests and stabilized the empire by establishing a loyal governing class and an effective modern

The Safavids built the Shah Mosque in Esfahan, Iran. Considered a masterpiece of Persian architecture, the mosque features a magnificent dome covered with colorful tiles.

government. He also allowed different religions to flourish in the empire. He even tried to end traditional conflicts between Muslims and Hindus by creating a new religion that mixed elements of both. His library was vast and included books in English, Greek, Persian, Hindi, and Arabic, and his court was cultured and learned.

The Mughal Empire reached its peak under Akbar's grandson, Shah Jahan, who reigned from 1628 to 1658. The empire became most famous for its dazzling splendor and wealth. Shah Jahan collected thousands of precious jewels and exported magnificent Indian art to Europe. He commissioned India's most famous building, the Taj Mahal, in memory of his beloved wife, who had died at a young age. Built of white marble, the monument served as a testament to the power and glory of Mughal rule. (This majestic tomb is pictured in Lesson 3.3.)

Mughal power eventually began to decline, however, as rebellious Hindus and European countries sought to gain control of India. In 1857, the British, who by then had gained control, sent the last Mughal ruler into exile.

REVIEW & ASSESS

1. **READING CHECK** What Muslim empires were rivals of the Ottoman Empire, and where were they located?

2. **COMPARE AND CONTRAST** How were the Safavid and Mughal Empires similar? How were they different?

3. **IDENTIFY PROBLEMS AND SOLUTIONS** How did Akbar the Great deal with the problem of religious conflicts?

7.2.4 Discuss the expansion of Muslim rule through military conquests and treaties, emphasizing the cultural blending within Muslim civilization and the spread and acceptance of Islam and the Arabic language.

Science and Philosophy

The knowledge in a book is useless if nobody reads it. But when people read a book and share its knowledge with others, the knowledge can become incredibly valuable. The leaders of various Muslim empires opened up whole libraries and shared their books with the world to stimulate learning. By doing so, Muslim empires advanced both science and philosophy.

MAIN IDEA

Under the leadership of Muslim dynasties, science and philosophy made important advances that spread across the world.

MATHEMATICS AND ASTRONOMY

Medieval times, which spanned from the 500s to the 1500s, saw the rise and fall of many Muslim empires. The vast extent of these empires and their religious tolerance allowed for a unique blending of cultures. Medieval Muslim leaders and scholars played a key role in preserving and building on the intellectual works of ancient Greece, Persia, and India. In this way, they helped build a foundation for modern civilization.

The field of mathematics provides an important example. Muslim scholars revived interest in the works of such Greek mathematicians as Euclid and Archimedes and further developed their ideas in geometry, trigonometry, and algebra. To simplify mathematics, they used the decimal number system and encouraged its adoption as the world's standard number system.

Muslim scholars also built upon ancient learning to extend their understanding of the universe. They constructed observatories to plot the movement of the stars, which enabled them to calculate dates for religious ceremonies and contributed to advances in navigation.

MEDICINE AND IDEAS

The Muslim quest for knowledge helped make the form of medicine practiced in Muslim lands the most advanced in the world. Following the Qur'an's instruction to care for the sick, Muslims built many hospitals. Muslim, Jewish, and Christian doctors collected the best available medical knowledge and organized it into reference books. These works helped spread the most advanced medical practices of the time throughout much of the world. They provided the basis for many Western medical treatments for centuries.

One of the most influential works was a 30-volume medical encyclopedia produced around 1000 by an Arab Muslim physician in al-Andalus known as **al-Zahrawi** (al-zuh-RAH-wee). This encyclopedia recommended treatments for a wide range of illnesses and included in-depth descriptions of surgeries. Al-Zahrawi pioneered surgical procedures and invented instruments, some of which are still used today.

Another Muslim physician from al-Andalus known as **Ibn Rushd** (ih-buhn RUSHT) wrote influential books on medicine. He was also a famous philosopher. His detailed studies of the Greek philosophers Aristotle and Plato were crucial in keeping alive the works of these two great thinkers. In his writings, Ibn Rushd tried to harmonize the ideas of Aristotle and Plato with Islam.

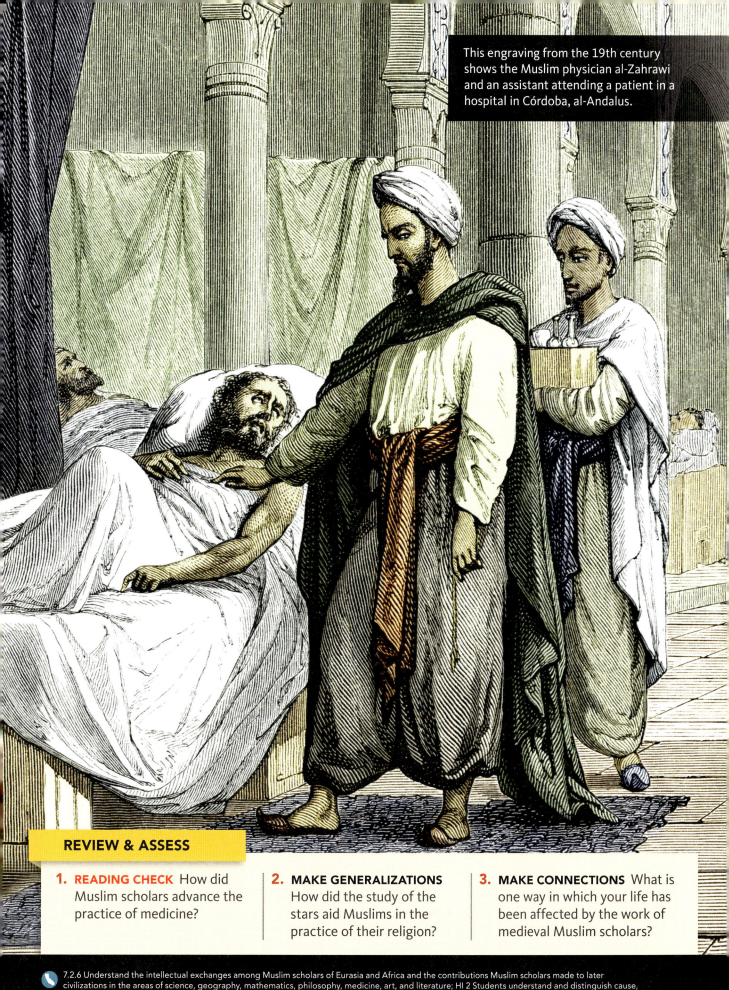

This engraving from the 19th century shows the Muslim physician al-Zahrawi and an assistant attending a patient in a hospital in Córdoba, al-Andalus.

REVIEW & ASSESS

1. **READING CHECK** How did Muslim scholars advance the practice of medicine?

2. **MAKE GENERALIZATIONS** How did the study of the stars aid Muslims in the practice of their religion?

3. **MAKE CONNECTIONS** What is one way in which your life has been affected by the work of medieval Muslim scholars?

7.2.6 Understand the intellectual exchanges among Muslim scholars of Eurasia and Africa and the contributions Muslim scholars made to later civilizations in the areas of science, geography, mathematics, philosophy, medicine, art, and literature; HI 2 Students understand and distinguish cause, effect, sequence, and correlation in historical events, including the long- and short-term causal relations; HI 3 Students explain the sources of historical

Aiding People Through Science

Hayat Sindi is acclaimed as one of the most influential Muslim women in the world. She is proud of her culture and its legacy of learning. "I've always admired people who do something for society," she says. One of her contributions fits on the tip of her finger. It's a tiny piece of paper that is helping save millions of lives around the world.

^
As a co-founder of Diagnostics for All, Hayat Sindi has traveled around the world. This photograph shows her in Brooklyn, New York.

Scientist Hayat Sindi is following Muslim tradition by promoting a medical device that benefits the world's poor people.

MEETING CHALLENGES

A fundamental belief of Islam is that the healthy should care for the sick, just as the wealthy should look after the poor. This belief motivated medieval Muslims to build hospitals and provide medical care to all groups of people at a time when medical care was extremely limited. The work of National Geographic Explorer Hayat Sindi carries on this tradition in the modern world. "Science can be such a powerful way to help humanity," says Sindi, a practicing Muslim from Mecca. "I'm using it to bring easy, affordable health diagnoses to the world's poorest people."

Postage-stamp-sized diagnostic tests developed by a scientific team at Harvard

Sindi was raised in a traditional Muslim family. Her passion for science drove her to leave Saudi Arabia, where women are not allowed to drive or vote. Even taking a job requires a male relative's permission. She traveled to England, where she taught herself English and won a place studying science at King's College in London. She went on to study at the University of Cambridge, the University of Oxford, the Massachusetts Institute of Technology, and Harvard University. "It was quite a journey," she says, "but when people tell me things are impossible, it just gives me energy."

A MISSION TO SAVE LIVES

Sindi's journey was certainly worth it. Today a medical invention she co-invented is helping millions of people from various ethnic groups and religions. "Essentially we've created a medical laboratory that can be taken anywhere because it's made of paper and is the size of a postage stamp," explains Sindi. The paper is etched with tiny channels that carry a single drop of saliva or other body fluid to tiny wells filled with chemicals. The chemicals change color, providing information on medical conditions, such as how well a person's liver is functioning.

The test costs less than a dime and requires no medical training to interpret. It is saving lives by identifying medical conditions early enough to be treated. "It's a tool that allows the poorest people in the most medically challenged places to get the tests they need," explains Sindi.

Just as Muslim physicians compiled books of medical knowledge and pushed the boundaries of medical understanding, Sindi is using the latest technology to ensure that more people receive better care. Sindi believes passionately in bringing science to everyone. "For me science is a universal language that transcends [rises above] nationality, religion, and gender. It can help solve any problem our world faces." Perhaps Muslim scholars before her felt the same way.

1. **READING CHECK** How does the medical device Sindi promotes benefit poor people?

2. **COMPARE AND CONTRAST** How is Sindi's work similar to the work of medieval Muslim physicians?

3. **DISTINGUISH FACT AND OPINION** Is the following statement a fact or an opinion: "[Science] can help solve any problem our world faces"? Explain your answer.

7.2.6 Understand the intellectual exchanges among Muslim scholars of Eurasia and Africa and the contributions Muslim scholars made to later civilizations in the areas of science, geography, mathematics, philosophy, medicine, art, and literature; REP 2 Students distinguish fact from opinion in historical narratives and stories.

83

3.3 Architecture, the Arts, and Literature

Have you ever drawn your name or other words in an artistic way? If so, you have something in common with medieval Muslim artists. These artists considered beautiful writing to be one of the highest forms of art and an expression of their religion, Islam. The Qur'an provided the passages for this beautiful writing.

MAIN IDEA

Medieval Muslim dynasties produced distinctive forms of architecture, art, and writing that are highly admired today.

BUILDING AND DESIGN

In medieval Islamic civilization, beautiful writing appeared not only in books but also in buildings. Those buildings, especially mosques, displayed many architectural features that were developed from Roman, Egyptian, Byzantine, and Persian models. However, the style of architecture soon became recognized as distinctly Islamic.

A typical mosque was topped by a large dome and had one or more **minarets**. These extremely tall, slender towers were designed to dominate the skyline and call attention to the importance of the mosque. From a minaret, a Muslim official known as a muezzin (moo-EH-zuhn) would call out a summons to prayer.

The inside of a mosque also had distinctive features. Under the dome was the prayer hall, a large open area designed to appear spacious and full of light. Set into one wall was the mihrab (MEE-ruhb), an often richly decorated archway that indicated the direction of Mecca. While sharing these common features, mosques also incorporated local influences, so they varied in design in different locations.

The decoration inside a mosque was often elaborate, featuring elegant writing called **calligraphy** and abstract design known as **arabesque**. Arabesque consists of patterns of flowers, leaves, vines, and geometric shapes. The patterns often repeat in a seemingly endless way, representing the Muslim belief in the infinity of God's creation. Muslim artists did not portray human figures or animals. According to an interpretation of the Qur'an, the depiction of people and animals imitates God's act of creation. Muslims feared the display of such works might encourage the worship of images.

LITERATURE

Besides distinctive architecture and art, medieval Islamic civilization also produced significant works of literature. Muslims consider the Qur'an to be the greatest literary work in the Arabic language. The best-known popular work of literature is *The Thousand and One Nights*, a collection of entertaining stories from India, Persia, and Arabia. It features such well-known characters as Aladdin and Sinbad the Sailor.

Muslims admired poetry more than any other form of literature. A four-line rhyming poem known as a quatrain was made popular by the Persian poet **Omar Khayyám** (ky-YAM), who lived from 1048 to 1131. *The Rubáiyát of Omar Khayyám*, a selection of his quatrains, is considered a masterpiece of world literature.

Critical Viewing The Taj Mahal in India was built in the mid-1600s by t Mughal emperor Shah Jahan. What features of Muslim architecture are apparent in the building's exterior?

REVIEW & ASSESS

1. READING CHECK What is a distinctive feature of the exterior architecture of a typical mosque?

2. DRAW CONCLUSIONS Would you expect to find statues in a mosque? Why or why not?

3. EVALUATE What qualities of Muslim architecture and art you find most appealing?

3.4

ISLAMIC ART

Islamic art features cultural influences from across vast empires. More importantly, it reflects the values and teachings of Islam. Muslim artists initially created calligraphy to beautify the Qur'an. The intricate floral and geometric patterns of arabesque emerged partly in response to an interpretation of the Qur'an. That interpretation discouraged the depiction of people and animals in art.

Mihrab
This archway comes from a mosque in Iran built in the 1300s. It features a mosaic of colorful tiles decorated with arabesque and calligraphy.

Caftan
This caftan, a long garment, belonged to Bayezid II, an Ottoman sultan who ruled from 1481 to 1512.

Ceramic Plate
This decorated plate was made in the 1700s in Morocco.

Stained Glass
This stained glass window appears in the Blue Mosque, which was built in the 1600s in Istanbul, Turkey.

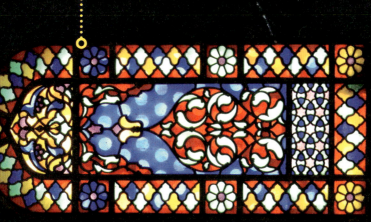

Calligraphy
This page of calligraphy comes from a Qur'an produced in Cairo, Egypt, around 1310.

Tile
This Turkish tile from about 1530 features floral patterns.

🔵 7.2.6 Understand the intellectual exchanges among Muslim scholars of Eurasia and Africa and the contributions Muslim scholars made to later civilizations in the areas of science, geography, mathematics, philosophy, medicine, art, and literature.

VOCABULARY

Use each of the following vocabulary words in a sentence that shows an understanding of the word's meaning.

1. **oasis** (HSS 7.2.1)

   An oasis was the only source of water for traders crossing the vast desert.

2. **medieval** (HSS 7.2)

3. **mosque** (HSS 7.2.3)

4. **pilgrimage** (HSS 7.2.2)

5. **caliph** (HSS 7.2.4)

6. **sultan** (HSS 7.2.4)

7. **janissary** (HSS 7.2.4)

8. **minaret** (HSS 7.2)

READING STRATEGY

9. **IDENTIFY MAIN IDEAS AND DETAILS** If you haven't already, complete your web with details that illustrate the legacy of Islamic culture. Then answer the question.

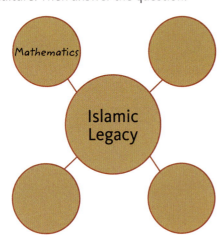

How is the influence of Islamic culture apparent in the present day? (HSS 7.2.6)

MAIN IDEAS

Answer the following questions. Support your answers with evidence from the chapter.

10. How were the Bedouin in Arabia organized in the 600s? **LESSON 1.1** (HSS 7.2.1)

11. Who was Muhammad? **LESSON 1.2** (HSS 7.2.2)

12. What happened to the Muslim state after Muhammad's death in 632? **LESSON 1.5** (HSS 7.2.1)

13. Why did Muslims split into two main sects in the late 600s? **LESSON 2.1** (HSS CST 1)

14. What dynasty transformed Muslim Spain into a center of Islamic culture between 756 and 1031? **LESSON 2.2** (HSS 7.2.6)

15. Who ruled the Ottoman Empire at its peak, and what were his major achievements? **LESSON 2.4** (HSS HI 1)

16. What major contributions did medieval Muslim scholars make to the field of mathematics? **LESSON 3.1** (HSS 7.2.6)

17. What are the advantages of the medical invention Hayat Sindi promotes? **LESSON 3.2** (HSS 7.2.6)

CRITICAL THINKING

Answer the following questions. Support your answers with evidence from the chapter.

18. **ESSENTIAL QUESTION** What is one major way in which medieval Muslim scholars helped build a foundation for modern civilization? (HSS 7.2.6)

19. **ANALYZE CAUSE AND EFFECT** How did the Qur'an affect the development of Islamic art? (HSS 7.2.3)

20. **MAKE INFERENCES** How did its geographic location contribute to the growth of the Safavid Empire? (HSS 7.2.5)

21. **YOU DECIDE** Which of the Muslim empires was the greatest? Be sure to explain what you mean by "great." (HSS REP 1)

INTERPRET MAPS

Study the map that shows the spread of Islam. Then answer the questions that follow.

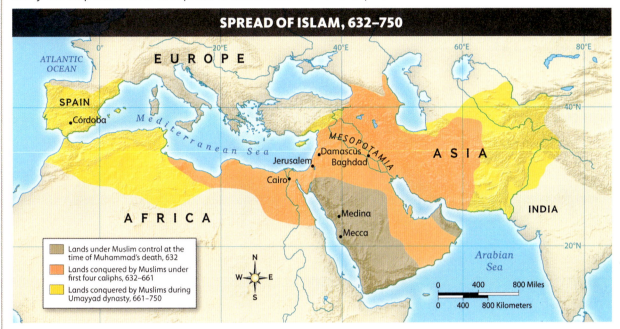

SPREAD OF ISLAM, 632–750

ATLANTIC OCEAN

EUROPE

SPAIN
•Córdoba

Mediterranean Sea

MESOPOTAMIA
•Damascus
Jerusalem• •Baghdad
Cairo•

AFRICA

Medina•

Mecca•

ASIA

INDIA

Arabian Sea

Lands under Muslim control at the time of Muhammad's death, 632

Lands conquered by Muslims under first four caliphs, 632–661

Lands conquered by Muslims during Umayyad dynasty, 661–750

0   400   800 Miles
0   400   800 Kilometers

22. Across what region had Islam spread by the time of Muhammad's death in 632? HSS CST 3

23. To what continents had Islam spread by 661? HSS CST 3

ANALYZE SOURCES

Read this part of an oath that was written by Moses Maimonides, a physician in Muslim Spain. Then answer the question that follows.

> May I never see in the patient anything but a fellow creature in pain. Grant me the strength, time and opportunity always to correct what [learning] I have acquired, always to extend its domain [sphere]; for knowledge is immense and the spirit of man can extend indefinitely to enrich itself daily with new requirements. . . . Oh, God, Thou has appointed me to watch over the life and death of Thy creatures; here am I ready for my vocation and now I turn unto my calling.

24. How do Maimonides' ideas about knowledge reflect achievements in Muslim Spain during its golden age? HSS REP 4

WRITE ABOUT HISTORY

25. INFORMATIVE Write a brief encyclopedia article that compares the main beliefs of Islam with those of Judaism and Christianity. HSS 7.2.2

TIPS

- Take notes on the beliefs of Islam described in Lesson 1.3.

- State the main idea about the similarities among the beliefs of Islam, Judaism, and Christianity in your beginning sentence.

- Develop the main idea by using relevant, well-chosen facts about the beliefs of each religion.

- Use appropriate transition words, such as *likewise*, *similarly*, and *also*, to clarify the similarities among the three religions' beliefs.

- Provide a concluding statement that follows from and supports the facts you have presented on the three religions' beliefs.

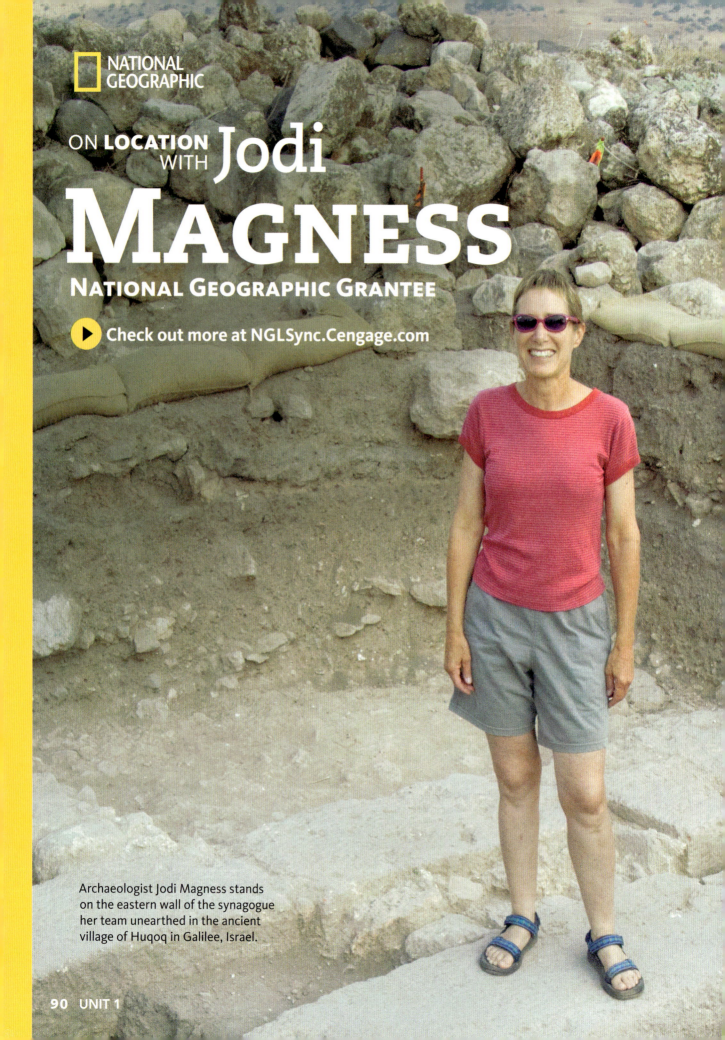

ON **LOCATION** WITH Jodi

MAGNESS

NATIONAL GEOGRAPHIC GRANTEE

▶ Check out more at NGLSync.Cengage.com

Archaeologist Jodi Magness stands
on the eastern wall of the synagogue
her team unearthed in the ancient
village of Huqoq in Galilee, Israel.

EXPLORING IN ISRAEL

I was just 12 when I decided I wanted to become an archaeologist. It is a passion I'm lucky enough to pursue as my career. I've taken part in over 20 excavations around the Mediterranean Sea. I now specialize in the history of ancient Palestine, the area that includes modern Israel, Jordan, and the Palestine territories. It's a land rich in history, and it's allowed me to study the city of Jerusalem, the fortress of Masada, and the Roman Army. But things really took off in 2011 when I came to study the ancient village of Huqoq (hoo-KOKE) in Galilee, Israel.

We were hunting for the remains of a fifth century synagogue. It was a big, overgrown site but our very first sounding came down right on the synagogue's eastern wall. We weren't able to use technologies like ground-penetrating radar to find the synagogue because it is covered by the bulldozed ruins of a modern village. We remove one rock at a time and record everything we do because you can never put the stones back the way they were.

Jodi Magness and her team are challenged by the summer heat, scorpions, and snakes in Huqoq.

HIDDEN MOSAICS

This is especially important because of what we are finding—mosaic floors made up of thousands of tiny cubes of stone. The very first mosaic that peered out of the dirt was the face of a woman. We've also uncovered spectacular mosaics depicting stories from the Hebrew Bible. We found a beautiful depiction of Samson taking revenge on the Philistines using foxes to carry torches and set fire to their fields. There's another mosaic showing Samson carrying the gate of Gaza in an incredible act of strength. We've even found one mosaic with elephants (see pages 344–345), which indicates that this is not a story from the Hebrew Bible. It might tell the story of Alexander the Great. So far, we have only uncovered a small part of the synagogue, and we hope our continued excavation will reveal more mosaics.

WHY STUDY HISTORY ❓

❝ The mosaics we are uncovering in Huqoq are not only beautiful, they are helping other archaeologists, scholars, and the general public to *better understand ancient Judaism*. Every year we come back and discover more, so it's really an extraordinary experience. ❞ —Jodi Magness

NATIONAL GEOGRAPHIC

The Stolen Past

BY KAREN LANGE

Adapted from "The Stolen Past," by Karen Lange,
in *National Geographic*, December 2008

For a thousand years, the ruins of Khirbet Tawas, a Byzantine jewel, stood southwest of Hebron. Then, in 2000, the second intifada began. As Palestinians fought Israeli troops, the West Bank became all but ungovernable. Soon the Israelis set up a web of security checkpoints, sealed off the region, and barred most Palestinians from working inside Israel. Jobless men looked for cash wherever they could find it. Armed with shovels, a small band descended on Khirbet Tawas. The looters searched for anything they could sell: Byzantine coins, clay lamps, glass bracelets.

Looters have overrun not just Khirbet Tawas but countless other archaeological sites located in the West Bank. They attack ancient sites with backhoes and small bulldozers, scraping away the top layer of earth across areas the size of several football fields. Guided by metal detectors—coins often give away the location of other goods—they take anything of value.

The West Bank is a cradle of civilization and a crossroads of empires. For Jews, Christians, and Muslims, it is sacred ground. Yet this priceless legacy is swiftly being lost. Archaeologist Salah Al-Houdalieh says, "They are destroying a cultural heritage that belongs to every Palestinian, to every human being."

Few jobs, inadequate law enforcement by both Palestinian and Israeli authorities, and demand for artifacts just across the border in Israel have created the perfect storm for looting.

Some looted artifacts are bought by middlemen who supply shops in Israel. Tourists eager to take home a piece of the Holy Land unknowingly support the trade. Other artifacts are smuggled into Jordan, then on to dealers elsewhere, who in turn sell the artifacts to outlets in Israel.

Alarmed by the spike in looting, Palestinian lawmakers have proposed increasing the maximum prison sentence for damaging archaeological sites from three years to five. Yet political circumstances and deep mutual distrust continue to hamper police on both sides of the border.

For more from National Geographic
Check out "The Wells of Memory" at NGLSync.Cengage.com

UNIT INQUIRY: MAKE AN IDEA MAP

In this unit, you learned about many cultural contributions of the Roman Empire, Byzantine Empire, and medieval Islamic civilizations. Based on your understanding of the text, what impact did these cultural contributions have on civilization as they spread throughout the world? How do these cultural contributions continue to make a major impact on our civilization today?

ASSIGNMENT Create an idea map that illustrates the cultural impact one of the major contributions of the Roman Empire, Byzantine Empire, or medieval Islamic civilizations has had (and continues to have) on our civilization today. Be prepared to present your idea map to the class and explain how the contribution or achievement is an example of cultural diffusion from ancient or medieval civilization to today.

Plan As you create your idea map, think about the many cultural achievements and contributions made by the Roman Empire, Byzantine Empire, and medieval Islamic civilizations. Select one major contribution or achievement that you think has had an impact on today's civilization. You might want to use a graphic organizer to help organize your thoughts. ▶

Produce Use your notes to produce descriptions of different ways the contribution or achievement you selected has impacted the world today. You might want to write them in outline or paragraph form.

Present Choose a creative way to present your idea map to the class. Consider one of these options:

- Create a multimedia presentation using photos to illustrate different ways the contribution/achievement impacts our civilization today.

- Write an introduction to your idea map that explains the significance of cultural diffusion in ancient and medieval civilization and the modern world.

- Draw a physical map to show the location where the contribution/achievement originated.

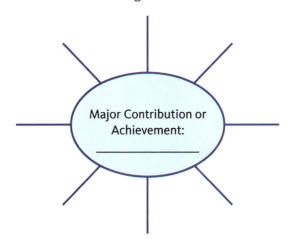

Major Contribution or Achievement:
_____

RAPID REVIEW
UNIT 1

ROMAN, BYZANTINE, AND ISLAMIC CIVILIZATIONS

TOP TEN

1. Internal problems and invasions by barbarians contributed to the fall of the Western Roman Empire in A.D. 476.

2. Byzantium was a center of trade and learning and the largest city in the medieval world.

3. The Roman Catholic Church split with the Eastern Orthodox Church in 1064.

4. Muhammad was a political and religious leader who founded Islam.

5. Islam spread across Southwest Asia, North Africa, India, and Europe through conquest and trade.

6-10. **NOW IT'S YOUR TURN** Complete the list with five more things to remember about Roman, Byzantine, and Islamic civilizations.

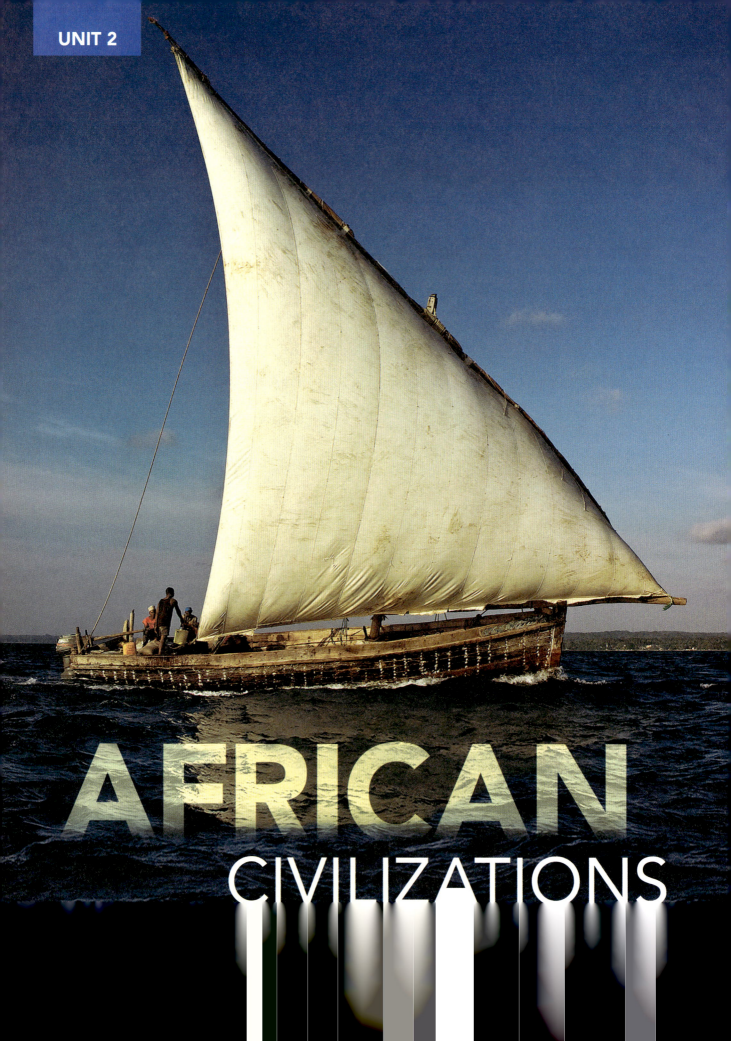

AFRICAN
CIVILIZATIONS

ON **LOCATION** WITH

Christopher DeCorse
Archaeologist

The story of Africa is an ancient one. The natural resources and movement of people across this huge continent have made the exchange of goods and ideas a major theme throughout its long history. Crossing the vast Sahara and sailing the waters of the Indian Ocean, Africans created some of the most successful trading networks in history. I'm Christopher DeCorse, and I'm an archaeologist and National Geographic Grantee. Join me on a journey to explore the civilizations of Africa!

< **CRITICAL VIEWING** Ships like this African dhow carried goods in and out of coastal trading cities. Why would a ship like this be good for sailing the open sea?

African Civilizations

c. A.D. 100
Aksum emerges as a prosperous trading kingdom in present-day Ethiopia.

c. 500 B.C.
The Nok people develop iron tools and terra cotta sculpture.
(terra cotta Nok head sculpture)

c. 300
The introduction of camels in North Africa allows for trans-Saharan trade.

A.D. 100

c. 1000 B.C.
The Bantu begin their slow migration across sub-Saharan Africa.

1000 B.C.

552 B.C. ASIA
Confucius is born in northeast China.

c. 500 B.C. AMERICAS
The Zapotec build the city of Monte Albán overlooking the Oaxaca Valley. *(statuette of a Zapotec god)*

The World

 CST 1 Students explain how major events are related to one another in time.

COMPARE TIME LINES

What two cultures had become highly developed by about 500 B.C.?

1324
Mansa Musa makes his pilgrimage to Egypt. *(illustration of Mansa Musa from an illuminated map)*

c. 1300
East African city-states, including Kilwa, arise along the East African coast.
(ruins at Kilwa)

c. 1230
The empire of Mali is founded by Sundiata Keita.

1400
The kingdom of Kongo emerges in the rain forests south of the Congo River.

c. 500
The trading kingdom of Ghana emerges west of the Sahara.

1250

1095
EUROPE
Pope Urban II initiates the first crusade to the Holy Land.

1500

330
EUROPE
Emperor Constantine makes Constantinople the capital of the Eastern Roman Empire.
(profile of Constantine on a gold coin)

1453
ASIA
Ottoman Turks capture Constantinople, ending the Byzantine Empire.

97

AFRICA

Land Use & Resources
2014

Africa is a huge land area that encompasses a wide variety of physical features and cultures. Trade has long been a part of many of these cultures, fueling the rise of kingdoms across the continent. West African civilizations were built on the trade of gold, salt, and slaves. The Indian Ocean trade made the ancient kingdom of Aksum a mighty power and later helped found the great city-states of East Africa.

With its plentiful natural resources, Africa plays a major role in international trade today. The highly detailed National Geographic map on the next page shows the continent's resources and land use systems. Many African nations are important trading partners of the United States. The graph below shows how much the United States spends on goods received from Africa (imports) and how much it earns on goods sent to Africa (exports).

What natural resources are found in West Africa?

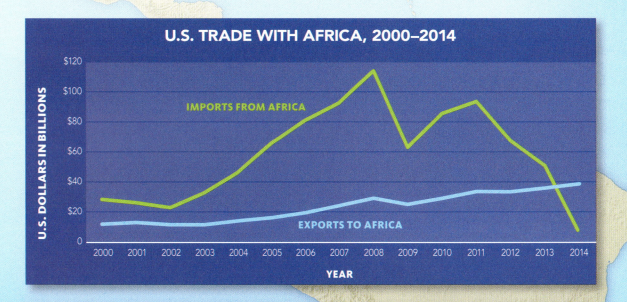

U.S. TRADE WITH AFRICA, 2000–2014

IMPORTS FROM AFRICA

EXPORTS TO AFRICA

(y-axis) U.S. DOLLARS IN BILLIONS: $120, $100, $80, $60, $40, $20, 0

(x-axis) YEAR: 2000 2001 2002 2003 2004 2005 2006 2007 2008 2009 2010 2011 2012 2013 2014

Imports Oil is among the top items imported to the United States from Africa, including that drilled from this oil rig in South Africa.

Exports The top items exported to Africa from the United States are machinery and equipment, including agricultural machines.

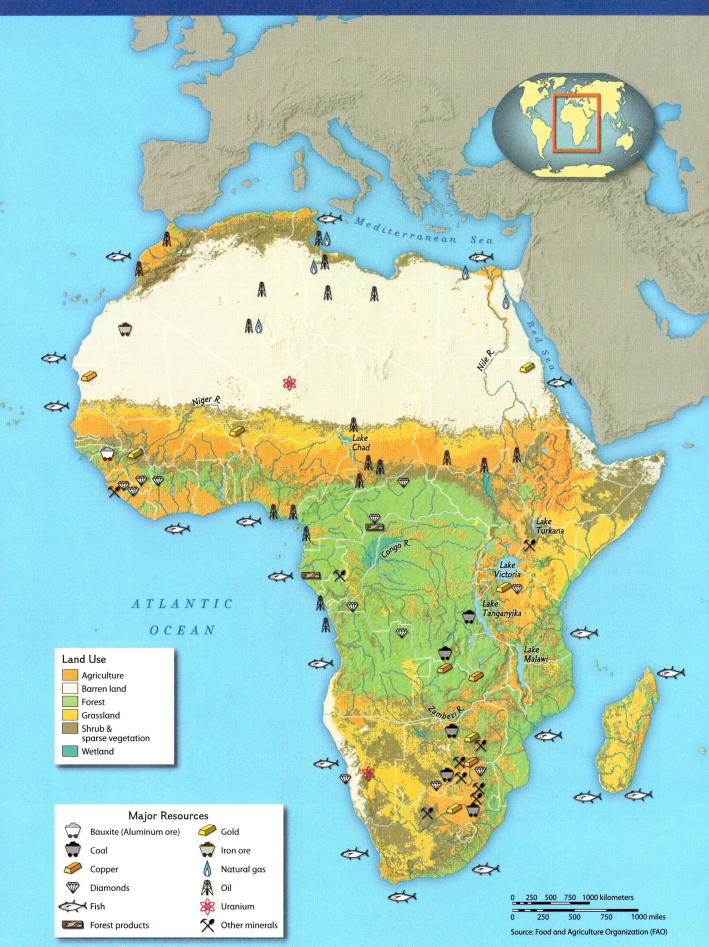

Mediterranean Sea

Red Sea

Nile R.

Niger R.

Lake Chad

Congo R.

Lake Turkana

Lake Victoria

Lake Tanganyika

Lake Malawi

Zambezi R.

ATLANTIC OCEAN

Land Use

Agriculture	
Barren land	
Forest	
Grassland	
Shrub & sparse vegetation	
Wetland	

Major Resources

	Bauxite (Aluminum ore)		Gold
	Coal		Iron ore
	Copper		Natural gas
	Diamonds		Oil
	Fish		Uranium
	Forest products		Other minerals

0 250 500 750 1000 kilometers

0 250 500 750 1000 miles

Source: Food and Agriculture Organization (FAO)

CST 3 Students use a variety of maps and documents to identify physical and cultural features of neighborhoods, cities, states, and countries and to explain the historical migration of people, expansion and disintegration of empires, and the growth of economic systems.

4

NORTH AND WEST AFRICA

1000 B.C. – A.D. 1500

ESSENTIAL QUESTION What impact did trade and technology have on North and West Africa?

SECTION 1 NORTH AFRICA

KEY VOCABULARY
caravan
commodity
desertification
savanna
scarcity
trans-Saharan

NAMES & PLACES
Berbers
Djenné
Sahara
Timbuktu

SECTION 2 WEST AFRICA

KEY VOCABULARY
griot
iron
mansa
oral tradition
terra cotta

NAMES & PLACES
Ghana
Iron Age
Mali
Mansa Musa
Nok
Sub-Saharan Africa
Sundiata Keita

READING STRATEGY

ANALYZE LANGUAGE USE
When you analyze language use, you determine the impact of the language a writer uses. Use a chart like this one to analyze the impact of language in the introductory paragraphs of the lessons in the chapter.

Language Example	What It Suggests

A woman wearing a traditional Songhai headdress poses in front of a decorative curtain in the town of Gao in northern Mali. The Songhai Empire was one of the great trading civilizations that flourished in West Africa between the 10th and 16th centuries A.D.

A **Vast** and **Varied Land**

The way that some modern maps are drawn magnifies the size of countries in the Northern Hemisphere. This projection disguises the huge scale of Africa, which is larger than the United States, Europe, Japan, and China combined. North Africa alone is a huge area that includes the Sahara, the world's largest desert.

MAIN IDEA

North Africa has a variety of landforms, including the vast Sahara.

THE LARGEST DESERT IN THE WORLD

The northern part of Africa borders the Mediterranean Sea. (See the map in Lesson 1.2.) At the entrance to the Mediterranean, North Africa lies only ten miles south of Europe. Lining the coast of North Africa are the rugged Atlas Mountains. For centuries, people have lived in villages scattered throughout these mountains.

South of the Atlas Mountains lies the **Sahara**, an important geographic feature of North Africa. Sahara, which means "desert," is the largest desert in the world. It stretches more than 3,000 miles across North Africa, spanning the continent from the Red Sea in the east to the Atlantic

Ocean in the west. Covering 3.5 million square miles, the Sahara is about the size of the continental United States, Alaska, and Hawaii combined. With its hot summers and warm winters, the Sahara is one of the hottest and driest places on Earth.

The Sahara's soaring mountains and vast seas of shifting sand provide a dramatic contrast to the desert's mostly flat and rocky terrain. In addition to the Atlas Mountains, two other mountain ranges, the Ahaggar and Tibesti, rise in the Sahara's interior.

For thousands of years, people found the Sahara almost impossible to cross. As a result, the peoples of North Africa, with their Mediterranean and Southwest Asian influences, developed independently from those living on the rest of the continent.

THE GREEN SAHARA

The hot, dry Sahara seems an unlikely place to find fossils of fish and rock paintings of lakes, forests, and herds of cattle. However, the Sahara has both, which offer clues to its past. The Sahara was not always a desert. Thirty million years ago, the Sahara was an ocean full of fish and whales. Over time, climate change drained the seas to leave lush tropical grasslands called the **savanna**. Many thousands of years ago, the Sahara was green. People farmed there and herded cattle.

Beginning around 5300 B.C., seasonal rains shifted southward. The Sahara's lakes, rivers, and grasslands dried up. As rain became scarce and temperatures soared up to 130°F, the Sahara's fertile soil dried, baked, and became unproductive. This process, called **desertification**, created the desert that exists today.

People and animals began migrating to better land with steady water supplies. Some people moved north, others south. Still others headed east toward the Nile River Valley, where they built one of Africa's greatest civilizations—Egypt.

Critical Viewing The Gao region of Mali is located in the southern Sahara along the Niger River, shown here. What traits of this area might enable people to live here?

REVIEW & ASSESS

1. **READING CHECK** What major landforms are found in North Africa?

2. **IDENTIFY MAIN IDEAS AND DETAILS** Why did North Africa develop independently from the rest of the African continent?

3. **ANALYZE CAUSE AND EFFECT** What effect did climate change have on the geography and climate of the Sahara?

Trans-Saharan Trade

The camel caravan snakes back and forth for miles across the desert. Thousands of camels trudge surefooted across the Saharan sand despite being loaded down with Mediterranean goods for trade. The caravan is a merchant's ticket to profit, but first the merchant must survive the journey.

MAIN IDEA

As North Africa developed a strong economy, trade between native and foreign communities brought the riches of the Sahara to Europe.

BERBER TRADERS

Trade in North Africa began with the **Berbers**. They were native to the region, and they lived in communities spread throughout areas in present-day Egypt, Libya, Tunisia, Algeria, and Morocco. Most Berbers farmed or herded cattle. Others lived as desert nomads or dwelled in the mountains. Despite these differences, they shared a broad Berber culture.

Around 800 B.C., the Phoenicians and Greeks arrived in North Africa and founded cities on the coast. The Phoenicians used these cities as staging areas for trade with Spain. One such city, Carthage, increasingly controlled Berber lands and peoples. Numidia, an early Berber kingdom, reacted to this invasion by helping the Romans overthrow Carthage.

Although clashes between Berbers and foreign rulers continued, trade relationships developed between the people of the desert and the people of the North African coast. The Berbers took an active role in this trade. Traveling along routes in the Sahara, they transported slaves, salt, semiprecious stones, and other goods for the Mediterranean market. In exchange, they received food, cloth, horses, weapons, and other manufactured goods.

A DIFFICULT PASSAGE

Carrying goods on trade routes in the desert was difficult and dangerous. Historians believe that around A.D. 300, the introduction of camels began to transform trade in North Africa, and the animals started to make large-scale **trans-Saharan** trade possible. That is, trade now crossed the Sahara. Camels were able to carry heavy loads over long distances and difficult terrain. They also needed little food and water.

Many independent merchants sought safety in numbers by traveling in a group called a camel **caravan**. Caravans had hundreds or even thousands of camels. Led by highly paid Berber guides, caravans would set off from North African cities and head into the Sahara. To avoid the worst of the desert heat, caravans only traveled in winter and most often at night.

Few merchants crossed the entire Sahara. Instead they exchanged their goods at an oasis, where they could find water. From there, other merchants would take the goods to the next oasis, and so on across the desert. In this way, trade routes connecting North and West Africa developed across the Sahara. The oases grew into towns and cities that became wealthy as centers of trade. However, the dangers of caravan travel remained. The possibility of dying from getting lost or from being caught in a sandstorm was just as real as the threat of attack by desert nomads. Trans-Saharan trade was a risky business.

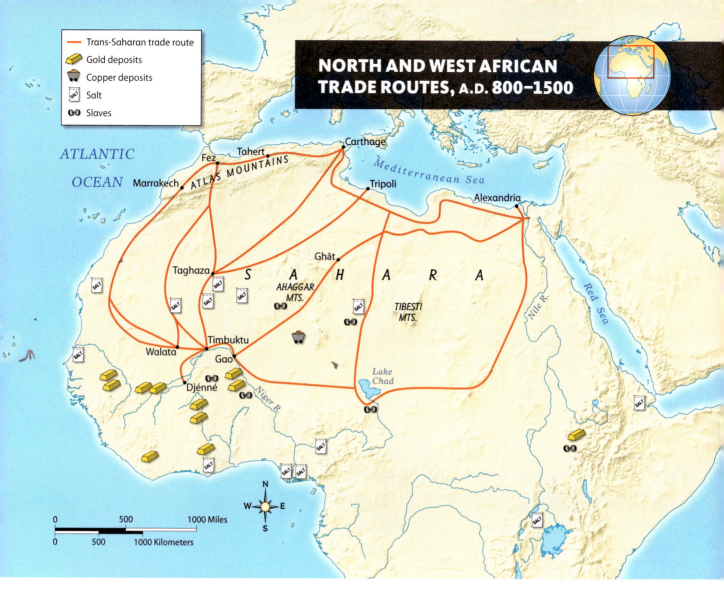

NORTH AND WEST AFRICAN TRADE ROUTES, A.D. 800–1500

Legend:
— Trans-Saharan trade route
- Gold deposits
- Copper deposits
- Salt
- Slaves

ATLANTIC OCEAN

Mediterranean Sea

Carthage
Tahert
Fez
Marrakech
ATLAS MOUNTAINS
Tripoli
Alexandria

S A H A R A

Ghāt
Taghaza
AHAGGAR MTS.
TIBESTI MTS.
Nile R.
Red Sea

Timbuktu
Walata
Gao
Djénné
Niger R.
Lake Chad

N W E S

0 500 1000 Miles
0 500 1000 Kilometers

TODAY'S MOUNTAIN BERBERS

Berbers now living in urban areas often lose touch with their traditions. However, the way of life of Berbers living in the Atlas Mountains of North Africa has remained basically unchanged for centuries.

Mountain Berber homes are simple structures of stone and wood. The ground floor is most often a stable, perhaps housing a cow or a few chickens. Their owners occupy the floor above. Instead of power tools, farmers use scythes and other hand tools. They plow using mules and harvest by hand.

Although mountain Berbers see few strangers, they are friendly and hospitable. They often greet Westerners with the ancient term *Arrumi*, meaning "Roman."

REVIEW & ASSESS

1. **READING CHECK** What was trans-Saharan trade?

2. **FORM AND SUPPORT OPINIONS** Was travel by caravan worth the risk? Support your opinion.

3. **INTERPRET MAPS** What valuable goods were exchanged on the trans-Saharan trade routes?

7.2.5 Describe the growth of cities and the establishment of trade routes among Asia, Africa, and Europe, the products and inventions that traveled along these routes (e.g., spices, textiles, paper, steel, new crops), and the role of merchants in Arab society; 7.4.1 Study the Niger River and the relationship of vegetation zones of forest, savannah, and desert to trade in gold, salt, food, and slaves; and the growth of the Ghana and Mali empires; 7.4.3 Describe the role of the trans-Saharan caravan trade in the changing religious and cultural characteristics of West Africa and the influence of Islamic beliefs, ethics, and law; CST 3 Students use a variety of maps and documents to identify physical and cultural features of neighborhoods, cities, states, and countries and to explain the historical migration of people, expansion and disintegration of empires, and the growth of economic systems.

Gold, Salt, and Slaves

"Pass the salt, please" is an everyday expression we use without thinking. Today, salt is so common we hardly notice it, but in the ancient world it was unbelievably rare and precious. Salt was literally worth its weight in gold, and the Sahara had vast quantities of it.

MAIN IDEA

Africa had many valuable resources that fostered trade with the Mediterranean world and beyond.

SALT

Too much salt is unhealthy, but a limited amount is crucial to a healthy body.

Salt assists in hydration, circulation, muscle contraction, and digestion. It's important to replace salt lost through perspiration.

PRECIOUS RESOURCES

Two of Africa's most valuable **commodities**, or trade goods, were gold and salt. Beginning in the 400s, these goods were traded for hundreds of years. The Western Sudan, the name for all of northern Africa west of Lake Chad, was especially rich in gold deposits.

Each year, perhaps a ton of gold crossed the Sahara, finding its way to Europe and Asia. African gold stimulated the flow of silk from China and spices from India. European kings used African gold to make coins.

Salt was worth almost as much as gold. Before there were refrigerators to keep food cold, people used salt to preserve meat and other foods. In some areas of the world, preservation with salt is still practiced. In much of the ancient world, salt was rare. Its **scarcity**, or small supply, made salt valuable. Africa, though, had large salt deposits, thanks to the Sahara. The desert had once been a shallow sea. As its waters dried up, salt deposits were left, especially in western Africa. Laborers extracted, or dug out, 200-pound slabs of salt, which they carved into blocks. Camels carried salt blocks hundreds of miles to be traded at a huge profit.

AFRICAN SLAVE TRADE

The labor needed for mining gold and salt came largely from slaves, who were traded across the desert beginning in the 600s. Like the

7.4.1 Study the Niger River and the relationship of vegetation zones of forest, savannah, and desert to trade in gold, salt, food, and slaves; and the growth of the Ghana and Mali empires; 7.4.3 Describe the role of the trans-Saharan

Critical Viewing A camel caravan moves through the desert. What does the image show about how camels are useful to traders?

Atlantic slave trade that would emerge in the 1500s, the trans-Saharan slave trade was a harsh and horrible business. Most slaves came from the Niger Delta region. (See the map in Lesson 1.2.) Once captured, they were chained together and forcibly marched through the desert.

The slave trade increased dramatically when Muslim traders arrived in North Africa in the 600s. However, the desert's vast expanse always limited the slave trade. Many slaves died during the terrible journey. The survivors were exchanged for trade goods, especially horses. A good horse was extremely valuable in the desert and cost a large number of slaves.

While some slaves were sold for labor, others satisfied a growing demand for slaves in the Mediterranean world. There, slaves were likely to become domestic servants, soldiers, artisans, or even important government officials. Nonetheless, these people had been taken from their families and cruelly treated, with little hope of ever returning home. It was a particularly brutal aspect of Africa's history.

REVIEW & ASSESS

1. **READING CHECK** Why were salt and gold such valuable resources?

2. **SEQUENCE EVENTS** What happened to greatly increase the slave trade?

3. **IDENTIFY MAIN IDEAS AND DETAILS** According to the text, what happened to slaves who reached North Africa?

caravan trade in the changing religious and cultural characteristics of West Africa and the influence of Islamic beliefs, ethics, and law; HI 2 Students understand and distinguish cause, effect, sequence, and correlation in historical events, including the long- and short-term causal relations; HI 6 Students interpret basic indicators of economic performance and conduct cost-benefit analyses of economic and political issues.

Islam Spreads to Africa

The mighty Muslim general Uqba fought his way across North Africa during the A.D. 600s. After his great triumphs, he rode his horse into the Atlantic Ocean, saying, "Oh God, if the sea had not prevented me, I would have galloped on forever . . . upholding your faith and fighting the unbelievers." Such determination helped assure the place of Islam in Africa.

MAIN IDEA

Islam spread through North and West Africa, affecting African culture.

MALI'S ANCIENT MANUSCRIPTS

Timbuktu and Djenné are home to hundreds of thousands of manuscripts dating back to the 1100s. These handwritten works contain invaluable insight into the history of Africa and Islam.

CONQUEST AND TRADE

After the prophet Muhammad's death in A.D. 632, Islam spread from its origins on the Arabian Peninsula to many other parts of the world. By 642, Arab armies had conquered Egypt. Over the next several centuries, Muslims would spread Islam throughout North and West Africa. At first, few Berbers converted to Islam, but eventually many did so. In time, most North Africans were Muslim. During the 1000s and the 1100s, first the Almoravids (al-muh-RAH-vuhdz) and then the Almohads (al-muh-HAHDZ) founded Berber dynasties that united northwestern Africa.

When the Arabs invaded North Africa, trans-Saharan trade with West Africa expanded greatly. Using camel caravans, Berber merchants carried their goods and religion across the Sahara. Many West African merchants saw a trading advantage and converted to Islam.

By the 1000s, West African rulers also began to convert to Islam, as did some of their subjects. Others continued their traditional beliefs, sometimes mixing them with Islamic practices. Muslim merchants established Islam as far away as the East African coast. By 1500, Islam had spread across North Africa, West Africa, and along the coast of East Africa.

THE IMPACT OF ISLAM

As Islam spread, so did Islamic culture. By the 1300s, Muslim leaders ruled several empires, and mosques were common in North and West Africa. Traditional mosque architecture was cleverly adapted to Africa's climate and materials. Builders used mud and even salt blocks. They created impressive buildings like the mud-built mosque in **Djenné** (jeh-NAY), shown opposite. Builders also designed rectangular mud-brick houses with flat roofs.

The Arabic language also spread. Literacy increased through the teaching of the Qur'an, and mosques became important centers of learning. Scholarship thrived. Cities like **Timbuktu** and Djenné became famous centers for Muslim art, literature, and science. Scholars in Timbuktu collected and wrote down Islamic teachings in many fields of knowledge, including astronomy, medicine, law, and mathematics.

Critical Viewing The Great Mosque of Djenné, Mali, is an architectural wonder. What distinctive features does the image show?

REVIEW & ASSESS

1. **READING CHECK** How did Islam spread throughout North and West Africa?

2. **MAKE INFERENCES** Why might West African merchants have viewed conversion to Islam as a trading advantage?

3. **ANALYZE LANGUAGE USE** How does the phrase "cleverly adapted" help explain the use of traditional mosque architecture in Africa?

7.2.5 Describe the growth of cities and the establishment of trade routes among Asia, Africa, and Europe, the products and inventions that traveled along these routes (e.g., spices, textiles, paper, steel, new crops), and the role of merchants in Arab society; 7.4.3 Describe the role of the trans-Saharan caravan trade in the changing religious and cultural characteristics of West Africa and the influence of Islamic beliefs, ethics, and law; 7.4.4 Trace the growth of the Arabic language in government, trade, and Islamic scholarship in West Africa.

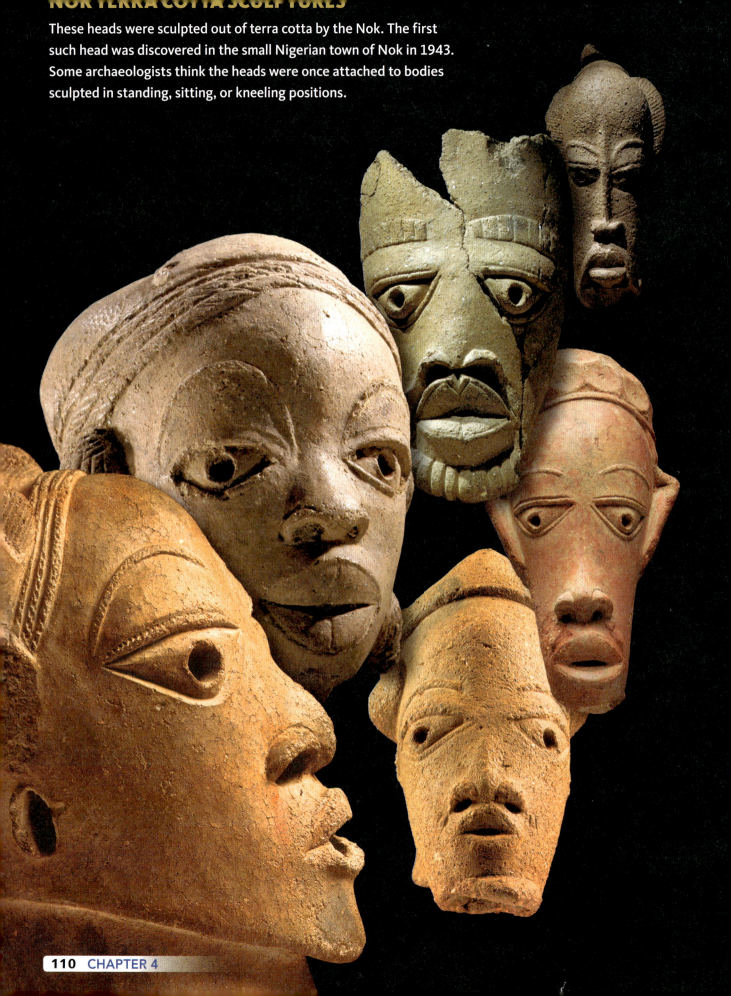

NOK TERRA COTTA SCULPTURES

These heads were sculpted out of terra cotta by the Nok. The first such head was discovered in the small Nigerian town of Nok in 1943. Some archaeologists think the heads were once attached to bodies sculpted in standing, sitting, or kneeling positions.

Nok Culture and Iron Technology

You put more wood into the blazing furnace and blow into it through long clay tubes. The injection of air makes the fire burn even hotter, and your body is almost scalded by the heat. But the results will be worth it when you succeed in extracting precious iron from rock.

MAIN IDEA

The Nok developed art forms and iron tools that brought great changes to West Africa.

THE NOK

West Africa juts out like the hump of a camel into the Atlantic Ocean. The region is part of **Sub-Saharan Africa**, which stretches south of the Sahara to the southern tip of the continent.

The **Nok** people settled in what is now the country of Nigeria. (See the map in Lesson 2.2.) Around 500 B.C., the Nok were among the first in West Africa to make tools from **iron**, a metal that is found in rock.

Nok artists also used **terra cotta**, which is fire-baked clay, to create unusual sculptures of humans. The sculpted heads of Nok figures, which are about 12 inches high and cone-shaped, are all that remain. These sculptures are the oldest known figurative sculptures south of the Sahara. They have elaborate hairstyles, triangular eyes, oversized features, and exaggerated expressions. This style heavily influenced West African art for centuries.

AFRICA'S IRON AGE

What archaeologists call the **Iron Age** was an important period during which the use of superior iron tools and weapons began and spread. The Nok were probably the first sub-Saharan people to smelt iron. They may have developed smelting independently or learned it through contact with other cultures.

Smelting is the process used to extract iron from a type of rock called iron ore. Using extraordinarily high temperatures, the iron is literally melted out of the rock. The Nok built clay furnaces with two chambers, one for the fire and the other for the ore. Smelters used clay pipes to blow air into the fire and increase its heat. Then they drained the liquid iron into stone molds to make strong iron tools and weapons.

The Nok used iron axes, picks, and hoes to clear huge areas of land for farming. With an increased food supply, the population grew.

At its peak, Nok culture covered about 350,000 square miles. However, deforestation, or cutting down forests, damaged the local ecosystem. At the same time, overuse made the soil infertile. Due to these geographic changes, Nok culture declined after about A.D. 200.

REVIEW & ASSESS

1. **READING CHECK** What Nok developments brought change to West Africa?

2. **ANALYZE CAUSE AND EFFECT** How did the use of iron tools affect Nok culture?

3. **DRAW CONCLUSIONS** How did the Nok use raw materials to advance their culture?

HI 2 Students understand and distinguish cause, effect, sequence, and correlation in historical events, including the long- and short-term causal relations.

The Kingdom of Ghana

During the 700s, Arab traders from North Africa began to cross the Sahara more frequently. When they reached West Africa, they talked glowingly of a "land of gold," where the king wore a hat made of gold and the horses were draped in stunning gold cloth. This was the land of Ghana, and for centuries, it was the wealthiest kingdom in West Africa.

MAIN IDEA

Trade, especially in gold, spurred the development of the powerful kingdom of Ghana in West Africa.

A KINGDOM OF GOLD

South of the Sahara was a region of grasslands that was ideally suited for agriculture. Iron tools helped the farmers grow more food. Surpluses of food allowed some family groups to specialize in other jobs, such as fishing or cloth-making. The people lived in villages, and the villages banded together to form the kingdom of **Ghana**.

By A.D. 500, Ghana had become the first great trading state in West Africa. Traders arrived there bringing salt and other commodities. The capital of Ghana,

Koumbi-Saleh (KUHM-bee SAHL-uh), stood midway between Africa's main sources of salt, most of which were in the Sahara, and West Africa's gold mines, which Ghana controlled. This control and a favorable location made Ghana's traders the ideal middlemen for trans-Saharan trade. (Middlemen are people who buy goods from one person and sell them to another.) The trade brought Ghana's traders wealth and power.

Ghana's kings made their money by taxing salt and other trade goods as they entered and departed Ghana. Ghana's rulers also strictly controlled the flow of gold. All gold nuggets automatically belonged to the king, and only gold dust could be traded. These rules ensured that gold remained scarce, which kept gold prices high. Trade goods also included textiles, weapons, horses, and even bananas. As trans-Saharan trade expanded, caravans carrying goods grew longer, sometimes numbering several hundred camels.

THE COMING OF ISLAM

Like all societies, Ghana was affected by outside influences. During the 700s, Arab traders brought Islam and Islamic laws to West Africa. Traders and others learned to speak and write in Arabic. Up to that point, people living in West Africa had not had a written language.

Around 1050, the Almoravids, whom you learned about earlier in this chapter, attacked Ghana and tried to force the leaders to become Muslims. The leaders fought back, but they had been greatly weakened by constant war. In 1076, the Almoravids captured Koumbi-Saleh.

In addition, Ghana's soil was worn out and could no longer support the population. By the early 1200s, Ghana's traders and farmers were migrating to richer lands to the south and west. The kingdom of Ghana had come to an end. However, Ghana's "land of gold" had played a major role in the development of trade and civilization in West Africa.

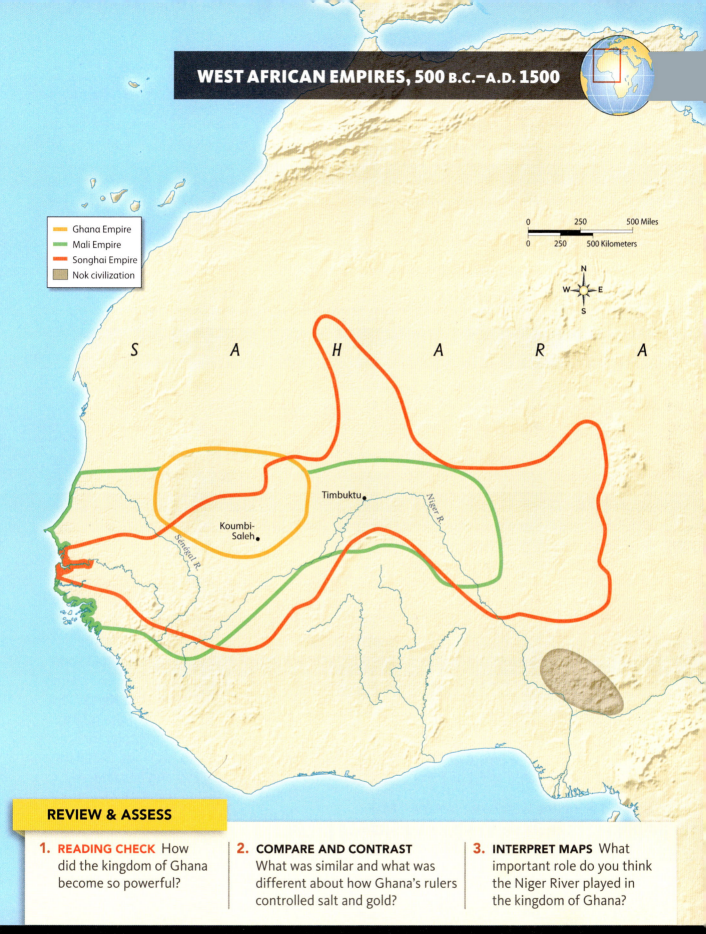

Ghana Empire
Mali Empire
Songhai Empire
Nok civilization

0   250   500 Miles
0   250   500 Kilometers

N
W   E
S

S   A   H   A   R   A

Timbuktu

Koumbi-
Saleh

Niger R.

Senégal R.

REVIEW & ASSESS

1. **READING CHECK** How did the kingdom of Ghana become so powerful?

2. **COMPARE AND CONTRAST** What was similar and what was different about how Ghana's rulers controlled salt and gold?

3. **INTERPRET MAPS** What important role do you think the Niger River played in the kingdom of Ghana?

7.4.1 Study the Niger River and the relationship of vegetation zones of forest, savannah, and desert to trade in gold, salt, food, and slaves; and the growth of the Ghana and Mali empires; 7.4.2 Analyze the importance of family, labor specialization, and regional commerce in the development of states and cities in West Africa; 7.4.3 Describe the role of the trans-Saharan caravan trade in the changing religious and cultural characteristics of West Africa and the influence of Islamic beliefs, ethics, and law; 7.4.4 Trace the growth of the Arabic language in government, trade, and Islamic scholarship in West Africa; CST 3 Students use a variety of maps and documents to identify physical and cultural features of neighborhoods, cities, states, and countries and to explain the historical migration of people, expansion and disintegration of empires, and the growth of economic systems; HI 6 Students interpret basic indicators of economic performance and conduct cost-benefit analyses of economic and political issues

The Empire of Mali

"This man flooded Cairo with his [gifts]. He left no . . . holder of a royal office without the gift of a load of gold."

This man, Mansa Musa, gave away so much gold that it led to a decline in the precious metal's value and ruined the Egyptian economy! African kings could grow unbelievably rich.

MAIN IDEA

Like Ghana, the powerful empire of Mali was built on trade and gold.

The Great Mosque, built by Mansa Musa after his pilgrimage to Mecca, had enough prayer space for 2,000 people.

Approximately 25,000 students were taught at the city's 180 schools and 3 universities.

THE EMERGENCE OF MALI

When Ghana declined in the 1200s, it left West Africa without a major power. Then a new power arose—the empire of **Mali**. Like Ghana, Mali built its wealth on gold, but it also boasted great achievements in culture and the arts. Word of Mali's achievements reached as far as Europe.

Located along the west coast of Africa, Mali had several geographic advantages. The land along the Niger River provided fertile farm land, and the river could be used to transport goods. The region received plenty of rain, so farmers could easily grow rice, millet, and other grains. Agricultural surpluses allowed Mali to engage in trade, acquire art, and construct impressive buildings.

MALI'S GREAT LEADERS

Mali was also fortunate because it had some very effective leaders. Popular legend claims extraordinary things of **Sundiata Keita** (sun-JAHT-ah KAY-tah), who founded the mighty empire. He brought peace and tolerance, as well as law and order, to his lands. Sundiata ruled from 1230 to 1255 and became incredibly rich by taxing trade. However, it was **Mansa Musa** (MAHN-sah MOO-sah) who introduced Mali to the world.

A descendant of Sundiata, Mansa Musa became **mansa**, or king, of Mali in 1307. Musa enlarged the empire and controlled trans-Saharan trade. Under his rule, Mali's population grew to about 40 million. Subject kings paid him tribute, and merchants

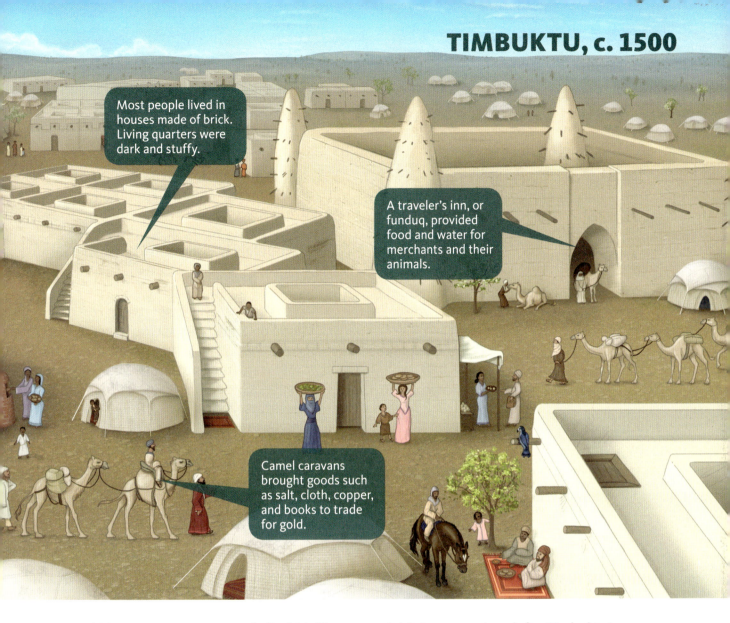

TIMBUKTU, c. 1500

Most people lived in houses made of brick. Living quarters were dark and stuffy.

A traveler's inn, or funduq, provided food and water for merchants and their animals.

Camel caravans brought goods such as salt, cloth, copper, and books to trade for gold.

paid him taxes. Musa owned all of Mali's abundant gold and was fabulously wealthy.

A devout Muslim, Musa provided strong support for the arts, learning, and Islam. He encouraged the trading city of Timbuktu to develop as a center of Islamic learning. He oversaw the construction of the city's Great Mosque, one the oldest mosques in Sub-Saharan Africa. Musa laid the groundwork for Timbuktu's emergence in the 1500s as the scholarly and religious center of West Africa. Although Musa ably ruled his vast empire, his successors were weak. As a result, Mali shrank to almost nothing as smaller kingdoms broke away and Berber nomads captured Timbuktu. One of the newly independent kingdoms, Songhai, eventually surpassed Mali in size and splendor.

REVIEW & ASSESS

1. **READING CHECK** In what ways were Mali and Ghana similar and different?

2. **DRAW CONCLUSIONS** What enabled Mansa Musa to support the arts and learning?

3. **SEQUENCE EVENTS** What events led to the decline of Mali?

7.2.5 Describe the growth of cities and the establishment of trade routes among Asia, Africa, and Europe, the products and inventions that traveled along these routes (e.g., spices, textiles, paper, steel, new crops), and the role of merchants in Arab society; 7.4.1 Study the Niger River and the relationship of vegetation zones of forest, savannah, and desert to trade in gold, salt, food, and slaves; and the growth of the Ghana and Mali empires; 7.4.4 Trace the growth of the Arabic language in government, trade, and Islamic scholarship in West Africa; CST 1 Students explain how major events are related to one another in time; HI 2 Students understand and distinguish cause, effect, sequence, and correlation in historical events, including the long- and short-term causal relations.

2.4 The Oral Tradition

You are exploring the past by reading this book. Written history is often considered the most accurate. But until very recently, people in much of the world, including Africa, didn't write down their history. Instead, special performers spoke or sang stories of the past, passing them from generation to generation.

MAIN IDEA

Africa has a rich tradition of oral history.

AN EPIC OF OLD MALI

One of the most famous griot stories is *Sundiata: An Epic of Old Mali*. This epic describes how Sundiata, the Lion King, defeated his enemies to found the empire of Mali. There is good evidence to suggest that at least some of the story is true.

ORAL HISTORY

Most early African civilizations, such as Ghana and Mali, did not develop a writing system until Muslim traders brought the Arabic language and writing system. Before the arrival of these traders, Africans passed on histories and stories orally, a method that historians call the ==oral tradition==. In this manner, history, culture, and social values were transmitted from one generation to the next.

A class of special storytellers emerged to relate the stories of villages, families, and kings. Known in West Africa as ==griots== (GREE-ohz), they spent years painstakingly memorizing family trees and learning stories.

Griots dramatically told their tales at public ceremonies, where excited crowds gathered to listen and learn. Stories about their ancestors and the exploits of kings were especially popular. Much of what historians know about early African history has been passed down through this oral tradition. It was not until the early 1900s that scholars wrote down these stories, fables, songs, and poems.

GRIOT TRADITION

Griots were highly respected members of African society who carried out many different roles. Most were men, but some were women. Griots served as historians, educators, and advisors. They also served as genealogists, or people who know how family members are related to one another and to their ancestors.

Griots were accomplished performers who could captivate their audiences. They often played drums or stringed instruments, such as the 21-string kora. Other musicians sometimes accompanied them as they told their stories.

Some griots wore costumes and masks. As the stories unfolded, actors and dancers sometimes interpreted the action. These dramatic aspects of griot performances added to the tales' excitement and helped make them more memorable.

In West Africa, the griot tradition is still very much alive. Famous griots are treated like rock stars, and the tradition has had a huge influence on modern West African music. In Western countries, young musicians with African roots are making the tradition their own.

Critical Viewing The griot is seated before a percussion instrument called a balafon. What instruments popular in the West are similar to the balafon?

Balafon
The balafon is a traditional African instrument made of wood and gourds.

Kora
The kora is a stringed instrument with a rounded back similar to that of a mandolin.

Koni
The koni has two strings and is made of wood and leather.

REVIEW & ASSESS

1. **READING CHECK** Why was oral tradition important in West Africa?

2. **ANALYZE LANGUAGE USE** How does the word *captivate* describe the ability of griots to perform?

3. **DRAW CONCLUSIONS** What might be the advantages and disadvantages of passing down history through oral tradition?

Trans-Saharan Travelers

Written accounts of early Africa have largely come from Muslim sources. Many manuscripts were kept in cities like Timbuktu and are still waiting to be studied. These accounts, written by people who were actually there, offer insights into early Africa and its place in the world.

This painting from a 13th-century manuscript shows a caravan of pilgrims.

from Al-Umari's account of Mansa Musa's visit to Cairo in 1324

Al-Umari, an Arabic historian, visited Egypt not long after Mansa Musa's famous visit. He was able to interview many firsthand witnesses to the event. His descriptions of Mansa Musa and his enormous wealth have greatly contributed to our knowledge of Mali. In this passage, Al-Umari recounts the experience of a government official who met the legendary ruler.

CONSTRUCTED RESPONSE What evidence from the text demonstrates that Mansa Musa was an immensely wealthy and religious man?

From the beginning of my coming to stay in Egypt I heard talk of the arrival of this sultan Musa on his Pilgrimage. . . . I asked the emir Abu . . . and he told me of the opulence [wealth], manly virtues, and piety of his sultan. "When I went out to meet him [he said] on behalf of the mighty sultan al-Malik al-Nasir, he did me extreme honour and treated me with the greatest courtesy. . . . Then he forwarded to the royal treasury many loads of unworked native gold and other valuables. I tried to persuade him to . . . meet the sultan, but he refused persistently saying: 'I came for the Pilgrimage and nothing else. I do not wish to mix anything else with my Pilgrimage.'"

from the *Catalan Atlas*, c. 1375

Mansa Musa's pilgrimage to Mecca literally put West Africa on the map. Stories of his extraordinary wealth stimulated international interest in West Africa, the land of gold. This made it a feature of medieval maps such as the *Catalan Atlas*, which gives West Africa considerable prominence. Abraham Cresques, a mapmaker, created the atlas in Majorca, an island that is part of Spain.

CONSTRUCTED RESPONSE Based on the map, what can you conclude about Mansa Musa's importance to West Africa?

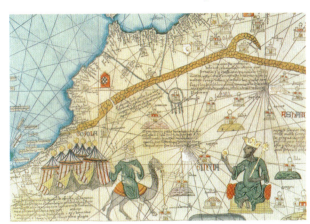

Detail showing West Africa and Mansa Musa (right)

SYNTHESIZE & WRITE

1. **REVIEW** Review what you have learned about West Africa and Mansa Musa in this chapter.

2. **RECALL** On your own paper, write down the main idea expressed in each primary source.

3. **CONSTRUCT** Write a topic sentence that answers this question: How did Mansa Musa affect Mali and the rest of the world?

4. **WRITE** Using evidence from the sources, write an argument to support the answer to the question in Step 3.

7.4.5 Describe the importance of written and oral traditions in the transmission of African history and culture; REP 4 Students assess the credibility of primary and secondary sources and draw sound conclusions from them.

119

VOCABULARY

Match each word in the first column with its definition in the second column.

WORD	DEFINITION
1. desertification HSS 7.4.1	a. a tradable good
2. trans-Saharan HSS 7.4.1	b. an area of lush tropical grasslands
3. caravan HSS 7.4.1	c. the practice of passing stories by spoken voice
4. commodity HSS 7.4.1	d. across the Sahara
5. scarcity HSS 7.4.1	e. a West African storyteller
6. savanna HSS 7.4.1	f. the process by which fertile land becomes a desert
7. griot HSS 7.4.5	g. people traveling together
8. oral tradition HSS 7.4.5	h. a shortage of something

READING STRATEGY

9. **ANALYZE LANGUAGE USE** Complete your chart to analyze language in at least three paragraphs. Then answer the question.

Language Example	What It Suggests
The caravan is a merchant's ticket to profit, but first the merchant must survive the journey.	The trip across the Sahara was very dangerous.

How does the writer's use of language in these examples help you understand what life was like in North and West Africa between 1000 B.C. and A.D. 1500? HSS 7.4.1

MAIN IDEAS

Answer the following questions. Support your answers with evidence from the chapter.

10. How did the geography and climate of the Sahara change over a long period of time? **LESSON 1.1** HSS 7.4.1

11. What impact did the development of trade between early colonists and Berbers have on North Africa? **LESSON 1.2** HSS 7.4.2

12. What valuable resources in Africa fostered trade? **LESSON 1.3** HSS 7.4.1

13. How did Islam spread throughout North and West Africa? **LESSON 1.4** HSS 7.4.3

14. What new technology was developed by the Nok people of West Africa? **LESSON 2.1** HSS 7.4.2

15. What factors led to the emergence of the powerful kingdom of Ghana? **LESSON 2.2** HSS 7.4.1

16. Why does Africa have a rich tradition of oral history? **LESSON 2.4** HSS 7.4.5

CRITICAL THINKING

Answer the following questions. Support your answers with evidence from the chapter.

17. **ESSENTIAL QUESTION** How did technology contribute to both the rise and the decline of Nok culture in West Africa? HSS HI 2

18. **ANALYZE CAUSE AND EFFECT** What effect did desertification have on the people and animals who inhabited the Sahara? HSS 7.4.1

19. **SEQUENCE EVENTS** How did vast salt deposits develop in the Sahara? HSS 7.4.1

20. **DRAW CONCLUSIONS** What was the cultural legacy of the spread of Islam in North and West Africa? HSS 7.4.3

21. **YOU DECIDE** If you were a trader in West Africa, would you rather have a pound of salt or a pound of gold? Support your opinion with evidence from the chapter. HSS REP 1

Study the map that shows the spread of ironworking in Africa. Then answer the questions that follow.

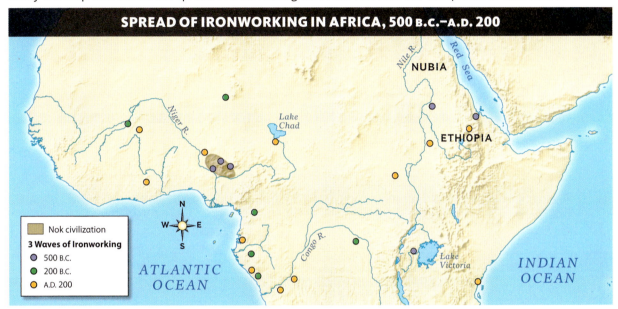

SPREAD OF IRONWORKING IN AFRICA, 500 B.C.–A.D. 200

Legend:
- Nok civilization
- **3 Waves of Ironworking**
  - 500 B.C.
  - 200 B.C.
  - A.D. 200

22. In what areas of Africa did people develop ironworking at the same time as the Nok? HSS CST 3

23. Where did ironworking spread between 500 B.C. and 200 B.C? HSS CST 3

ANALYZE SOURCES

Alvise Cadamosto was an Italian explorer who wrote one of the earliest known accounts of West Africa. Read his description of the salt-gold trade in the 1450s.

> Having reached these waters [the upper Niger] with the salt, they proceed in this fashion: all those who have the salt pile it in rows, each marking his own. Having made these piles, the whole caravan retires half a day's journey. Then there come another [group] who do not wish to be seen or to speak . . . they place a quantity of gold opposite each pile and then turn back, leaving salt and gold. When they have gone [those] who own the salt return: if they are satisfied with the quantity of gold, they leave the salt and retire with the gold. . . . In this way, by long and ancient custom, they carry on their trade without seeing or speaking to each other.

24. What is distinctive about how transactions in the salt-gold trade were carried out? HSS REP 4

WRITE ABOUT HISTORY

25. NARRATIVE Suppose you were able to travel to the trading city of Timbuktu at the time of its greatest influence and importance. Write a brief account of your time there and describe what you see. Use the tips below to help you plan, organize, and revise your narrative. HSS HI 1

TIPS
- Take notes from the lesson about the empire of Mali.
- Select relevant, well-chosen facts, concrete details, and examples that will be the basis of your narrative.
- Use transitions to make your account of your trip clear to readers.
- Use vocabulary from the chapter as appropriate.
- Use word-processing software to produce and publish your final account.

5

EAST, CENTRAL, AND SOUTHERN AFRICA

1000 B.C. – A.D. 1500

ESSENTIAL QUESTION How did trade influence the growth and culture of East, Central, and Southern Africa?

SECTION 1 EAST AFRICA

KEY VOCABULARY	NAMES & PLACES
city-state	Aksum
dhow	Ezana
hub	Kilwa
mariner	Swahili
monsoon	
sultan	

SECTION 2 CENTRAL AND SOUTHERN AFRICA

KEY VOCABULARY	NAMES & PLACES
deplete	Afonso I
lingua franca	Bantu
migration	Great Zimbabwe
tribute	Kongo
	Shona

READING STRATEGY

ORGANIZE IDEAS: ANALYZE CAUSE AND EFFECT
When you analyze cause and effect, you note the consequences of an action. Often, a cause will have multiple effects. As you read the chapter, use a diagram like this one to identify effects of the Bantu migrations across sub-Saharan Africa.

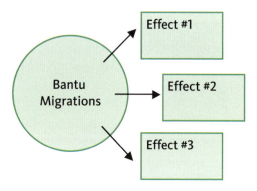

Bantu Migrations → Effect #1
Bantu Migrations → Effect #2
Bantu Migrations → Effect #3

HI 2 Students understand and distinguish cause, effect, sequence, and correlation in historical events, including the long- and short-term causal relations.

Farmers sell their produce next to one of the main roads on the outskirts of Nairobi, Kenya.

The **Kingdom** of **Aksum**

Around A.D. 250, a Persian prophet listed the four great empires in the world: Rome, Persia, China, and Aksum. Two thousand years ago, Aksum was the jewel of East Africa. It was an organized and prosperous kingdom built on trade.

MAIN IDEA

The prosperous kingdom of Aksum rose to power in East Africa.

IVORY TRADE

Ivory comes from the tusks of animals, especially elephants. Ivory exports, such as this mask, brought the African elephant close to extinction. Today these exports are regulated, but illegal trade still threatens elephants.

THE RISE OF AKSUM

The geography of East Africa made it ideally suited for trade. The region is shaped like a rhinoceros horn, earning it the nickname the Horn of Africa. The Red Sea connects East Africa with the Persian Gulf, the Mediterranean Sea, and the Indian Ocean. These bodies of water can carry Africa's vast resources around the world. From very early times, trade was central to East Africa's development.

Aksum (AHK-soom) began around 500 B.C. in what is now Ethiopia. By A.D. 100, Aksum had emerged as a prosperous trading kingdom. Its territory stretched from the Sahara to the Red Sea, where ports enabled it to dominate trade with Arabia, Persia, India, China, and Europe.

Around A.D. 350, King **Ezana** (AY-zah-nah) of Aksum conquered its great trading rival, Kush (which you read about in Chapter 4), and seized control of the valuable ivory trade. He also converted to Christianity and made it the official religion of Aksum. Ezana declared his faith on a solid stone pillar called a stela (STEE-luh). Aksum's kings built these monuments as symbols of their power.

TRADE AND ISOLATION

Aksum's location made it a major international trading hub, or center. The kingdom's economy grew through the trade of ivory, spices, and slaves. Aksum spent its wealth on textiles, metal, and olive oil from its trading partners. Its wealth also fueled cultural achievements. Artisans produced luxury goods, and the kingdom minted its own coins. Aksum developed a written language, which was used to create a rich body of literature. However, this time of prosperity did not last.

Beginning in the A.D. 500s, regional wars and Arab expansion closed off some of Aksum's key trade routes. The kingdom also suffered the effects of deforestation, droughts, and overfarming, which reduced the availability of food. Aksum declined, and Muslim invaders shrank its borders. Christian Aksum became surrounded by Muslim territories.

By A.D. 800, Christians in the region had retreated into the mountains of Ethiopia. Isolated, the Christians were mostly left alone, and their legacy still thrives there today.

Giant stelae from the kingdom of Aksum can still be seen today in Ethiopia.

EAST AFRICAN TRADE, c. A.D. 100

REVIEW & ASSESS

1. **READING CHECK** Why was East Africa a good location for trade?

2. **MAKE INFERENCES** How did King Ezana of Aksum help spread Christianity throughout the region?

3. **INTERPRET MAPS** What bodies of water were important to trade routes that extended from East Africa to Europe, India, and the African interior?

CST 3 Students use a variety of maps and documents to identify physical and cultural features of neighborhoods, cities, states, and countries and to explain the historical migration of people, expansion and disintegration of empires, and the growth of economic systems; HI 6 Students interpret basic indicators of economic performance and conduct cost-benefit analyses of economic and political issues.

125

Indian Ocean Trade

In 1980, an adventurer recreating the legendary voyage of Sinbad the Sailor came to a halt near the island of Sri Lanka. The winds propelling his ship suddenly stopped, and for 35 days he went nowhere. Ancient East African sailors could have predicted this occurrence because they understood exactly when the Indian Ocean's winds blew—and when they did not.

MAIN IDEA

The Indian Ocean was a key part of East Africa's far-reaching trade network.

MONSOON WINDS

The East African coast became important for trade because the area could easily be reached by land or sea. Traders could bring goods from inland areas and load them onto ships in the Red Sea. However, even experienced sailors clung to coastlines because their ships and navigational skills were not good enough to sail safely out to sea. Beginning around A.D. 800, however, East African **mariners**, or sailors, developed the skills and ships to cross the Indian Ocean, which is the world's third largest ocean. They also learned how to use the wind to carry them all the way to India and back—if they timed it right.

From April to October, strong winds called **monsoons** blow northeast from Africa toward India. Between November and March, the winds reverse direction and blow southwest from India to Africa. They are extremely reliable and make it possible for a sailing ship to make the long journey from Africa to India and back. Even with the winds, however, the round trip could take as long as a full year.

Sailors learned to predict these winds and plan their journeys around them. Merchants who needed to move their goods between Africa and India hired experienced sailors who knew the winds. This trade across the Indian Ocean helped the economic development of both regions.

INDIAN OCEAN TRADE NETWORK

Over time, mariners and merchants continued working together to create an extensive trade network around the Indian Ocean. This network directly linked East Africa with Arabia, Persia, India, and Southeast Asia. Traders could transport goods to Europe, the Middle East, and even China.

New sailing technology made the trade network possible. Trading goods across the ocean required a sturdy ship that could carry a large amount of goods. In the Indian Ocean trade, that ship was called a **dhow** (dow). Dhows not only carried goods, but they also transported important elements of culture, such as language and religion.

With the expansion of trade, more Muslim merchants settled on the East African coast and married into local ruling families. Coastal villages grew into important trading towns controlled by Muslim rulers called **sultans**. As Muslim sailors and merchants traveled for trade, they introduced Islam to people throughout East Africa. As a result, the region developed a distinctive African-Arabic culture. It was an example of how people from other regions would influence Africa.

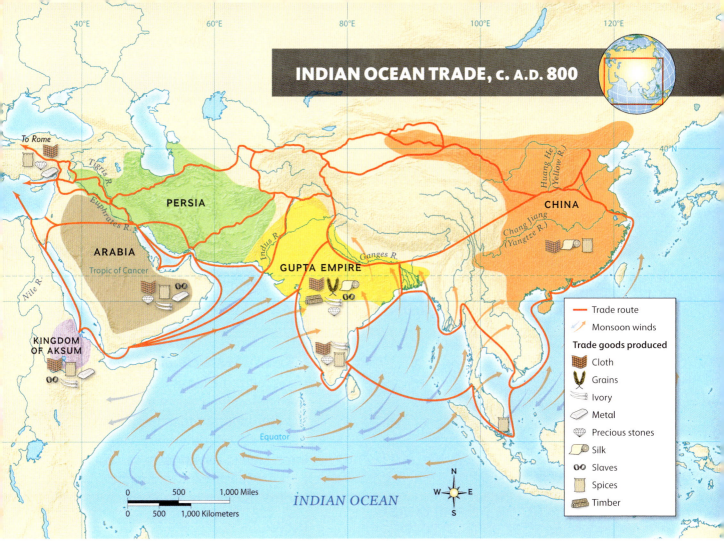

INDIAN OCEAN TRADE, c. A.D. 800

Legend:
- Trade route
- Monsoon winds

Trade goods produced
- Cloth
- Grains
- Ivory
- Metal
- Precious stones
- Silk
- Slaves
- Spices
- Timber

Map labels: To Rome, Tigris R., Euphrates R., PERSIA, ARABIA, Tropic of Cancer, Nile R., KINGDOM OF AKSUM, Indus R., GUPTA EMPIRE, Ganges R., CHINA, Huang He (Yellow R.), Chang Jiang (Yangtze R.), Equator, INDIAN OCEAN

Scale: 0 500 1,000 Miles / 0 500 1,000 Kilometers

DHOW SHIPS

Dhows typically had long, thin hulls and triangular sails that were good at catching the monsoon winds. The winds were critical for successful voyages.

The early dhows were able to carry relatively large shipments of trade goods. They would travel across the Indian Ocean, trade their cargo, and return to Africa with silks and other valuables.

Today many types of dhows are still used along the East African coast.

REVIEW & ASSESS

1. READING CHECK How did monsoon winds affect trade between Africa and India?

2. IDENTIFY MAIN IDEAS AND DETAILS How did trade networks across the Indian Ocean develop?

3. INTERPRET MAPS What products did East Africans produce to trade with other countries?

 7.2.5 Describe the growth of cities and the establishment of trade routes among Asia, Africa, and Europe, the products and inventions that traveled along these routes (e.g., spices, textiles, paper, steel, new crops), and the role of merchants in Arab society; CST 3 Students use a variety of maps and documents to identify physical and cultural features of neighborhoods, cities, states, and countries and to explain the historical migration of people, expansion and disintegration of empires, and the growth of economic systems; HI 6 Students interpret basic indicators of economic performance and conduct cost-benefit analyses of economic and political issues.

127

1.3 East African City-States

The streets of Kilwa were packed with a diverse mix of people from all over the world. Their different clothing, customs, and languages made for an exciting atmosphere. Trade brought all these influences to this vibrant city-state.

MAIN IDEA

City-states with a distinctive culture developed in East Africa.

Habari "Hello"

SWAHILI TODAY

Today, Swahili is an official language of Tanzania and a common language among many East African peoples. There are about 15 major Swahili dialects, or variations of the language. More than 30 million people speak Swahili. The word above is Swahili for "hello."

TRADE ON THE COAST

As Arab merchants settled in East African towns, they brought Islam. As you have read, these Arabic immigrants married local ruling families, and Muslims came to control trade.

The Arabs encountered Africans who spoke Bantu languages. The Bantu, whom you will learn more about in the next lesson, were people who migrated from West Africa into sub-Saharan Africa. These migrations began more than two thousand years ago. The Bantu established trade networks. In time, their trade networks grew.

As a result, East Africa had a rich mix of cultures. The East African and Arabic Muslim cultures combined to form the unique **Swahili** (swah-HEE-lee) culture.

Swahili became the name used to describe the African-Arabic people of East Africa. Swahili is also the name of their language, which became the language of trade and a common language of all East Africans. The Swahili language and culture, together with the widespread adoption of Islam, helped unify the people of East Africa.

The Swahili people also developed a political system based on independent **city-states**. These are cities that control the surrounding villages and towns. By 1300, there were at least 35 trading cities along the coast. These strongly Islamic cities felt more closely connected to their foreign trading partners than to their non-Muslim African neighbors. Although they were not interested in territorial expansion, East African city-states fought to control as much trade as possible.

KILWA

One of the richest and most powerful city-states in Africa was **Kilwa**. (See the map in the Chapter Review.) It was located on an island that was as far south along the East African coast as trading ships could reach in one season. Any merchants from southern Africa had to come to Kilwa if they wanted foreign goods. Africa's main sources of gold were also south of Kilwa, which meant that the city-state controlled the overseas trade in gold.

To reinforce its control of the gold trade, Kilwa took over the port of Sofala. Sofala was farther south than Kilwa, but Sofala was closer to the gold mines. By controlling Sofala, Kilwa could more easily move gold to its ports for the arrival of seasonal trading ships.

Kilwa's social classes were rigid, and it was difficult to move from one class to another. This was true for most East African city-states. Kilwa's sultan stood at the top of the society. Below the sultan were Muslim merchants, who were taxed heavily by the sultan but still grew rich. Merchants built ornate palaces, mosques, and homes of coral stone. Below the merchants were the majority of the townspeople, who were artisans, officials, and sailors. At the bottom of society were non-Muslim farmers, fishers, and, below them, slaves.

Kilwa and other East African city-states thrived for centuries until the arrival of the Portuguese in the late 1400s. These European explorers and traders stumbled upon the previously unknown East African trade network. They quickly recognized that the network moved a great deal of wealth. Just as quickly, they decided they wanted a piece of that wealth. Through political pressure and sometimes direct force, the Portuguese gained increasing control over East Africa's city-states, coastline, and commerce.

REVIEW & ASSESS

1. **READING CHECK** What effect did trade have on the culture of East African city-states?

2. **ANALYZE CAUSE AND EFFECT** What factors helped Kilwa become one of the richest and most powerful city-states in Africa?

3. **ANALYZE LANGUAGE USE** The text uses the word *stumbled* to describe how the Portuguese discovered Kilwa's trade network. What does this word suggest about this discovery?

7.2.5 Describe the growth of cities and the establishment of trade routes among Asia, Africa, and Europe, the products and inventions that traveled along these routes (e.g., spices, textiles, paper, steel, new crops), and the role of merchants in Arab society; HI 2 Students understand and distinguish cause, effect, sequence, and correlation in historical events, including the long- and short-term causal relations; HI 6 Students interpret basic indicators of economic performance and conduct cost-benefit analyses of economic and political issues.

Bantu Migrations

More than two thousand years ago, people in western Africa started migrating east and south, spreading their language and culture. These were the Bantu-speaking people, and their migration is one of the great stories in African history. They have played a major role in the development of sub-Saharan Africa—and they show the role that migration has played in world history.

MAIN IDEA

The Bantu populated much of Africa.

MOVEMENTS EAST

Bantu means "people" and is a general name for many different peoples of Africa who speak more than 500 different languages yet share a common ancestry. By studying the different Bantu languages, linguists, people who study human speech, know that the Bantu originated in western Africa around present-day Nigeria and Cameroon.

The **migration**, or movement, of the Bantu people was slow through the dense forest at the equator but accelerated across the open savanna. By the end of the A.D. 300s, Bantu speakers dominated all of sub-Saharan Africa except in the southwest, where the dry and hot climate was much more harsh.

The earliest Bantu speakers were probably fishers and farmers. Along the way, they learned how to work metals to create tools and weapons. The Bantu carried their metalworking skills with them. They traveled in small family groups and chose the best land for farming.

The Bantu's numbers grew, thanks to their mastery of iron, which allowed them to prepare land for planting crops. They relied on a method in which they used iron tools and fire to clear land for cultivation. They adapted the environment to better suit their needs. When the soil was exhausted, they simply moved to the next fertile area.

One crop that became widespread actually originated from Indonesia—bananas. Bananas became a staple crop in East Africa, where more varieties have developed than anywhere else in the world. Communities had rapid population growth if they had good growing conditions, plentiful rainfall, and an absence of the disease-carrying tsetse flies.

The Bantu spread across Africa in phases. Their migration was not constant and the speed of their migration could be altered by many factors including vegetation, disease, and climate.

IMPACT OF THE MIGRATIONS

At the time the Bantu began migrating, hunter-gatherers populated most of Africa, but both populations remained relatively low. As a result, there was plenty of room for the Bantu and hunter-gathers to coexist peacefully—or to avoid each other if they wanted.

At times, the Bantu and the people they encountered even helped each other by exchanging information. One skill the Bantu learned along the way was how to raise animals. When arguments over territory did occur, however, the Bantu's iron weapons gave them a clear and deadly advantage.

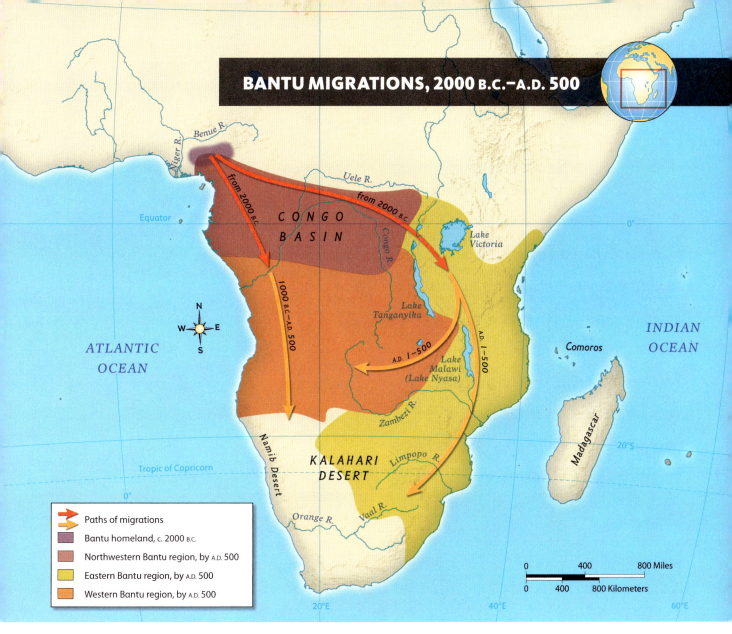

Benue R.

Niger R.

Uele R.

Equator

CONGO BASIN

from 2000 B.C.

from 2000 B.C.

Congo R.

Lake Victoria

1000 B.C.–A.D. 500

Lake Tanganyika

A.D. I–500

A.D. I–500

ATLANTIC OCEAN

A.D. I–500

Lake Malawi (Lake Nyasa)

INDIAN OCEAN

Comoros

Zambezi R.

Namib Desert

KALAHARI DESERT

Limpopo R.

Madagascar

20°S

Tropic of Capricorn

0°

Orange R.

Vaal R.

Paths of migrations

Bantu homeland, c. 2000 B.C.

Northwestern Bantu region, by A.D. 500

Eastern Bantu region, by A.D. 500

Western Bantu region, by A.D. 500

0   400   800 Miles

0   400   800 Kilometers

20°E   40°E   60°E

As they migrated, the Bantu had a great impact on the people of eastern and western Africa. They married into local families and spread the technology of making weapons and tools from iron, bronze, and copper. They also affected how people organized and governed themselves. Some of these influences are felt in Africa even today.

At the same time, the Bantu who migrated down the east coast of Africa also absorbed the influences of Arabic settlers. As you have read, this led to the region's distinctive African-Arabic culture and the Swahili language. Swahili became the widespread language of trade and a **lingua franca** (LING-gwuh FRANG-kuh), or a language commonly used by many different groups of people.

REVIEW & ASSESS

1. READING CHECK What is one impact the Bantu-speaking people had on Africa?

2. COMPARE AND CONTRAST In what ways were the Bantu different from other groups of people who lived in Africa at this time?

3. INTERPRET MAPS What physical features may have limited Bantu migration into the far south and southwest?

CST 3 Students use a variety of maps and documents to identify physical and cultural features of neighborhoods, cities, states, and countries and to explain the historical migration of people, expansion and disintegration of empires, and the growth of economic systems.

131

2.2 Great Zimbabwe

Meeting Great Zimbabwe's king means walking a narrow path between towering stone walls. Reaching out, you can easily touch each wall, but the sky is just a sliver high above you. You feel closed in, fearful, and very, very small. And that's the idea. These imposing stone structures express the enormous power of the king.

MAIN IDEA

Great Zimbabwe was a wealthy trading empire that expressed its power through enormous stone structures.

A SOUTHERN TRADING CITY

One group of the Bantu-speaking migrants that you learned about in the previous lesson settled on a plateau between two rivers in southern Africa. They were the **Shona** (SHOH-nuh), who established **Great Zimbabwe**. The site of their capital was probably chosen for its climate and agricultural potential. But it was also on the route traders used to carry gold to the coast, where Kilwa was located. (See the map in the Chapter Review.) Great Zimbabwe and Kilwa thrived and grew together. Great Zimbabwe's rulers grew rich and powerful by taxing trade goods. They controlled a vast empire with more than 300 towns.

GREAT STONE HOUSES

Great Zimbabwe's rulers expressed their power and wealth through extraordinary stone structures. *Zimbabwe* means "place of stone houses" in Bantu, and over 300 zimbabwes are scattered throughout southern Africa.

The ruins of Great Zimbabwe are still impressive today. The Great Enclosure is an imposing circular wall over 30 feet tall and 15 feet thick. The stones are cut so carefully and wedged in so tightly that they hold together without mortar. Behind the wall lived Great Zimbabwe's elite, separated from the ordinary people.

The massive circular wall in Great Zimbabwe surrounds an area known as the Great Enclosure.

After A.D. 1450, however, Great Zimbabwe declined and was abandoned. The arrival of Portuguese traders on the coast shifted the gold trade away from Great Zimbabwe, which led to a decrease in wealth. Historians also theorize that the city's citizens may have **depleted**, or used up, the local resources, such as soil, water, and wood.

SHONA SCULPTURE

The only surviving sculptures from Great Zimbabwe are stylized birds carved out of soapstone. The bird was adopted as the symbol of present-day Zimbabwe. Modern Shona have revived traditional sculpture by carving pieces influenced by their Great Zimbabwe traditions.

REVIEW & ASSESS

1. **READING CHECK** What was the source of Great Zimbabwe's wealth?

2. **DESCRIBE GEOGRAPHIC INFORMATION** How did the location of Great Zimbabwe affect its role as a trading civilization?

3. **IDENTIFY MAIN IDEAS AND DETAILS** According to the text, what key factors probably led to the decline and abandonment of Great Zimbabwe?

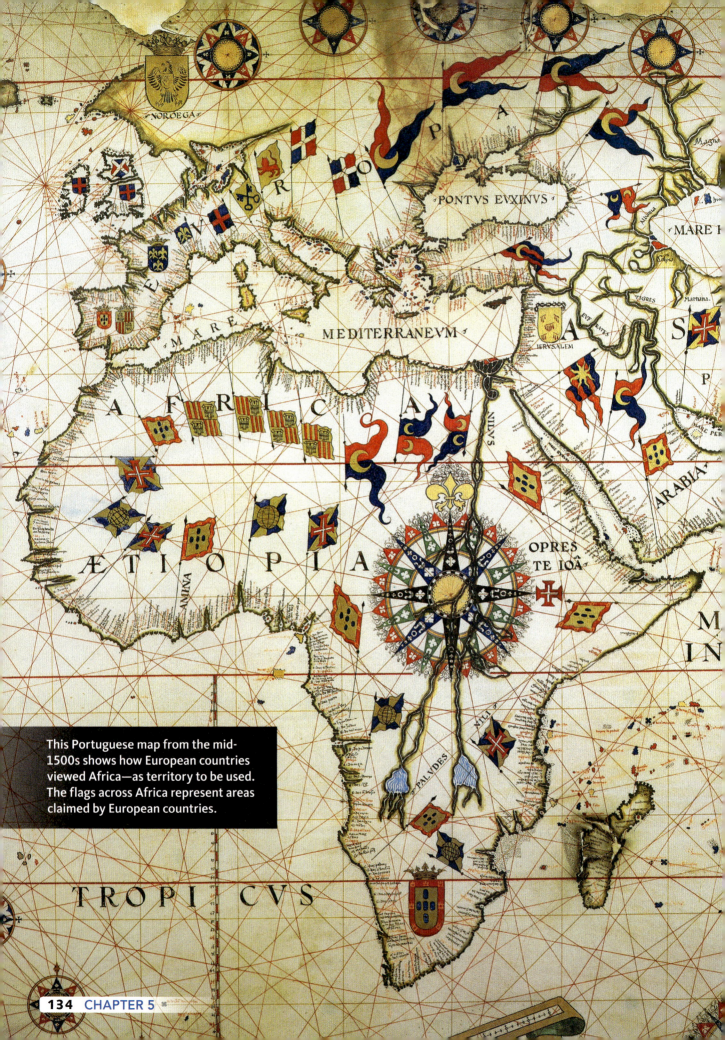

This Portuguese map from the mid-1500s shows how European countries viewed Africa—as territory to be used. The flags across Africa represent areas claimed by European countries.

2.3 The Kingdom of Kongo

"Great and powerful, full of people, having many vassals [loyal landowners]." This is how Portuguese explorers described the African kingdom of Kongo. They were soon responsible for changing every bit of that description.

MAIN IDEA

Kongo grew rich on the gold trade but would lose everything to the Europeans.

KINGDOM OF THE RAIN FOREST

The kingdom of **Kongo** emerged in the rain forests south of the Congo River around 1400. Like other regions of Africa, Kongo was influenced by migrating Bantu speakers who took advantage of the area's fertile soil. The people also knew how to make weapons and tools from iron and copper. They eventually formed a loose partnership of farming villages. Wise kings known as *manikongo* (MA-nuh-kahng-go) led the people and united the kingdom, which expanded through conquest, marriages, and treaties.

By the 1480s, the *manikongo* ruled more than half a million people in a large and well-ordered state. The *manikongo* grew wealthy through an organized tribute system. In this system, local rulers took **tribute**, or goods and services, from their subjects and passed them on to the king and his royal court. The tribute system actually increased trade and strengthened the economy.

The people of Kongo were not only good farmers, but they were also skilled metalworkers, potters, and weavers. Kongo's kings also sought to improve their understanding of science and the arts. When the Europeans arrived, the *manikongo* saw it as an opportunity to make great leaps in understanding. They were wrong.

THE ARRIVAL OF THE PORTUGUESE

In 1483, the Portuguese arrived in Kongo. An alliance was arranged, and, eight years later, the king converted to Christianity. The king's son, **Afonso I** (uh-FOHN-soo), became *manikongo* in 1509. He was a devout Christian and strongly pro-Portuguese. With Portuguese soldiers and weapons, Afonso extended his kingdom and took many prisoners, who were sold to the Portuguese as slaves.

However, the Portuguese wanted more than Kongo's many natural resources. They wanted cheap labor and began enslaving the people of Kongo. Afonso tried to resist slavery, but despite his best efforts, the slave trade grew. The drain of people, especially the agricultural workforce, greatly weakened the kingdom. For the next four centuries, European and American slavery would have a devastating impact on all of Africa.

REVIEW & ASSESS

1. **READING CHECK** What caused the kingdom of Kongo to weaken and lose its wealth and power to Portugal?

2. **DESCRIBE GEOGRAPHIC INFORMATION** What role did the location of Kongo play in the kingdom's settlement and prosperity?

3. **SEQUENCE EVENTS** Describe the turning points in the interaction between Kongo and Portugal.

7.2.6 Understand the intellectual exchanges among Muslim scholars of Eurasia and Africa and the contributions Muslim scholars made to later civilizations in the areas of science, geography, mathematics, philosophy, medicine, art, and literature; CST 1 Students explain how major events are related to one another in time; HI 2 Students understand and distinguish cause, effect, sequence, and correlation in historical events, including the long- and short-term causal relations; HI 6 Students interpret basic indicators of economic performance and conduct cost-benefit analyses of economic and political issues.

VOCABULARY

Use each of the following vocabulary words in a sentence that shows an understanding of the term's meaning.

1. **hub**
   Aksum's prime location made it a hub of international trade.

2. **monsoon**

3. **dhow**

4. **city-state**

5. **migration**

6. **deplete**

7. **lingua franca**

READING STRATEGY

8. **ORGANIZE IDEAS: ANALYZE CAUSE AND EFFECT** If you haven't already, complete your diagram to identify effects of the Bantu migrations across sub-Saharan Africa. Then answer the question.

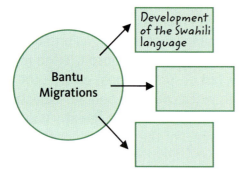

How did the Bantu migrations affect culture in sub-Saharan Africa? (HSS HI 2)

MAIN IDEAS

Answer the following questions. Support your answers with evidence from the chapter.

9. Why was East Africa a good location for trade? **LESSON 1.1** (HSS CST 3)

10. What helped sailors navigate across the Indian Ocean? **LESSON 1.2**

11. How did Kilwa become an important trading city? **LESSON 1.3** (HSS HI 1)

12. How did the Bantu come to populate much of sub-Saharan Africa? **LESSON 2.1** (HSS CST 3)

13. What was the purpose of Great Zimbabwe's imposing stone structures? **LESSON 2.2**

14. What effect did the arrival of the Portuguese have on the kingdom of Kongo? **LESSON 2.3** (HSS HI 2)

CRITICAL THINKING

Answer the following questions. Support your answers with evidence from the chapter.

15. **ESSENTIAL QUESTION** What evidence demonstrates that Aksum made many cultural achievements while it was an international trading hub? (HSS HI 1)

16. **ANALYZE CAUSE AND EFFECT** How did advances in sailing make long-distance trade across the Indian Ocean possible? (HSS HI 2)

17. **DRAW CONCLUSIONS** In what way was Swahili the result of the blending of cultures? (HSS HI 3)

18. **MAKE INFERENCES** How did their method of farming influence the Bantu's movement across Africa? (HSS CST 3)

19. **ANALYZE CAUSE AND EFFECT** What impact did Portugal have on the development of the kingdom of Kongo? (HSS HI 2)

20. **YOU DECIDE** What was the greatest cultural achievement of eastern, central, and southern Africa? Support your opinion with evidence from the chapter. (HSS REP 1)

INTERPRET MAPS

Study the map that shows the location of kingdoms and city-states in sub-Saharan Africa. Then answer the questions that follow.

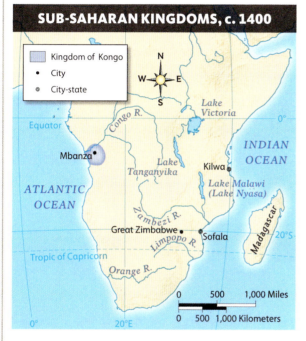

SUB-SAHARAN KINGDOMS, c. 1400

Legend:
- Kingdom of Kongo
- • City
- ⊙ City-state

Labels on map: Congo R., Lake Victoria, Equator, 0°, INDIAN OCEAN, Mbanza, Lake Tanganyika, Kilwa, ATLANTIC OCEAN, Lake Malawi (Lake Nyasa), Zambezi R., Great Zimbabwe, Sofala, Madagascar, 20°S, Limpopo R., Tropic of Capricorn, Orange R., 0°, 20°E

Scale: 0 500 1,000 Miles / 0 500 1,000 Kilometers

21. What do trading city-states—such as Sofala and Kilwa—have in common? (HSS CST 3)

22. What rivers could traders from Great Zimbabwe have used to trade with Mbanza? (HSS CST 3)

ANALYZE SOURCES

Look at the photograph below of one of the 11 medieval Christian churches of Lalibela, Ethiopia, all of which were carved and chiseled out of rock. Known as House of St. George, this church is isolated from the other 10 churches.

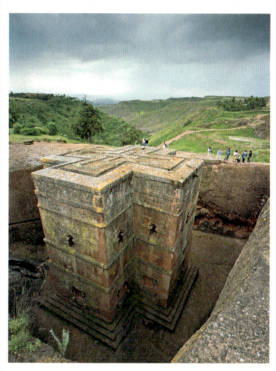

23. What is unique about the construction of this church? (HSS REP 4)

WRITE ABOUT HISTORY

24. INFORMATIVE Write an outline of the causes and effects of the slave trade between the kingdom of Kongo and Portugal. (HSS HI 2)

TIPS

- Take notes from the lesson about the kingdom of Kongo.
- List your topic at the beginning of the outline.
- Create two sections under the topic: one to focus on causes and another to focus on effects.
- List relevant facts, concrete details, and examples under each section of the outline.
- Use at least two vocabulary words from the chapter in your outline.

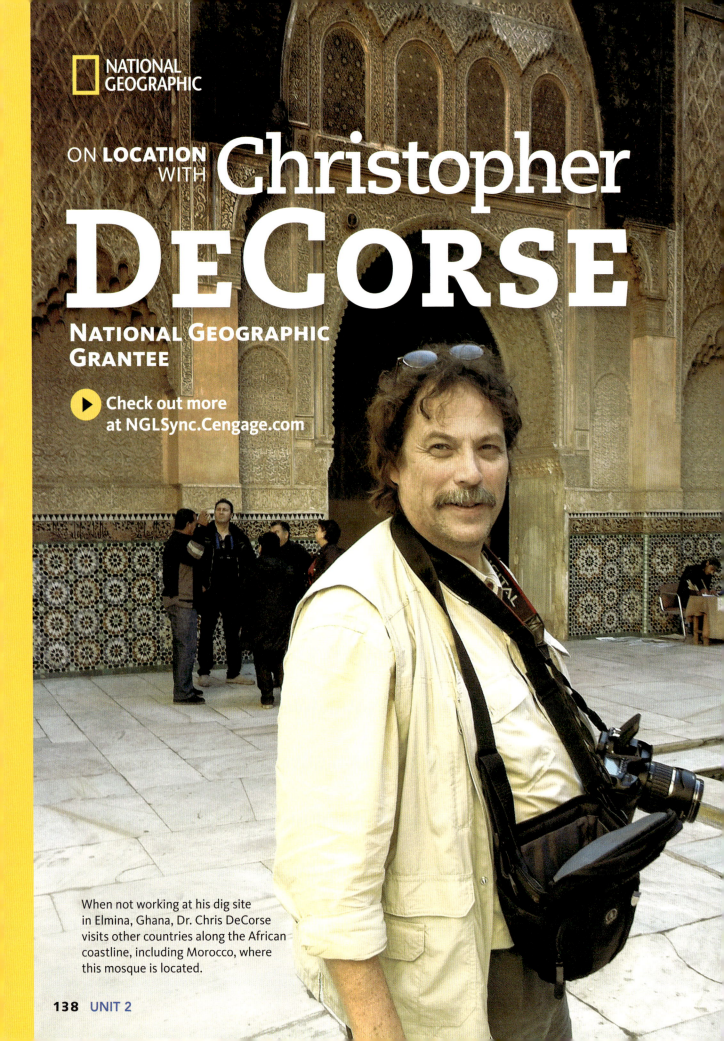

NATIONAL GEOGRAPHIC

ON **LOCATION** WITH **Christopher DeCorse**

NATIONAL GEOGRAPHIC GRANTEE

▶ **Check out more** at NGLSync.Cengage.com

When not working at his dig site in Elmina, Ghana, Dr. Chris DeCorse visits other countries along the African coastline, including Morocco, where this mosque is located.

EARLY INTEREST

Who isn't fascinated by archaeology? Lost civilizations, undisturbed tombs, and golden idols captivate us all! When I was five years old, my grandfather took me to museums and I was entranced by the models and displays. My parents indulged my interest with family trips to archaeological sites, taking the bus in our muddy field clothes with our digging equipment—people thought we were nuts. By sixth grade I had decided to be an archaeologist in Africa.

Chris DeCorse and his team visit Freetown, Sierra Leon, the capital city and a major African port in the Atlantic Ocean.

EXCAVATING ELMINA

Africa is believed to be the place where humankind likely emerged, but many parts of the vast continent remain largely unexplored by archaeologists. Given the lack of early written information about most of sub-Saharan Africa, archaeology is the key to revealing a relatively unknown past. I really want to know what the civilizations and societies of the region were like before the Europeans arrived in the 15th century. I'd also like to know how this area was changed by the Atlantic trade, and especially the slave trade that brought millions of Africans to the Americas. Archaeology holds the answers to these questions.

My research into the African settlement of Elmina in coastal Ghana allows me to examine the interactions and exchanges of Africans and Europeans over the past 500 years. In 1482, the Portuguese built a castle next to an existing African settlement. It was the first and largest European outpost in sub-Saharan Africa, and a center of European trade for the next four centuries. By studying the growth of the African settlement of Elmina from a small village to a town of perhaps 20,000, we can chart the changes in the lives of its inhabitants.

Previous studies had suggested there would be few traces of the early Elmina settlement, but I discovered a remarkably preserved site filled with intact artifacts from the town's occupants. While the vast majority of archaeological artifacts are rarely exciting to the average person, every bit of broken pottery or fragment of iron has a story to tell and forms part of the bigger story of how this West African trading city developed. Elmina was part of a changing landscape that marks the emergence of the modern world.

WHY STUDY HISTORY ❓

❝ *History is part of modern life;* it shaped the world we live in and it continues to influence the present in a myriad of ways. Sites like Elmina are a testament to the exchanges that have shaped the modern world. ❞ —Christopher DeCorse

NATIONAL GEOGRAPHIC

The Telltale Scribes of Timbuktu

BY PETER GWIN

Adapted from "The Telltale Scribes of Timbuktu," by Peter Gwin, in *National Geographic*, January 2011

Abdel Kader Haidara is one of Timbuktu's leading historians. He is also a man obsessed with the written word. Books, he said, are part of his soul, and books, he is convinced, will save Timbuktu. Words form the muscle that hold societies upright, Haidara argues. Consider the Qur'an, the Bible, the American Constitution, but also letters from fathers to sons, last wills, or blessings. Thousands of words infused with emotions fill in the nooks and corners of human life. "Some of those words," he says triumphantly, "can only be found here in Timbuktu."

Haidara's family controls Timbuktu's largest private library. The collection of around 22,000 manuscripts dates back to the 11th century. Most are written in Arabic, but some are in Haidara's native Songhai. Others are written in Tamashek, the Tuareg language.

The mosaic of Timbuktu that emerges from its manuscripts describes a city made wealthy by its position at the intersection of the trans-Saharan caravan routes and the Niger River. As its wealth grew, the city built grand mosques, attracting scholars who formed academies and imported books from throughout the Islamic world. New books arrived, and scribes copied facsimiles for the private libraries of local teachers and their wealthy patrons.

Timbuktu's downfall came when one of its conquerors valued knowledge, too. When the Moroccan army arrived in 1591, its soldiers looted the libraries and sent the books back to the Moroccan ruler. The remaining collections were scattered. Scholars estimate many thousands of manuscripts lie buried in the desert or forgotten in hiding places, slowly yielding to heat, rot, and bugs.

Three new state-of-the-art libraries have been constructed to collect, restore, and digitize Timbuktu's manuscripts. Haidara heads one of these new facilities. When asked about tensions in the region, he points to pages riddled with tiny holes and remarks, "Criminals are the least of my worries. Termites are my biggest enemies."

For more from National Geographic
Check out "Rift in Paradise" at NGLSync.Cengage.com

UNIT INQUIRY: CREATE A LOCAL TRADE EXCHANGE

In this unit, you learned how trade influenced the growth and cultures of African civilizations. Based on your understanding of the text, what natural resources were Africa's most valuable commodities? For what other goods were these commodities traded? How did Africa's valuable resources stimulate trade in the region and throughout the world?

ASSIGNMENT Create a local trade exchange that focuses on selling a commodity that is plentiful in your local area in exchange for goods and/or services that are needed in your local area. Be prepared to present your trade exchange plan to the class and explain how it will benefit the growth of your community.

Plan As you create your local trade exchange, think about some of the trade items that were highly valuable to African trading kingdoms—salt, for example. To begin creating your local trade exchange, identify trade items (goods and services) that are plentiful in your community, as well as goods and services that are needed. You might want to use a graphic organizer to help organize your thoughts. ▶

Produce Use your notes to produce descriptions of the goods and services you will sell and buy through your local trade exchange. Think about the value of these goods and services and why they are important to your community.

Present Choose a creative way to present your local trade exchange to the class. Consider one of these options:

- Create a multimedia presentation to promote the local goods and services for sale on your trade exchange.

- Write an advertisement for a media site that describes your local trade exchange and its importance to the community.

- Draw a map of your community and provide icons in the map key to identify commodities that are traded on the exchange.

Trade Commodities

Goods and Services to Sell	
Goods and Services to Buy	

1. Berbers from North Africa established profitable trans-Saharan trade routes with West Africa for gold, salt, and slaves.

2. The Nok people were the first to raise cattle and use iron, and they dominated West Africa.

3. The empires of Ghana and Mali grew powerful by controlling trans-Saharan trade routes.

4. Wealthy civilizations emerged on the East African coast as the monsoon winds helped a sea trade develop in the Indian Ocean.

5. Groups of people in Central Africa migrated east and south, carrying with them their Bantu language and iron making skills.

6-10. **NOW IT'S YOUR TURN** Complete the list with five more things to remember about African civilizations.

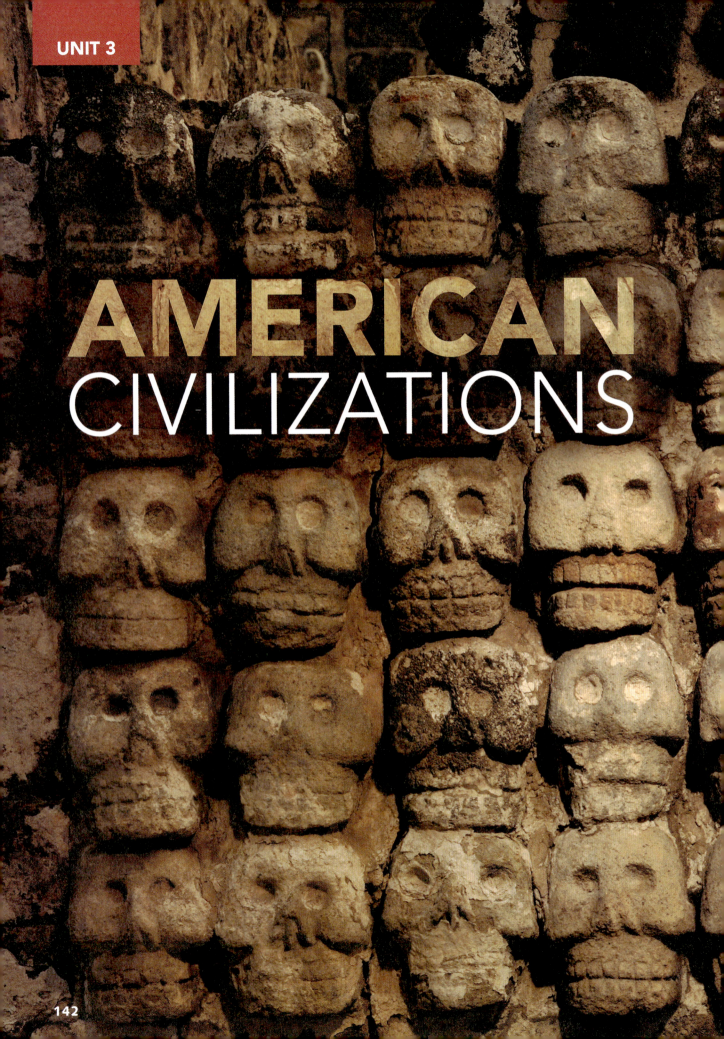

AMERICAN
CIVILIZATIONS

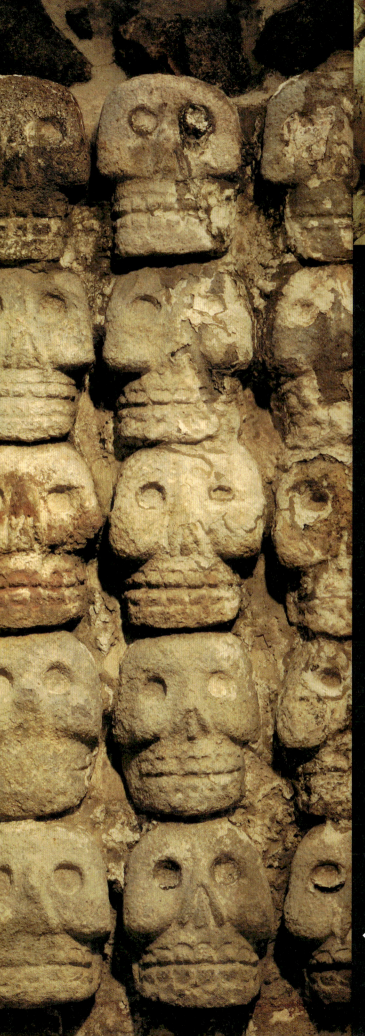

NATIONAL GEOGRAPHIC

ON **LOCATION** WITH

Francisco Estrada-Belli
Archaeologist

When I was seven years old, my parents introduced me to one of the most amazing American civilizations in history: the Maya. As an archaeologist, I've rediscovered lost cities in the jungles of Guatemala and have learned much about Maya culture and history. Part of my job is teaching Guatemalan children about the Maya and instilling a sense of pride in their homeland. My name is Francisco Estrada-Belli, and I'm a National Geographic Explorer. Join me in exploring the many civilizations of the Americas.

< **CRITICAL VIEWING** The Tzompantli, or "Wall of Skulls," is located at the Maya site of Chichén Itzá on the Yucatán Peninsula. What does this carving tell you about the Maya culture?

UNIT 3

TIME LINE OF WORLD EVENTS

American Civilizations

1200 B.C.
The Olmec civilization begins in Mesoamerica.

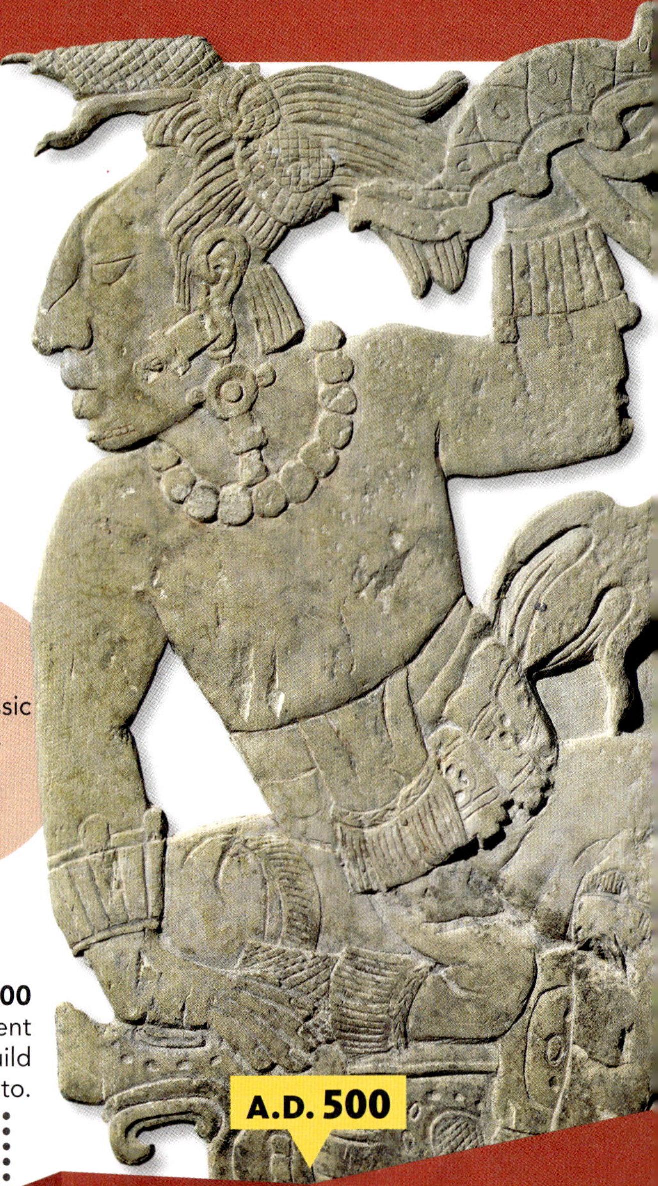

500 B.C.
The Zapotec build Monte Albán.

A.D. 250
The Maya Classic Period begins.
(carving on a Maya stele)

900
The ancient Pueblo build Pueblo Bonito.

1200 B.C. — **A.D. 500**

The World

1045 B.C.
ASIA
Zhou dynasty begins 800-year rule in China.

500 B.C.
ASIA
Buddhism emerges in India. *(Indian Buddha sculpture)*

476
EUROPE
The Western Roman Empire falls.

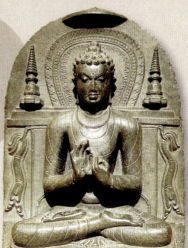

CST 1 Students explain how major events are related to one another in time.

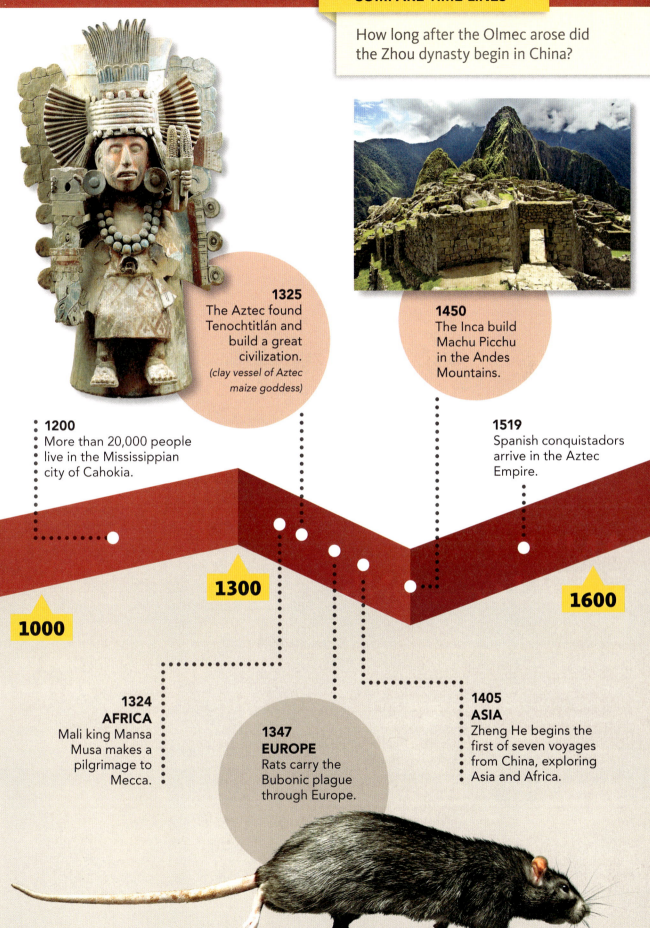

How long after the Olmec arose did the Zhou dynasty begin in China?

1325
The Aztec found Tenochtitlán and build a great civilization.
(clay vessel of Aztec maize goddess)

1450
The Inca build Machu Picchu in the Andes Mountains.

1200
More than 20,000 people live in the Mississippian city of Cahokia.

1519
Spanish conquistadors arrive in the Aztec Empire.

1300

1600

1000

1324
AFRICA
Mali king Mansa Musa makes a pilgrimage to Mecca.

1347
EUROPE
Rats carry the Bubonic plague through Europe.

1405
ASIA
Zheng He begins the first of seven voyages from China, exploring Asia and Africa.

145

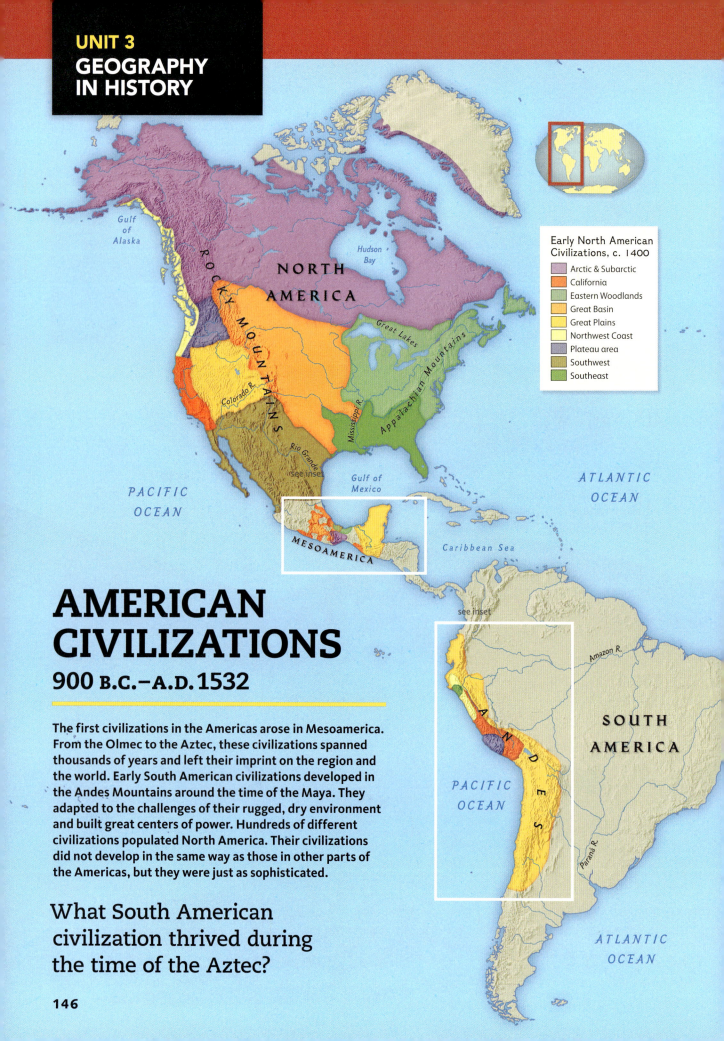

Early North American Civilizations, c. 1400
- Arctic & Subarctic
- California
- Eastern Woodlands
- Great Basin
- Great Plains
- Northwest Coast
- Plateau area
- Southwest
- Southeast

AMERICAN CIVILIZATIONS
900 B.C.–A.D. 1532

The first civilizations in the Americas arose in Mesoamerica. From the Olmec to the Aztec, these civilizations spanned thousands of years and left their imprint on the region and the world. Early South American civilizations developed in the Andes Mountains around the time of the Maya. They adapted to the challenges of their rugged, dry environment and built great centers of power. Hundreds of different civilizations populated North America. Their civilizations did not develop in the same way as those in other parts of the Americas, but they were just as sophisticated.

What South American civilization thrived during the time of the Aztec?

EARLY MESOAMERICAN CIVILIZATIONS

Gulf of Mexico

YUCATÁN PENINSULA

Caribbean Sea

PACIFIC OCEAN

Early Mesoamerican Civilizations
- Olmec, c. 900 B.C.
- Zapotec, c. 500 B.C.
- Maya, c. A.D. 900
- Aztec, c. A.D. 1519

EARLY SOUTH AMERICAN CIVILIZATIONS

AMAZON BASIN

Amazon R.

Marañón R.

Ucayali R.

Madre de Dios R.

A N D E S

Cuzco

Lake Titicaca

PACIFIC OCEAN

Early South American Civilizations
- Moche, c. A.D. 700
- Nazca, c. A.D. 600
- Wari, c. A.D. 1000
- Sican, c. A.D. 1400
- Inca, c. A.D. 1532

INCA BY THE NUMBERS

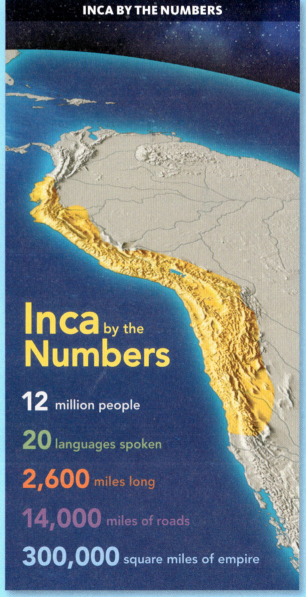

Inca by the Numbers

12 million people

20 languages spoken

2,600 miles long

14,000 miles of roads

300,000 square miles of empire

CST 3 Students use a variety of maps and documents to identify physical and cultural features of neighborhoods, cities, states, and countries and to explain the historical migration of people, expansion and disintegration of empires, and the growth of economic systems.

6

MESOAMERICA

1200 B.C. – A.D. 1521

ESSENTIAL QUESTION How did Mesoamerican civilizations adopt and adapt the cultures of earlier civilizations?

SECTION 1 THE OLMEC AND THE ZAPOTEC

KEY VOCABULARY
cacao
highland
lowland
maize
mother culture
slash-and-burn
  agriculture
terrace

NAMES & PLACES
Mesoamerica
Monte Albán
Olmec
Yucatán Peninsula
Zapotec

SECTION 2 THE MAYA

KEY VOCABULARY
codex
creation story
glyph

NAMES & PLACES
El Mirador
Maya
Popol Vuh

SECTION 3 THE AZTEC

KEY VOCABULARY
chinampa
communal
conquistador
noble
serf

NAMES & PLACES
Hernán Cortés
Moctezuma II
Templo Mayor
Tenochtitlán
Teotihuacán

READING STRATEGY

IDENTIFY MAIN IDEAS AND DETAILS
When you identify key topics in a text, you need to support them with details from the text. As you read the chapter, use diagrams like this one to identify details about each Mesoamerican civilization.

Main-Idea Diagram

Main Idea: Olmec Civilization
Detail:
Detail:
Detail:
Detail:
Detail:

The Temple of the Great Jaguar at Tikal, Guatemala, served as a tomb for a Maya ruler. Its steep staircase is divided into nine levels and may represent the nine levels of the underworld in Maya religious belief.

The Geography of Mesoamerica

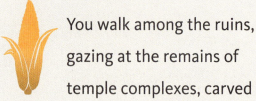

You walk among the ruins, gazing at the remains of temple complexes, carved stone sculptures, and towering pyramids. Are you visiting a city that thrived during the time of ancient Egypt? No. You're in the middle of a jungle in a region of North America known as Mesoamerica.

MAIN IDEA

Geographic factors greatly influenced the development of civilizations in Mesoamerica.

HIGHLANDS AND LOWLANDS

Thousands of years ago, advanced civilizations arose in **Mesoamerica**, which stretches from southern Mexico into part of Central America. The region's climate and fertile land helped the civilizations thrive.

Mesoamerica's landscape is divided into two main geographic areas: **highlands**, or land high above the sea, and **lowlands**, or land that is low and level. The highlands lie between the mountains of the Sierra Madre, a mountain system in Mexico, and consist of fairly flat and fertile land. This land was good for agriculture, but it also posed some challenges for its early residents. They were rocked from time to time by volcanic eruptions and powerful earthquakes. The lowlands are less active. They lie along the coast of the Gulf of Mexico. They are also found in the jungles of the **Yucatán** (you-kuh-TAN) **Peninsula**, which is located between the Gulf of Mexico and the Caribbean Sea.

If you hiked from the lowlands to the highlands, you would experience a wide variety of climates, from tropical rain forests to very cold, dry zones in the higher mountains. In general, the climate in the highlands is cooler and drier than that in the lowlands, where it can rain more than 100 inches a year. The lowlands are also crisscrossed by many rivers. Some of these rivers flood during heavy seasonal rains and wash fertile silt onto their floodplains.

AGRICULTURE

Early Mesoamerican farmers learned what crops would grow well in the different climates of the highlands and lowlands. In the drier highland areas, the main crops included **maize** (also known as corn), squash, and beans. These three crops are often called the Three Sisters because they benefit from being planted close together. The beans grow up the maize stalks, while the squash spreads over the ground, preventing the growth of weeds. Farmers in the lowlands grew these three crops as well as palm, avocado, and **cacao** (kuh-COW) trees. Cacao beans were used to make chocolate. Sometimes the beans were even used as money.

Mesoamerica's farmers developed different agricultural practices in the region's varied landscapes. In drier areas, farmers redirected the course of streams to irrigate their fields. In the dense lowland jungles, farmers cleared fields through a technique known as **slash-and-burn agriculture**, shown on the opposite page. These agricultural techniques helped ancient cultures produce food surpluses and allowed people to do jobs other than farming. As a result, civilizations began to arise in Mesoamerica more than 3,000 years ago—first the Olmec and later the Zapotec.

7.7.1 Study the locations, landforms, and climates of Mexico, Central America, and South America and their effects on Mayan, Aztec, and Incan economies, trade, and development of urban societies; CST 3 Students use

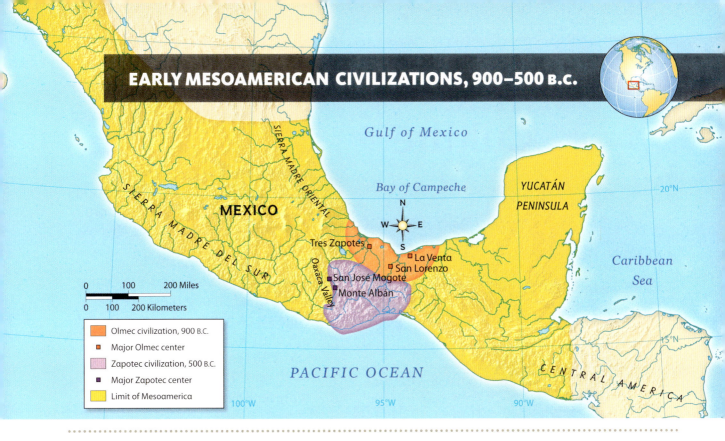

EARLY MESOAMERICAN CIVILIZATIONS, 900–500 B.C.

Gulf of Mexico

SIERRA MADRE ORIENTAL

Bay of Campeche

YUCATÁN PENINSULA

20°N

MEXICO

SIERRA MADRE DEL SUR

Tres Zapotes

La Venta
San Lorenzo

Oaxaca Valley

San José Mogote
Monte Albán

Caribbean Sea

PACIFIC OCEAN

CENTRAL AMERICA

15°N

0   100   200 Miles
0   100   200 Kilometers

■ Olmec civilization, 900 B.C.
■ Major Olmec center
■ Zapotec civilization, 500 B.C.
■ Major Zapotec center
■ Limit of Mesoamerica

100°W   95°W   90°W

SLASH-AND-BURN AGRICULTURE

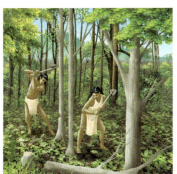

1 Slash
Wooded areas and jungles are too thick to plant crops. Farmers slash, or cut down, trees.

2 Burn
Fallen trees and leaves are burned to clear the land. Ash produced by the fires is used as fertilizer.

3 Fertilize and Plant
Cleared land is fertilized with ash. Farmers plant crops such as maize and squash.

4 Migrate
Farmers move on to new locations after soil on cleared land becomes less productive.

REVIEW & ASSESS

1. **READING CHECK** What geographic factors influenced the development of civilizations in Mesoamerica?

2. **INTERPRET MAPS** Why do you think the Olmec and Zapotec civilizations developed along coastal areas?

3. **COMPARE AND CONTRAST** How did agricultural techniques differ in Mesoamerica's highlands and lowlands?

a variety of maps and documents to identify physical and cultural features of neighborhoods, cities, states, and countries and to explain the historical migration of people, expansion and disintegration of empires, and the growth of economic systems.

Olmec Culture

After a long search, the foreman has finally found the right rock. It's huge and heavy. He directs his men to begin their work. Their task: to haul the rock 50 miles through the jungle to the city where an artist will carve it into a sculpture. Their challenge: to move the rock without using a wheeled cart or animals. Welcome to the world of the Olmec.

MAIN IDEA

The Olmec civilization that arose in Mesoamerica was one of the region's earliest civilizations and influenced later cultures.

JAGUAR GOD

The Olmec worshipped many gods, but one of the most important was the jaguar god. When Olmec priests visited the spirit world, the priests believed they transformed into powerful jaguars.

OLMEC CITIES

The **Olmec** (AHL-mehk) culture began along Mexico's Gulf Coast around 1200 B.C. The development of this culture led to the birth of Mesoamerica's first civilization.

Like the ancient civilizations of Mesopotamia, Egypt, India, and China, the Olmec emerged on the floodplains of rivers. Heavy rains caused these rivers to flood and deposit fertile silt on their plains. The rich soil allowed farmers to grow abundant crops. In time, the culture's economy expanded and cities, including San Lorenzo, La Venta, and Tres Zapotes, began to develop. (See the map in Lesson 1.1.)

Olmec cities contained pyramids and temples built on earthen mounds. The Olmec also built courts where athletes played a game that was a sort of combination of modern soccer and basketball. You will learn more about this game later in the chapter.

Archaeologists have also found extraordinary works of art in Olmec cities. Chief among these are the huge stone heads the Olmec carved out of rock. The heads stand as tall as 10 feet and can weigh up to 20 tons. They are believed to represent different Olmec rulers.

DAILY LIFE AND LEGACY

Workers, including those who hauled the rocks for the stone sculptures, and farmers made up most of Olmec society. They were at the bottom of the civilization's class structure. Rulers were at the top, followed by priests, merchants, and artists. The farmers and workers lived in simple houses made of wood or mud. The upper classes lived in more elaborate stone structures and wore fine clothes and precious jewelry.

Archaeologists are not sure why, but around 400 B.C., the Olmec civilization disappeared. However, elements of the civilization's legacy can be seen in later civilizations. The Olmec had established an extensive trade network. In addition to the exchange of goods, the trade routes carried Olmec culture throughout Mesoamerica. As new civilizations arose, their people were influenced by Olmec art and religious practices. As a result, many archaeologists consider the Olmec to be the **mother culture** of Mesoamerica.

Critical Viewing The rock this head was carved out of may have been rolled onto a log raft and floated downriver. Why might Olmec laborers have chosen to use this method to move the head?

REVIEW & ASSESS

1. **READING CHECK** What geographic features played a key role in the development of Olmec civilization?

2. **INTERPRET VISUALS** What does the stone head suggest about the power and authority of Olmec rulers?

3. **DRAW CONCLUSIONS** What conclusions can you draw about daily life for most of the Olmec people?

Critical Viewing This mural by Mexican artist Diego Rivera shows Zapotec artists at work. What details in the mural convey class differences in the society?

The Zapotec and Monte Albán

As the Olmec declined, the Zapotec people were developing an advanced society to the southwest. Although their culture reflected Olmec influence, the Zapotec developed their own distinct and powerful civilization. They became a leading player in Mesoamerica.

MAIN IDEA

The Zapotec established a civilization and controlled the Oaxaca Valley for more than 1,000 years.

PEOPLE OF THE VALLEY

The **Zapotec** people would build one of the first major cities in Mesoamerica, but their beginnings were humble. They developed their society in the Oaxaca (wuh-HAH-kah) Valley, a large, open area where three smaller valleys meet. (See the map in Lesson 1.1.) This fertile area, with its river, mild climate, and abundant rainfall, proved excellent for growing crops, especially maize.

For centuries, the Zapotec lived in farming villages located throughout the Oaxaca Valley. Then, around 1300 B.C., a settlement called San José Mogote (san ho-ZAY moh-GOH-tay) emerged as the Zapotec center of power. Leaders built temples there and had artists decorate them with huge sculptures. In time, nearly half of the Zapotec people lived in San José Mogote.

URBAN CENTER

Around 500 B.C., the center of power shifted when the Zapotec built a city known now as **Monte Albán** (MAHN-tay ahl-BAHN) high atop a mountain. The site overlooked the Oaxaca Valley. Its location helped the Zapotec defend themselves against their enemies. Monte Albán must have been a spectacular sight. The city's rulers flattened the top of the mountain and built great plazas on it filled with pyramids, palaces, and even an astronomical observatory.

Monte Albán became the center of the Zapotec civilization. There, the Zapotec built magnificent tombs in which they buried the bodies of wealthy people wearing their gold jewelry. The Zapotec believed the deceased would carry the jewelry into the afterlife. Artificial **terraces**, or stepped platforms built into the mountainside, provided additional area for building and agriculture.

Around A.D. 750, Monte Albán's power began to weaken. By 900, the city had disappeared. Economic difficulties may have caused the decline, but no one knows for sure. Like the fall of the Olmec, the decline of the Zapotec civilization remains a mystery.

REVIEW & ASSESS

1. **READING CHECK** What geographic features of the Oaxaca Valley encouraged the development of the Zapotec civilization?

2. **MAKE INFERENCES** How do you think the location of Monte Albán helped the Zapotec defend themselves from their enemies?

3. **DETERMINE WORD MEANINGS** What does *deceased* mean in the phrase, "the deceased would carry the jewelry into the afterlife"?

7.7.1 Study the locations, landforms, and climates of Mexico, Central America, and South America and their effects on Mayan, Aztec, and Incan economies, trade, and development of urban societies; 7.7.2 Study the roles of people in each society, including class structures, family life, warfare, religious beliefs and practices, and slavery.

Maya Society

Can people be made of corn? According to Maya tradition, they can. But it took the Maya gods a while to figure out how to do it. At first, they made people out of things like mud and wood, but these creatures couldn't speak. Finally, the gods mixed their blood with maize flour. The result? Walking, talking human beings. No wonder the early Maya called themselves "the people of the maize."

MAIN IDEA

Maya society was structured according to a class system, and religion shaped daily life.

CLASS SYSTEM

The **Maya** emerged around the same time as the Zapotec. Their culture began to develop to the east of the Zapotec in areas of present-day southern Mexico and Central America around 1500 B.C. These areas included lowlands in the north, highlands in the south, the forests of the Yucatán Peninsula, and the tropical jungles of Mexico and Guatemala.

Like Olmec farmers, Maya farmers developed successful agricultural practices. They produced surpluses of crops, including beans, chili peppers, cacao beans, and, of course, maize, which the Maya considered sacred. These surpluses allowed some people to become priests, merchants, and craftspeople and some villages to gain great wealth. Wealthier villages with religious ceremonial centers arose around 500 B.C. In time, these villages grew into cities.

The development of Maya cities produced a class system with four main classes. At the top was the king, who performed religious ceremonies and was believed to have descended from the gods. Next came priests and warriors. The priests decided when farmers could plant and when people could marry. They also conducted important religious rituals and ceremonies. Warriors were well respected and well trained.

Merchants and craftspeople followed these upper classes. Craftspeople made articles out of pottery and designed buildings and temples. The merchants sold and traded goods—often with buyers in other Maya cities. Finally, farmers—who made up the majority of the population—and slaves were at the bottom of the heap. Most of the slaves were prisoners of war. They were given the worst jobs and were often killed when their masters died.

DAILY LIFE

Class determined where people lived and how they dressed. People who belonged to the upper classes lived in stone buildings and wore colorfully decorated clothes and jewelry. Farmers wore plain clothes and lived in mud huts.

While the wealthy enjoyed a comfortable lifestyle, farmers worked hard in the heat to grow their crops. On hillsides they carved out terraces on which to grow their maize, cacao beans, and chili peppers. In drier areas they dug channels that carried river water to their fields. In addition to doing their own work, sometimes farmers had to tend the king's fields and build monuments and temples in his cities.

7.7.1 Study the locations, landforms, and climates of Mexico, Central America, and South America and their effects on Mayan, Aztec, and Incan economies, trade, and development of urban societies; 7.7.2 Study the roles of people in each society, including

MAYA MAIZE GOD

The maize god was one of the most important Maya gods. The god often appeared as a handsome young man with hair made of maize silk. The god represented the cycle of life (birth, death, rebirth) as well as the cycle of maize (planting, harvesting, replanting).

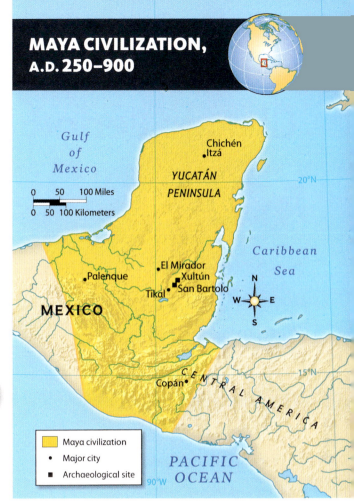

MAYA CIVILIZATION, A.D. 250–900

Eventually the Maya learned how to track seasonal changes. This knowledge helped them predict the best time to plant and harvest their crops. You will learn more about how the Maya measured time later in the chapter.

Above all, however, the farmers looked to their gods to control the weather and increase their harvests. Religion was central to everyone's lives, and the Maya worshipped many gods, including the gods of fire, sun, war, rain, and maize. (You can learn more about the importance of the maize god in the feature above.) All of these gods were

thought to influence every aspect of the people's lives—in both good and bad ways.

To please the gods, the Maya made frequent offerings of food, animals, plants, and precious objects. As you have already learned, the Maya believed that the gods had given their blood to create people. In return, the Maya sometimes offered their own blood or made human sacrifices to honor the gods. Just as maize nourished people, the Maya believed that blood nourished the gods. Rather than sacrifice one of their own, however, the Maya often sacrificed a member of the lowest class in their society: a slave.

REVIEW & ASSESS

1. **READING CHECK** What were the four main classes of early Maya society?

2. **INTERPRET MAPS** On what geographic landform were many of the major Maya cities located?

3. **COMPARE AND CONTRAST** How did the daily life of farmers differ from that of people belonging to the wealthier classes?

class structures, family life, warfare, religious beliefs and practices, and slavery; 7.7.3 Explain how and where each empire arose and how the Aztec and Incan empires were defeated by the Spanish; CST 3 Students use a variety of maps and documents to identify physical and cultural features of neighborhoods, cities, states, and countries and to explain the historical migration of people, expansion and disintegration of empires, and the growth of economic systems.

The Maya Classic Period

In the 1800s, explorers battled mosquitoes, illness, and thick jungle growth in their search for the ruined remains of the Maya civilization. Their efforts paid off. When they came upon the half-buried monuments in the ancient Maya city of Copán, one of the explorers—John Lloyd Stephens—was so fascinated by what he saw that he purchased the site on the spot.

MAIN IDEA

The Maya built sophisticated cities that contained impressive structures and artwork.

CITIES

Many of the great Maya cities lay hidden beneath the jungle growth for centuries. One of the earliest of these cities was **El Mirador**, which has been called the "cradle of the Maya civilization." (See the map in Lesson 2.1.) The city flourished from about 300 B.C. to A.D. 150 and was home to as many as 200,000 people. Most Maya cities, however, developed during the Classic Period, which lasted between A.D. 250 and 900. These cities included Copán (koh-PAHN), Tikal (tee-KAHL), Chichén Itzá (chee-CHEHN ee-TSAH), and Palenque (pah-LEHNG-keh). Although each was an independent city-state ruled by a king, trade linked the city-states. Merchants from the cities exchanged goods such as salt and jade jewelry and often paid for them with cacao beans.

Most Maya cities followed a similar layout. A large plaza in the center of the city served as both a public gathering place and market. Each city also contained a palace for the king, administrative buildings, temples, and stepped pyramids. The pyramids rose hundreds of feet in the air and were lined with steep staircases. Many of the pyramids featured platforms at the top. Priests conducted ceremonies on the platforms so that the entire population could witness them.

The Maya built temples on the top of some of the pyramids. A huge ball court was constructed at the foot of at least one of these pyramids in each city to allow athletes to play the sacred Mesoamerican ball game. The Maya played this game, which began with the Olmec, to honor their gods. The illustration on the opposite page shows Maya athletes in action on the court.

CULTURE AND ART

Like the ball game, many other aspects of Maya culture and art were linked to religion. Artists made sculptures that honored and brought to life the various Maya gods. They also carved stone slabs called stelae to honor their kings. Artists carved a king's likeness on the slab and recorded his actions on it as well—actually setting his story in stone.

All of these stories were probably passed down orally from generation to generation. This oral tradition continued long after the great Maya civilization had come to an end. It may have been weakened by war, food shortages, or overcrowding. For whatever reason, by A.D. 900, the Maya had abandoned many of their cities. When Spanish conquerors arrived in the 1500s, only weakened city-states had been left behind—a shadow of their former glory.

MESOAMERICAN BALL GAME

The game the Maya and other Mesoamerican peoples played on a court like this one was much more than a game. It was often a matter of life and death. The captain of the losing Maya team probably climbed the temple steps to be sacrificed to the gods.

Players weren't allowed to touch the ball with their hands. They could only bounce the ball off their knees, hips, and elbows.

The solid ball was hard enough to break bones, so the players wore some heavy padding.

The goal of the game was to launch the ball through a stone ring. Since this wasn't easy, a game could go on for days.

REVIEW & ASSESS

1. **READING CHECK** What was the layout of most of the great Maya cities?

2. **INTEGRATE VISUALS** Based on the illustration and what you have learned about the Mesoamerican ball game, what qualities were probably necessary to play the game?

3. **MAKE INFERENCES** How do you think the Maya reacted as they witnessed a religious ceremony performed at the top of a towering pyramid?

7.7.2 Study the roles of people in each society, including class structures, family life, warfare, religious beliefs and practices, and slavery; 7.7.4 Describe the artistic and oral traditions and architecture in the three civilizations.

Uncovering Maya Murals

Sometimes you're just lucky. Ask **William Saturno**. He had spent three days—instead of the three hours he thought the trip would take—trudging through the jungles of Guatemala looking for carved Maya monuments. During the search, he and his team had been lost and near death. When a pyramid appeared in the midst of the dense undergrowth, Saturno ducked inside it to escape the terrible heat. He turned around to find a stunning Maya mural of the maize god looking right back at him. Now Saturno's lucky find is rewriting Maya history.

^
William Saturno is dedicated to preserving and interpreting the remains of the early Maya. In this photo, he removes debris from a mural he uncovered at the Maya site of Xultún.

MAIN IDEA

Archaeologist William Saturno's discoveries have challenged ideas about the early Maya and provided insight into their way of thinking.

A LUCKY FIND

National Geographic Explorer William Saturno has spent his life studying the Maya and searching out the civilization's secrets. His greatest discovery occurred in 2001, when he found the mural at a site he later named San Bartolo.

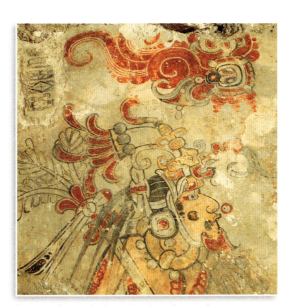

Portrait of a scholar in the San Bartolo mural

Saturno spent several years excavating the wall painting, which represented the Maya creation story in graceful and sophisticated detail. However, when Saturno dated the work of art, he found that it had been created around 100 B.C.—more than 300 years before the Maya Classic Period had even begun. As Saturno says, "Clearly Maya painting had achieved glory centuries before the great works of the Classic Maya."

The far end of the mural revealed another surprise—the portrait of a king. "Some scholars thought that at this early stage in Maya history, the Preclassic, city-states had not yet evolved into full-fledged monarchies, with all the trappings seen later," explains Saturno. "But here was a king, named and titled, receiving his crown. In short, this one chamber upended much of what we thought we knew about the early Maya."

ROOM OF WONDER

About ten years later and just five miles from San Bartolo, Saturno got lucky again. He was digging under a mound in the Maya site of Xultún (shool-tuhn) when a student assistant claimed he'd found traces of paint on a wall. "I was curious," Saturno says. "So I excavated to the back wall, and I saw a beautiful portrait of a king. There he was in Technicolor, with blue feathers."

After more painstaking work, Saturno uncovered an entire room with paintings of other figures and a wall covered with columns of numbers. He thinks that mathematicians had been using the walls like a whiteboard to see whether the movements of the moon and planets matched the dates they had calculated. The mural and numbers dated back to about A.D. 750, around the time Xultún was beginning to decline.

According to Saturno, the Maya knew the collapse of their city had begun. Still, as he says, "They wanted to tie events in their king's life to larger cosmic cycles. They wanted to show that the king would be okay and that nothing would change. We keep looking for endings. It's an entirely different mind-set. I would never have identified this nondescript [uninteresting] mound as special. But this discovery implies that special things are everywhere."

REVIEW & ASSESS

1. **READING CHECK** Why are William Saturno's discoveries so remarkable?

2. **DRAW CONCLUSIONS** Saturno emphasizes the luck he's had in his explorations, but what other qualities must he possess to carry out his work?

3. **ANALYZE LANGUAGE USE** Saturno says that the Maya had "an entirely different mind-set." What do you think he is suggesting about how the Maya viewed the world?

7.7.4 Describe the artistic and oral traditions and architecture in the three civilizations; HI 5 Students recognize that interpretations of history are subject to change as new information is uncovered.

161

Legacy of the Maya

In 2012, the prediction went viral: On December 21, the world was going to end. The prediction was based on the Maya calendar, which some people claimed would end on that day. But the date simply marked the completion of a 5,125-year cycle. The Maya had calculated that a new cycle would begin on the 22nd.

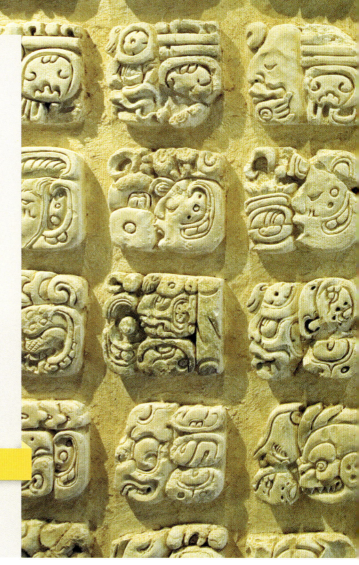

MAIN IDEA

Important advances in mathematics, astronomy, and writing allowed the Maya to create their calendar.

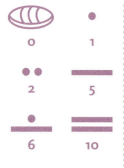

0	1
2	5
6	10

MAYA NUMBERS

The Maya represented numbers using only three symbols: a shell for zero, a dot for one, and a bar for five. A few of the numbers are shown above. Try using the symbols to create some simple subtraction problems.

MATH AND ASTRONOMY

The Maya were superb mathematicians. Like the people of ancient India, they developed the concept of zero. They also developed a sophisticated number system using positions to show place value and to calculate sums up to the hundreds of millions.

Such calculations were used to record astronomical observations as well. Maya astronomers observed the sun, moon, planets, and stars and were able to predict their movements with great accuracy—all without the aid of any instruments. Instead, they studied the sky from temples and observatories. Astronomers used their observations to calculate the best times for planting and harvesting crops and for religious celebrations.

These astronomical observations and calculations were used to develop an elaborate 365-day calendar that was nearly as accurate as our own. Remember the room that William Saturno uncovered in Xultún? The mathematical calculations on its walls were probably used to work out dates in the calendar.

WRITING SYSTEM AND BOOKS

Archaeologists gained a better understanding of the Maya people's scientific achievements and culture

The Maya calendar is actually a system of several calendars used together to track days and cycles. Glyphs, like those you see here, represent days and months in the complex calendar.

once they began to crack the code of their writing system. The Maya used symbolic pictures called **glyphs** (glihfs) to represent words, syllables, and sounds that could be combined into complex sentences.

The Maya carved glyphs into their monuments, stelae, and tombs. Maya writers, called scribes, also used them to record their people's history in a folded book made of tree-bark paper called a **codex**. The Spanish conquerors destroyed most of the codices in the 1500s. However,

after the Spanish arrived, the Maya wrote other books in which they recorded Maya history and culture. The most famous of these books is called the ***Popol Vuh***, which recounts the Maya creation story.

As you've already learned, the Maya civilization had greatly declined by A.D. 900. However, Maya people today still keep their culture alive. Many of them speak the Maya languages and tell their ancestors' stories. They are a living legacy of the Maya civilization.

REVIEW & ASSESS

1. **READING CHECK** What important mathematical ideas did the Maya develop?

2. **IDENTIFY MAIN IDEAS AND DETAILS** According to the text, why did Maya astronomers study the sun, moon, planets, and stars?

3. **ASK QUESTIONS** Frame a question about Maya culture that can be answered by historical research.

 7.7.5 Describe the Meso-American achievements in astronomy and mathematics, including the development of the calendar and the Meso-American knowledge of seasonal changes to the civilizations' agricultural systems; REP 1 Students frame questions that can be answered by historical study and research.

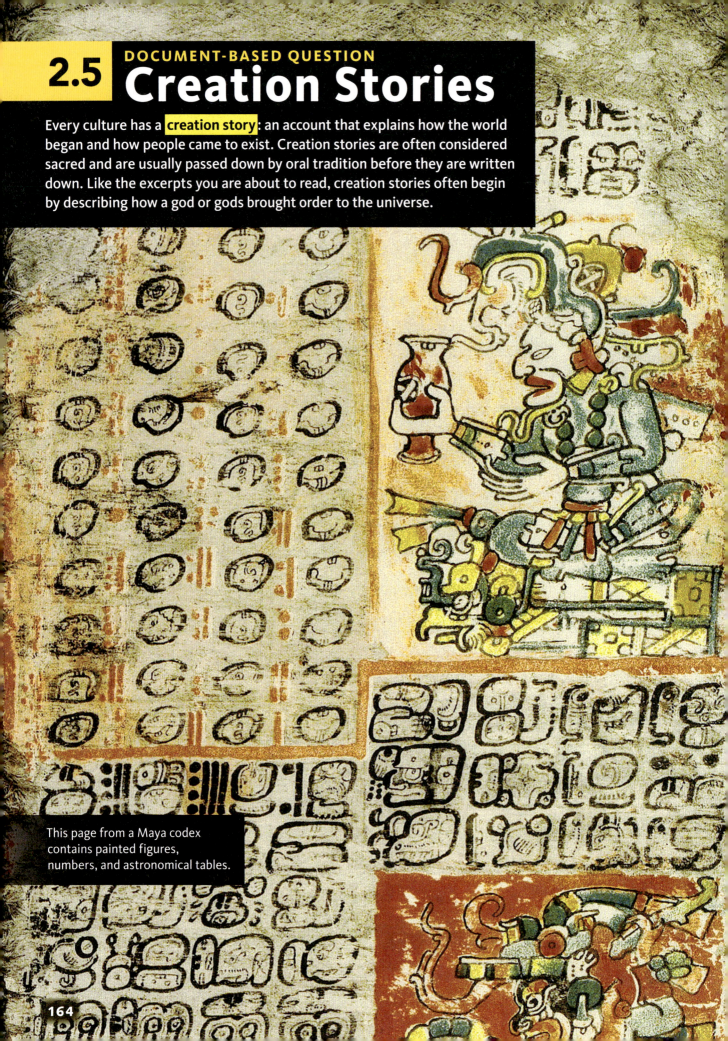

DOCUMENT-BASED QUESTION
Creation Stories

Every culture has a <mark>creation story</mark>: an account that explains how the world began and how people came to exist. Creation stories are often considered sacred and are usually passed down by oral tradition before they are written down. Like the excerpts you are about to read, creation stories often begin by describing how a god or gods brought order to the universe.

This page from a Maya codex contains painted figures, numbers, and astronomical tables.

DOCUMENT ONE

Primary Source: Sacred Text

from the *Popol Vuh*, translated by Dennis Tedlock

Spanish conquerors destroyed much of Maya culture in the 1500s. To preserve their sacred stories for future generations, Maya scribes wrote them down in the *Popol Vuh*. In this passage, two Maya gods form Earth from a world that contains only the sea.

CONSTRUCTED RESPONSE According to this passage, how did the Maya gods form Earth?

"Let it be this way, think about it: this water should be removed, emptied out for the formation of the earth's own plate and platform . . ." they said. And then the earth arose because of them, it was simply their word that brought it forth. For the forming of the earth they said, "Earth." It arose suddenly, just like a cloud, like a mist, now forming, unfolding.

DOCUMENT TWO

Primary Source: Sacred Text

from the Book of Genesis

Genesis is the first book of the Hebrew Bible, a collection of sacred Jewish texts. It is also the first book of the Old Testament in the Christian Bible. Followers of both religions believe in a single God. In this passage from Genesis, which means "the origin, or beginning," God creates night and day.

CONSTRUCTED RESPONSE In this excerpt, what was the world like before God brought light to the earth?

When God began to create heaven and earth—the earth being unformed and void [empty]. . .—God said, "Let there be light"; and there was light. God saw that the light was good, and God separated the light from the darkness. God called the light Day, and the darkness He called Night. And there was evening and there was morning, a first day.

DOCUMENT THREE

Primary Source: Myth

from *Pan Gu Creates Heaven and Earth*, translated by Jan and Yvonne Walls

Pan Gu is a god in an ancient Chinese creation story that has been told and passed down for more than 2,000 years. According to the story, Pan Gu created heaven and earth. In this passage, Pan Gu bursts from a disordered universe that is shaped like an egg.

CONSTRUCTED RESPONSE In this myth, what elements formed heaven and what elements formed the earth?

Pan Gu, an enormous giant, was being nurtured [cared for] in the dark chaos of that egg. . . . Then one day he woke and stretched himself, shattering the egg-shaped chaos into pieces. The pure lighter elements gradually rose up to become heaven and the impure heavier parts slowly sank down to form the earth.

SYNTHESIZE & WRITE

1. **REVIEW** Review what you have learned about the creation stories and religious beliefs of early civilizations.

2. **RECALL** On your own paper, write down the main idea expressed in each document.

3. **CONSTRUCT** Write a topic sentence that answers this question: What are some common characteristics of creation stories?

4. **WRITE** Using evidence from the documents, write a paragraph to support your answer in Step 3.

7.7.4 Describe the artistic and oral traditions and architecture in the three civilizations; REP 4 Students assess the credibility of primary and secondary sources and draw sound conclusions from them.

Tenochtitlán: An Aztec City

Thriving cities, massive temples, fierce warriors, strong armies. These are only a few characteristics of the Mesoamerican civilization called the Aztec. The Aztec were nomads from a mysterious land known as Aztlán—the origin of the name *Aztec*. Starting from only an island city in a swamp, the Aztec founded a powerful empire.

MAIN IDEA

The Aztec developed a mighty empire in central Mexico.

SETTLING IN CENTRAL MEXICO

Around A.D. 1300, Aztec nomads migrated into the Valley of Mexico, a thriving and populous region in the central part of Mexico. When the Aztec arrived, the valley was dominated by rival city-states. The Aztec settled there, adopted local ways, and served powerful kings as farmers and warriors. Then, in 1325, the Aztec founded their own city, **Tenochtitlán** (tay-nohch-teet-LAHN). Today Tenochtitlán is known as Mexico City.

The Aztec built Tenochtitlán on two islands in a swamp in the western part of Lake Texcoco. To feed their growing population, they constructed artificial fields called chinampas (chee-NAHM-pahz). Chinampa farmers piled layers of mud and vegetation to raise the soil level above the water. Then they planted trees alongside to mark off planting areas. Finally, they covered the areas with more soil, dug up from the bottom of the lake. Farmers planted maize, beans, and different kinds of squash on the chinampas. These remarkable fields produced many crops, and the Aztec population thrived.

One advantage of living in a lake was that canoes made transport easy, so trade flourished. In time, the Aztec established a twin city called Tlatelolco (tlaht-el-OHL-koh) in the northern part of Lake Texcoco. Tlatelolco had a huge marketplace. Every day, thousands of people crossed the lake in canoes and visited Tlatelolco's bustling market.

BUILDING AN EMPIRE

The Aztec developed into skilled warriors. At first they fought for other kings, but then they overthrew their masters and began fighting for themselves. They allied with two other cities, Texcoco and Tlacopan (tlaht-oh-PAHN), to form a powerful Triple Alliance that the Aztec would control by 1428. Well-trained Aztec armies marched steadily through Mesoamerica, forcing hundreds of small city-states to surrender to Aztec rule.

Aztec bureaucrats, or government officials, kept order and enforced the supply of tribute to Tenochtitlán. Tribute, or a payment for protection, was made in food, raw materials, goods, or labor. Over time, the Aztec grew rich and commanded a vast empire stretching from the Pacific Ocean to the Gulf of Mexico. Around six million people lived in the Aztec Empire at its height.

By 1519, about 200,000 people lived in Tenochtitlán, which had become the largest city in Mesoamerica. It was one of the most magnificent cities of its time. The pyramid of **Templo Mayor**, or the Great Temple, towered above the city. Dozens more temples and many beautiful palaces surrounded Templo Mayor. Four roads

THE AZTEC EMPIRE, 1503–1519

HUASTEC
CHICHIMEC
Oxitipán
METZTITLÁN
Zimapán
TARASCANS
Vinazco R.
Cazones R.
El Tajín
Tula Valley of
Totlantzinco
Lake Cuitzeo
Mexico
Lake Texcoco
TEXCOCO
Xocotla
Jalapa
20°N
TLACOPÁN
Tlatelolco
TLAXCALA
Zempoala (Cempoala)
TENOCHTITLÁN
Tlaxcala
Ixhuacán
Huexotzinco
Veracruz
Balsas R.
Cholula
Orizaba
Gulf of Mexico
Nexapa R.
Atoyac R.
Mixtlán
Oztoma
TEOTITLÁN
San Juan R.
Xicallanco
Teloloapán
Usumacinta R.
Zacatula
Yanhuitlán
Tetela
YOPITZINCO
Achiotla
Zozollán
Grijalva R.
Nochcoc
Milta
Acapulco
Monte
Grijalva R.
Ayutla
Grande R.
Albán
MIXTEC
Tehuantepec
Tototepec
XOCONOCHO
PACIFIC OCEAN
Huiztlán
Mazatlán

Legend:
- Aztec Empire, 1503
- Moctezuma II's conquests
- **TEXCOCO** Triple Alliance
- Moctezuma II's offensives
- Route of Hernán Cortés, 1519

Scale:
0 · 50 · 100 Miles
0 · 50 · 100 Kilometers

---

divided the city into quarters, each with distinct neighborhoods, leaders, farmland, markets, and temples. The island city was crisscrossed by canals and connected to the mainland by long causeways, or roads across the water. When Spanish explorers arrived in 1519, they marveled at Tenochtitlán's size and splendor.

PRECIOUS MASKS

This turquoise mask depicts the Aztec god Quetzalcoatl (kweht-sahl-koh-AHT-uhl), believed to be part bird, part snake. Aztec sculptors carved masks from volcanic rock and precious stones such as turquoise and jade.

REVIEW & ASSESS

1. **READING CHECK** What features made Tenochtitlán an awe-inspiring city?

2. **ANALYZE CAUSE AND EFFECT** How were the Aztec able to develop productive farm fields in the swampy lands around Tenochtitlán?

3. **INTERPRET MAPS** Use the map scale to determine how far the Aztec Empire extended from north to south in 1503.

7.7.1 Study the locations, landforms, and climates of Mexico, Central America, and South America and their effects on Mayan, Aztec, and Incan economies, trade, and development of urban societies; 7.7.3 Explain how and where each empire arose and how the Aztec and Incan empires were defeated by the Spanish; CST 3 Students use a variety of maps and documents to identify physical and cultural features of neighborhoods, cities, states, and countries and to explain the historical migration of people, expansion and disintegration of empires, and the growth of economic systems.

Aztec Culture

In any big city, you will find people from all walks of life. The same was true for the great Aztec city of Tenochtitlán, where you might have met nobles, priests, soldiers, artisans, and slaves.

MAIN IDEA

Class structure and religious practices defined Aztec society.

CLASS STRUCTURE

The emperor was the most powerful person in Aztec society. He controlled all political and spiritual matters and served for life. Below him were the **nobles**. Nobles were the smallest but most powerful class. They inherited their status and held the top jobs as generals, priests, tax collectors, and judges. Some nobles even governed cities for the Aztec emperor.

Most Aztec belonged to the commoner class, which included merchants and artisans, farmers, and soldiers. Merchants and artisans were highly respected, and they lived in their own communities. Merchants traveled throughout the empire, trading goods. Artisans made and sold jewelry, ornaments, and clothes. Many Aztec were farmers who worked **communal**, or shared, land and had to give part of their harvest as a tax to the empire. Others were professional soldiers, some of whom gained wealth and privilege by distinguishing themselves on the battlefield.

Serfs and slaves occupied the lowest level of Aztec society. **Serfs** lived and worked on the private land of nobles. In addition to providing agricultural labor, serfs performed household tasks for landowners. Slaves were considered property and were usually prisoners of war. Slave status was not based on race, and children of slaves were born free.

AZTEC GODS

Religion was central to all classes of Aztec society. The Aztec were polytheistic. They worshipped as many as 1,000 gods and built hundreds of magnificent temples and religious structures in Tenochtitlán to honor those gods. Though people's individual homes were simply constructed, they almost always featured a shrine to the gods.

The Aztec followed many traditions that they shared with other Mesoamerican cultures. They believed they could please the gods with offerings and sacrifices. Some of these sacrifices were human.

Critical Viewing The skulls of sacrificed prisoners fill the Wall of Skulls in Templo Mayor. What message did the wall probably send to enemies of the Aztec?

Most of the human sacrifices were prisoners of war. The Aztec considered themselves "the People of the Sun" and believed they nourished the sun with these sacrifices.

An important site for the Aztec was **Teotihuacán** (tay-oh-TEE-wah-khan), or "the place where the gods were born." Teotihuacán was located north of Tenochtitlán and built by an earlier people. This once-great city became sacred to the Aztec, who came later. The Aztec built onto the ruins they found there and revived worship at its many temples, including two vast pyramids dedicated to the sun and moon.

WARRIOR SCHOOLS

This Aztec sculpture depicts an Eagle Warrior. Much of the success of the Aztec Empire was due to its fierce warriors. All boys attended military training schools from a young age. At these schools, boys learned to fight in formation and use weapons.

REVIEW & ASSESS

1. **READING CHECK** Which social class in Aztec society had the most members?

2. **DRAW CONCLUSIONS** Why do you think merchants and artisans were highly respected members of the commoner class?

3. **COMPARE AND CONTRAST** In what ways were some Aztec religious practices similar to practices of other Mesoamerican cultures?

7.7.2 Study the roles of people in each society, including class structures, family life, warfare, religious beliefs and practices, and slavery; 7.7.4 Describe the artistic and oral traditions and architecture in the three civilizations.

3.3

Aztec
Defeat and Legacy

The Aztec founded thriving cities, developed rich cultures, and built a strong military. However, their empire lasted barely 200 years. It came to a sudden end when the Spanish arrived in the early 1500s.

MAIN IDEA

European invaders defeated the Aztec, who left behind a rich cultural legacy.

END OF THE EMPIRE

Aztec power depended on the empire's huge military, which conquered many people and then demanded tribute from defeated populations. Constant wars and regular rebellions, though, kept the Aztec Empire unstable. The unrest in the empire was made worse by the rule of **Moctezuma II** (mok-tih-ZOO-muh), who became emperor in 1502. He considered himself an equal to the gods. He also kept pressuring defeated peoples for more and more tribute to pay for his luxurious, wasteful lifestyle. Until 1519, he crushed one rebellion after another. Then the unthinkable happened.

That year **conquistadors** arrived from Europe. Conquistadors were Spanish conquerors who were greedy for gold and other riches from South and Central America. Although few in number, they were able to overpower the Aztec with superior weapons, such as guns and cannons, as well as horses. Aztec warriors armed with spear throwers and swords were no match for Spanish conquistadors. Spanish invaders also brought diseases such as smallpox that would eventually kill millions of native people throughout the Americas.

Believing the Spanish would liberate them from the tyranny of their rulers, some Aztec joined the conquistadors' leader, **Hernán Cortés**, in his battles. (See Cortés' route on the map in Lesson 3.1.) The conquest ended with a great siege of Tenochtitlán in 1521. The Spanish surrounded and systematically destroyed the great city. They rebuilt over the ruins, and that city became present-day Mexico City, Mexico.

AZTEC LEGACY

Because of their ruthless approach to conquest, the Spanish destroyed Aztec buildings, art, and literature. However, some Aztec ruins, artifacts, and writings survived the conquest. Archaeologists and historians study them to learn more about the Aztec.

The Aztec built huge monuments, especially temples for their gods. Aztec temples were positioned to line up with the sun and stars. The Aztec were skilled astronomers who could predict the movements of the sun, moon, planets, and stars. Like the Maya, the Aztec believed these movements directly affected their lives. They also used complex calendars to chart and record events, such as important religious rituals and the planting and harvesting of crops.

Aztec writing also gives archaeologists and historians a picture of their society. The Aztec recorded historical events, and they wrote inspiring speeches, poetry, legends, and prayers to their gods. Glyphs represented words that were painted into codices. Although few of the original codices survived, many were copied and translated by Spanish scholars. These colorful books offer a detailed and artistic picture of Aztec society.

Portrait of Montezuma II, European School, 16th century

This painting of Moctezuma II reflects how Europeans viewed him. Moctezuma expanded the Aztec Empire and made Tenochtitlán its capital city.

On your paper, match the vocabulary word in the first column with its definition in the second column.

WORD	DEFINITION
1. terrace HSS 7.7.1	**a.** a civilization that greatly influences other civilizations
2. mother culture HSS HI 3	**b.** a stepped platform built into a mountainside
3. codex HSS 7.7.4	**c.** a symbolic picture used to represent a word, syllable, or sound
4. glyph HSS 7.7.4	**d.** a Spanish conqueror who overpowered the Aztec
5. chinampa HSS 7.7.1	**e.** a folded book made from tree-bark paper
6. conquistador HSS 7.7.3	**f.** an artificial field

READING STRATEGY

7. IDENTIFY MAIN IDEAS AND DETAILS If you haven't already, complete your diagram for each Mesoamerican civilization. Then answer the question.

Main-Idea Diagram

Main Idea: Olmec Civilization
Detail: Developed along a floodplain
Detail:
Detail:
Detail:
Detail:

What feature do you think was the greatest legacy of each civilization? Explain. HSS 7.7.5

MAIN IDEAS

Answer the following questions. Support your answers with evidence from the chapter.

8. Why is the Olmec civilization considered to be Mesoamerica's mother culture? **LESSON 1.2** HSS HI 3

9. Why is Monte Albán considered one of the first major cities in Mesoamerica? **LESSON 1.3** HSS 7.7.1

10. Which groups of people made up the largest social class in the Maya civilization? **LESSON 2.1** HSS 7.7.2

11. During what time period did most of the great Maya cities develop? **LESSON 2.2** HSS CST 2

12. What did the Maya use to develop their elaborate 365-day calendar? **LESSON 2.4** HSS 7.7.5

13. Describe the class structure of society in the Aztec Empire. **LESSON 3.2** HSS 7.7.2

14. How did instability contribute to the end of the Aztec Empire? **LESSON 3.3** HSS 7.7.3

CRITICAL THINKING

Answer the following questions. Support your answers with evidence from the chapter.

15. ESSENTIAL QUESTION How did the Olmec civilization influence the Maya civilization? HSS HI 3

16. ANALYZE CAUSE AND EFFECT What happened as a result of the Olmec's trade network? HSS HI 2

17. COMPARE AND CONTRAST What are some of the similarities surrounding the decline of the Zapotec and Maya civilizations? HSS HI 2

18. COMPARE AND CONTRAST What distinguishes the Aztec from the early river valley civilizations of Mesopotamia, Egypt, India, and China? HSS HI 2

19. FORM AND SUPPORT OPINIONS In your opinion, was Moctezuma II an effective leader of the Aztec Empire? Why or why not? HSS HI 1

20. YOU DECIDE What do you think is the Maya civilization's greatest legacy? Support your opinion with evidence from the chapter. HSS REP 1

Study the images of a Maya pyramid and an ancient Egyptian pyramid. Then answer the questions that follow.

Maya pyramid

Egyptian pyramid

21. How are the pyramids alike, and how do they differ? (HSS 7.7.4)

22. What challenges did both pyramid styles present to the people who built them? (HSS 7.7.4)

ANALYZE SOURCES

This jade mask was placed over the face of King Pacal, a great ruler of Palenque, when he died. The mask shows the king's own features.

23. The Maya highly valued jade and often used it to represent the maize god. Study the mask. Why do you think the Maya associated jade with the maize god? (HSS REP 4)

WRITE ABOUT HISTORY

24. EXPLANATORY How were the Olmec, Zapotec, Maya, and Aztec civilizations similar? How did they differ? Write a paragraph comparing and contrasting the civilizations for tourists who are planning to visit some of the civilizations' archaeological and historic sites. Consider such aspects of the civilizations as religion, art, architecture, daily life, social structure, and the sciences. (HSS 7.7)

TIPS

• Take notes from the lessons about the Olmec, Zapotec, Maya, and Aztec civilizations. You might jot down your comparisons in a chart using the aspects listed above as headings in the chart.

• State your main idea clearly at the beginning of the paragraph. Support your main idea with relevant facts, details, and examples.

• Use vocabulary from the chapter in your paragraph.

• Provide a concluding statement about the similarities and differences among the Olmec, Zapotec, Maya, and Aztec civilizations.

7

SOUTH AND NORTH AMERICA

100 B.C. – A.D. 1600

ESSENTIAL QUESTION In what ways do civilizations adapt to the environments in which they live?

SECTION 1 PERUVIAN CULTURES

KEY VOCABULARY	NAMES & PLACES
geoglyph	Atahualpa
quarry	Francisco Pizarro
quinoa	Machu Picchu
terrace farming	Moche
	Nasca
	Pachacuti
	Sicán
	Wari

SECTION 2 NORTH AMERICAN CULTURES

KEY VOCABULARY	NAMES & PLACES
adobe	Algonquin
confederation	Cahokia
kiva	Cherokee
mound builder	Creek
potlatch	Great Plains
shaman	Iroquois
totem pole	Mesa Verde
wigwam	Pueblo Bonito

READING STRATEGY

ORGANIZE IDEAS: SEQUENCE EVENTS In this chapter, the sequence of historical events is divided by geographic location. First you'll learn about events in South America, and then you'll learn about events in North America. Use a time line like this one to place all the events in the chapter in order so you can see what was happening in both locations at a specific time.

PERUVIAN CULTURES

NORTH AMERICAN CULTURES

CST 1 Students explain how major events are related to one another in time; CST 2 Students construct various time lines of key events, people, and periods of the historical era they are studying.

The fine-line art that wraps around this Moche stirrup pot shows warriors running to the top of a mountain and back down again.

(Banco Central de Reserva Del Perú, Lima, Perú)

Pre-Inca Cultures

Humans have treasured gold for centuries. When people mold gold into necklaces and bracelets, the beautiful finish outshines all other metals. In the northern and western parts of South America, four cultures developed extraordinary skill in working with gold and other precious metals. These cultures lived in present-day Peru, which the Inca would dominate by A.D. 1400.

MAIN IDEA

Beginning around A.D. 100, four complex cultures thrived in Peru.

THE MOCHE AND THE NASCA

On the northwest coast of South America, the **Moche** (MOH-chay) culture flourished between A.D. 100 and 700. Their land was harsh—a desert that was squeezed between the Andes Mountains to the east and the Pacific Ocean to the west. Like other pre-Inca cultures and the Inca who came later, the Moche showed great creativity in adapting to this challenging environment. To irrigate the farm fields in their arid region, they built complex irrigation systems. They also developed a strong military and ruled nearly 400 miles of the Peruvian coast.

The Moche were also artists, as shown by the artifacts archaeologists have discovered. Moche artisans created beautiful ceramics, or bowls, statues, and other objects made from clay and then hardened under intense heat. The artisans decorated the vessels with detailed line drawings of animals and people, such as rulers and warriors. Just as impressive was Moche artists' work with gold, which they shaped into exquisite jewelry. One pair of solid gold peanuts looked just like the real things—except they were three times larger.

In south Peru, the **Nasca** culture thrived from about A.D. 200 to 600. It was one of the earliest complex cultures in South America. Nasca artisans were as highly skilled as those of the Moche culture, creating magnificent jewelry from gold, silver, and copper. They also formed ceramic pottery and decorated it with intricate designs from nature, such as birds and fish.

The Nasca left behind a mystery, though. They created enormous ==geoglyphs==, or large geometric designs and shapes drawn on the ground. The shapes often took the form of animals or birds. The dry climate where the Nasca lived helped preserve the geoglyphs. However, archaeologists are still not absolutely certain what the purpose of the designs was.

THE WARI AND THE SICÁN

The greatest military power among pre-Inca cultures was the **Wari** culture, which dominated the high desert of central Peru from about A.D. 500 to 1000. With their strong military, the Wari overran the Nasca and other people and established the first empire in the region of the Andes Mountains. The Wari were also skilled farmers. To cultivate crops on the rugged terrain of the Andes, they created terraced fields, or flat fields dug out of the sides of hills.

In a recent find at El Castillo, a Wari city along the Peruvian coast, archaeologists

Critical Viewing This giant spider geoglyph created by the Nasca still exists in the Nasca Desert of Peru. What clues in the photo reveal the geoglyph's size?

unearthed a royal tomb that revealed a great deal about Wari culture. The tomb contained the remains of four queens or princesses and other members of the nobility. Buried with the remains were golden earrings, copper axes, and silver bowls. The discovery indicates that not only did the Wari worship their ancestors but they were, like other pre-Inca cultures, gifted artisans with precious metals.

While the Wari ruled central Peru, the **Sicán** culture flourished in the mountains of northern Peru from about A.D. 800 to 1400. The Sicán created delicate jewelry from

gold, silver, and copper. They perfected a technique of pounding gold into extremely thin sheets. Archaeologists found two strips of metal that were only 0.006 inches thick—almost as thin as a piece of paper.

The Sicán showed great respect for the creatures of the natural world. Artists created a mural that was decorated with waves, fish, the sun, and the moon. When the Sicán buried the dead, they prepared them for the next world by burying them with gold, copper, and shells to carry water. This practice revealed their belief in an afterlife.

REVIEW & ASSESS

1. **READING CHECK** Where did the pre-Inca cultures live?

2. **SUMMARIZE** What have discoveries of tombs revealed about pre-Inca cultures?

3. **COMPARE AND CONTRAST** In what ways were these four pre-Inca cultures similar?

7.7.1 Study the locations, landforms, and climates of Mexico, Central America, and South America and their effects on Mayan, Aztec, and Incan economies, trade, and development of urban societies.

1.2 PERUVIAN GOLD

Pre-Inca Peruvians were master artisans who created fine jewelry and adornments with precious metals such as gold, silver, and copper. They also made pottery that was both beautiful and functional. The artifacts shown here were part of a special exhibition by the National Geographic Museum in partnership with the government of Peru. What common themes do you notice in the artifacts featured below?

Nasca Bee

Pre-Inca artisans decorated clothing with gold appliqués like this bee, which mimics a Nasca geoglyph of the same shape.
(Banco Central de Reserva Del Perú, Lima, Perú)

El Tocado

The Sicán crafted this headdress with movable parts and radiating feathers. Note the enormous gold ear spools on each side.
(Y. Yoshii/PAS)

Diadem

This Moche headpiece, called a diadem, symbolizes power and authority. It is 12 inches wide, made from a single sheet of copper, and coated with gold.
(Museo Larco Lima-Perú)

Nose Ornament
Gold and silver are fused together in this bi-metal piece. Cats, which represented strength and fierceness, made frequent appearances in pre-Inca art.
(Banco Central de Reserva Del Perú, Lima, Perú)

Moche Mask
When copper is exposed to the elements, it changes in color from a shiny red-brown to a pale green, as it did on this funeral mask.
(Museo Larco Lima-Perú)

7.7.4 Describe the artistic and oral traditions and architecture in the three civilizations.

179

Inca Society and Government

The civilization known as the Inca began as a small mountain culture that lived high in the Andes Mountains. In only a few hundred years, the Inca had conquered large parts of South America and governed a huge empire.

MAIN IDEA

The Inca created and controlled a large empire in South America.

ORGANIZED EMPIRE

About the same time as the Aztec emerged in Mesoamerica, the Inca began their conquest of western South America. In A.D. 1200, the Inca were one of many small states occupying the Urubamba Valley, high in the Andes Mountains of present-day Peru. By 1440, the Inca ruled the region.

Under the leadership of the emperor **Pachacuti** (pah-chah-KOO-tee), the empire expanded rapidly. The name *Pachacuti* means "he who changed the world"—and this ambitious man certainly did that. Pachacuti conquered and ruled widespread areas through a powerful military and a strong central government. He also transformed the Inca capital, Cusco (KOO-skoh), into an impressive stone city of 100,000 people.

The Inca Empire stretched 2,600 miles from present-day Colombia to Argentina and included about 12 million people who spoke more than 20 languages. Despite its size, the Inca Empire was well organized. The hierarchy of Inca society helped rulers maintain tight control of the large empire.

At the top, the emperor had absolute power. Below him, four regional officials called prefects oversaw provincial governors, district officers, and local chiefs. Foremen supervised ten families each and helped carry out the policies of the emperor. The Inca government viewed the empire's subjects as a resource, like gold or timber. It demanded that whole populations relocate if the state needed their labor elsewhere. Commoners farmed communal land and worked on state-owned farms while also serving in the army or on building projects.

In order to manage the many details involved in running an empire, the Inca also had a large bureaucracy, or system of state officials. In fact, for every 10,000 Inca, there were 1,331 administrators. These administrators kept detailed records about all parts of the empire, from population to farm animals to trade.

MOUNTAIN LIFE

Like other early civilizations, the Inca Empire was built on agriculture. However, farming was difficult in the steep Andes. The Inca made up for the lack of flat farmland with a type of farming called **terrace farming**. They cut flat steps, or terraces, on the sides of mountains and then built stone walls to keep the terraces in place. Terrace farming produced potatoes, maize, and **quinoa** (KEEN-wah), a high-protein grain native to the Andes. In addition to farming, the Inca raised llamas and alpacas for meat and wool and for transporting goods and people across the mountains.

Inca religious rituals centered on the need to guarantee a good harvest. The Inca worshipped their emperor as the son of Inti, the sun god, and believed the emperor helped humans communicate with the gods.

THE INCA EMPIRE, 1400–1532

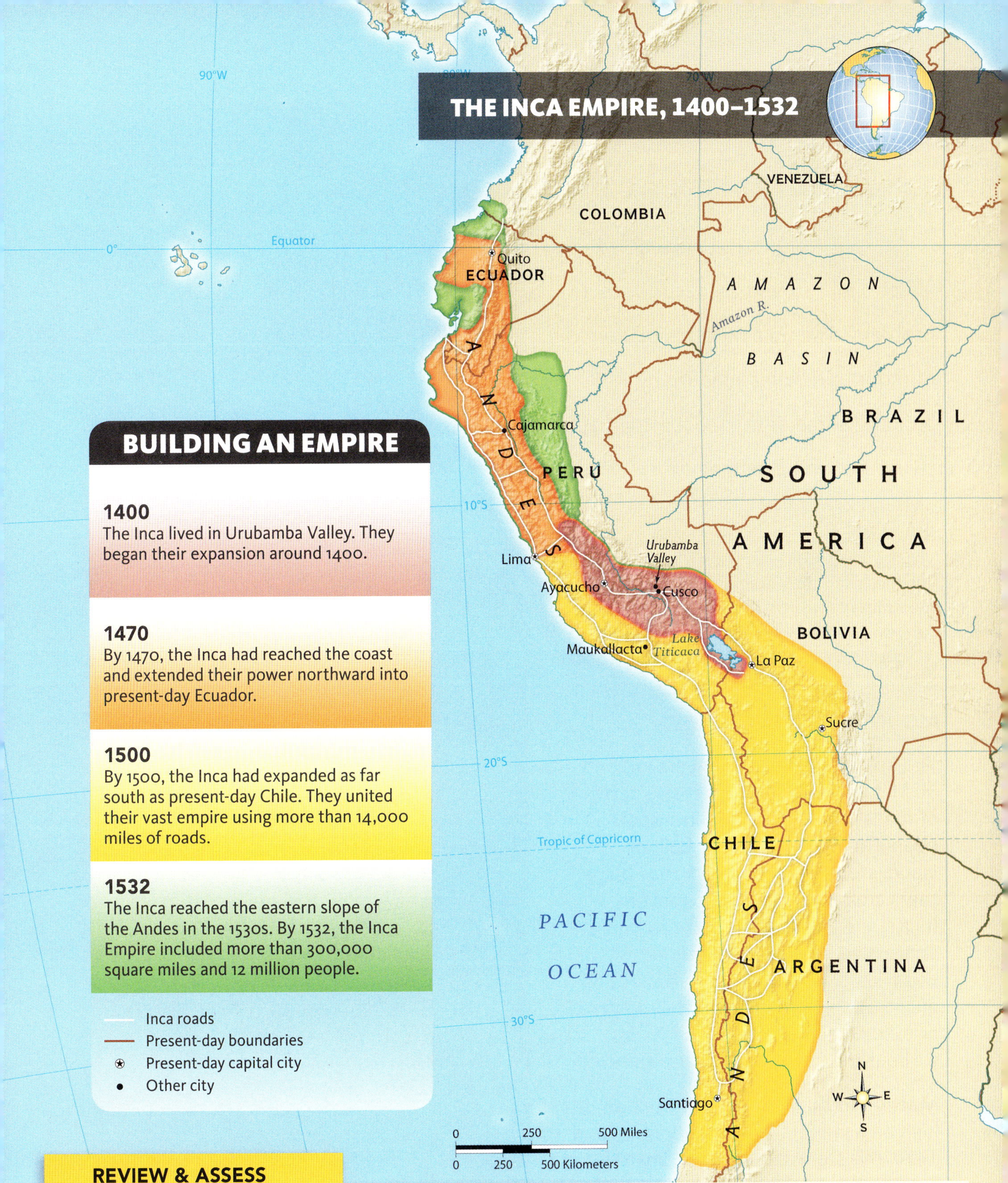

90°W
80°W
70°W
0°
Equator
10°S
20°S
Tropic of Capricorn
30°S
VENEZUELA
COLOMBIA
Quito
ECUADOR
A M A Z O N
Amazon R.
B A S I N
B R A Z I L
S O U T H
A M E R I C A
A N D E S
Cajamarca
PERU
Lima
Urubamba Valley
Ayacucho
Cusco
Lake Titicaca
Maukallacta
La Paz
BOLIVIA
Sucre
CHILE
PACIFIC OCEAN
A N D E S
ARGENTINA
Santiago
N
W
E
S
0 250 500 Miles
0 250 500 Kilometers

BUILDING AN EMPIRE

1400
The Inca lived in Urubamba Valley. They began their expansion around 1400.

1470
By 1470, the Inca had reached the coast and extended their power northward into present-day Ecuador.

1500
By 1500, the Inca had expanded as far south as present-day Chile. They united their vast empire using more than 14,000 miles of roads.

1532
The Inca reached the eastern slope of the Andes in the 1530s. By 1532, the Inca Empire included more than 300,000 square miles and 12 million people.

- Inca roads
- Present-day boundaries
- ⊛ Present-day capital city
- • Other city

REVIEW & ASSESS

1. **READING CHECK** How did Pachacuti unify and control the Inca Empire?

2. **ANALYZE CAUSE AND EFFECT** What method did the Inca use to farm in the Andes Mountains?

3. **INTERPRET MAPS** What physical features limited eastward and westward expansion of the Inca Empire?

7.7.1 Study the locations, landforms, and climates of Mexico, Central America, and South America and their effects on Mayan, Aztec, and Incan economies, trade, and development of urban societies; 7.7.2 Study the roles of people in each society, including class structures, family life, warfare, religious beliefs and practices, and slavery; 7.7.3 Explain how and where each empire arose and how the Aztec and Incan empires were defeated by the Spanish; CST 3 Students use a variety of maps and documents to identify physical and cultural features of neighborhoods, cities, states, and countries and to explain the historical migration of people, expansion and disintegration of empires, and the growth of economic systems.

1.4 Inca Architecture

What do you do when you are faced with a problem? The Inca met the challenge of mountain living head-on by building some of the most remarkable structures you can imagine.

MAIN IDEA

The Inca used their building skills to adapt to their mountain surroundings.

MOUNTAIN BUILDERS

The Inca were gifted engineers and builders. They built an extensive network of roads that helped them transport people and goods. Bridges built of wood, stone, and even thick rope helped them cross rivers and deep canyons. Inca stone architecture was even more impressive. The Inca constructed walls, buildings, and entire cities out of enormous blocks of stone. They **quarried**, or extracted, the stone in the Andes without the use of iron or steel tools.

Machu Picchu (MAH-choo PEE-choo) sits high on a mountain in Peru. Built around 1450, this stone city survived Spanish conquest in the 1530s because the Spanish never found it. Machu Picchu included religious temples, royal residences, and homes for workers as well as waterworks and terraces for farming. Aqueducts made of stone carried water to the city—just as aqueducts carried water in ancient Rome.

Critical Viewing Machu Picchu sits 8,000 feet above sea level. Why might the Inca have built this city in such a remote place?

REVIEW & ASSESS

1. **READING CHECK** Why are the Inca known as highly skilled engineers and builders?

2. **MAKE INFERENCES** How did bridges and roads help the Inca manage their empire?

3. **DRAW CONCLUSIONS** Why did Machu Picchu survive the Spanish conquest?

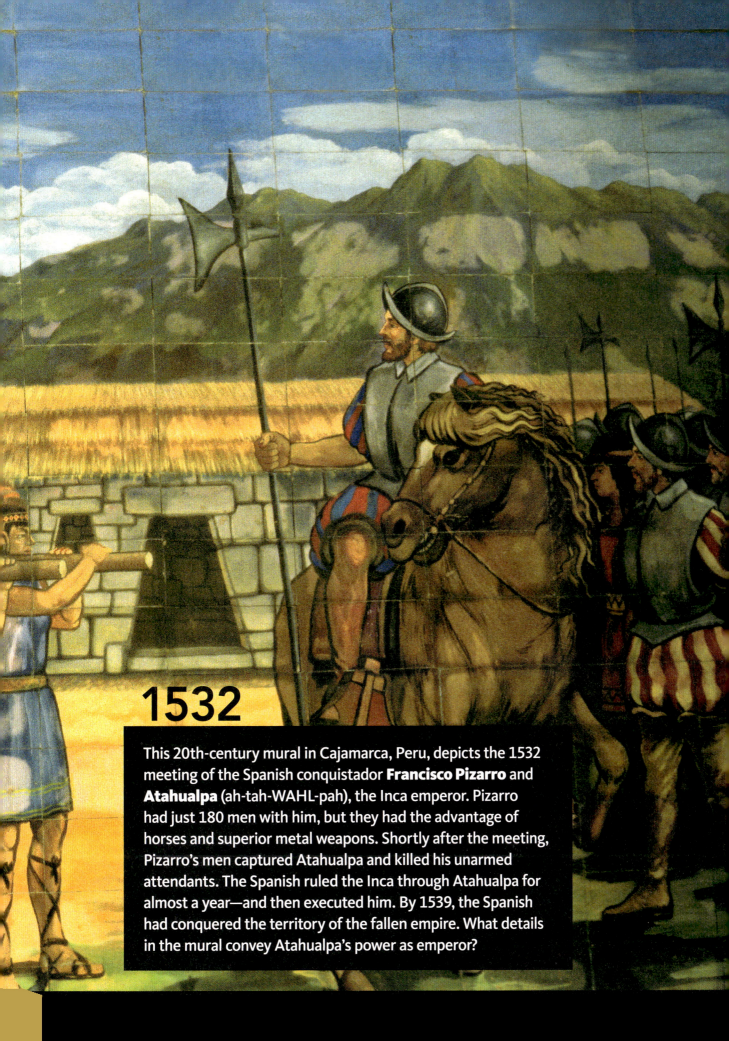

1532

This 20th-century mural in Cajamarca, Peru, depicts the 1532 meeting of the Spanish conquistador **Francisco Pizarro** and **Atahualpa** (ah-tah-WAHL-pah), the Inca emperor. Pizarro had just 180 men with him, but they had the advantage of horses and superior metal weapons. Shortly after the meeting, Pizarro's men captured Atahualpa and killed his unarmed attendants. The Spanish ruled the Inca through Atahualpa for almost a year—and then executed him. By 1539, the Spanish had conquered the territory of the fallen empire. What details in the mural convey Atahualpa's power as emperor?

Northwest Coast Cultures

North America is made up of vastly different landscapes, including rain forests, mountains, deserts, prairies, and woodlands. The hundreds of Native American cultures varied as much as North America's geography. In the Pacific Northwest, the forests and seacoast provided a hospitable environment for several cultures.

MAIN IDEA

Native American cultures of the Pacific Northwest thrived in a land of plentiful rainfall and dense forests.

NORTHWEST COAST TRIBES

Thirty distinct cultures lived in the Pacific Northwest region. This narrow strip of mountains and woodland followed the coast from present-day northern California to Alaska. It was one of the most densely populated parts of North America. The lakes, rivers, and ocean provided fish, shellfish, and whales. The forests offered plentiful plants and game. With such abundance, populations grew, and complex societies developed without any need to farm.

Along the southern coast of what is now the state of Alaska, the Tlingit (KLING–kit) people developed a thriving culture that was closely tied to the Pacific Ocean and the many rivers. In fact, the word *Tlingit* means "the People of the Tides." The Tlingit were superb sailors and fishers, and their most important food was salmon.

Because the Pacific Northwest receives ample rainfall, forests carpet the region. As a result, wood was central to Tlingit culture. Around A.D. 500, the Tlingit developed tools for splitting and carving wood. With those tools, they built permanent homes and crafted everyday necessities such as plates and utensils. They also used tools and fire to carve dugout canoes from logs. The canoes, some as long as 60 feet, were seaworthy and could sail for miles into the Pacific Ocean, allowing the Tlingit to hunt for whales.

Two other important Northwest Coast tribes—the Kwakiutl (kwahk-ee-YOU-tuhl) and the Haida (HIGH-dah)—lived south of the Tlingit. Both lived by hunting and gathering but settled in permanent villages. They used the forests' cedar trees to build large family houses. Like the Tlingit, they also built excellent seagoing canoes.

These tribes also traded extensively with neighboring cultures. Over time, trade allowed some families to become wealthy, and social classes developed. Social rank became hereditary and certain families had great influence based on their wealth and ancestry. These families demonstrated and shared wealth through gift-giving ceremonies called **potlatches**, in which they gave away gifts and food to their communities.

TOTEM POLES AND MASKS

The skillful wood carvings of Northwest Coast cultures reveal their relationship to the natural world and their belief in a spirit world. One example of their artistry is found in the intricate masks they carved and painted and then wore at ceremonies. A **shaman**, or a person who is believed to be able to help others communicate with the spirit world, guided the mask carving and led the ceremonies.

Critical Viewing These modern totem poles in southeastern Alaska demonstrate Northwest Coast cultures' wood carving tradition. What features do you see on these totem poles?

Totem poles are another example of Northwest Coast wood carving artistry. Totem poles are tall, elaborately carved and painted tree trunks that honor a revered being or guardian associated with a family. Totem pole carvings included colorful representations of animals of the region, such as bears, whales, and eagles. Other carvings included human figures, such as chiefs or ancestors and supernatural spirits. Totem poles told stories and legends as well as family and tribal histories. Wood rots easily in the region's damp climate, so few totem poles have survived more than 100 years. However, totem pole carving remains a Northwest Coast tradition today.

REVIEW & ASSESS

1. **READING CHECK** In what ways did the geography of the Pacific Northwest influence the culture of the Tlingit people?

2. **DRAW CONCLUSIONS** What was the function of the potlatch in the Kwakiutl and Haida societies?

3. **EVALUATE** What role did totem poles and masks play in the cultures of Pacific Northwest tribes?

The Ancient Pueblo

The American Southwest could not be more different from the Pacific Northwest. The Southwest is a harsh land of mountains and deserts, where temperatures can reach a scorching 120 degrees Fahrenheit. In this forbidding land, the ancient Pueblo developed a vibrant culture that was closely tied to the land.

MAIN IDEA

The ancient Pueblo adapted to their environment by farming the arid land and building complex structures.

DESERT DWELLERS

As early as 1000 B.C., the ancient Pueblo began to farm in various parts of the arid Southwest desert. They inhabited the Four Corners region, where present-day Arizona, Colorado, Utah, and New Mexico come together. Little by little, they began to build villages with permanent structures on high plateaus or in canyons. Some structures were dwellings made of stone and **adobe**, a clay used for building. Farm fields surrounded the villages. Using a technique called dry farming, the ancient Pueblo grew crops on the dry land, using very little water. The three staples of their diet were corn, beans, and squash.

The ancient Pueblo were skilled artisans who created baskets and pottery that were beautiful yet practical. They wove lightweight baskets and threaded together different materials to create brightly colored patterns. They used the baskets to carry objects and even to cook by placing hot stones in the baskets to heat the food. As they settled in permanent villages, the ancient Pueblo began to create extraordinary pottery, which was heavier but more permanent than baskets. They molded clay into jars, bowls, and pitchers.

PUEBLO BONITO AND MESA VERDE

One of the most impressive ancient Pueblo settlements was **Pueblo Bonito**, located in Chaco Canyon in northern New Mexico. It housed as many as 1,200 people and had more than 600 rooms and 30 kivas. **Kivas** were circular-shaped chambers in the ground used for ceremonies and social gatherings. Construction on Pueblo Bonito began around A.D. 850 and continued for another 200 years. The ancient Pueblo abandoned Pueblo Bonito sometime during the 1200s. Archaeologists are not sure why, but they believe that a severe drought may have forced people to migrate to other parts of the Southwest.

By 1200, the ancient Pueblo who lived in present-day southwestern Colorado built a series of dwellings into the sides of cliffs at **Mesa Verde**. They did this to defend themselves from invaders and provide protection from rain and the intense sun. Using advanced architectural skills, they built structures with several stories underneath cliff overhangs. The largest dwelling, Cliff Palace, featured more than 200 rooms and housed about 250 people. In all, the dwellings at Mesa Verde sheltered as many as 5,000 people.

The ancient Pueblo abandoned Mesa Verde by about 1300. In the late 1800s, two local ranchers discovered the ruins there, and in 1906, it became a U.S. National Park.

Critical Viewing Pueblo Bonito (top) and Mesa Verde (bottom) demonstrate the building skills of the ancient Pueblo. At both sites, individual dwellings are connected to each other. Why might the ancient Pueblo have used this building strategy?

REVIEW & ASSESS

1. **READING CHECK** How did the ancient Pueblo survive on the harsh land?

2. **DRAW CONCLUSIONS** How did the ancient Pueblo show their skill as artisans?

3. **COMPARE AND CONTRAST** In what ways were Pueblo Bonito and Mesa Verde similar? How were they different?

Peoples of the Great Plains

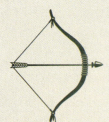

Hunting might be a sport for some people in the 21st century, but for early Great Plains cultures, hunting was key to survival. Farming on dry grasslands did not always produce good harvests. So Great Plains tribes relied on other natural resources, such as the buffalo.

MAIN IDEA

Native Americans on the Great Plains depended on the land and especially on the buffalo for survival.

PLAINS DWELLERS

The **Great Plains** is a wide area of flat, windswept grasslands that stretches north from present-day Texas into Canada. Early tribes settled along the region's major rivers and established permanent villages.

To survive the bitter winters, some tribes built earth lodges out of soil and grasses to house whole families. They relied mostly on hunting, gathering, and fishing because farming was not easy on the dry grasslands of the plains.

The different tribes of the Great Plains each had their own spiritual beliefs and traditions. Many homes had altars for burning incense during prayers. Farming communities practiced religious ceremonies centered on a good harvest. Hunting tribes had ceremonies focused on visions and spirit beings that might enhance their hunting abilities. For example, young men participated in vision quests where they put their bodies through strenuous ordeals. The goal was to achieve a trancelike state and have a vision—often of an animal. Shamans would interpret their visions.

Another important spiritual practice for Great Plains people was the Sun Dance. The Sun Dance was an annual ceremony of drumming, dancing, singing, and praying for harmony among people and giving thanks for prosperity.

BUFFALO HUNTERS

One animal was central to the livelihood and the culture of the Great Plains people— the buffalo. Large herds grazed on the wide-open grasslands, and nomadic tribes followed their migrations. These tribes had no horses, so they traveled on foot.

Because buffalo are more aggressive than cattle, they will attack if provoked. Hunting buffalo was a risky business. Hunters agitated the herd into a thunderous stampede. Then they drove the buffalo over cliffs or into corrals where they killed the animals with arrows or spears.

Buffalo were a useful resource. Great Plains people ate buffalo meat raw, roasted, or as smoked jerky. They used buffalo skins for clothes and tents, bones for tools, sinew, or tendons, for bowstrings, boiled hooves for glue, and even buffalo dung for fuel.

In the 1500s, the Spanish introduced horses to North America, and some Great Plains people began to use them to hunt. Horses allowed the tribes to follow buffalo migrations across the plains. As hunting became more efficient, more tribes moved to the plains and became buffalo hunters. White settlers in the 1800s also hunted the buffalo, resulting in its near extinction.

Critical Viewing Before 1500, about 50 million buffalo roamed freely on the plains. By 1889, commercial hunting with horses and guns had reduced buffalo numbers to just 1,000. How might this overhunting have affected tribes on the Great Plains?

REVIEW & ASSESS

1. **READING CHECK** Why were buffalo important to the people of the Great Plains?

2. **ANALYZE CAUSE AND EFFECT** How did the introduction of the horse to North America affect life for tribes on the Great Plains?

3. **COMPARE AND CONTRAST** How were the religious practices of Great Plains tribes similar? How did they differ?

The Mound Builders and Cahokia

The Mississippi River Valley and prairies and woodlands further east supported many different Native American cultures. Some built mounds, others built cities—including one of the largest cities in North America.

MAIN IDEA

Native Americans from the Great Lakes to the Gulf of Mexico developed complex societies, large cities, and organized governments.

MOUND BUILDERS

East of the Mississippi River, woodlands and prairies covered the lands that stretch between the Great Lakes and the Gulf of Mexico. Between 1000 B.C. and A.D. 500, the Adena and then the Hopewell lived in this region. They are known as mound builders because they built huge mounds of earth. The mounds served religious and ceremonial purposes. Some mounds, such as the Great Serpent Mound built by the Adena in southern Ohio, formed the shape of animals.

The mound builders relied mostly on hunting and gathering, but they also tamed wild plants and farmed crops such as barley. Maize—called corn today—appeared around A.D. 100, probably brought there by traders. The Adena and Hopewell cultures developed highly organized and complex societies. Living in villages that dotted the region, they hunted, farmed, and traded. The Hopewell culture collapsed by A.D. 500 for reasons that remain unknown.

From 800 to 1700, a different mound building culture—the Mississippians—emerged in the Mississippi River Valley. The Mississippians eventually populated the region from present-day Ohio, Indiana, and Illinois, south to the Gulf of Mexico. Like the Adena and Hopewell, Mississippians built mounds that had sloping sides, steps, and flat tops. However, the Mississippians built their mounds around a central plaza, where they held feasts and ceremonies.

The fertile floodplains of the Mississippi River Valley supported farming. Because of the fertility of their lands, the Mississippians grew ample quantities of maize, beans, and squash. They also hunted, skillfully using bows and arrows. Because of their plentiful food, Mississippian settlements supported large populations. In fact, they were the most populous Native American settlements north of Mexico.

CAHOKIA

The largest and most complex city that the mound builders created was at **Cahokia**, in southwest Illinois. Cahokia contained more than 120 mounds covering 6 square miles and supported more than 30,000 people. A series of stockades surrounded much of the city and a grand plaza provided space for ceremonies and celebrations.

The centerpiece of Cahokia was Monks Mound, which rose 100 feet above the flat prairie and covered 16 acres. This mound contained 814,000 cubic yards of soil—enough to fill 45,000 dump trucks. The Cahokians moved all this earth without the use of dump trucks, though. They used baskets instead.

Building the mounds required a highly organized society. A powerful chief who lived in a palace on top of one of the mounds ruled the city. Archaeologists believe that

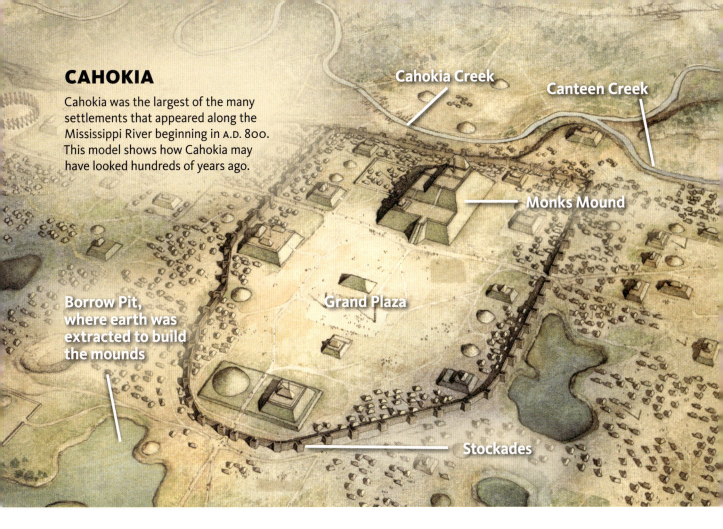

CAHOKIA

Cahokia was the largest of the many settlements that appeared along the Mississippi River beginning in A.D. 800. This model shows how Cahokia may have looked hundreds of years ago.

Cahokia Creek

Canteen Creek

Monks Mound

Grand Plaza

Borrow Pit, where earth was extracted to build the mounds

Stockades

when the chief died, the people destroyed the palace, added more earth to the mound, and built a new palace for the next ruler.

Cahokians engaged in widespread trade with other Mississippian cities and towns. Using the Mississippi River and other waterways, they exchanged freshwater pearls, silver, copper, beads, and pottery.

By 1400, Cahokia had been abandoned. Archaeologists are not sure why, but many think this once-mighty city may have been weakened by less abundant crop production, disease, overpopulation, or warfare.

Archaeologists found this artifact, called the Rattler Frog Pipe, in a burial mound near Cahokia. They think it may represent a shaman in an amphibian disguise.

REVIEW & ASSESS

1. **READING CHECK** What purposes did mounds serve in the Adena, Hopewell, and Mississippian cultures?

2. **DRAW CONCLUSIONS** How was agriculture important to the way of life of Mississippian cultures?

3. **ANALYZE VISUALS** Based on the text and illustration of Cahokia, what purpose might the stockades have served?

Cultures in the East and Southeast

Like cultures in the Pacific Northwest, Native Americans who lived on the opposite side of North America relied on the plentiful wood and game from the forests and woodlands that surrounded them. Over time, they developed sophisticated ways of governing themselves.

MAIN IDEA

Native American cultures in the East and Southeast developed complex political organizations.

THE CHEROKEE AND THE CREEK

The **Cherokee** lived in the forests of the present-day states of Georgia, Tennessee, North Carolina, and South Carolina. They built permanent log cabins using the wood from the forests that surrounded them. The Cherokee hunted deer, elk, and bear, and they also farmed, growing crops such as corn, beans, and squash.

Individual Cherokee villages formed complex alliances with each other and with other cultures. During wartime, some villages were known as "red towns," where the people held war councils and ceremonies. Other villages were considered "white towns," or towns devoted to peace. Spanish explorers arrived in the mid-1500s, and

British colonists moved into the region in the 1700s. The Cherokee traded extensively with both groups, exchanging furs and animal hides for horses, fabrics, and firearms.

The **Creek** lived south and west of the Cherokee, in what are now the states of Alabama, Mississippi, Florida, Georgia, South Carolina, and Tennessee. Like the Cherokee, the Creek formed alliances with different tribes that spoke related languages.

The Creek had great respect for fire. Each settlement had a permanent fire, which the people believed was a symbol of the life-giving powers of the sun. The female head of each household lit a fire from the village's flame and then carried it to her family. With this custom, the Creek developed a strong sense of unity within the community.

An important custom that the Cherokee and the Creek shared was the Green Corn Ceremony. Corn was an important crop for both groups. The Cherokee and Creek held this ceremony when their corn first ripened, in early to mid-summer. Over a period lasting from four to eight days, they feasted, held dances, and repaired buildings. At the height of the ceremony, they relit the sacred fire at the center of the village's plaza.

THE ALGONQUIN AND THE IROQUOIS

The **Algonquin** and **Iroquois** dominated the woodlands of the Northeast, in present-day southern Canada, upper New York, and Pennsylvania. Each culture included different tribes with their own languages and customs. The woodlands provided wood, plants, and animals, but they could not support enough farming to sustain large cities.

Instead, farmers in temporary villages relied on slash-and-burn techniques. Algonquin and Iroquois farmers burnt fields out of the forests and grew crops such as corn, beans, and squash until the soil was exhausted, or depleted of nutrients. Entire villages would then move on and create new fields elsewhere.

This reproduction shows what an Iroquois longhouse may have looked like. Like wigwams, longhouses had domed roofs and were covered with tree bark for protection.

The Algonquin lived in **wigwams**, or domed huts built on a framework of poles and covered with skins or bark. Wigwams could be quickly moved and easily adapted to the changing weather. The Algonquin farmed for much of the year, but in winter moved around because they were hunting game. Chiefs led villages made up of related families. Villages traded and formed loose **confederations**, or groups of allies, to help each other through war or hardship.

In contrast to the Algonquin, the Iroquois developed a more formal political structure. They called themselves the "people of the longhouse." They lived in villages of longhouses, in which as many as 10 families lived. Iroquois tribes fought each other until the 1500s, when they formed the Iroquois League. This agreement formally bound together five tribes—Onondaga, Seneca, Mohawk, Oneida, and Cayuga—in a representative and democratic alliance.

REVIEW & ASSESS

1. **READING CHECK** What was the function of the Green Corn Ceremony in Cherokee and Creek culture?

2. **COMPARE AND CONTRAST** How did the political structures of the Algonquin and Iroquois differ?

3. **MAKE INFERENCES** How might the Iroquois League have helped end fighting among the Iroquois tribes?

VOCABULARY

Use each of the following vocabulary words in a sentence that shows an understanding of the term's meaning.

1. quinoa HSS 7.7.1
   The Inca grew quinoa, a high-protein grain native to the Andes Mountains.

2. wigwam

3. totem pole

4. terrace farming HSS 7.7.1

5. adobe

6. confederation

7. potlatch

8. quarry

9. geoglyph HSS 7.7.1

READING STRATEGY

10. ORGANIZE IDEAS: SEQUENCE EVENTS
If you haven't already, complete your time line to sequence events that occurred in civilizations in South and North America. Then answer the question.

● A.D. 100
The Moche civilization began to flourish.

PERUVIAN CULTURES

NORTH AMERICAN CULTURES

A.D. 500 ●
The Tlingit developed tools for splitting and carving wood.

What event affected civilizations in both South and North America in the 1500s?
HSS HI 2

MAIN IDEAS

Answer the following questions. Support your answers with evidence from the chapter.

11. What have archaeologists learned about pre-Inca cultures from various discoveries in Peru? **LESSON 1.1**

12. Why did the Inca Empire develop rapidly under the leadership of Pachacuti? **LESSON 1.3**

13. What factors helped Machu Picchu survive the Spanish conquest? **LESSON 1.4**

14. On what natural resources did Northwest Coast cultures rely? **LESSON 2.1**

15. How did the beginning of pottery making signal a shift in ancient Pueblo culture? **LESSON 2.2**

16. Why were buffalo important to the people of the Great Plains? **LESSON 2.3**

17. What made it possible for the Mississippi River Valley to support large cities? **LESSON 2.4**

CRITICAL THINKING

Answer the following questions. Support your answers with evidence from the chapter.

18. **ESSENTIAL QUESTION** Were the cultures in South and North America successful in adapting to their environments? Explain your answer.

19. **COMPARE AND CONTRAST** Consider what you know about early civilizations in north Africa and Asia. What distinguishes pre-Inca civilizations from the early river valley civilizations of Mesopotamia, Egypt, India, and China?

20. **MAKE INFERENCES** Why was a network of roads important to the success of the Inca Empire?

21. **ANALYZE CAUSE AND EFFECT** How were complex societies in the Pacific Northwest able to develop and grow without farming?

22. **YOU DECIDE** Did the size of the Inca Empire contribute to its fall? Support your opinion with evidence from the chapter.

INTERPRET VISUALS

Study the photograph showing farming terraces built by the Inca. Then answer the questions that follow.

23. Use details in the photo to describe the method of terrace farming the Inca used. HSS 7.7.1

24. Why might Inca farmers have preferred flat surfaces on which to grow crops? HSS 7.7.1

ANALYZE SOURCES

While on an expedition in the Andes in 1911, American explorer Hiram Bingham and his guide discovered a city that had been hidden for nearly 400 years: Machu Picchu. Read the passage and then answer the question.

> We were confronted with an unexpected sight, a great flight of beautifully constructed stone-faced terraces, perhaps a hundred of them, each hundreds of feet long and ten feet high. . . . The flowing lines, the symmetrical arrangement of the [large stones], and the gradual gradation of the [layers], combined to produce a wonderful effect, softer and more pleasing than that of the marble temples of the Old World.
>
> from *Lost City of the Incas*, by Hiram Bingham, 1952

25. What were Bingham's impressions of the architecture at Machu Picchu? HSS REP 4

WRITE ABOUT HISTORY

26. INFORMATIVE Suppose you are contributing to a booklet about Native American cultures. Write a paragraph that explores the impact of the Spanish use of guns and horses on the Great Plains peoples. Use the tips below to plan, organize, and revise your paragraph. HSS HI 2

TIPS

- Take notes from the lesson about the Great Plains peoples.
- Begin the paragraph with a clear topic sentence.
- Develop the paragraph with supporting details.
- Use vocabulary from the chapter as appropriate.
- Conclude with a general statement about the effect of guns and horses on the lives of the Great Plains peoples.
- Use word-processing software to produce and publish your final paragraph.

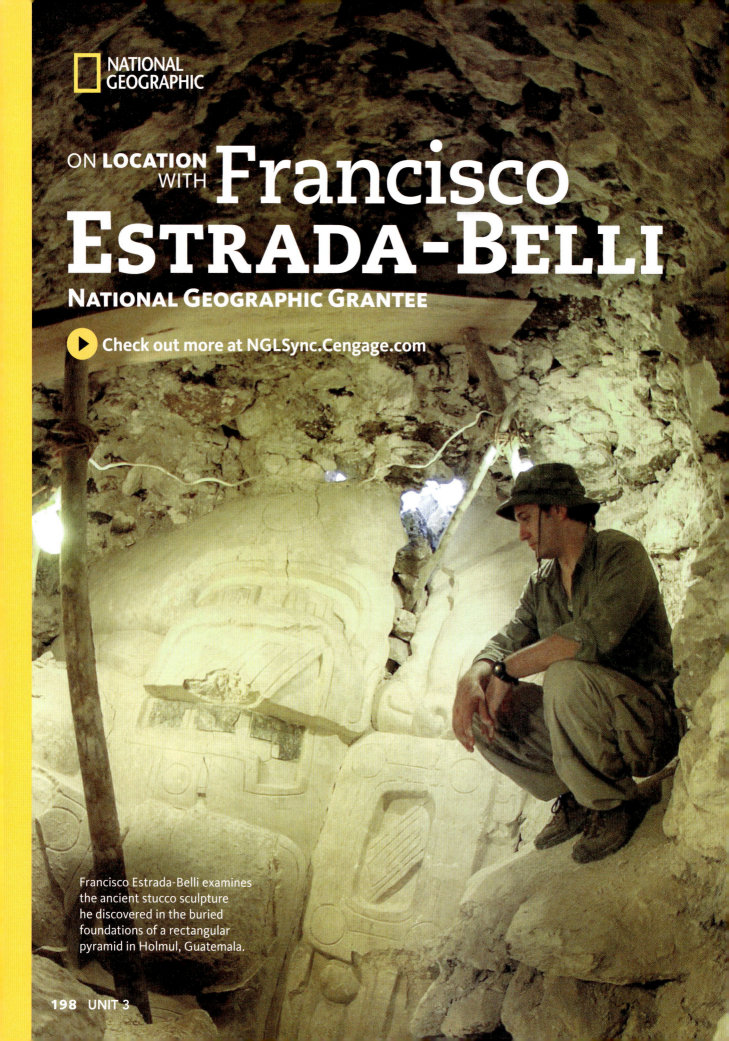

ON **LOCATION** WITH Francisco ESTRADA-BELLI

NATIONAL GEOGRAPHIC GRANTEE

▶ Check out more at NGLSync.Cengage.com

Francisco Estrada-Belli examines the ancient stucco sculpture he discovered in the buried foundations of a rectangular pyramid in Holmul, Guatemala.

HIDDEN CITIES

Exploring lost Mayan cities hidden deep in the jungles of Guatemala—that's my job! Every year we discover additional sites to explore to learn more about the Maya civilization, which thrived in Central America for nearly 1,500 years. It seems incredible, but in Guatemala you can still hack your way through the vegetation and come face-to-face with a long lost city.

As a child I visited the magnificent Mayan ruins of Tikal. I had so many questions! How did the Maya build such a great civilization in a jungle? Why did they leave their city? That's why I became an archaeologist: to try and answer some of those questions. I wanted to shed light on the beginnings of Maya civilization, so I chose to study the buried Maya city of Holmul, which had been partially excavated a hundred years ago and then forgotten. It was a good place to start. Exploring nearby, I found another lost Maya city called Cival. This turned out to be one of the earliest cities the Maya built, around 800 B.C. This was over 1,000 years before classic Maya civilization blossomed in cities like Tikal. By showing the complexity and innovation of early Maya settlements, including their architecture, our findings challenge the common belief that the early Maya were simple village farmers.

BURIED SCULPTURES

We've made many important discoveries, including a massive sculpture buried beneath a temple's rubble at Holmul. The site already had been ransacked by looters,

Archaeology can be messy. Here, Estrada-Belli uses a tractor to tow a car through the muddy Guatemalan jungle.

and if they had dug for another ten minutes, they might have found the sculpture. It's amazingly well-preserved—it even has a little color left on it—and it had almost been lost forever. That makes me feel as if we really rescued the past. I feel like I have made a really important contribution.

I love sharing all this new knowledge with others, not just academics but ordinary people and students. I want to help the modern Maya who live in the area, especially the children, reconnect with their glorious Maya past. Right now, they have little or no knowledge of their heritage, and I believe that people who know their past can live a better life.

WHY STUDY HISTORY ❓

❝ The past is irreplaceable, but the past is disappearing because of development, looting, and erosion. I study history because *the past is not a luxury, but instead a necessity* for cultures and for humanity as a whole to be able to live in peace. ❞   — Francisco Estrada-Belli

NATIONAL GEOGRAPHIC

Unburying the Aztec

BY ROBERT DRAPER

Adapted from "Unburying the Aztec," by Robert Draper, in *National Geographic*, November 2010

Archaeologists reassemble an earth goddess monolith at Templo Mayor.

Archaeologist Leonardo López Luján might be on the verge of a major discovery. Since the Spanish conquest of Mexico in 1521, no Aztec emperor's remains have been discovered. Yet historical records say that three Aztec rulers were cremated and their ashes buried at the foot of Templo Mayor, in present-day Mexico City.

In 2008, López Luján unearthed a 12-ton monolith representing an earth goddess near Templo Mayor. Immediately, López Luján noticed that the monolith depicted a figure holding a rabbit, with ten dots above it. In the Aztec writing system, 10-Rabbit is 1502— the year that the empire's most feared ruler, Ahuitzotl (ah-WEE-tzoh-tuhl), died. López Luján is convinced that Ahuitzotl's tomb is somewhere near where the monolith was found.

Aztec power was fleeting. They ruled their empire for less than a century before the Spanish demolished it. The Aztec maintained what some scholars call "a cheap empire." The conquered were allowed to continue governing themselves as long as they paid tribute.

Ahuitzotl assumed the throne in 1486. As the eighth emperor, he stretched the empire to its breaking point. His armies made 45 conquests over 16 years, conquering areas along the Pacific coast, down into present-day Guatemala. He also sealed off trade from rivals to the west and increased control over subjugated territories. "He was more forceful, more brutal," says archaeologist Raúl Arana. "When people didn't want to pay tribute, he sent in the military. With Ahuitzotl, the Aztec went to the maximum expression of everything. And perhaps it was too much. All empires have a limit."

López Luján's work at the Templo Mayor site is slow, partly because of the challenges excavating in a modern city. Urban archaeologists have to dig around sewer and subway lines, avoid underground telephone, fiber optic, and electric cables, and maintain security for a dig in the middle of a city. "Sooner or later, we'll find Ahuitzotl's tomb," López Luján hopes. Whether or not he does, the Aztec mystique will continue to occupy modern Mexico's imagination.

For more from National Geographic
Check out "People of the Horse" at NGLSync.Cengage.com

UNIT INQUIRY: DESIGN AN ADAPTATION STRATEGY

In this unit, you learned how civilizations in North and South America adapted to the environments in which they lived. Based on your understanding of the text, what were the environments like in which these different civilizations lived? In what ways did people adapt to survive or become better suited to their environment?

ASSIGNMENT Design an adaptation strategy that you think would be helpful to people moving to a new environment. The strategy should identify the specific environment, such as a new school, neighborhood, or city. The strategy should also include a series of actions/steps people could take to adapt to their new environment. Be prepared to present your strategy to the class and explain how it will help people adapt successfully to the new environment.

Plan As you design your strategy, think about the role adaptation has played in the survival and success of past civilizations. Adaptation—no matter when and where it occurs—does not happen overnight. Think about the steps that would ensure successful adaptation in a new environment today. You might want to use a graphic organizer to help organize your thoughts. ▶

Produce Use your notes to produce descriptions of the elements of your adaptation strategy. You might want to write them in outline or paragraph form.

Present Choose a creative way to present your strategy for adaptation to the class. Consider one of these options:

- Create a multimedia presentation using photos to illustrate the series of actions/steps in your strategy.

- Write a slogan for your strategy that communicates the importance of successful adaptation in a new environment.

- Describe how a potential problem or difficulty in the new environment might be turned into an opportunity.

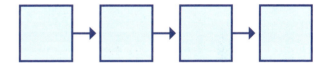

RAPID REVIEW
UNIT 3

AMERICAN CIVILIZATIONS

TOP TEN

1. The Maya developed an advanced writing system, and they studied mathematics and astronomy.
2. The Aztec Empire grew powerful through conquest by its formidable army.
3. Spanish conquistadors used steel weapons and horses to overthrow the Aztec and the Inca.
4. The Inca established a massive empire that included more than 12 million people.
5. The Mississippians built many cities in the Mississippi River Valley, including Cahokia.

6-10. NOW IT'S YOUR TURN Complete the list with five more things to remember about American civilizations.

TO UNDERSTAND THE SIMILARITIES AND DIFFERENCES AMONG CIVILIZATIONS

You just plowed through three units introducing civilizations with similar but different languages, cultures, and religions. As global citizens, our call to action is to understand that each civilization has its own unique identity. Recognizing the inherent worth and equality of all civilizations and cultures—and, in fact, of all people—is at the heart of global citizenship.

On the Framework of World History chart at the beginning of this text, the civilizations in Unit 1 fall under "World Systems." The Roman, Byzantine, and Islamic civilizations continued to build on the foundations that early civilizations had established. Some of the civilizations in Africa and the Americas fall under the second and third levels of that chart. Yet all these civilizations established sophisticated cultures. Understanding the similarities and differences among them is one reason we study history.

Fred Hiebert
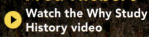 **Watch the Why Study History video**

WHAT COMES NEXT? PREVIEW UNITS 4–5

4

HORSE RACE, MONGOLIA

EMPIRES OF ASIA

Follow the inventions and advancements in technology that would open the globe to exploration and trade, cause an explosion in communication, and make human conflict more deadly.

5

SAN GIOVANNI

MEDIEVAL, RENAISSANCE, AND REVOLUTIONARY EUROPE

Learn how the cultures and empires of medieval and early modern Europe further developed technology and artistic expression to set the stage for today's modern, global world.

KEY TAKEAWAYS UNITS 1–3

PATTERNS IN HISTORY: SIMILAR DEVELOPMENTS ACROSS LOCATIONS

- Continued environmental adaptations in Africa and the Americas improve agricultural production.
- Trade takes off on a global scale, including trans-Saharan movement of gold and salt and Indian Ocean trade between East Africa and Asia.

GOVERNMENT

- In Europe, the Justinian Code preserves basic concepts of Roman law.
- Mighty empires form in Mali and Aksum in Africa.
- In the Americas, the Maya and Inca rise to power.

MOVEMENT OF PEOPLE AND IDEAS

- Roman culture spreads through colonization and trade.
- As a trading crossroads, the Byzantine capital of Constantinople becomes a center of cultural diversity.
- Islamic culture spreads through trade and conquest.

ARTISTIC EXPRESSION

- In Europe, new art forms include mosaics and frescoes of ancient Rome and calligraphy and arabesques of Islam.
- The Nok in Africa produce terra cotta sculptures.

TECHNOLOGY & INNOVATION

Engineering and architectural developments include

- improved concrete and arches from ancient Rome
- the iron technology of the Nok
- the monumental structures of the Maya, Aztec, and Inca

These massive Roman aqueducts in Segovia, Spain, are evidence of ancient Roman technological advances in arch-building.

AS YOU READ ON

You've got a whole backdrop of complex civilizations to draw on as you read about key civilizations in Asia in Unit 4. Think about how these civilizations helped set the stage for the deep changes that would occur by the 1600s (Unit 5).

Remember that as global citizens, you know that throughout history all civilizations made enduring contributions to the human community. The diversity of those cultures and their contributions is what makes our world a rich and exciting place to live.

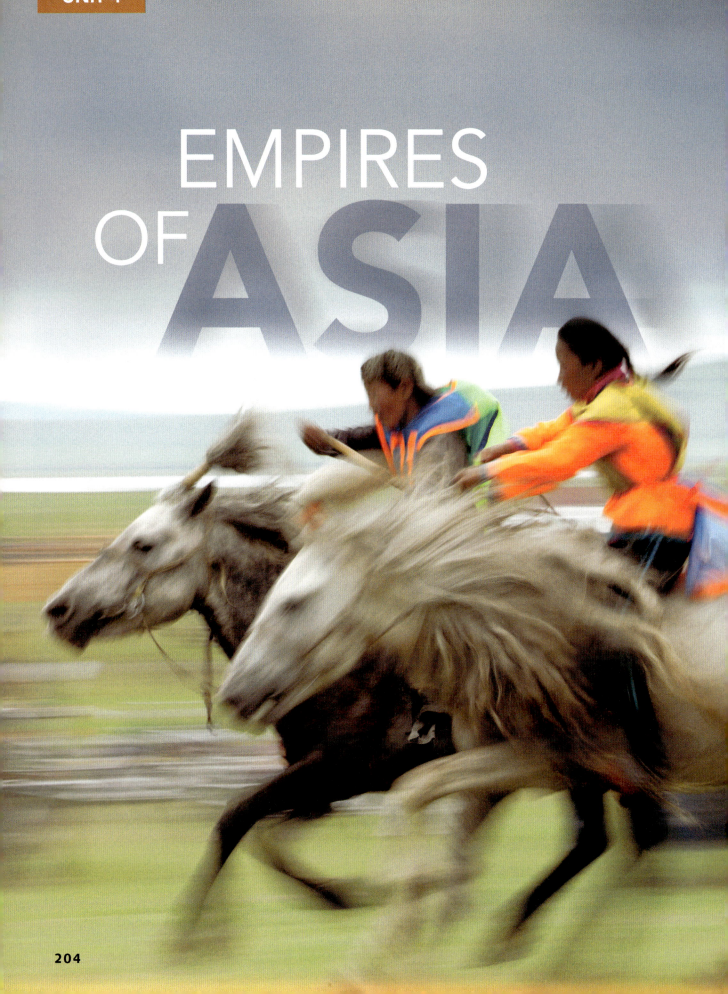

EMPIRES OF ASIA

ON **LOCATION** WITH

Albert Lin
Research Scientist/Engineer

Looking for the unknown burial ground of the Mongol emperor Genghis Khan is a big challenge. The vast and unending steppe landscape of Mongolia makes it hard to know where to search. Add to that the fact that the Mongolians consider the tomb of their great leader to be sacred and off-limits to the traditional methods of archaeology— digging in the earth. I'm Albert Lin, and I'm using innovative technology such as satellite imagery and remote sensors to search for Genghis Khan's tomb without ever touching a shovel.

< CRITICAL VIEWING Children race horses across Central Mongolia during a summer festival. What can you infer about the geography of this region?

UNIT 4

TIME LINE OF WORLD EVENTS

Asian Civilizations

China, Japan, Korea, India, and Southeast Asia

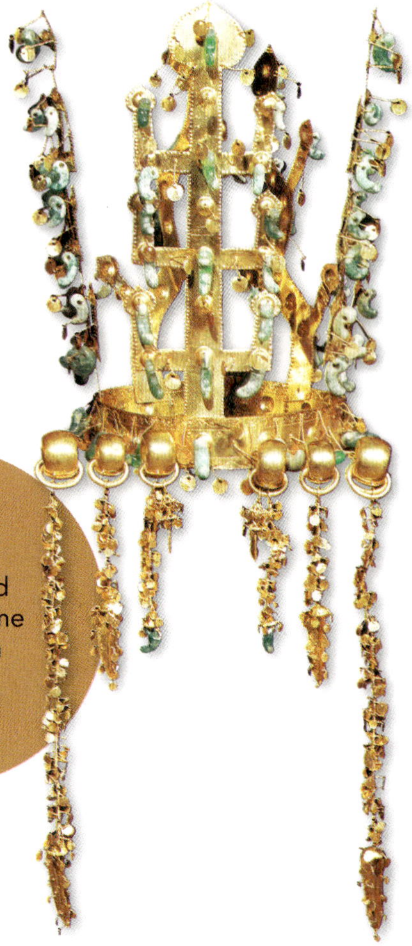

500

c. 570
ASIA
The prophet Muhammad is born in Mecca.

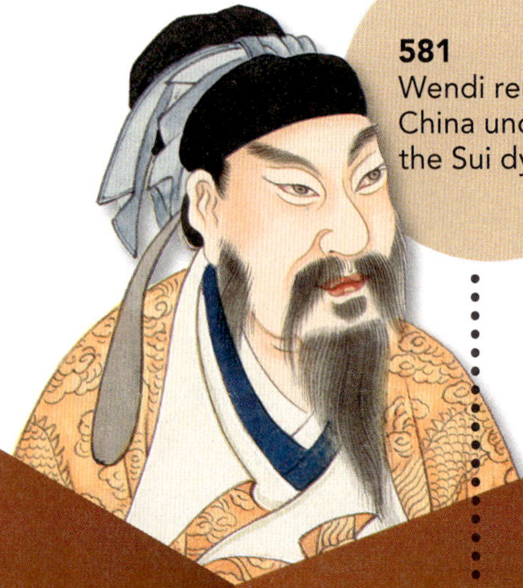

581
Wendi reunifies China under the Sui dynasty.

676
Korea is united for the first time under the Silla kingdom.
(Silla crown)

800
EUROPE
Charlemagne becomes the first Holy Roman Emperor.

900

938
The Dai Viet state (Vietnam) gains independence from China.

1000

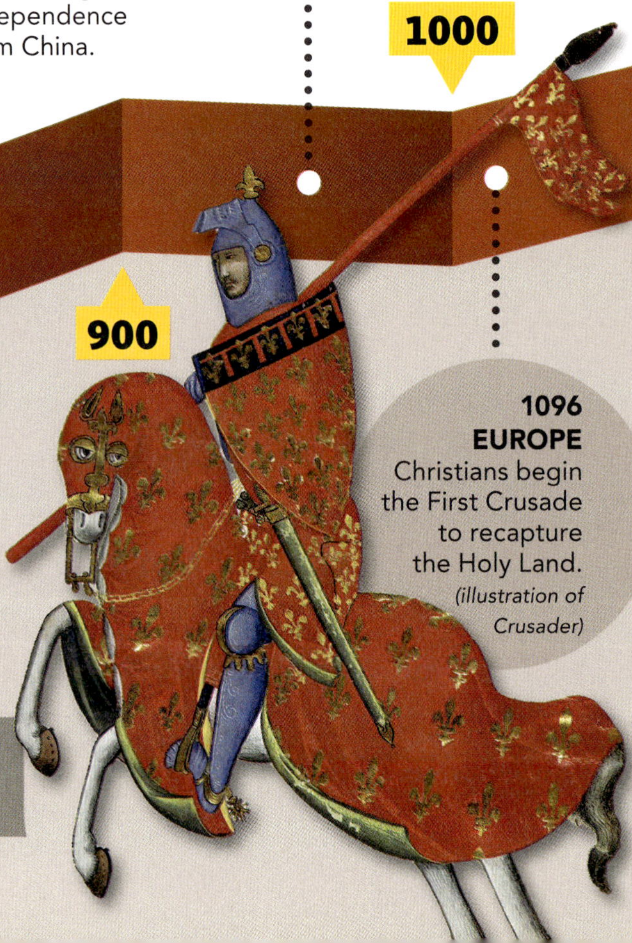

1096
EUROPE
Christians begin the First Crusade to recapture the Holy Land.
(illustration of Crusader)

The World

CST 1 Students explain how major events are related to one another in time.

What Asian civilizations did the Mongols invade and conquer for a time?

1206
The Delhi Sultanate is established in northern India after years of invasions by Muslim Turks.

1603
Tokugawa Ieyasu establishes a shogunate.
(samurai helmet)

1912
Revolutionary forces overthrow the Qing dynasty.

1867
Tokugawa shogunate is overthrown and the emperor takes control of Japan.

1392
The Choson dynasty emerges in Korea after nearly 100 years of Mongol rule.

1209
The Mongols, led by Genghis Khan, invade northern China.

1644
The Manchus overthrow the Ming and found the Qing dynasty.

1800

1400

1230
AFRICA
Sundiata Keita founds the Empire of Mali.

1453
EUROPE
The Turks gain control of Constantinople, ending the Byzantine Empire.
(Hagia Sophia, Istanbul)

1776
AMERICAS
The American colonies declare their independence.

1884–1885
AFRICA
Africa is divided up among European nations at the Berlin Conference.

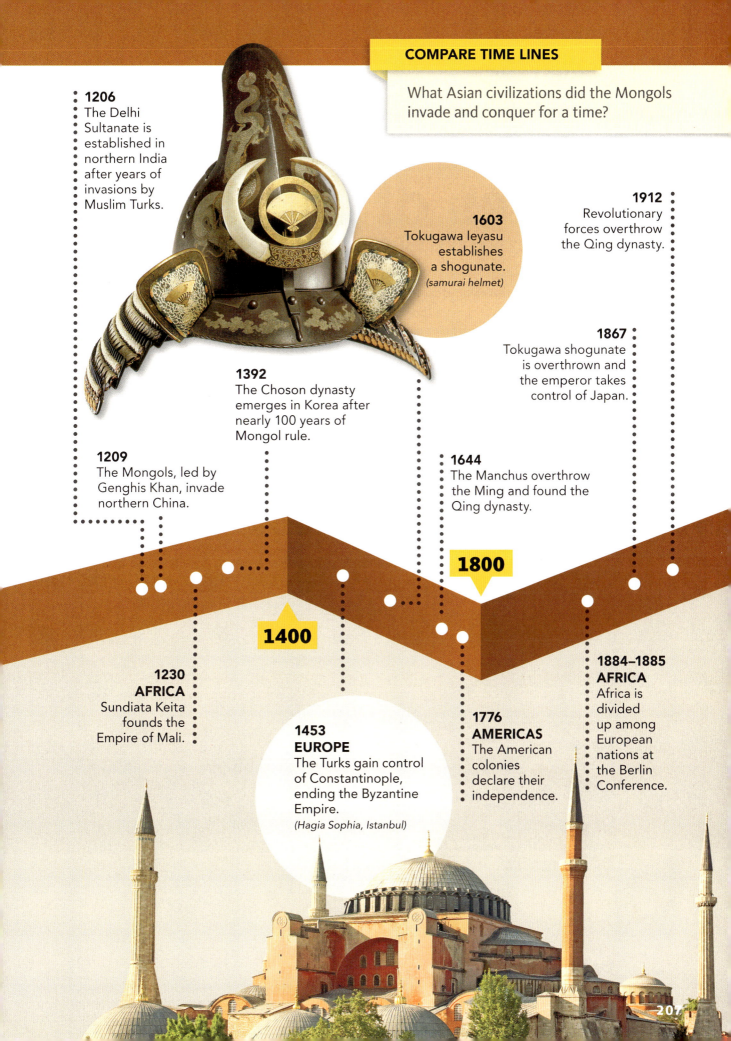

207

Empires of Asia

1000–1300

Between 1100 and 1200, many great empires existed almost side by side in Asia. The Song dynasty, with its many inventions and booming economy, made China the world's most advanced society of the time. Chinese ideas had influenced kingdoms on the Korean Peninsula for centuries. However, the Koryu dynasty adapted Chinese practices, including the idea of a centralized government, to meet their own needs. In the 1200s, both China and the Koryu were conquered by the Mongols, who would establish the largest land empire in history.

East of the Korean Peninsula lay Japan, which was under military rule in the 1100s. In the strictly structured society of Japan at that time, armies of samurai fought to protect their ruler. In the south, the Chola Empire ruled over much of southern India and established maritime trade networks, while northern India was conquered by Muslim Turks from Central Asia. The southeast was dominated by the prosperous Khmer Empire. Only the Dai Viet also ruled in the region. This state began a thousand years of independence for Vietnam.

Where were most of the Asian empires located?

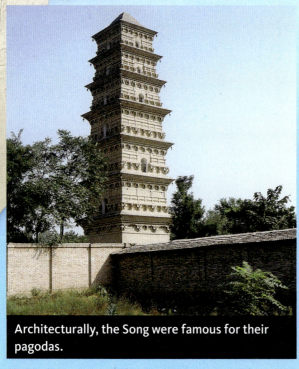

Architecturally, the Song were famous for their pagodas.

CST 3 Students use a variety of maps and documents to identify physical and cultural features of neighborhoods, cities, states, and countries and to explain the historical migration of people, expansion and disintegration of empires, and the growth of economic systems.

Empires of Asia

	Chola, 1050
	Delhi Sultanate, 1300
	Japan, 1100
	Khmer, 1100
	Koryu Dynasty (Korea), 1100
	Mongol homeland, 1200
	Song Dynasty (China), 1100
	Dai Viet (Vietnam), 1200
	Grand Canal
	Great Wall

MONGOL HOMELAND

Karakorum

G O B I

SONG DYNASTY (CHINA)

Huang He (Yellow R.)

Huang He (Yellow R.)

Kaifeng

Yangzhou

Chang Jiang (Yangtze R.)

Chang Jiang (Yangtze R.)

Hangzhou

Yangtze R.

Mekong R.

Guangzhou

DAI VIET (VIETNAM)

Hanoi

Hainan

KHMER

Angkor

Mekong R.

KORYU DYNASTY (KOREA)

Yellow Sea

East China Sea

Sea of Japan

JAPAN

Heian (Kyoto)

PACIFIC OCEAN

South China Sea

Philippines

Borneo

Sumatra

Celebes

Java

0   200   400   600   800 kilometers

0   200   400   600   800 miles

8

DYNASTIES OF CHINA

581 – 1912

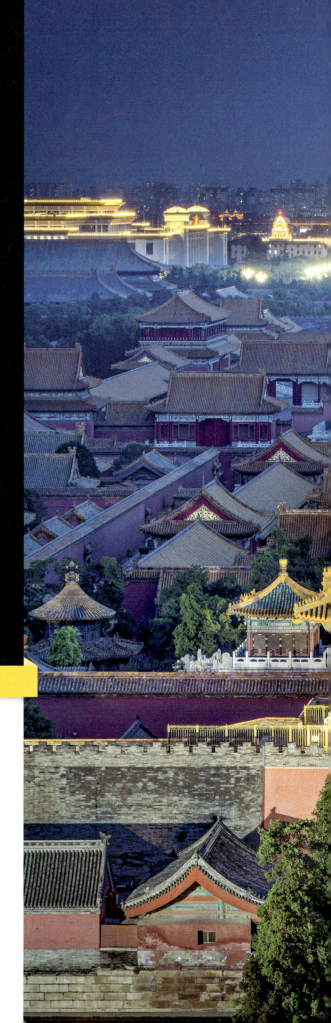

ESSENTIAL QUESTION What legacy did China leave to the modern world?

SECTION 1 A GOLDEN AGE OF PROSPERITY

KEY VOCABULARY	NAMES & PLACES
commerce	Song
movable type	Sui
nirvana	Taizong
porcelain	Tang
reincarnation	Wendi
reunify	Yangdi
staple	

SECTION 2 THE MONGOL EMPIRE

KEY VOCABULARY	NAMES & PLACES
khanate	Genghis Khan
steppe	Kublai Khan
	Marco Polo
	Yuan

SECTION 3 THE MING DYNASTY

KEY VOCABULARY	NAMES & PLACES
isolationism	Hongwu
	Manchus
	Ming
	Qing
	Yongle
	Zheng He

READING STRATEGY

DRAW CONCLUSIONS When you draw conclusions, you support them with evidence from the text. Use a graphic organizer like this one to draw conclusions about the impact of the Tang, Song, and Ming dynasties on Chinese civilization.

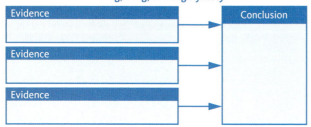

Tang, Song, or Ming Dynasty

Evidence	→	Conclusion
Evidence	→	
Evidence	→	

The north gate of Beijing's Forbidden City, known as the Gate of Divine Prowess, served as an entrance and exit for China's empresses.

Reunification
Under the
Sui Dynasty

 A famous Chinese proverb says, "After a long split, a union will occur; after a long union, a split will occur." This saying reflects the belief that Chinese history has been a series of cycles alternating between strength and weakness. After a period of unrest, a strong leader establishes a powerful dynasty. It flourishes and then eventually declines until the people rebel and a new dynasty gains power. This dynastic cycle is a repeating theme in Chinese history.

MAIN IDEA

The short-lived Sui dynasty reunified China after centuries of civil war.

WENDI'S RULE

The Han dynasty, which began its rule of China in 206 B.C., ruled China for centuries, until weak rulers, rebellions, and powerful warlords caused its collapse in A.D. 220. China was plunged into nearly 400 years of civil war among many small kingdoms. The state belief system of Confucianism declined, though its ethical ideals and Chinese culture survived.

Then, in 581, the dynastic cycle turned again. A general named **Wendi** seized power and established a new dynasty called the **Sui** (sway). Wendi's conquests allowed him to **reunify**, or join together again, northern and southern China. He then faced the enormous challenge of restoring order across a vast and culturally diverse land.

To reunify China, Wendi strengthened the central government, limiting the power of local nobles and the bureaucracy. The government selected new officials by written examination and made sure they better reflected China's diverse ethnic groups. The military was organized and brought under Wendi's control.

Wendi also issued a new law code that combined northern and southern traditions. He gave farming land to former soldiers, established agriculture in the border regions of the empire, and extended the canal system. Wendi encouraged religious tolerance but also promoted the popular religion of Buddhism. When he died unexpectedly in 604, he left a strong empire for his son and successor, **Yangdi**.

THE GRAND CANAL

Yangdi loved luxury and built extravagant palaces in his new eastern capital at Luoyang (lu-WOH-YAHNG). Yangdi extended some of his father's useful public projects, such as restoring and expanding the Great Wall to help protect China's long and vulnerable northern border, and building state granaries to protect the food supply.

He also built the Grand Canal, connecting the southern Chang Jiang with the northern Huang He. This incredible 1,200-mile waterway had a road alongside it and became a vital communication link. It united China's economy, allowing southern China's plentiful resources to flow north where the government and armies were located. However, it came at a cost. Millions of peasants were forced to work on it, and many of them died.

Beijing

Luoyang

Xi'an

Huang He (Yellow R.)

Grand Canal

Yangzhou

CHINA

Chian Jiang (Yangtze R.)

Hangzhou

Yellow Sea

East China Sea

PACIFIC OCEAN

South China Sea

N
W E
S

INDIAN OCEAN

▨	Sui dynasty, 581–618
▨	Tang dynasty, 618–907
—	Grand Canal
⋌⋌⋌	Great Wall
—	Boundary of modern China

0   200   400 Miles

0   200   400 Kilometers

The people of China hated this forced labor and the high taxes imposed by both Wendi and Yangdi to pay for such projects. Yangdi also launched expensive and unsuccessful wars against Korea. The military campaign required more money and service from his unhappy subjects.

Yangdi grew increasingly unpopular until, in 611, a famine finally pushed the people to rebel. It was the dynastic cycle at work. Rich and poor rose up against Yangdi's harsh rule, and he was assassinated. The Sui dynasty proved to be short-lived. In 618, a new dynasty—the Tang—rose to power. These leaders would continue to unify China.

REVIEW & ASSESS

1. **READING CHECK** What is the Sui dynasty known for?

2. **MAKE INFERENCES** How did the Sui dynasty reflect the pattern of the dynastic cycle?

3. **INTERPRET MAPS** How might the Grand Canal have improved China's trade network?

7.3.1 Describe the reunification of China under the Tang Dynasty and reasons for the spread of Buddhism in Tang China, Korea, and Japan; CST 3 Students use a variety of maps and documents to identify physical and cultural features of neighborhoods, cities, states, and countries and to explain the historical migration of people, expansion and disintegration of empires, and the growth of economic systems; HI 6 Students interpret basic indicators of economic performance and conduct cost-benefit analyses of economic and political issues.

The Spread of Buddhism

When bad things happen, it's common to question our beliefs and re-examine our understanding of the world. In trying to make sense of the suffering, we might find comfort in the spirituality of religion—the belief that a higher power can end the misery. The Chinese people found comfort in religion when they most needed it.

MAIN IDEA

In troubled times, many Chinese turned to Buddhism.

BUDDHISM IN CHINA

The collapse of the Han dynasty in A.D. 220 plunged China into chaos for a period that would last hundreds of years. In such troubled times, many Chinese turned from the practical belief system known as Confucianism to a new, more spiritual religion—Buddhism.

As you learned in Chapter 6, Buddhism was based on an understanding of life founded by Siddhartha Gautama in India around 500 B.C. He taught that the keys to a good life were revealed in the Four Noble Truths: Life is full of suffering; the cause of suffering is desire and ignorance; to end the cycle of desire is to end suffering; and one can be free of desires by following the Eightfold Path. The path promoted a balanced life in which the sum of a person's deeds, or karma, results in reincarnation, or rebirth, into another life. Through good karma over successive lifetimes, a person could reach the state of nirvana—an end of reincarnation and the suffering of life.

Foreign traders and missionaries brought Buddhism to China during the first century A.D. During the collapse of the Han dynasty and the civil war that followed, Buddhism's teachings provided comfort and offered a clear path beyond suffering. Buddhist texts were translated, and Buddhist practices were adapted into a distinctive Chinese form, which became very popular among all classes of people.

Over the following centuries, Buddhism's popularity rose and declined, but emperors often promoted it to gain the people's support, as Wendi had done. This promotion included building magnificent monuments and not taxing Buddhist religious lands. Meanwhile, Buddhism continued to spread rapidly across the east and southeast areas of Asia, especially Korea and Japan.

IMPACT ON CONFUCIANISM

After the chaotic period of civil war ended, Confucianism made a comeback during the 600s. The government reintroduced traditional Confucian-style tests for the civil service. Confucian principles of respect, responsibility, loyalty, and duty to family and the state became popular once again.

In contrast, Buddhism encouraged moral behavior but played down the importance of obedience to outside authority in favor of inner guidance. Daoism, which emphasized our essential unity with nature, also had a strong following. These three competing belief systems became interwoven. Confucianism's concern with earthly duty influenced the religious spirituality of Buddhism and Daoism. As a result, Confucianism once more emerged as an important part of Chinese society.

Critical Viewing This Buddhist cave painting from China shows a seated figure meditating. What do the details in this painting suggest about Buddhism?

REVIEW & ASSESS

1. **READING CHECK** After the collapse of the Han dynasty, why did many Chinese turned to Buddhism?

2. **SEQUENCE EVENTS** How was Buddhism first introduced in China?

3. **COMPARE AND CONTRAST** How do the main principles of Confucianism and Buddhism differ?

7.3.1 Describe the reunification of China under the Tang Dynasty and reasons for the spread of Buddhism in Tang China, Korea, and Japan; 7.3.3 Analyze the influences of Confucianism and changes in Confucian thought during the Sung and Mongol periods; CST 1 Students explain how major events are related to one another in time.

1.3 Tang and Song Dynasties

A picture is worth a thousand words—but it often does not last as long. Only words remain to capture the brilliance of Chinese painting from this era. For example, legend tells how the acclaimed Tang artist Wu Daozi (woo dow-dzuh) painted a mural that was so lifelike, he walked into it and disappeared forever.

MAIN IDEA

Under the Tang and Song dynasties, China grew and prospered.

THE TANG DYNASTY

Although unpopular, the Sui dynasty established solid foundations of government for future dynasties to build on. After the rulers of the **Tang** dynasty seized power in 618, they continued the project of reunifying China, which had begun under the short-lived Sui dynasty. They encouraged economic growth through agricultural reform and trade. The dynasty also strengthened the government by using civil service examinations to select government officials. These well-educated scholar-officials carried out government policy. They helped keep the government stable from one emperor to the next.

These reforms helped the Tang expand the empire into central and southern Asia.

(See the map in Lesson 1.1.) Meanwhile, literature and art flourished in a golden age. Few paintings survive, but beautiful sculptures reveal the talent of the artists of this period. Also, around 48,000 poems exist from this time. Tang officials were encouraged to write poetry.

Taizong (ty-johng) was the second Tang emperor and an admired figure in Chinese history. From 626 to 649, he used Confucian ideas to organize his government. Later, Wu Zhao (woo jow), the wife of Taizong's son and successor Gaozong, became China's only official female emperor by ruthlessly eliminating her rivals, including her own children. Despite the stormy succession, Wu Zhao had inherited a peaceful and well-run country. Her policies were sensible, improved the life of the people, and helped strengthen the empire. Later Tang emperors were less successful. Political instability sparked a long civil war in which millions died. Poor rulers, corruption, and rebellion weakened Tang authority until the dynasty lost power in 907. Once again, China plunged into chaos.

THE SONG DYNASTY

In 960, over 50 years later, the **Song** dynasty restored order. Though the Song rulers did not expand the territory of the empire, they introduced domestic improvements that made Song China the world's most advanced society of the time. Confucianism again became the state philosophy. Art and literature thrived while technology led to new inventions. Agriculture expanded with new techniques in drainage, irrigation, and terrace farming. Strains of rice from Southeast Asia doubled the harvest, and rice became China's **staple**, or main crop. In a short period, from 750 to 1100, China's population doubled to 100 million.

Meanwhile, this growth led to more rapid trade, and China's economy boomed. Farmers grew sugar cane, tea, bamboo, and hemp for trade, and the traditional crafts of

7.3.1 Describe the reunification of China under the Tang Dynasty and reasons for the spread of Buddhism in Tang China, Korea, and Japan; 7.3.2 Describe agricultural, technological, and commercial developments during the Tang and Sung

silk, paper, and ceramics grew in popularity. Improved roads and canals carried goods within China, while bigger ships carried exports overseas. For the first time, the state made more money from trade than from agriculture. Because of the strong economy, China started banks and printed the world's first paper money. Economic prosperity led to the growth of cities, which became busy centers of culture and **commerce**, or the buying and selling of goods.

REVIEW & ASSESS

1. READING CHECK How did China change during the Song dynasty?

2. MAKE INFERENCES How did reforms introduced under the Tang dynasty contribute to China's golden age?

3. ANALYZE CAUSE AND EFFECT How did the growth of trade during the Song dynasty affect China?

periods; 7.3.5 Describe the development of the imperial state and the scholar-official class; HI 2 Students understand and distinguish cause, effect, sequence, and correlation in historical events, including the long- and short-term causal relations; HI 6 Students interpret basic indicators of economic performance and conduct cost-benefit analyses of economic and political issues.

The **Legacy** of **Chinese Inventions**

Imagine using dimes to buy a car. Maybe you'd start counting but soon give up. Dollar bills are far more convenient. Printed money was a Chinese invention, as were printed books, porcelain, navigational compasses, and gunpowder. All these new inventions were created during the Tang and Song dynasties. It's difficult to imagine our world without these items.

MAIN IDEA

Chinese inventions have helped shape the world we live in today.

PRINTING AND PAPER MONEY

The Chinese had invented paper around A.D. 100. About five hundred years later, they contributed another bookmaking breakthrough—block printing. This technique involved carving the text in reverse to stand out on a block of wood. The block was painted with ink and pressed onto paper to create a printed page. Carving the blocks for each page of each book was a long process.

Around 1041, the innovation of **movable type**, which used individually carved characters, made it easier and cheaper to print books. The new widespread distribution of books helped spread government regulations, literature, and the ideas of Confucianism and Buddhism.

Meanwhile, China's booming population and economy created a large demand for coins—by 1085 six billion coins were minted per year. The coins were too bulky for large transactions, so merchants began exchanging paper notes as IOUs. The money stayed in a bank but was owned by whoever held the note. Around 1100, the first government-backed currency was issued. Over time, the use of bank seals and increasingly complex designs helped discourage counterfeiting.

GUNPOWDER, THE MAGNETIC COMPASS, AND PORCELAIN

Gunpowder was an accidental discovery by Chinese alchemists attempting to turn worthless metals into gold. These early chemists found that sulfur, saltpeter, and charcoal made a powerful explosive when mixed together. The military found that gunpowder confined in an iron tube could shoot objects great distances. This discovery led to the development of cannons, guns, and fireworks. Later, Chinese armies used gunpowder in Central Asia, and the secret spread.

The Chinese had long used magnetic compasses for ceremonies, but in the 1100s they began using them for navigation. A sliver of magnetized iron hanging from a silk thread or floating in water would point north and south. This property allowed sailors to tell their direction without the sun or stars. Longer sea journeys also became possible, which increased China's maritime trade.

One especially prized trade item was **porcelain**—a strong, light, and nearly see-through ceramic. Porcelain's closely guarded secret was the blending of unique minerals and a glaze at very high temperatures. Because of these secret techniques, porcelain—or china, as it came to be called—was incredibly rare and precious.

CHINESE INVENTIONS

Antique block characters for printing

Song porcelain vase with celadon glaze

Movable Type

The Chinese created block characters for use in movable type, a development that made printing easier. Artisans carved characters as individual clay tablets that could be arranged on a board to form text. After printing, the characters could be reused.

Porcelain

Techniques for creating porcelain were perfected during the Tang dynasty and reached the height of artistry under the Song. The formula used to create porcelain was a closely guarded secret.

Ancient Chinese nautical compass

Fireworks display

Compass

The ancient Chinese had developed a compass that was used in rituals. During the Song dynasty, they discovered the secret to making a magnetic compass used for navigation.

Gunpowder

After the invention of gunpowder, the military experimented with explosive arrows, grenades, rockets, and land mines, and finally developed firearms and fireworks.

REVIEW & ASSESS

1. **READING CHECK** What inventions occurred during the Tang and Song dynasties?

2. **DRAW CONCLUSIONS** Why did the invention of movable type help increase the spread of ideas?

3. **ANALYZE CAUSE AND EFFECT** How did the use of magnetic compasses for navigation affect China's trade?

7.3.2 Describe agricultural, technological, and commercial developments during the Tang and Sung periods; 7.3.5 Trace the historic influence of such discoveries as tea, the manufacture of paper, wood-block printing, the compass, and gunpowder; HI 2 Students understand and distinguish cause, effect, sequence, and correlation in historical events, including the long- and short-term causal relations.

GENGHIS
KHAN

A.D. **1162 – 1227**

Forget Rome or Britain. It was the Mongols who ruled the largest land empire in history. It stretched from present-day Korea to Hungary and included more than 100 million people of widely differing cultures. And the Mongols conquered all this territory in less than 100 years, thanks to the determination of one man—Genghis Khan.

💼 **Job:** Universal ruler
✏️ **Education:** His harsh childhood
🌐 **Home:** Near the Onon River
　　 Real Name: Temujin

FINEST HOUR

When he died, Genghis Khan had united the nomadic tribes, conquered China, and extended his rule over all of central Asia.

WORST MOMENT

The death of his father, a defeated Mongol chieftain, left young Temujin and his mother to eke out a living on the harsh steppe.

FRIENDS

Jamuka was a friend and rival whom Temujin later defeated to become universal ruler.

TRIVIA

It is said that Temujin was born grasping a clot of blood in his hand, which has been viewed throughout history as a mixed sign—an omen of his future fame (and notoriety).

THE MONGOL CONQUEST

The Mongols were a loose collection of independent nomadic tribes from the **steppes**—or vast, grassy plains—of northwest China. They spent their lives roaming, raiding, herding, and fighting across this landscape.

A child named Temujin (TEH-moo-juhn) was born on this landscape. He was the son of a defeated Mongol chieftain, and his childhood was harsh. However, Temujin was ambitious, clever, charismatic, and a great warrior. He became a tribal leader and, in 1206, the Mongol people gave him the title **Genghis Khan** (JEHNG-gihs KAHN), meaning "universal ruler."

Despite conflicts among the tribes, there was one thing they all needed—more grazing lands. Genghis Khan organized the diverse bands into a powerful military machine that would sweep mercilessly across Asia in one of history's most impressive conquests.

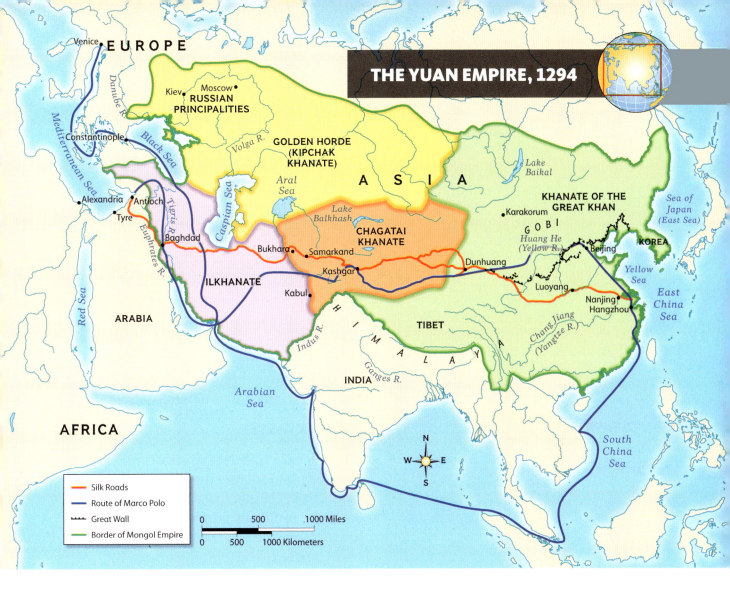

Legend:
- Silk Roads
- Route of Marco Polo
- Great Wall
- Border of Mongol Empire

In 1212, Genghis Khan and the Mongols invaded northern China, destroying more than 90 cities and killing their inhabitants. Turning west, he destroyed an empire in what is now Iran. He then invaded southern Russia and, in 1215, destroyed China's capital.

When Genghis Khan died around 1226, he had conquered much of central Asia. Four of his sons shared his vast empire, dividing it into four **khanates**, or regions, and expanded their rule into Europe and southern China.

KUBLAI KHAN

China's next great leader was Genghis Khan's grandson, **Kublai Khan** (KOO-bluh KAHN). He rose to become leader of the Mongol Empire in 1264. Kublai Khan was determined to add to his empire by conquering all of southern China. By 1271, he had succeeded, giving the Mongols control over most of China. That year he declared himself emperor, adopting the dynastic name **Yuan** (yoo-ahn) and preparing to help his army meet new challenges.

REVIEW & ASSESS

1. **READING CHECK** How did the Mongols gain power?

2. **COMPARE AND CONTRAST** How were Genghis and Kublai Khan alike?

3. **INTERPRET MAPS** Which cities in the northwest were part of the Mongol Empire?

CST 3 Students use a variety of maps and documents to identify physical and cultural features of neighborhoods, cities, states, and countries and to explain the historical migration of people, expansion and disintegration of empires, and the growth of economic systems.

Life in Yuan China

You love your country but hate your rulers. The Mongols are in charge, and they discriminate against you. You pay higher taxes than foreigners, receive less justice, and are excluded from the best jobs—all because you're Chinese.

MAIN IDEA

The Mongols set up strict rules to control China.

YUAN GOVERNMENT

Kublai Khan adopted a less destructive approach to governing than that of his predecessors, trying to win over the Chinese people and preserve conquered towns instead of destroying them. Even so, any resistance was brutally punished. During the 1270s, Song loyalists continued to fight the Mongols in southern China. The Mongols defeated the Song uprising of 200,000 troops—and then killed the entire population of Hangzhou (hahng-joh) city. To avoid further suffering, remaining officials of the Song dynasty surrendered in 1279.

Kublai Khan was now ruler of all China—the first to unite all China since the end of the Tang dynasty, which ended in 907—and its first foreign ruler ever. He would rule for 15 years, until his death in 1294. His Yuan dynasty led China for a century, but it was not an easy time for the Chinese.

The Mongols were more used to fighting than governing, and controlling a country as large and sophisticated as China demanded a highly organized government. Under the Yuan dynasty, Chinese government continued much as before, with a strong central state built around a bureaucracy with Confucian rituals and ceremonies.

The big difference was that the Mongols excluded Chinese people from higher positions to stop them from having too much power. Instead, Mongols and foreigners, especially Muslims, received the top jobs. Foreigners migrated to China, including the famous Italian merchant **Marco Polo**, who served as a tax collector and special envoy to the emperor. However, Chinese scholars still had a strong unofficial influence, and Kublai Khan relied on Chinese advisors.

SOCIAL CLASSES

Most Chinese hated living under the Mongols, who treated them as second-class citizens in their own country. Society was divided into four classes. At the top were the Mongols, followed by non-Chinese foreigners. Then came the northern Chinese, who had lived longest under Yuan rule. At the very bottom of society were the southern Chinese, who made up 80 percent of the population.

Many peasant farmers in the bottom bracket of society were forced off their land when they could not pay their taxes. Unable to feed their families, many sold themselves into slavery far from home. The government forced peasants to work on extravagant imperial projects. The Yuan dynasty rebuilt Beijing as a wealthy city filled with magnificent palaces and pleasure gardens enjoyed by rich foreigners.

All this luxury came at a cost for the Chinese. The Mongols feared rebellion because of the pressures they placed on the Chinese. Looking for signs of revolt, agents working for the government kept a close eye on neighborhoods. They forced

7.3.3 Analyze the influences of Confucianism and changes in Confucian thought during the Sung and Mongol periods; 7.3.4 Understand the importance of both overland trade and maritime expeditions between China and other civilizations

People in China still use the Grand Canal, shown in this photograph, to move goods up and down the river.

every ten Chinese families to share a single knife. The government banned meetings and fairs and prevented the Chinese from going out at night or playing sports, thinking it was too much like military exercise.

The Yuan dynasty did make significant contributions, though. During its reign, trade and agriculture expanded. The Yuan built roads and extended the Grand Canal. The Mongol postal service provided efficient communication, and the government introduced an accurate calendar of 365.2

days. Also, with many Chinese scholars out of work, they had more time to write, and Chinese literature flourished.

Still, the Chinese remained hostile to Mongol rule and formed secret societies to plot rebellions. After Kublai Khan's death in 1294, the Yuan dynasty gradually declined. There were seven emperors in 40 years, none of them as gifted as Kublai Khan. Rebellions started to break out, and, by 1368, China was poised for yet another change in dynasties.

REVIEW & ASSESS

1. **READING CHECK** How did the Mongols treat the Chinese under their rule?

2. **MAKE INFERENCES** Why did Kublai Khan exclude the Chinese from important jobs in government?

3. **ANALYZE CAUSE AND EFFECT** Under the Yuan dynasty, how did the Mongols open China to foreigners?

in the Mongol Ascendancy and Ming Dynasty; 7.8.3 Understand the effects of the reopining of the ancient "Silk Road" between Europe and China, including Marco Polo's travels and the location of his routes.

223

Travels on the
Silk Roads

Under the Mongols, China continued to produce goods that were popular all around the world, especially silk and porcelain. The Mongols wanted to encourage commerce, and their control of China and all the lands that connected it to Europe helped trade flourish. The ancient trade routes, the Silk Roads, were revitalized, and new routes reached north to the Mongol capital of Karakorum. From here, great caravans could now travel in safety and ease across the lush plains that had previously been too dangerous because of tribal wars and banditry.

In this illustration from Marco Polo's book of his travels, traders bring spices from the western part of the Mongol Empire to the east.

from *Book of the Wonders of the World* by **Marco Polo and Rustichello, 15th century**

from *Genghis Khan and the Making of the Modern World* by Jack Weatherford

Anthropologist Jack Weatherford presents a fairly positive view of the rule of the Mongols. Silk was one of China's most valued exports, and here Weatherford notes how Genghis Khan shaped its distribution.

CONSTRUCTED RESPONSE Why might the people living on the steppes benefit from Genghis Khan's rerouting of exports through their territory?

> A river of brightly colored silk flowed out of China. It was as though Genghis Khan had rerouted all the different twisting channels of the Silk Route, combined them into one large stream, and redirected it northward to spill out across the Mongol steppes.

---

from *Travels* by Marco Polo

Marco Polo was a merchant from Venice whose adventures in Asia have become the most celebrated of the medieval world. His colorful descriptions of life in Mongol China paint a vivid picture of the court of Kublai Khan.

CONSTRUCTED RESPONSE Why would using experts to determine prices make trade fairer and easier?

> Several times a year, parties of traders arrive with pearls and precious stones and gold and silver and other valuables, such as cloth of gold and silk, and surrender them all to the Great [Kublai] Khan. The Khan then summons twelve experts . . . and bids them examine the wares that the traders have bought and pay for them what they judge to be their true value.

Passport Medallion, c. 1300

Kublai Khan issued a medallion like the one at right to Marco Polo before he set off on his travels. It acted as a passport, helping Marco Polo access difficult areas and secure help and supplies from subjects of the Khan.

CONSTRUCTED RESPONSE How might Marco Polo have helped expand China's foreign contact and trade during the Mongol Empire?

SYNTHESIZE & WRITE

1. **REVIEW** Review what you have learned about the Mongol Empire.

2. **RECALL** On your own paper, write down the main idea expressed through each document and artifact.

3. **CONSTRUCT** Write a topic sentence that answers this question: During the Mongol Empire, how did Genghis Khan and Kublai Khan promote and increase trade?

4. **WRITE** Using evidence from the documents and artifact, write an informative paragraph to support the answer to the question in Step 3.

7.8.3 Understand the effects of the reopening of the ancient "Silk Road" between Europe and China, including Marco Polo's travels and the location of his routes; REP 4 Students assess the credibility of primary and secondary sources and draw sound conclusions from them.

Return to Chinese Rule

After a challenging period of Mongol rule, the Chinese people found an unlikely rescuer in a peasant who led China's rebellion. China's next two emperors set out to restore the country to greatness. The Ming dynasty's capital was a spectacular new seat of power that would be used continuously for 500 years.

MAIN IDEA

The Ming dynasty restored China to greatness.

A NEW LEADERSHIP

By the 1360s, Mongol rule had weakened and rebellions broke out. The son of a peasant, Zhu Yuanzhang (joo yoo-ahn-jahng), emerged as a leader. In 1368, the rebels began driving the Mongols north of the Great Wall, eventually bringing an end to Mongol rule. Zhu declared himself **Hongwu** (hung-woo), or the first emperor of the **Ming** dynasty.

The Chinese again ruled China, and Hongwu set out to restore the country to greatness. He could be paranoid, controlling, and cruel, but he worked hard to improve the lives of peasants. Hongwu rebuilt China's agriculture system and supported the growth of manufacturing. He cut government spending and established efficient taxation. He based his rule on the principles of the Tang and Song dynasties and strengthened the system of civil service exams that were used to select scholar-officials to operate the government.

Hongwu's son **Yongle** (yung-loh) was, like his father, a suspicious, ruthless, and tyrannical ruler. However, he also effectively continued his father's work rebuilding China. Yongle sponsored sea expeditions and encouraged local governments to build schools for commoners. He also sponsored great literary works and led armies to suppress China's neighbors.

IMPERIAL PALACE

Like many Chinese emperors, Yongle moved the imperial capital—this time north, to Beijing. This location placed Yongle near his supporters and closer to his armies guarding China's borders. Beijing was well organized. It was laid out in a grid aligned with the points of the compass and surrounded by 14 miles of 40-foot walls. To feed the vast numbers of people who flocked to the capital, Yongle extended the Grand Canal even farther, using advanced engineering to carry boats uphill.

At Beijing's heart was the Imperial Palace, or Forbidden City—so named because few were admitted and only with the emperor's permission. The Forbidden City would be the center of imperial power and government for the next 500 years. It took an estimated one million workers nearly 15 years to complete the palace, which was an architectural marvel. The huge complex boasted hundreds of buildings that towered over Beijing. It included luxurious private residences for the imperial family and more than 100,000 servants. The city's rectangular, symmetrical, and compass-aligned design was said to be in perfect harmony with the world. It remains the world's largest palace—the perfect place for the emperor to fulfill his role as a connection between the will of heaven and the practical rule of Earth.

FORBIDDEN CITY

Governments are often housed in imposing buildings that reflect the power of politics. But few are as impressive as the Imperial Palace in Beijing.

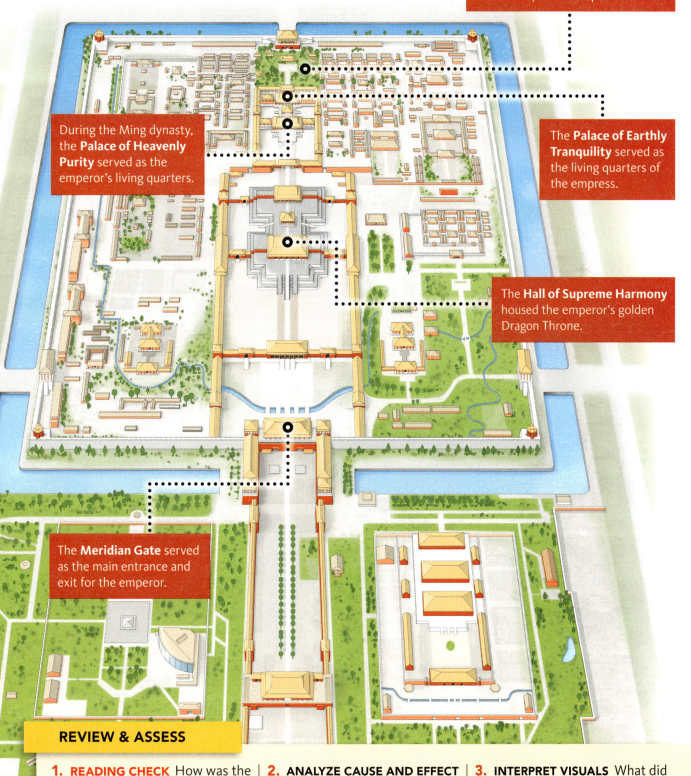

The **Imperial Garden** was filled with fragrant flowers, plants, and trees as well as sculptures and pavilions.

During the Ming dynasty, the **Palace of Heavenly Purity** served as the emperor's living quarters.

The **Palace of Earthly Tranquility** served as the living quarters of the empress.

The **Hall of Supreme Harmony** housed the emperor's golden Dragon Throne.

The **Meridian Gate** served as the main entrance and exit for the emperor.

7.3.6 Describe the development of the imperial state and the scholar-official class; HI 2 Students understand and distinguish cause, effect, sequence, and correlation in historical events, including the long- and short-term causal relations.

227

Zheng He's Explorations

The sea beckoned to a young Chinese Muslim named **Zheng He** (jung huh), who rose through the ranks of the navy and, in 1405, began a series of seven voyages to Asia and Africa. His success was built on the accuracy of Chinese navigation—the best in the world.

MAIN IDEA

Chinese ships and navigational tools allowed China to spread its power and influence by sea.

THE VOYAGES OF ZHENG HE

Zheng He's expeditions included more than 300 ships and nearly 30,000 sailors. This show of force was about more than exploration and trade. It also communicated political power. Zheng He's main mission was to glorify Yongle by asserting Chinese control over trade routes and weaker countries. For three decades, Zheng He sailed 40,000 miles around Southeast Asia, East Africa, and the Middle East.

His ships returned to China laden with treasure and exotic luxuries such as gold, gems, rare spices, giraffes, and zebras. These expeditions established China's international reputation as goods and ideas were exchanged with more countries than ever before. However, not everyone was happy that China was reaching out to other lands.

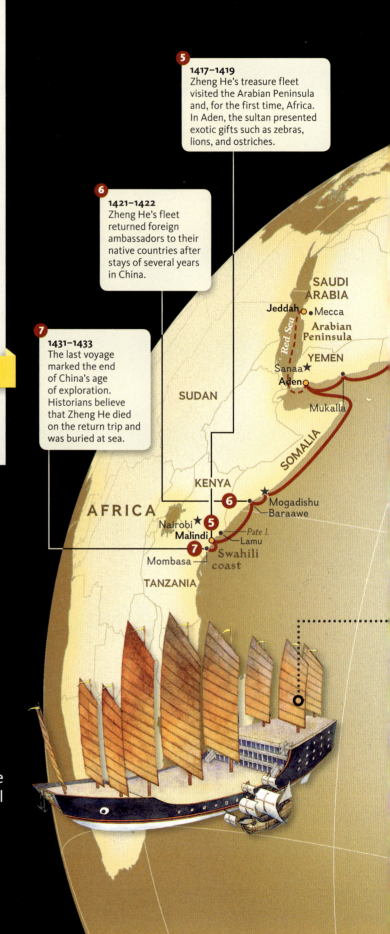

5 1417–1419
Zheng He's treasure fleet visited the Arabian Peninsula and, for the first time, Africa. In Aden, the sultan presented exotic gifts such as zebras, lions, and ostriches.

6 1421–1422
Zheng He's fleet returned foreign ambassadors to their native countries after stays of several years in China.

7 1431–1433
The last voyage marked the end of China's age of exploration. Historians believe that Zheng He died on the return trip and was buried at sea.

SAUDI ARABIA
Jeddah • Mecca
Arabian Peninsula
Red Sea
YEMEN
Sanaa ★
Aden
Mukalla
SUDAN
SOMALIA
AFRICA
KENYA
Mogadishu
Baraawe
Nairobi ★
Malindi
Pate I.
Lamu
Mombasa
Swahili coast
TANZANIA

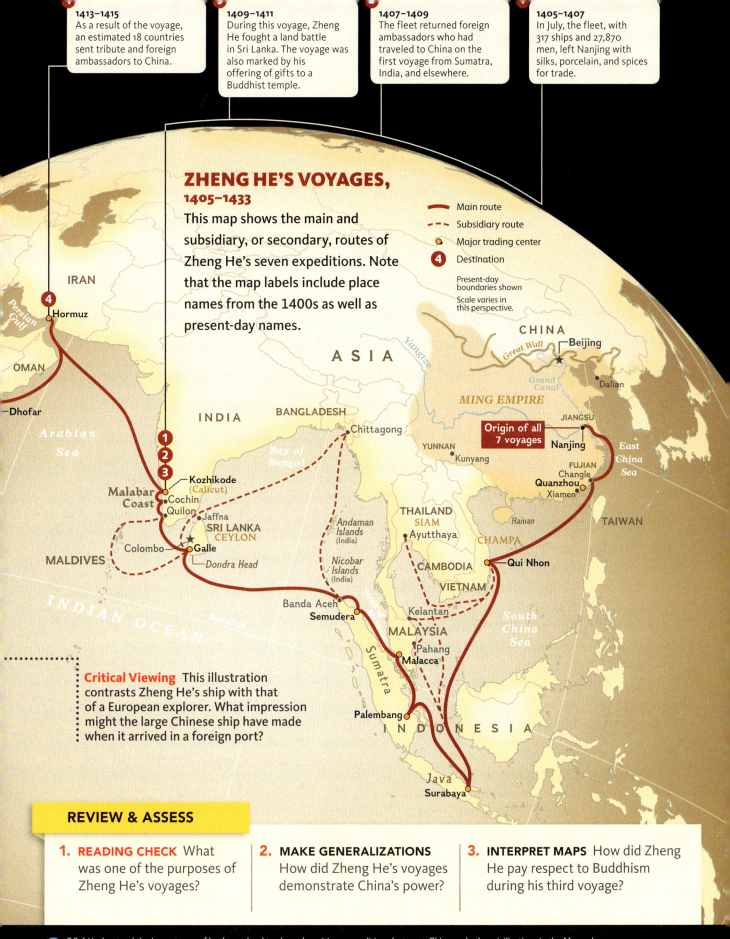

1413–1415
As a result of the voyage, an estimated 18 countries sent tribute and foreign ambassadors to China.

1409–1411
During this voyage, Zheng He fought a land battle in Sri Lanka. The voyage was also marked by his offering of gifts to a Buddhist temple.

1407–1409
The fleet returned foreign ambassadors who had traveled to China on the first voyage from Sumatra, India, and elsewhere.

1405–1407
In July, the fleet, with 317 ships and 27,870 men, left Nanjing with silks, porcelain, and spices for trade.

ZHENG HE'S VOYAGES,
1405–1433

This map shows the main and subsidiary, or secondary, routes of Zheng He's seven expeditions. Note that the map labels include place names from the 1400s as well as present-day names.

— Main route
-- Subsidiary route
● Major trading center
④ Destination

Present-day boundaries shown
Scale varies in this perspective.

Critical Viewing This illustration contrasts Zheng He's ship with that of a European explorer. What impression might the large Chinese ship have made when it arrived in a foreign port?

REVIEW & ASSESS

1. READING CHECK What was one of the purposes of Zheng He's voyages?

2. MAKE GENERALIZATIONS How did Zheng He's voyages demonstrate China's power?

3. INTERPRET MAPS How did Zheng He pay respect to Buddhism during his third voyage?

7.3.4 Understand the importance of both overland trade and maritime expeditions between China and other civilizations in the Mongol Ascendancy and Ming Dynasty.

China Turns Inward

An ostrich is believed to bury its head in the sand to avoid seeing its enemies. But that doesn't stop its enemies from seeing it—or attacking it. China could have learned a valuable lesson on what not to do from this bird.

MAIN IDEA

China isolated itself from the world, but foreign influences still brought the downfall of the dynastic system.

ISOLATION POLICY

China's great explorer, Zheng He, died during his seventh voyage and was buried at sea. His death marked the end of China's maritime expeditions. There were competing government factions for and against exploration, and when the emperor Zhengtong (jung-tung) took power in 1435, he stopped all future voyages, claiming that they were too expensive and they imported dangerous foreign ideas.

The Chinese considered themselves the most civilized people on Earth. They felt they were surrounded by barbarians and did not need the rest of the world. After a period of foreign rule and much instability in their history, it was understandable that the Chinese reacted this way. However, the effect of Zhengtong's decision was to surrender control of the region's seas and trade to ambitious European nations and Japanese pirates.

In the following centuries, China entered a long period of **isolationism**, during which it rejected foreign contact and influences. The government took up a defensive attitude and geared the economy toward self-sufficiency. Rulers banned foreign trade, kicked out foreigners, and tried to eliminate foreign influences from Chinese society.

Symbolic of this effort was the extension of the Great Wall, which the government rebuilt entirely in stone and completed with 25,000 watchtowers along its 5,500-mile length. The wall was a formidable physical sign of China's defensive isolation.

THE LAST DYNASTY

The world, however, would not leave China alone. Starting in the mid-1500s, the Ming dynasty faced more and more challenges. Pirate raids were common along the southeast coast. The Mongols invaded the north, and Japan conquered Chinese-protected Korea. The cost of these wars, on top of a lavish imperial lifestyle and corruption at court, spelled financial difficulties. The peasants paid taxes for all this while they were already coping with widespread crop failures, famine, and disease. The people rebelled, and Ming authority crumbled.

In 1644, rebels took over Beijing. In despair, the last of the Ming emperors hanged himself from a tree. Tribes north of the wall, the **Manchus**, united and took advantage of the confusion to seize power. They easily defeated the rebels and founded the **Qing** (chihng) dynasty.

China would remain under the Qing's foreign rule for nearly 300 years. The Qing kept native customs and the Ming government structure but also introduced some of their own traditions. They forced Chinese men to wear their hair as the Qing did, in a long braid. The Qing continued

Dynastic Time Line of China

👑 Important Rulers
⭐ Major Accomplishments

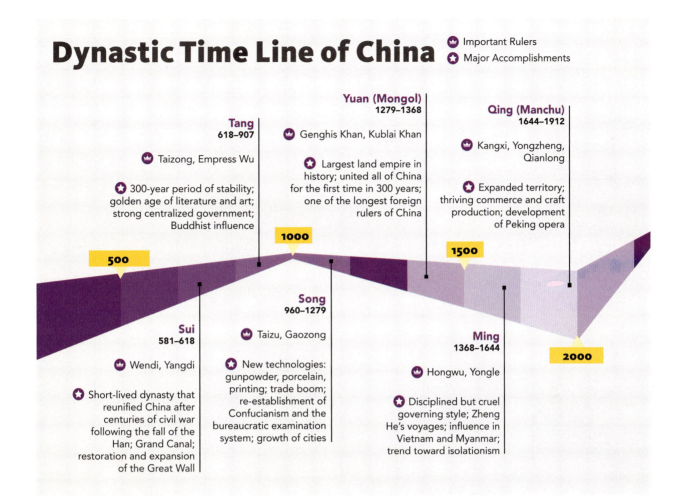

Tang
618–907

👑 Taizong, Empress Wu

⭐ 300-year period of stability; golden age of literature and art; strong centralized government; Buddhist influence

Yuan (Mongol)
1279–1368

👑 Genghis Khan, Kublai Khan

⭐ Largest land empire in history; united all of China for the first time in 300 years; one of the longest foreign rulers of China

Qing (Manchu)
1644–1912

👑 Kangxi, Yongzheng, Qianlong

⭐ Expanded territory; thriving commerce and craft production; development of Peking opera

500

1000

1500

2000

Sui
581–618

👑 Wendi, Yangdi

⭐ Short-lived dynasty that reunified China after centuries of civil war following the fall of the Han; Grand Canal; restoration and expansion of the Great Wall

Song
960–1279

👑 Taizu, Gaozong

⭐ New technologies: gunpowder, porcelain, printing; trade boom; re-establishment of Confucianism and the bureaucratic examination system; growth of cities

Ming
1368–1644

👑 Hongwu, Yongle

⭐ Disciplined but cruel governing style; Zheng He's voyages; influence in Vietnam and Myanmar; trend toward isolationism

China's isolationism, although they did embark on some successful wars that expanded the empire by the end of the 18th century. With peace and prosperity, the population started to increase again, reaching 300 million by 1800. At that time, many Chinese began to migrate to new lands that the Ming had conquered earlier.

Since 1514, European traders had been traveling to China. The Europeans were building strong trading colonies across Asia. The Qing tried to restrict European trade and refused to buy European goods. During the late 1700s, frustrated British merchants began smuggling the drug opium into China. They soon had a successful trade, but addiction ruined countless Chinese lives. The resulting Opium Wars weakened China internally and internationally. European powers seized Chinese territories and took control of the economy. After 1850, a string of rebellions weakened China, and, in February 1912, revolutionary forces overthrew the Qing dynasty. Two thousand years of imperial rule had come to a decisive end.

REVIEW & ASSESS

1. **READING CHECK** How did China try to isolate itself from foreign influences?

2. **COMPARE AND CONTRAST** How did China's policy toward the outside world at the beginning of the Ming dynasty differ from that at the end of the Ming Dynasty?

3. **INTEGRATE VISUALS** How does the time line illustrate the recurring theme of the "dynastic cycle" in Chinese history?

🌀 CST 1 Students explain how major events are related to one another in time.

231

Exploring China's
Diverse Cultures

"When I was little I would identify the pieces of our Thanksgiving turkey and then reassemble the bones after the meal," laughs Christine Lee, a bioarchaeologist and a National Geographic Explorer. "My parents thought I was going to be a doctor!" Instead, she entered a relatively new science, bioarchaeology, which combines biology and archaeology, using the tools of both sciences to find out about the way ancient people lived.

^
This pit of human skulls was found during the excavation of Zhengzhou, a city from the Shang period about 3,750 years ago. Burial customs varied among several distinct cultures in early China.

Bioarchaeology is providing insights into ancient China and Mongolia.

SKELETAL SECRETS

Christine Lee uses biological techniques to examine human skeletons found in archaeological sites. These new techniques allow researchers to piece together clues that tell the stories of long-dead individuals and groups. It is amazing what Dr. Lee can learn from even a single tooth.

A skeleton reveals even more. "Bones can tell me a person's sex, age, and whether they worked hard or had an easy life," she says. "Were they right- or left-handed, did they walk long distances, ride horses, or spend lots of time kneeling? Did they have arthritis, leprosy, tuberculosis? Did they get kicked by a cow, fall off a horse, break their nose in a fight? Bones show me all this and more," says Dr. Lee. By comparing particular skeletal characteristics across populations, she can see how ancient peoples were connected. She can also find details that provide clues to ancient people's ancestral origins, movements, and marriages.

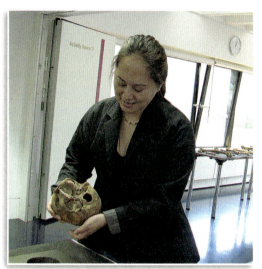

Dr. Christine Lee in the field

PUZZLES FROM THE PAST

Dr. Lee has worked all over the world but has a particular interest in Asia. In Mongolia, she was the lead bioarchaeologist on a team excavating a cemetery of the Xiongnu (shung-noo) people. These were the nomads whose raids drove China to build the 2,000-mile-long Great Wall to keep them out. The dig site was in the middle of the desert, a thousand miles from the Mongolian capital. "We stopped in a village and asked for directions and were told the site was cursed," she says. "When we got there it was eerily quiet . . . I always said if I ever felt the skeletons didn't want me there I would leave. I decided we could study the skeletons when they were brought to the museum—then we left."

Back at the museum, Dr. Lee's studies highlighted cultural differences between the ancient Xiongnu and their Chinese neighbors to the south. "The ancestors of today's Mongolians rode horses, ate meat, and had a certain cowboy wildness compared to the rigid society and structure on the other side of the Great Wall," she notes. This cultural contrast was reinforced by her excavations of another independent kingdom, the Dian (dee-ahn), a city society of farmers and fishers in southern China. Dr. Lee's findings suggest that the Xiongnu and the Chinese had very little interaction and almost never intermarried.

Dr. Lee feels a responsibility to uncover the stories of these cultures in China's history: "When I look at a 2,000-year-old skull it's like I'm saying, 'Don't worry. I will tell the world about you—I'll describe what your life was like and prove it had meaning.'"

1. **READING CHECK** How is bioarchaeology helping scientists gain insights into ancient China and Mongolia?

2. **IDENTIFY MAIN IDEAS AND DETAILS** What can Dr. Lee tell about ancient people's lives from their bones?

3. **COMPARE AND CONTRAST** According to Dr. Lee's studies, what important cultural differences existed between the Xiongnu people and their Chinese neighbors?

VOCABULARY

On your paper, write the vocabulary word that completes each of the following sentences.

1. General Wendi's conquests managed to _____ north and south China and establish a strong new dynasty called the Sui. HSS 7.3.1

2. During the Song dynasty, agricultural techniques improved and rice became China's _____. HSS 7.3.2

3. A strong, nearly see-through ceramic called _____ was an especially valuable trade item. HSS 7.3.2

4. The Mongols were a loose collection of nomadic tribes who roamed, raided, herded, and fought across the vast _____ of northwest China. HSS 7.3.4

5. During Emperor Zhengtong's rule, China pursued a policy of _____, rejecting foreign contact and influences. HSS HI 1

6. The goal of Buddhism is to achieve _____, an end of reincarnation and the suffering of life. HSS 7.3.1

READING STRATEGY

7. DRAW CONCLUSIONS If you haven't already, complete your graphic organizer to draw conclusions about the impact of the Tang, Song, and Ming dynasties on Chinese civilization. Then answer the question.

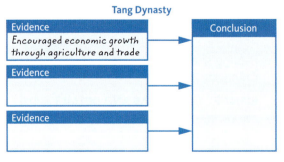

Tang Dynasty

Evidence	Conclusion
Encouraged economic growth through agriculture and trade	
Evidence	
Evidence	

Which dynasty do you think had the greatest impact on Chinese civilization? Explain your reasoning. HSS HI 1

MAIN IDEAS

Answer the following questions. Support your answers with evidence from the chapter.

8. What happened after the collapse of the Han dynasty in A.D. 220? **LESSON 1.1** HSS 7.3.1

9. Why did many Chinese turn away from traditional Confucianism and embrace Buddhism? **LESSON 1.2** HSS 7.3.1

10. What factors contributed to China's growth during the Tang and Song dynasties? **LESSON 1.3** HSS 7.3.2

11. How did the Mongols gain power in China? **LESSON 2.1** HSS HI 1

12. During the Yuan dynasty, how did the Mongols treat the Chinese under their rule? **LESSON 2.2** HSS HI 1

13. How did the Ming dynasty restore Chinese rule to China? **LESSON 3.1** HSS HI 1

14. What were the goals of Zheng He's voyages through Asia and Africa? **LESSON 3.2** HSS 7.3.4

15. Why did China adopt a policy of isolationism during the Ming dynasty? **LESSON 3.3** HSS HI 1

CRITICAL THINKING

Answer the following questions. Support your answers with evidence from the chapter.

16. ESSENTIAL QUESTION Which ancient Chinese invention benefitted people most: movable type, porcelain, gunpowder, or the compass? HSS 7.3.5

17. ANALYZE CAUSE AND EFFECT Why was Wendi able to win the support of China's population? HSS 7.3.1

18. ANALYZE CAUSE AND EFFECT How did Buddhism and Daoism influence Confucianism? HSS 7.3.3

19. SEQUENCE EVENTS Describe the order of events in the Mongol creation of the world's largest empire. HSS CST 1

20. MAKE INFERENCES How did Zheng He's maritime expeditions expand Chinese influence and demonstrate China's power and wealth? HSS 7.3.4

21. YOU DECIDE Was Mongol rule good or bad for China? Support your opinion with evidence from the chapter. HSS REP 5

Study the photograph of the seated Buddha statues in the Yungang Grottoes, a UNESCO World Heritage site in the Shanxi province of China. Then answer the questions that follow.

22. What spiritual qualities are conveyed through these statues of Buddha? (HSS REP 4)

23. Why do you think these statues were carved in such a large scale? (HSS REP 4)

ANALYZE SOURCES

Read the following poem, written by Li Po, one of the most popular Chinese poets of the Tang dynasty.

> **Zazen on Ching-t'ing Mountain**
>
> The birds have vanished down the sky.
> Now the last cloud drains away.
>
> We sit together, the mountain and me,
> Until only the mountain remains.

24. What is one Daoist or Buddhist ideal that is reflected in this poem? (HSS REP 4)

WRITE ABOUT HISTORY

25. EXPOSITORY Suppose you are a historian being interviewed about China. The interviewer asks you, "How did the Great Wall become a symbol of China's policy of isolationism at the end of the Ming dynasty?" Write your answer in a brief paragraph. (HSS HI 1)

TIPS

- Take notes from Lesson 3.3, "China Turns Inward."
- Begin the paragraph with a clear topic sentence.
- Develop the paragraph with supporting details and examples of the steps China took to pursue its policy of isolationism, particularly the expansion and fortification of the Great Wall.
- Use at least two vocabulary terms from the chapter.
- Conclude with an explanation of why the Great Wall became a symbol of China's policy of isolationism.

JAPANESE CIVILIZATION

400 – 1868

ESSENTIAL QUESTION How was Japanese civilization influenced by neighboring cultures?

SECTION 1 EARLY JAPAN

KEY VOCABULARY

archipelago
aristocracy
calligraphy
clan
embassy
regent
ritual

NAMES & PLACES

Prince Shotoku
Ring of Fire
Shinto

SECTION 2 JAPANESE ART AND CULTURE

KEY VOCABULARY

haiku
kabuki
meditation
noh

NAMES & PLACES

Matsuo Basho
Murasaki Shikibu
Sei Shonagon
Zen Buddhism

SECTION 3 JAPANESE FEUDALISM

KEY VOCABULARY

bushido
daimyo
feudalism
samurai
shogun
shogunate
vassal

NAMES & PLACES

Tokugawa Ieyasu

READING STRATEGY

MAKE INFERENCES To make an inference, you combine what the text says with what you already know. As you read this chapter, think back to what you read about Chinese culture in the previous chapter. Use a graphic organizer like the one below to make inferences about how the Japanese felt about Chinese culture.

 What Text Says **+** What I Know **→** Inference

Mount Fuji, on the island of Honshu,
is the highest mountain in Japan.
Many Japanese regard the mountain
as sacred.

The Geography of Japan

From studying its geography, no one would expect Japan to have become the industrial superpower it is today. This small country consists of thousands of isolated, mostly mountainous islands. Japan has little land for agriculture and few natural resources or navigable rivers. In addition, catastrophic natural disasters are common.

MAIN IDEA

Japan's geography has greatly affected its historical and cultural development.

AN ISLAND NATION

Japan is an **archipelago** (AHR-kuh-peh-luh-goh), or group of islands, located in the vast Pacific Ocean. The country's thousands of islands stretch out in a long arc along the east coast of Asia.

Most of Japan's population lives on four main islands: Hokkaido (hoh-KY-doh), Honshu (HAHN-shoo), Shikoku (shih-KOH-koo), and Kyushu (keh-shoo). These four islands have a total area of about 145,000 square miles—roughly the size of the state of Montana—and thousands of miles of coastline. Honshu is by far Japan's largest island. Along with Kyushu, it has been the historic heartland of political, economic, and social development in Japan.

Japan's neighbor, South Korea, is more than 120 miles away. China is about 500 miles away. Japan's isolation has had a huge impact on its culture. For much of its history, Japan was far enough away from mainland Asia to escape invasions and major migrations. As a result, the Japanese nation developed largely from one ethnic group. This common ethnicity gave the Japanese a strong sense of unity.

However, Japan's nearest neighbors still influenced the country's culture. Japan imported many ideas and institutions from China and Korea and adapted them to form a unique Japanese culture. You will learn more about these countries' influence on Japan later in this chapter.

A MOUNTAINOUS LAND

The islands of Japan are actually the peaks of mostly submerged mountains and volcanoes. Japan lies along the **Ring of Fire**, an area of intense earthquakes and volcanic activity that arcs around the basin of the Pacific Ocean. About 1,500 earthquakes and thousands of volcanic eruptions rock Japan every year.

Because of underwater earthquakes, Japan also is at risk from huge ocean waves called tsunamis (su-NAH-mees). In addition, destructive storms called typhoons (ty-FOONS) are common. In the Atlantic Ocean, these storms are called hurricanes.

Japan's mountainous terrain limits the amount of space available for farming and for building homes. Only about 12 percent of the country's land can be farmed, and Japan's population is crowded onto a few coastal plains.

Apart from seafood and vast forests, Japan lacks any important natural resources, such as metals or coal. However, its geographic difficulties have helped make the Japanese a hardy people.

GEOGRAPHY OF JAPAN

120°E 130°E 140°E

Hokkaido

Sea of Japan (East Sea)

CHOSON DYNASTY (KOREA)

Yellow Sea

Honshu

JAPAN
Edo (Tokyo)
Fuji ▲

Heian (Kyoto)
Nara

Shikoku

PACIFIC OCEAN

CHINA

Kyushu

30°N

Elevation

feet	meters
10,000+	3,050+
5,000	1,524
2,000	610
1,000	305
500	152
0	0

0   100   200 Miles
0   100   200 Kilometers

RING OF FIRE

ASIA

NORTH AMERICA

JAPAN

PACIFIC OCEAN

SOUTH AMERICA

AUSTRALIA

0   2,000 Miles
0   2,000 Kilometers

Ring of Fire
△ Volcano active within the past 12,000 years

REVIEW & ASSESS

1. READING CHECK What is the relationship between Japan's geography and its culture?

2. ANALYZE CAUSE AND EFFECT How did Japan's geography affect where people settled?

3. INTERPRET MAPS What are some advantages and disadvantages of Japan's location and terrain?

7.5.1 Describe the significance of Japan's proximity to China and Korea and the intellectual, linguistic, religious, and philosophical influence of those countries on Japan; CST 3 Students use a variety of maps and documents to identify physical and cultural features of neighborhoods, cities, states, and countries and to explain the historical migration of people, expansion and disintegration of empires, and the growth of economic systems; HI 2 Students understand and distinguish cause, effect, sequence, and correlation in historical events, including the long- and short-term

Early Beliefs and Cultures

Many people feel a great sense of awe when they witness a vibrant sunset, a stunning mountain view, or another wonder of nature. In early Japan, the beauty of the natural world became the basis of a religion.

MAIN IDEA

Religion was at the center of a society organized into family groups in early Japan.

TRADITIONAL RELIGION

With its rugged mountains and lush forests, Japan has an especially beautiful landscape. Its breathtaking views inspired Japan's most ancient religion, **Shinto** (SHIHN-toh), which means "way of the gods."

Shinto is based on the belief that spiritual powers reside in nature. Followers of Shinto worship divine spirits or gods called *kami*. The religion recognizes millions of kami, ranging from the sun, moon, and storms to individual animals, trees, streams, and rocks. Anything in nature that inspires a sense of religious wonder is considered a kami or the home of a kami. Followers of Shinto regard mountains as especially important homes for Shinto gods. Perhaps because of its size, Mount Fuji, near Tokyo, has long been considered particularly sacred.

Shinto has no founder, no holy scriptures, no moral code, and no clear date of origin. It also does not have elaborate temples. Instead, worshippers focus on simple shrines, or places that are considered sacred. Gates called torii (TAWR-ee-ee) often mark a shrine's entrance.

Shinto worship is relatively simple. Worshippers typically visit a shrine, purify themselves by washing, clap their hands to attract the god's attention, and then whisper a short prayer. Shinto priests perform more elaborate **rituals**, or religious ceremonies, that often involve bells, music, and dancing.

SOCIAL STRUCTURE

People from Siberia and Korea first settled Japan about 30,000 years ago. The first culture, the Jomon (JOH-mahn), emerged about 10,000 years ago. The Jomon people were hunters, gatherers, and fishers who lived in caves and shallow pit dwellings. They made simple pottery, baskets, and clothes from natural materials. Around 3000 B.C., they began basic farming.

Critical Viewing Fushimi Inari Shrine in Kyoto, Japan, is noted for its many entrance gates, called torii. What are some distinctive features of the torii?

About 300 B.C., a new wave of immigrants with a significantly more advanced culture—the Yayoi (YAH-yoy)—arrived from mainland Asia. They knew how to grow rice, work metal, and weave. Their skills changed Japan dramatically. As farming flourished, people built villages that grew into larger communities.

A powerful **clan** ruled each community. A clan is a group of families who share a common ancestor. Each clan had a chief who was a religious leader or a mighty warrior. The chief, who could be male or female, headed a social class system in which a small **aristocracy**, or group

of wealthy people, was supported by many farmers, artisans, and slaves.

After A.D. 300, the power of the aristocracy increased. This growth in power was reflected in the large tombs built for people of high social status. Vast earthen mounds covered the tombs. The largest of these tombs rivals Egypt's great pyramids in scale.

The Shinto religion served as a strong unifying factor in early Japanese society. The worship of particular gods bound together families, clans, and regions. Later, Shinto would help unite Japan's many independent kingdoms under a single leader.

REVIEW & ASSESS

1. **READING CHECK** What inspired the development of the ancient Japanese religion called Shinto?

2. **DESCRIBE** What are some distinctive features of the Shinto religion?

3. **ANALYZE CAUSE AND EFFECT** How did the Yayoi culture affect Japan?

 7.5.1 Describe the significance of Japan's proximity to China and Korea and the intellectual, linguistic, religious, and philosophical influence of those countries on Japan; HI 2 Students understand and distinguish cause, effect, sequence, and correlation in historical events, including the long- and short-term causal relations.

This bronze statue stands before the entry gate of Horyu-ji, a Buddhist religious center founded by Prince Shotoku in the 600s.

1.3 Prince Shotoku

"In a country, there are not two lords; the people have not two masters. The sovereign is the master of the people of the whole country." In this strong statement, **Prince Shotoku** (shoh-toh-ku) of Japan sent a clear message to the people. He wanted them to know that Japan was now a united nation under a single ruler, or sovereign.

MAIN IDEA

Between 593 and 622, Prince Shotoku unified Japan under a Chinese model of centralized government and promoted other Chinese ideas.

A POWERFUL CLAN

Before the 400s, hundreds of Japan's independent clans ruled their own territories and often battled one another. Amid the many clans, one grew increasingly powerful: the Yamato (YAH-mah-toh). The Yamato rode into battle on horses, recently introduced from Korea. With their military superiority, they won control over many of the clans. By the 400s, these clans had united under the leadership of a Yamato emperor and his successors. To support the idea that they were the rightful rulers of Japan, the Yamato claimed their line of emperors was directly descended from the chief Shinto deity, the sun goddess Amaterasu (ah-mah-teh-RAH-soo). The Yamato effectively established a hereditary monarchy, in which rule passes from one member of a royal family to another.

In 593, Japan took another political leap. Empress Suiko (soo-EE-koh) won the throne and named her 21-year-old nephew, Prince Shotoku, as her **regent**. A regent is a person who rules when a monarch or emperor is unable to do so. However, Shotoku held most of the real power in Japan. He established the Japanese practice of having both a ruler in name only and an actual ruler. Between 593 and 622, Shotoku and Suiko laid the foundations of Japanese government.

CENTRALIZED GOVERNMENT

Greatly impressed by China's culture, Prince Shotoku introduced Chinese ideas and practices to help unite the Japanese people and strengthen imperial control over them. The religion of Buddhism and a centralized government were among these ideas and practices.

In 604, Shotoku issued Japan's first constitution, which skillfully mixed Confucian and Buddhist ideas. The constitution emphasized obedience to the emperor and the emperor's duty to care for his subjects. Shotoku introduced ideas for Japanese government that lasted for centuries.

REVIEW & ASSESS

1. **READING CHECK** How did Prince Shotoku unify the Japanese people?

2. **MAKE INFERENCES** Why do you think Prince Shotoku stressed the fact that Japan had only one ruler?

3. **FORM AND SUPPORT OPINIONS** What do you consider to be Prince Shotoku's greatest accomplishment? Why?

7.5.1 Describe the significance of Japan's proximity to China and Korea and the intellectual, linguistic, religious, and philosophical influence of those countries on Japan; 7.5.2 Discuss the reign of Prince Shotoku of Japan and the characteristics of Japanese society and family life during his reign.

1.4 Influences from China and Korea

When you see a hairstyle you like, you might decide to copy it. But you might change it slightly to fit your own taste, type of hair, or facial shape. In a similar way, the Japanese copied and adapted aspects of the cultures of China and Korea.

MAIN IDEA

Japan adopted ideas from Korea and China but adapted them to fit Japanese culture.

SPREADING NEW IDEAS

Korea is Japan's closest neighbor and also borders China. Many elements of Chinese culture spread from Korea to Japan. To learn directly about Chinese culture, Japan sent many embassies to China beginning in the early 600s. An **embassy** is a group of official representatives from one country who have been sent on a mission to another country. Between 607 and 839, Japan sent hundreds of people on more than 12 official missions to China. They brought back knowledge that influenced many aspects of Japanese life, including agriculture, art, government, religion, and technology.

As a result, China's influence extended to such everyday practices as drinking tea, cooking, and gardening. Even the name the Japanese use to refer to their country, *Nippon*, comes from the Chinese language. *Nippon* means "Land of the Rising Sun" and refers to Japan's location east of China—toward the rising sun.

China had a major impact on Japanese writing, even though the Japanese and Chinese languages are completely unrelated. For example, most Chinese words are just one syllable, while Japanese words combine many syllables. The differences made it extremely difficult to write Japanese using the Chinese alphabet, so at first the Japanese wrote in the Chinese language. Later, the Japanese added new characters to the Chinese alphabet, which made writing Japanese much easier.

The Chinese also influenced how the Japanese viewed writing. Initially, the Japanese considered writing to be a purely functional activity, useful for such purposes as keeping records. Japanese aristocrats did not bother to learn to write. However, interaction with China encouraged writing for cultural reasons, such as telling stories. The Japanese also adopted the practice of **calligraphy**, or beautiful writing, from China.

ADAPTING INFLUENCES

The Japanese did not simply imitate everything Chinese. They carefully selected what suited them and then adapted it to their own needs, which led to a distinctive Japanese culture. For example, the Japanese copied the Chinese civil service system, which established a hierarchy, or ranking, of government officials. In China, government officials earned their positions based on examinations and good work. However, members of Japan's aristocracy wanted to keep power to themselves. In Japan, the emperor appointed government officials based on heredity, not on ability.

Japan continued adopting and adapting Chinese practices into the early 800s. By then, however, Japan's own culture was flourishing. After 839, Japan no longer sent any major missions to China. Nevertheless, China's influence on Japanese culture can still be seen today.

These students are participating in an annual calligraphy contest in Tokyo.

REVIEW & ASSESS

1. READING CHECK How does Japan's name reflect the influence of the Chinese?

2. MAKE INFERENCES How does the Japanese system of writing demonstrate Japan's tendency to adopt—and adapt—ideas from China?

3. COMPARE AND CONTRAST What was a major difference between the civil service systems in China and Japan?

7.5.1 Describe the significance of Japan's proximity to China and Korea and the intellectual, linguistic, religious, and philosophical influence of those countries on Japan.

Literature
and the Arts

If you look at a time line of early English literature, you'll notice that all the best known authors—like William Shakespeare—are male. That's *not* the case with early Japanese literature. Two of the most famous authors are female, and one introduced a new form of literature to the world.

MAIN IDEA

Japan's rich cultural heritage includes unique forms of literature and art.

BONSAI

The Japanese imported the tradition of bonsai (bohn-SY) from China. To create a bonsai, a gardener painstakingly prunes and trains an ordinary plant to grow into a miniature tree that perfectly reflects its full-size relative.

LITERATURE AND DRAMA

A Japanese woman named **Murasaki Shikibu** (MOO-rah-SAH-kee SHEE-kee-boo) wrote the world's first novel in the 1000s. Her novel, *The Tale of Genji*, paints a vivid picture of life at the emperor's court. Her much admired masterpiece is still read today.

Another female writer of the same time, **Sei Shonagon** (SAY SHOW-nah-gohn), wrote a collection of reportedly true stories about court life called *The Pillow Book*. The book's title probably comes from the practice of keeping paper by the bedside for writing down thoughts.

Other Japanese writers developed a form of poetry called haiku (HY-koo), which has 17 syllables in three unrhymed lines of 5, 7, and 5 syllables. Traditional haiku evokes aspects of nature and often employs striking comparisons. One of the great masters of haiku was **Matsuo Basho** (MAHT-soo-oh bah-SHAW). In 1666, he abandoned his warrior life to write verses inspired by Buddhism. His poetry provided deep insights into human nature, turning haiku into a popular and beloved art form.

In the field of drama, Japan developed two forms that are still popular today. Noh (noh) emerged in the 1300s and kabuki (kuh-BOO-kee) in the 1600s. Noh grew out of Shinto rituals and often retold well-known folktales. Performing on a simple wooden stage, the actors wore elaborate masks and many layers of clothing to appear larger than life. Their movements were deliberately slow and choreographed to music to create a powerful effect.

Kabuki developed as a contrast to noh and was more lively and understandable. The actors performed on a large stage with trapdoors, revolving sections, and a raised walkway for dramatic effects. They wore luxurious costumes that reflected their characters' status. Their elaborate makeup highlighted important facial expressions, such as smiling or frowning.

PAINTING AND GARDENING

As you have learned, the Japanese adopted the Chinese art of calligraphy, which is traditionally produced with a brush and ink. China also influenced painting in Japan. Japanese artists adapted a form of Chinese ink painting to create paintings called *suiboku*

(soo-ee-BOH-koo), using bold strokes of black and white ink. Artists later created vibrant watercolors and prints. Early Japanese painting focused on religious subjects, but landscapes, scenes of daily life, legends, and battles also became popular.

Following the Shinto tradition of seeking harmony with nature, the Japanese became dedicated gardeners. They developed various types of gardens with the aim of creating symbolic miniature landscapes. Paradise gardens re-created the Buddhist idea of paradise. Dry-landscape gardens consisted of carefully chosen stones arranged in raked gravel as a focus for meditation. Stroll gardens featured carefully designed landscapes along a walking path. Tea gardens had neatly trimmed plants along a short path leading to a special house for drinking tea.

REVIEW & ASSESS

1. **READING CHECK** What new forms of literature and drama did the Japanese develop?

2. **COMPARE AND CONTRAST** How are the literary works of Murasaki Shikibu and Sei Shonagon similar?

3. **MAKE GENERALIZATIONS** How did Japanese gardens reflect both Shinto and Buddhist ideas?

7.5.5 Study the ninth and tenth centuries' golden age of literature, art, and drama and its lasting effects on culture today, including Murasaki Shikibu's *Tale of Genji.*

Poetry and Prose

During the Heian (HAY-ahn) period, from 794 to 1185, Japan enjoyed a golden age in literature. The ruling class in the capital city of Heian, modern Kyoto (kee-OH-toh), filled their time with cultural pursuits. Both male and female aristocrats, including warriors, engaged in writing as a cultural activity. The common literary subjects of nature and beauty had wide appeal to Japanese audiences. Literature also flourished during the later Edo (eh-doh) period, from 1603 to 1867.

This woodblock print by Japanese artist Utagawa Kunisada (1786–1864) depicts a scene from *The Tale of Genji*.

Primary Source: Diary

from *The Pillow Book* by Sei Shonagon

In keeping with the traditional Japanese love of nature, artists and writers found a source of inspiration in the changing seasons. Here, Sei Shonagon paints a timeless portrait of the seasons to set the scene at the start of *The Pillow Book*.

CONSTRUCTED RESPONSE Which parts of the day does Sei Shonagon find most beautiful in the spring and summer seasons? Why?

> In spring, the dawn [is most beautiful]— when the slowly paling mountain rim is tinged with red, and wisps of faintly crimson-purple cloud float in the sky.
>
> In summer, the night—moonlit nights, of course, but also at the dark of the moon, it's beautiful when fireflies are dancing everywhere in a mazy [confused] flight.

DOCUMENT TWO

Primary Source: Novel

from *The Tale of Genji* by Murasaki Shikibu

Prince Genji is the central character in Murasaki's novel. Although most of the story is told in prose, Murasaki includes many poems that are spoken by the characters. Here, the writer sets the scene as Genji says farewell to a former love.

CONSTRUCTED RESPONSE How does the writer use images of nature to express Genji's feelings?

> No one could ever convey all that passed between those two [Genji and the lady], who together had known such uncounted sorrows. The quality of a sky at last touched by dawn seemed meant for them alone.
>
> "Many dews attend any reluctant parting at the break of day but no one has ever seen the like of this autumn sky," Genji said.

DOCUMENT THREE

Primary Source: Poetry

Haiku by Matsuo Basho

A traditional haiku has 17 syllables, arranged in three lines of 5, 7, and 5 syllables, though the syllable count is sometimes lost in translation, as in the one shown here. In the 1600s, Matsuo Basho developed haiku into a distinct art form.

CONSTRUCTED RESPONSE What feelings about nature does this haiku express?

> The quiet pond
> A frog leaps in,
> The sound of water

SYNTHESIZE & WRITE

1. **REVIEW** Review what you have learned from this chapter about Japanese literature.

2. **RECALL** On your own paper, write down the main idea expressed in each document above.

3. **CONSTRUCT** Write a topic sentence that answers this question: What can you infer about early Japanese authors' relationship to nature?

4. **WRITE** Using evidence from the documents, write a paragraph that supports your topic sentence in Step 3.

7.5.5 Study the ninth and tenth centuries' golden age of literature, art, and drama and its lasting effects on culture today, including Murasaki Shikibu's *Tale of Genji*; REP 4 Students assess the credibility of primary and secondary sources and draw sound conclusions from them.

249

Zen Buddhism

The world's religions prescribe a variety of ways for people to seek salvation, enlightenment, or meaning in life. Many encourage followers to study holy books, perform rituals, say prayers, and do good deeds. A religion called **Zen Buddhism**, which took root in Japan in the 1100s, takes a different approach. Its followers focus on clearing their minds and simplifying their lives.

MAIN IDEA

In the 1100s, Zen Buddhism developed a small but elite following that allowed it to greatly influence Japanese culture.

A NEW FORM OF BUDDHISM

Buddhism originally spread to Japan in the 500s. Over time, many sects, or forms, of Buddhism emerged, the best-known being Zen Buddhism. This sect arrived from China in the 1100s.

While traditional Buddhists sought salvation by studying scriptures, performing rituals, and doing good deeds, Zen Buddhists focused on **meditation**. In fact, *Zen* is the Japanese pronunciation of the Chinese word *Ch'an*, which roughly translates as "meditation." In meditation, a person remains still and enters a trancelike state of thought. True meditation requires self-discipline and concentration. For Zen Buddhists, the goal is to achieve inner peace and to realize that there is something divine in each person. To help focus and escape worldly distractions, Zen Buddhists embrace simplicity in all things, including home furnishings, food, clothing, and art.

INFLUENCE ON CULTURE

Zen Buddhism influenced Japanese culture far more than any other form of Buddhism. Many Japanese poets and artists, for example, embraced the religion's guiding principles of simplicity, understatement, and grace. The content and form of haiku reflect not only these principles but also the religion's focus on the present moment. Artists inspired by Zen Buddhism challenged themselves to convey complex natural scenes with as few brushstrokes as possible, using only black ink on white paper. A typical painting might capture the essence of a mountain-filled landscape.

You read about the different types of Japanese gardens in a previous lesson. These gardens were all influenced by Zen Buddhism. For example, the religion inspired gardeners to create dry-landscape gardens, also called viewing gardens, that represented the world in miniature. In these gardens, simple objects typically stood for something much bigger. An arrangement of rocks might convey a waterfall, or a collection of pebbles might depict a stream. Ryoanji (roh-AHN-gee) Temple in Kyoto has a celebrated Zen viewing garden. It consists of a rectangle of raked sand and 15 pebbles surrounded by clay walls and tall trees.

The main purpose of Zen viewing gardens was to promote a calm state of mind for meditation. As a result, the gardens made a perfect setting for the highly ritualized Zen tea ceremony. This ceremony involved drinking bitter tea in precisely

Critical Viewing A Buddhist monk meditates by a Zen viewing garden. What mood or state of mind might such a garden inspire?

three and a half sips while sitting on the floor of a bare hut. The simplicity of the tea ceremony focused attention on the beauty of an everyday activity.

Many people considered Zen Buddhism a difficult religion to practice. However, Zen Buddhism won a strong following among the warrior class that was developing in Japan. The religion's focus on simplicity, self-discipline, and the contemplation of life and death appealed to warriors, who regularly faced deadly challenges on the battlefield. Their support ensured Zen Buddhism an important place in Japanese society.

REVIEW & ASSESS

1. **READING CHECK** Which guiding principles of Zen Buddhism had an impact on Japanese society and culture?

2. **COMPARE AND CONTRAST** How do traditional Buddhism and Zen Buddhism differ?

3. **MAKE INFERENCES** How do Zen viewing gardens reflect the values of Zen Buddhism?

7.3.1 Describe the reunification of China under the Tang Dynasty and reasons for the spread of Buddhism in Tang China, Korea, and Japan; 7.5.5 Trace the development of distinctive forms of Japanese Buddhism.

Samurai and Shoguns

The year is 1195. A Japanese warrior strides confidently past a group of peasant farmers. He looks magnificent in his colorful and decorative armor. But with his swords and spears, he is also deadly. The warrior hardly notices the peasants, but they bow their heads anyway. They know their place in Japanese society.

MAIN IDEA

Between 1192 and 1867, powerful military families ruled Japan with the support of armies of hired warriors.

FEMALE WARRIORS

Some Japanese women were well-trained, skillful fighters. Women of the samurai class were expected to defend their homes from attack by enemy warriors. A few female warriors also rode into battle.

A STRUCTURED SOCIETY

By the mid-1000s, the power of the central government in Japan was fading. The emperor's responsibilities were limited to religious functions. The real rulers of Japan were the **daimyo** (DY-mee-oh), the leaders of large landowning families.

As the power of the central government decreased, the daimyo grew stronger and more independent. They transformed their local estates into self-governing states, wielding the power of life and death over those under them.

Each daimyo had an army of hired warriors called **samurai** (SAM-uh-ry). Individual samurai swore allegiance to a daimyo and were duty-bound to fight for their lord. In return, the samurai received money and land. The samurai were **vassals** of the daimyo. A vassal is a person who receives land from a feudal lord in exchange for obedience and service.

This order of allegiance, called **feudalism**, was the main system of government in medieval Europe as well as Japan. The greatest daimyo came to command the allegiance of many lesser lords and their armies, creating powerful rival groups that battled for control of Japan.

7.5.3 Describe the values, social customs, and traditions prescribed by the lord-vassal system consisting of shogun, daimyo, and samurai and the lasting influence of the warrior code in the twentieth century; 7.5.6 Analyze the rise of a military society in the late twelfth century and the role of the samurai in that society.

MILITARY RULE

Japan's daimyo fought one another until the Minamoto (MEE-nah-moh-toh) family defeated them all. In 1192, the family's leader, Yoritomo (yoh-REE-toh-moh), became **shogun**, which means "general." As shogun, Yoritomo effectively governed Japan, and the emperor became a figurehead. The Minamoto family began a long line of hereditary rulers. The dynasty held power until the 1300s.

The warrior culture of this period was based on a strict code of behavior called **bushido** (buh-SHEE-doh) or "the way of the warrior." Bushido fused aspects of three religions: Shinto's devotion to family and ruler, Zen Buddhism's focus on inner peace and fearlessness, and Confucianism's service to state and country. The code promoted loyalty, bravery, and honor, much like the code of chivalry followed by knights, a warrior class that arose in Europe around the 800s.

REVIEW & ASSESS

1. **READING CHECK** What were the roles of the emperor, the daimyo, and the samurai in feudal Japan?

2. **IDENTIFY PROBLEMS AND SOLUTIONS** What problem in Japan's central government did feudalism help solve?

3. **MAKE INFERENCES** What were some benefits and drawbacks of being a samurai?

3.2 HISTORY THROUGH OBJECTS

TOOLS OF THE SAMURAI

A samurai riding into battle on horseback must have been quite a sight. The colorful, complicated armor was made to be both beautiful and useful. The armor included metal or leather scales laced together to protect the warrior's body while allowing quick, easy movement. A samurai was armed with two swords, a long curved one and a short one, as well as a spear or gun.

Spear
This spear from the 1800s is made of iron, wood, and crushed mother of pearl.

Sword
Samurai highly valued their razor-sharp swords.

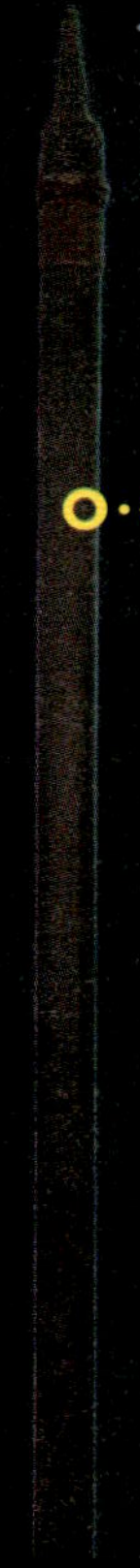

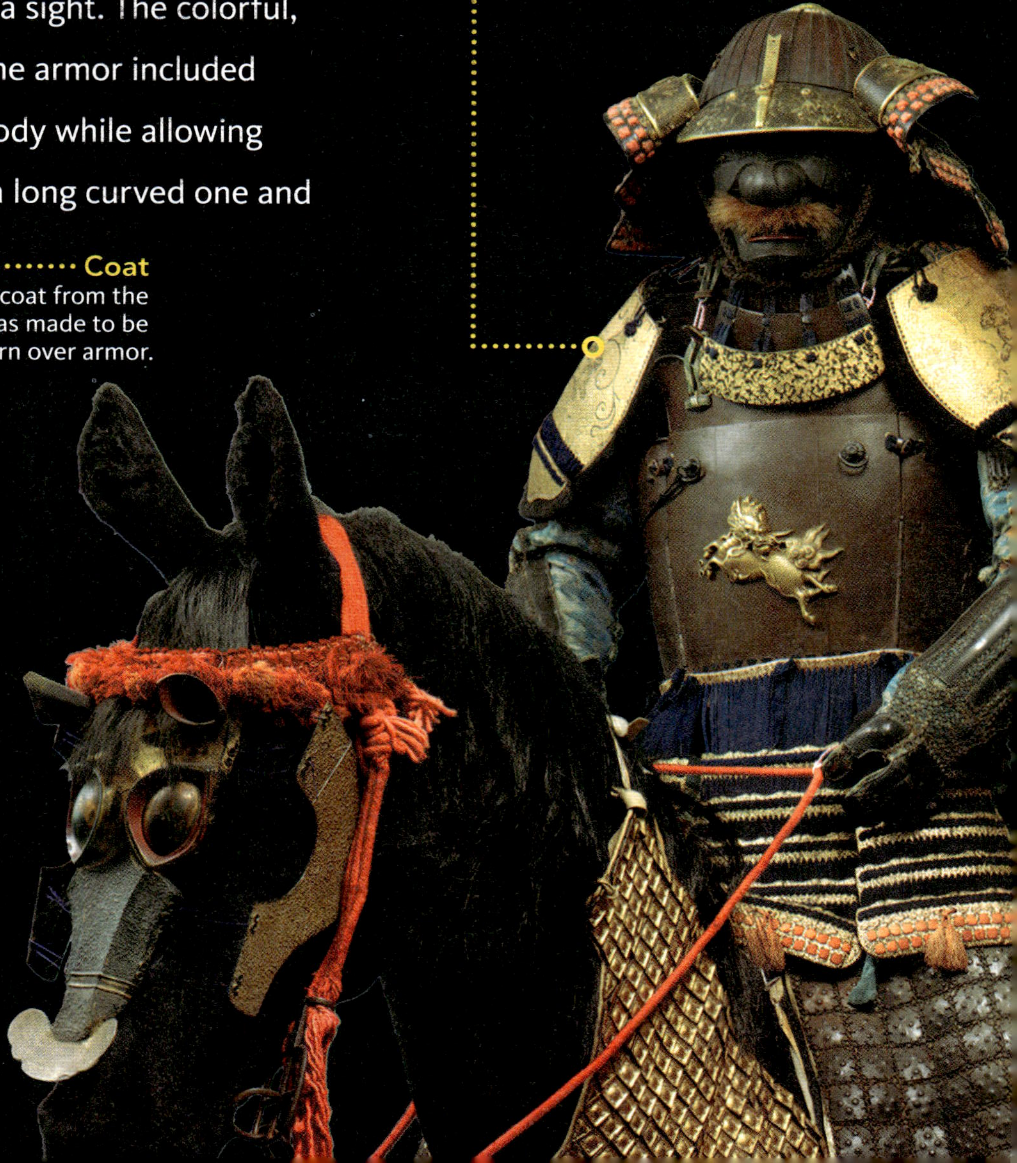

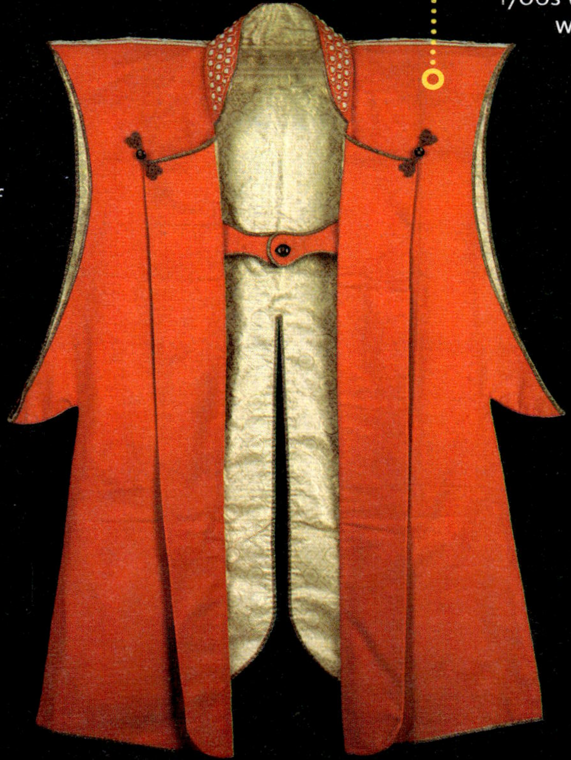

Coat
This surcoat from the 1700s was made to be worn over armor.

Armor
A great deal of care and effort went into making the elaborate armor for a samurai.

Helmet Crest
The creature depicted in this helmet crest has the head of a tiger and the body of a fish.

Helmet
This helmet from about 1550 is made of iron, wood, leather, gilt copper, and lacing.

Gun
The Portuguese introduced the first guns into Japan in the 1500s.

Face and Neck Guard
Samurai wore terrifying masks like this one.

7.5.3 Describe the values, social customs, and traditions prescribed by the lord-vassal system consisting of shogun, daimyo, and samurai and the lasting influence of the warrior code in the twentieth century.

255

Unification and Isolation

In some developing countries today, people protest against Western influence on their cultures. They fear losing their own unique cultures as their countries become more and more westernized. In the 1600s, Japan's rulers not only complained, they did something. They closed the country's doors to foreigners.

MAIN IDEA

After centuries of intense power struggles, Japan was reunified in the 1600s under a strong central government that rejected contact with foreigners.

THE WARRING STATES PERIOD

Japan faced a major threat in 1274: invasion by the Mongols, the great Asian superpower you learned about in the previous chapter. The Mongols had already conquered China and Korea. Now the Mongol leader Kublai Khan wanted to control Japan, too. In their initial attack, the Mongols captured many outlying islands. Then they retreated after a typhoon wrecked many of their ships.

Kublai Khan did not launch another invasion of Japan until 1281. However, this time he assembled the largest seaborne invasion force the world had yet seen—4,400 ships carrying about 150,000 men. The daimyo put aside their differences and focused all their resources on defeating the Mongols. The Japanese warriors fought the invaders for about two months. Then a typhoon smashed into the Mongol fleet, killing tens of thousands. Japan claimed that heaven had saved the country by sending a *kamikaze*, or "divine wind," to stop the Mongols.

Instead of unifying Japan, however, this victory against the Mongols tore the country apart. A vast amount of money had been spent on the defense, but the Japanese gained no valuable rewards to repay the nobles and warriors. This inability to pay undermined the shogun's authority. Steadily, the daimyo seized control of their regions and then ruled them independently. Japan became divided among some 300 daimyo, all plotting and fighting for power.

This period of the "Warring States" lasted from 1467 until 1568. Then a powerful leader named Oda Nobunaga (oh-dah noh-boo-nah-gah) brought most of Japan under his control. In 1603, a leader named **Tokugawa Ieyasu** (toh-koo-gah-wah ee-yeh-yah-soo) finally broke the power of the daimyo and reunified all of Japan under a **shogunate**, or rule by a shogun.

THE TOKUGAWA SHOGUNATE

Ieyasu's rule ushered in a period of stability and peace that lasted nearly 300 years. Ieyasu and his successors feared that foreign contact was corrupting the people and upsetting the traditional balance of power. As a result, by 1639, the shoguns had begun a national policy of isolation and cut Japan off from outside influence. They stopped almost all foreign trade and travel and expelled certain groups of foreigners, including Europeans and Christians. Japan's isolation continued for more than 200 years. Then, in 1854, the United States pressured Japan to reopen for foreign trade. In 1867, the Tokugawa shogunate was overthrown and the emperor took control of Japan.

TOKUGAWA IEYASU

Fuji from Suruga Street, Yedo, Ando Hiroshige (1797-1858)

- 💼 **Job:** Shogun of all of Japan
- 📝 **Education:** Learned the art of war and government while being held hostage by a neighboring clan
- 🌐 **Home:** Ruled from Edo (present-day Tokyo)

FINEST HOUR

He defeated the rebellious daimyo at the Battle of Sekigahara in 1600 to become shogun of Japan.

TRIVIA

Ieyasu built a castle at Edo that was gradually expanded until it became the world's largest at the time. The families of the daimyo were forced to live in mansions around the castle. Ieyasu effectively made the families hostages to guarantee good behavior by the daimyo.

This print shows a busy street in Edo during the period of Japan's isolation from the West.

REVIEW & ASSESS

1. **READING CHECK** What were the key events in Japan's unification and isolation?

2. **ANALYZE CAUSE AND EFFECT** Why did the Tokugawa shogunate decide to isolate Japan from foreign influence?

3. **FORM AND SUPPORT OPINIONS** Do you think a policy of isolation was wise for Japan? Why or why not?

7.5.6 Analyze the rise of a military society in the late twelfth century and the role of the samurai in that society; HI 2 Students understand and

257

Use each of the following vocabulary words in a sentence that shows an understanding of the word's meaning.

1. **archipelago** (HSS 7.5)
   Japan is an archipelago, or chain of islands, located in the Pacific Ocean.

2. **daimyo** (HSS 7.5.3)

3. **clan** (HSS 7.5)

4. **regent** (HSS 7.5.2)

5. **haiku** (HSS 7.5.5)

6. **samurai** (HSS 7.5.3)

7. **shogun** (HSS 7.5.3)

8. **bushido** (HSS 7.5.3)

READING STRATEGY

9. **MAKE INFERENCES** If you haven't already, complete the graphic organizer to make inferences about how the Japanese viewed Chinese culture. Then answer the question.

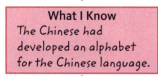

What Text Says
The Japanese added new characters to the Chinese alphabet.

+

What I Know
The Chinese had developed an alphabet for the Chinese language.

↓

Inference

Based on what you've read, how did the Japanese view Chinese culture? Support your response with evidence from the chapter. (HSS 7.5.1)

MAIN IDEAS

Answer the following questions. Support your answers with evidence from the chapter.

10. In what ways did Japan's geography affect its sense of unity? **LESSON 1.1** (HSS 7.5)

11. What belief forms the basis of Japan's ancient religion of Shinto? **LESSON 1.2** (HSS 7.5)

12. What ideas did Japan borrow from China's civilization? **LESSON 1.4** (HSS 7.5.1)

13. What new forms of literature and drama did the Japanese develop? **LESSON 2.1** (HSS 7.5.5)

14. What is the goal of meditation in Zen Buddhism? **LESSON 2.3** (HSS 7.5.4)

15. How did Japan come to be ruled by powerful military families between 1192 and 1867? **LESSON 3.1** (HSS 7.5.3)

16. How was Japan reunified after the Warring States period? **LESSON 3.3** (HSS 7.5.6)

CRITICAL THINKING

Answer the following questions. Support your answers with evidence from the chapter.

17. **ESSENTIAL QUESTION** How did China and Korea influence Japanese culture? (HSS 7.5.1)

18. **ANALYZE CAUSE AND EFFECT** Why was the Shinto religion a strong unifying factor in early Japanese society? (HSS HI 2)

19. **DRAW CONCLUSIONS** Which government probably had more qualified officials—the Chinese or the Japanese? Why? (HSS HI 2)

20. **COMPARE AND CONTRAST** How did Japan open itself to other cultures? How did it close itself off? (HSS HI 1)

21. **MAKE GENERALIZATIONS** How did feudalism benefit both the daimyo and vassals? (HSS 7.5.3)

22. **YOU DECIDE** Was China's influence on Japan beneficial or harmful? Support your opinion with evidence from the chapter. (HSS REP 1)

INTERPRET CHARTS

Study this chart, which illustrates Japan's society in the feudal period. Then answer the questions that follow.

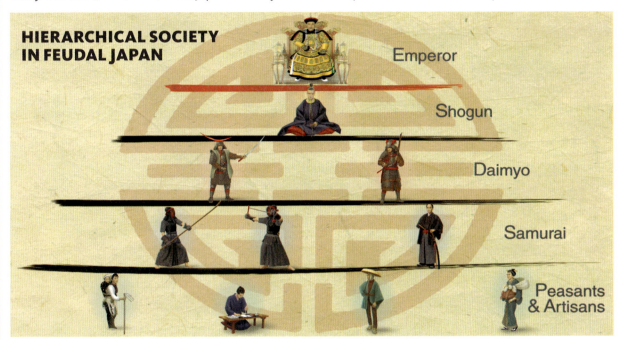

HIERARCHICAL SOCIETY IN FEUDAL JAPAN

Emperor

Shogun

Daimyo

Samurai

Peasants & Artisans

23. Who held the real power in feudal Japan's military society? HSS 7.5.3

24. Which class of people probably created the most wealth for feudal Japan? Why? HSS 7.5.1

ANALYZE SOURCES

Read the following haiku written by a modern Japanese poet. Then answer the question that follows.

I kill an ant . . .

and realize my three children

were watching

—Shuson Kato (1905–1993)

25. What enduring values of Japanese culture are reflected in this haiku? HSS REP 4

WRITE ABOUT HISTORY

26. INFORMATIVE Write a short encyclopedia article for fellow students comparing or contrasting the rule of Prince Shotoku and the rule of Tokugawa Ieyasu. HSS HI 1

> **TIPS**
>
> • Take notes on each ruler from Lessons 1.3 and 3.3.
>
> • State your main idea about the similarities or differences between the two rulers in your beginning sentence.
>
> • Develop the main idea with relevant facts, details, or examples about the rule of each leader.
>
> • Use transitions, such as "in a similar way" or "unlike," to clarify the relationships between ideas.
>
> • Provide a concluding statement that follows from and supports the information presented.

10 KOREA, INDIA, AND SOUTHEAST ASIA

320 – 1910

ESSENTIAL QUESTION How did Asian civilizations influence each other?

SECTION 1 KOREA'S EARLY HISTORY

KEY VOCABULARY	NAMES & PLACES
adapt	Choson
celadon	Koguryo
hanbok	Koryo
kimchi	Paekche
ondol	Silla
rivalry	Tripitaka Koreana

SECTION 2 SOUTH AND SOUTHEAST ASIA

KEY VOCABULARY	NAMES & PLACES
bas-relief	Angkor Wat
bodhisattva	Chandra Gupta I
cultivate	Dai Viet
golden age	Hinduism
impose	Kalidasa
karma	Khmer
reincarnation	Nam Viet
	Sikhism
	Trung Nhi
	Trung Trac

READING STRATEGY

DETERMINE WORD MEANINGS When you come across an unfamiliar word in a text, you can use context clues to help you figure out the word's meaning. Signal words like *or*, *is*, and *such as* often indicate that a word is going to be defined in the text. As you read the chapter, use a chart like this one to keep track of vocabulary words and their definitions.

Word	Definition	Example from My Life

Sokkuram, a cave temple in Korea, is home to this huge statue of Buddha.

The Three Kingdoms

 What might happen if your teachers lost control of your school? Groups of friends would stick together and do their own thing. Some small groups might band together to form larger ones based on shared friends and interests. In time, the whole school might be split into a few large groups ruling themselves and maybe even trying to control their rivals. This is what happened in Korea.

MAIN IDEA

Three kingdoms with strong Chinese cultural influences ruled early Korea.

FORMATION OF KOREA

Korea is a large, mountainous peninsula that juts out from the Asian continent. Its population became concentrated in the coastal plains and river valleys, where the land was fertile and could be cultivated.

Korea's nearest neighbors are China and Japan. The three countries have always influenced one another, both culturally and politically. In 108 B.C., the Chinese Han dynasty conquered northwest Korea. Chinese settlers followed, bringing their culture with them. But as the Han dynasty declined, its grip on Korea weakened. Korea's scattered native tribes began taking control of their lands and gradually formed three kingdoms.

Tradition claims that the **Silla** (SIHL-uh) kingdom was formed in southeast Korea around 57 B.C. About 37 B.C., the **Koguryo** (koh-gur-YOO) kingdom emerged in the north. Then, around 18 B.C., the **Paekche** (pahk-chay) kingdom was founded in the southwest. For centuries, the three kingdoms grew, developed, and fought one another for control of Korea. At first, Koguryo was by far the strongest, even as it fought off Chinese invasions. But by the A.D. 300s, Koguryo had managed to dominate most of the peninsula. Paekche's strength was largely economic due to extensive trade. Over time, Silla increased its political, military, and economic power.

RIVALRY

Despite their bitter rivalry, or competition, the three kingdoms had very similar cultures. They each developed feudal-style societies, with kings commanding a warrior aristocracy and an educated bureaucracy. Poor peasants provided the labor for agriculture. The kingdoms shared a common language and adopted Chinese writing. Their economies were similar as well. All three exported leather goods, tools, and wool clothing in exchange for Chinese paper, porcelain, silk, and weapons.

Chinese culture greatly influenced Korea in the areas of art, architecture, literature, government, and religion. From China, the kingdoms imported the Buddhist religion, as well as Confucian ideas for government and society. They also adopted Chinese writing. Despite these strong Chinese influences, Korea managed to maintain its own distinct culture.

In A.D. 660, the Silla king entered into an alliance with the Tang dynasty in China. Together, Silla and the Tang conquered Paekche in A.D. 660 and Koguryo in A.D. 668. For the first time, Korea was unified.

THE THREE KINGDOMS OF KOREA, A.D. 500s

CHINA

KOGURYO

Sea of Japan
(East Sea)

40°N

Yellow
Sea

Kongju

PAEKCHE

SILLA

Kyongju

JAPAN

Kyoto

Osaka

35°N

125°E

130°E

135°E

0   100   200 Miles
0   100   200 Kilometers

Some historians see Silla's alliance with Tang China as a national betrayal that encouraged China's ambition to control the peninsula. Nevertheless, the alliance turned out to be a brilliant move for Silla. After the two allies conquered Paekche, the Tang seized complete control of the conquered lands and reduced the Silla king's powers. Silla waited patiently for revenge. It did not have long to wait.

Following the alliance's defeat of Koguryo, Silla took control of Paekche. Then China tried to depose the Silla king, an action that led to war between the two former allies. After a series of battles, Silla defeated the Chinese army in A.D. 675 and then fought off the Chinese navy the following year. China withdrew from the peninsula in A.D. 676, leaving Silla in control of a unified Korean kingdom.

REVIEW & ASSESS

1. **READING CHECK** How did China influence early Korea?

2. **SYNTHESIZE** What political goal did Silla, Koguryo, and Paekche have in common?

3. **INTERPRET MAPS** Why has human movement between China and Korea been relatively easy throughout history?

 7.3.1 Describe the reunification of China under the Tang Dynasty and reasons for the spread of Buddhism in Tang China, Korea, and Japan; CST 3 Students use a variety of maps and documents to identify physical and cultural features of neighborhoods, cities, states, and countries and to explain the historical migration of people, expansion and disintegration of empires, and the growth of economic systems; HI 6 Students interpret basic indicators of economic performance and conduct cost-benefit analyses of economic and political issues.

1.2 KOREAN ARTIFACTS

Archaeologists have discovered many beautiful artifacts from early Korea. These artifacts range from pottery to jewelry to religious figures. In Silla, sometimes called "the land of gold," artisans often used gold to create precious objects, including a number of gold crowns. Uniquely Korean, the crowns' designs incorporate chains with mirrors or jewels as well as elements of trees and antlers.

Crown of Silla
This ornate crown of gold was discovered in the tomb of a Silla king and queen.

Gogok
This jade teardrop, or *gogok*, probably once adorned a crown, belt, or bracelet.

Earrings
This pair of gold earrings from the early 400s were probably worn by a Silla noblewoman.

Tile
The monster mask on this roof tile was thought to ward off evil spirits.

Vase
Tiny figures of animals decorate this gray stoneware vase.

Dragon's Head
This gilded bronze dragon's head reflects the skill of Silla artisans.

Necklace
This ornate gold necklace is adorned with a jade gogok.

Bodhisattva
This statue of an enlightened being, or bodhisattva, is made of gilded bronze.

1.3 Koryo and Choson Dynasties

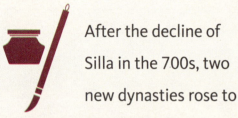

After the decline of Silla in the 700s, two new dynasties rose to power. During the Koryo and Choson dynasties, Korea enjoyed proud independence. Then new rulers forbade Koreans from meeting freely, speaking their mind, practicing their culture, or even using their family name.

MAIN IDEA

Two great dynasties ruled for nearly a thousand years before Korea lost its independence.

KORYO

In the 700s, after a golden age, Silla began to decline. Its rulers fought among themselves. Nobles seized large areas of farmland, while peasants rebelled against poor government. In A.D. 918, General Wang Kon founded a rival dynasty called the **Koryo**. After a long war, the Silla king surrendered in 935. Then, for more than 450 years, Korea was ruled by the Koryo, from which Korea takes its name.

Chinese ideas and practices continued to flow south, although they were ==adapted==, or changed, to meet Koryo's own needs. For example, Koryo adapted Chinese-style centralized government but gave special preference to aristocrats. As a result, Koryo's professional bureaucracy came almost entirely from its hereditary nobility. Koryo potters also imported advanced Chinese techniques but again developed a uniquely Korean style.

Yet Chinese influence remained strong. As in China, Buddhism greatly inspired art. Korea's literary language remained Chinese for centuries, and Chinese poetry was much imitated. Even the oldest surviving book on Korea's history, the *Samguk Sagi*, mentions almost twice as many Chinese sources as Korean.

CHOSON

In 1231, the Mongols invaded Koryo and took control. The Mongols were harsh rulers. They demanded tribute from the Koryo rulers, who had to send them a million soldiers and 20,000 horses. Mongol domination ended in 1336. Soon, a new dynasty arose.

In 1392, the **Choson** dynasty replaced the Koryo dynasty. Choson ruled Korea for the next 518 years. Like Koryo, Choson adapted many elements of Chinese culture. Choson rulers created a strong, centralized Confucian-style government with a strict political and social hierarchy. However, over the following centuries, Korea developed its own alphabet, artistic styles, and other distinctive cultural characteristics.

Then, in 1894, disaster struck. Both China and Japan invaded Korea to help crush a people's rebellion. The rebels quickly surrendered, but Japan fought on and won control of the peninsula. In 1910, Korea was formally made part of Japan, which imposed a harsh military rule.

The Japanese occupied Korea until 1945. During this occupation, life in Korea contrasted sharply with life during the Choson dynasty. The Japanese required Koreans to adopt Japanese culture and even to use Japanese-style names. Koreans considered this a heartbreaking betrayal of their ancestry and a bitter end to Korean independence.

Critical Viewing This detail from an 18th-century silk banner shows a group of women during the Choson Dynasty. What indicates that the women are from different social classes?

后妃

REVIEW & ASSESS

1. **READING CHECK** What common influence helped shape the Koryo and Choson dynasties?

2. **CATEGORIZE** During the Choson dynasty, which cultural characteristics were distinctively Korean?

3. **ANALYZE CAUSE AND EFFECT** What caused the end of Korean independence in 1910?

Korean Culture

When we pose for a picture, we say "cheese" to produce a smile. In Korea, they say "kimchi"—a word that ends with a similar sound. Koreans have been making kimchi for hundreds of years. It is one of many examples of Korea's distinctive culture.

MAIN IDEA

Korea developed their own culture despite many Chinese influences.

RELIGION, POTTERY, AND PRINTING

While Chinese ideas and practices were certainly influential, Korea developed its own culture. Chinese Confucianism and Buddhism were adapted to Korean needs. Inspired by Song China's advanced glazed ceramics, Korean potters developed **celadon** (SEH-luh-dahn), a type of pottery with a unique blue-green color. Korean celadon is considered among the finest porcelain in the world.

Similarly, Chinese woodblock printing reached new heights in Korean hands. Korean monks spent years painstakingly carving Buddhist teachings onto more than 80,000 wooden blocks known collectively as the **Tripitaka Koreana**. After the blocks were burned during the Mongol invasion in 1231, Buddhist monks made and recarved all new blocks, which are kept at Haeinsa Temple in present-day South Korea.

Built in the 1400s, the complex of four buildings that house the Tripitaka Koreana is also remarkable. These structures create an environment that has preserved the woodblocks for centuries. The floor contains a mixture of soil, charcoal, salt, clay, sand, and plaster powder that regulates moisture, while strategically placed windows ensure consistent air quality.

In 1377, Korea produced *Jikji*, the world's oldest book printed with movable metal type. Reusable metal characters arranged on a board created a printing plate that was tough and flexible, allowing for mass printing. Korea used metal type 78 years before it was first used in Europe.

FOOD, CLOTHING, AND HEATING

Other aspects of daily life illustrate Korea's distinctive culture. **Kimchi**, for example, is Korea's national dish. This dish is made

of spicy pickled vegetables and is as full of flavor as it is rich in vitamins and minerals. People began making kimchi as a way of preserving vegetables, especially cabbage. Once sliced and seasoned, the vegetables were placed in large jars of salt water and buried. About a month later, the kimchi was ready to eat. Today, there are more than 160 varieties of kimchi.

For centuries, Koreans wore traditional clothing called **hanbok**. A woman's hanbok included seven layers of undergarments covered by a long billowing skirt and a short, tight-fitting jacket. Men wore full-length pants and a long jacket with wide sleeves. The material ranged from hemp to silk but was usually brightly colored with beautiful designs. Today, most Koreans wear hanbok only on special occasions.

From as early as the first century, Korean homes benefited from a unique system of heating called **ondol**. Hot air from fireplaces was drawn through passageways beneath the floors. The heated air warmed both the floors and the rooms above. Even today, Koreans use an updated version of ondol.

REVIEW & ASSESS

1. **READING CHECK** What aspects of Chinese culture did Koreans adapt to develop their own distinct culture?

2. **ANALYZE CAUSE AND EFFECT** Why were the Tripitaka woodblocks carved a second time?

3. **DETERMINE WORD MEANINGS** In the phrase "the complex of four buildings," what does the word *complex* mean?

THE GUPTA EMPIRE, c. A.D. 400

HINDU KUSH
HIMALAYA
Indus R.
Ganges
Ayodhya
R.
Pataliputra
MAGADHA
Tropic of Cancer
*Arabian
Sea*
Bay of
Bengal

Gupta Empire

0   300   600 Miles
0   300   600 Kilometers

N W E S

Dedicated to the God Vishnu, the Dashavatar Temple in northern India is an example of Gupta architecture.

The Gupta Empire

As Korea's Three Kingdoms battled for control of the peninsula, a similar struggle was occurring on the Indian subcontinent. After 500 years of fighting, however, a unifying power arose and ushered India through a golden age.

MAIN IDEA

The Gupta Empire brought 200 years of peace and prosperity to India.

A WISE RULER

India was united for the first time under the rule of Chandragupta Maurya around 320 B.C. His grandson, Asoka, was a strong ruler and helped spread Buddhism throughout Asia. After his death, however, the Maurya Empire collapsed into many warring kingdoms. Then around A.D. 320, a new unifying power arose. A leader from the kingdom of Magadha called **Chandra Gupta I** began gaining new land and established the Gupta Empire. A dynasty of strong Gupta kings continued to expand the empire until it covered most of northern India. The Guptas allowed defeated kings to continue to rule and, in exchange, required obedience and tribute from them.

Gupta rulers brought India 200 years of political stability, peace, and prosperity. The expanding empire and its extensive trade routes spread Indian cultural influences around Asia and beyond.

GOLDEN AGE AND DECLINE

Chandra Gupta II, grandson of Chandra Gupta I, ruled during India's **golden age**, a period of great cultural achievement. **Kalidasa** (kah-lih-DAH-suh), one of India's greatest writers, composed poems and plays in Sanskrit. Scribes, or writers, wrote down ancient spoken stories, including Hindu epic poems such as the *Mahabharata* and the *Ramayana*. Architects designed and built elegant new temples.

Indian mathematicians developed the concept of zero, which is crucial to mathematics and computing. Indian astronomers calculated the length of the solar year. They also asserted that Earth traveled around the sun and proved that the world was round 1,000 years before Columbus's voyage to the Americas.

After the decline of the Gupta Empire in the mid-500s, northern India was split into several smaller kingdoms. In southern India, the powerful Chola Empire arose around A.D. 900 and dominated due to its control of trade across the Indian Ocean. The Cholas also built many ornate and beautiful Hindu temples and spread their cultural influence across Southeast Asia.

REVIEW & ASSESS

1. **READING CHECK** How did both the Guptas and the Cholas spread Indian culture beyond South Asia?

2. **INTERPRET MAPS** In which directions did the Gupta Empire spread out from Magadha?

3. **FORM AND SUPPORT OPINIONS** Which achievement during India's golden age do you think was most significant? Explain your answer.

CST 3 Students use a variety of maps and documents to identify physical and cultural features of neighborhoods, cities, states, and countries and to explain the historical migration of people, expansion and disintegration of empires, and the growth of economic systems.

2.2 Religion in South Asia

Religion is an important part of South Asia's history because it has shaped borders and cultures. Two of the world's main religions—Hinduism and Buddhism—were founded in India and spread around the world. Islam, while founded on the Arabian Peninsula, quickly spread to South Asia. After Hinduism, it is the second-largest religion in the region.

MAIN IDEA

India played an important role in the development and spread of world religions.

HINDUISM AND BUDDHISM

During the Gupta Empire, Hinduism flourished and eventually became India's main religion. Scholars believe that Hinduism evolved over many centuries from the ideas and practices of diverse communities. Its many Gods and Goddesses, or Deities, are representations of Brahman, a universal spirit. The three most widely worshipped Gods are Brahma (the creator), Vishnu (the preserver), and Shiva (the transformer).

A key belief of Hinduism is the concept of **reincarnation**, or the rebirth of the soul. After death, a person's soul is reborn into another physical life. The kind of life is determined by a soul's **karma**, or actions during a life. If a soul has lived a good life, it is reborn into a more spiritually evolved life. If the soul has lived an evil life, it is reborn into a life with greater suffering. This process continues until the soul lives a perfect life.

Toward the end of the 600s, a Hindu spiritual movement known as the Bhakti movement began in southern India and, over centuries, spread to other parts of the Indian subcontinent. This movement placed less importance on the rituals of early Hinduism and social hierarchy and emphasized a personal devotion to a Deity. It also emphasized social and religious equality. Prominent Bhakti saints included Meera Bhai and Ramananda.

As with Hinduism, Buddhism changed over time to became a more devotional religion. The Buddha came to be treated as a god and was worshipped along with **bodhisattvas** (boh-dih-SUHT-vuhz), or enlightened beings.

As Hinduism regained popularity, the practice of Buddhism in India began to decline. However, as you've already learned in Chapter 8, it spread to Central and East Asia via merchants and missionaries along the Silk Roads. Both Hinduism and Buddhism also spread to Southeast Asian kingdoms through trade across the Indian Ocean. You will learn more about these kingdoms and India's influence later in this chapter.

THE ARRIVAL OF ISLAM

Islam arrived in India via trade with Africa and through invasions by Turks from Central Asia. By the early 1200s, most of northern India was under Muslim rule in the established Delhi sultanate. The sultanate lasted for nearly three centuries and is credited with preventing the Mongols from invading South Asia.

Many Muslim rulers practiced tolerance with their Hindu subjects, and Hinduism remained India's main religion. However, Islam did become an established religion through forced conversion by some rulers and by

Schoolgirls offer a prayer before a performance of Indian classical dance in honor of Lord Shiva.

the voluntary conversion of Indians who wanted to avoid paying a special tax. Many Indians were converted by Sufi missionaries. Sufis are Muslims who believe in a personal, emotional, and devotional relationship with God and focus less on formal religious teachings.

Muslim rule in India reached its peak with the Mughal Empire, which you read about in Chapter 3. However, Islam remained popular and soon became India's second-largest religion.

SIKHISM

In the midst of northern India's Hindu and Muslim population, a new religion, Sikhism, emerged in 1469 in Punjab. It was based on the religious experience of ten gurus, or teachers, whose teachings were collected in a scripture called the Guru Granth Sahib.

Sikhs believe in one God who is formless, all-powerful, all-loving, and without fear or hate toward anyone. They also believe that an individual can achieve unity with God through service to others, meditation, and honest labor. Sikhs do not use tobacco or alcohol, and they often follow a strict dress code, which includes never cutting their hair.

REVIEW & ASSESS

1. **READING CHECK** What role did India play in the development and spread of world religions?

2. **DESCRIBE** How did Hinduism change as a result of the Bhakti movement?

3. **MAKE INFERENCES** Why might members of India's lower social classes have been attracted to Sufi beliefs?

273

2.3 Vietnamese Kingdoms

Are there people you admire but also dislike? Perhaps you appreciate their skill in sports but dislike their superior attitude in the classroom. Vietnam appreciated Chinese culture but hated Chinese domination.

MAIN IDEA

Vietnam followed more than a millennium of foreign occupation with a thousand years of independence.

CHINESE RULE

Although the origins of modern Vietnam are shrouded in myth, Vietnamese history most likely began with the migration of settlers from southern China into the Red River delta. As in Korea, Vietnam's challenge was maintaining political and cultural independence from China, its powerful neighbor.

In 207 B.C., an ambitious Chinese governor incorporated the Red River delta into his breakaway kingdom of **Nam Viet**. Barely a century later, in 111 B.C., the Han Chinese seized control of Nam Viet, and it became a Chinese-ruled province for more than a thousand years. The province provided China with valuable ports for traders sailing to India and Southeast Asia.

Nam Viet's Chinese rulers increasingly **imposed**, or forced, Chinese culture onto the Nam Viet people. Yet the harder China pushed, the more the people resisted, which led to many violent uprisings. The most famous was in A.D. 39, when sisters **Trung Trac** and **Trung Nhi** led a rebellion against Chinese rule. Having raised an army, the sisters rode into battle on the backs of elephants. Within a year, the two women and their allies had driven out the Chinese. The sisters ruled for three years before being defeated by Chinese forces. Today the Trung sisters are still honored as national heroes.

DAI VIET

In A.D. 938, Ngo Quyen (noh kwehn) led an uprising that finally defeated the Chinese. In a decisive battle, he sank China's warships by planting iron-tipped stakes in a riverbed. China acknowledged the independence of the new **Dai Viet** state in exchange for tribute payments. This began a thousand years of independence for Vietnam.

The Ly dynasty's strong leadership from 1009 to 1225 moved the Vietnamese capital to what is now Hanoi, established a strong central government, and built an effective road network. Ly rulers reinforced Buddhism as the state religion and promoted Confucian values in government and society. They developed a code of law and recruited a professional army.

From 1225 to 1400, the equally dynamic Tran dynasty further reformed the administration, agriculture, and economy. Tran rulers succeeded in fighting off a major Mongol invasion in 1257 and expanded south into the rival kingdom of Champa. Then, in 1407, the Ming Chinese invaded and brutally enforced Chinese culture.

When, in 1428, Le Thanh Tong restored native rule, he actively promoted China's government systems as well as its language, art, and literature. His reforms may have had a greater effect on making Vietnam Chinese than a thousand years of occupation. In 1471, Dai Viet reconquered Champa, creating what is now recognized as Vietnam.

EARLY CHINESE INFLUENCE IN ASIA

Sea of Japan
(East Sea)

KOREA

JAPAN

Yellow
Sea

CHINA

East
China
Sea

PACIFIC
OCEAN

DAI VIET

KHMER

South
China
Sea

Legend

- Buddhism
- Civil service
- Agriculture
- Porcelain
- Printing
- System of writing

0   300   600 Miles

0   300   600 Kilometers

N
W   E
S

100°E   120°E   130°E
10°N
20°N
30°N
40°N
50°N

REVIEW & ASSESS

1. READING CHECK Why did the Han Chinese want to occupy and control Nam Viet?

2. COMPARE AND CONTRAST How was Le Thanh Tong's rule similar to the Ming Chinese rule of Vietnam?

3. INTERPRET MAPS Where did Buddhism spread from China?

2.4 The Khmer Empire

 Dark and threatening skies mean the monsoon is coming. However, you are confident that the efficient network of dams, dikes, and canals will save your rice paddy from flood damage. Rice is the backbone of the Khmer economy.

MAIN IDEA

Rice agriculture helped the Khmer dominate Southeast Asia for centuries.

INDIAN AND CHINESE INFLUENCES

Present-day Cambodia was the heartland of one of Southeast Asia's most powerful states. The **Khmer** (kuh-MAIR) people migrated south from China. By A.D. 500, they were founding small city-states known collectively as Chenla. To their south lay the powerful trading kingdom of Funan, which was probably founded by Indian traders who valued its strategic location between India and China. Funan introduced many Indian influences to Cambodia, including irrigation, centralized government, the Sanskrit language, and the Hindu religion.

In the mid-600s, Chenla extended into Funan. Threatened by strong island nations like Java, the Chenla kingdoms rallied together for protection. In 802, they formally united under the "universal ruler" Jayavarman II (JEYE-ah-var-mahn). This was the beginning of the Khmer Empire, which dominated Southeast Asia until 1431.

THE ANGKOR ERA

The Khmer established their capital in Angkor, which means "city." The city's art and architecture were Indian in style, and the layout reflected the Hindu vision of the universe. Khmer religious beliefs were a complex mixture of Hinduism, Buddhism, and native religions. The Khmer adopted the Indian idea of kings as gods who ruled with divine authority.

A large central bureaucracy governed the Khmer Empire, which included vassal states. These states paid tribute, which, along with trade, contributed to the empire's economy. Yet the mainstay of the Khmer economy was rice.

The Khmer were skilled rice farmers, having learned how to grow rice from the Chinese. The Khmer region's many wet and fertile river deltas were ideal for **cultivating**, or growing, rice. Khmer farmers built a brilliant water-management system to control and harness the heavy monsoon rains. The system combined immense storage tanks with canals, dikes, and dams. As a result, farmers were able to produce three or four rice harvests a year. By 1250, rice fed Angkor's population of 1.5 million and produced a huge surplus for export. This intensive rice cultivation was the foundation of Khmer prosperity, stability, and power, which expanded across Southeast Asia.

The Khmer Empire reached its peak under Jayavarman VII, who ruled from 1181 to 1218. Jayavarman VII built roads and a new capital city called Angkor Thom. He also supported Buddhism by building an estimated 20,000 Buddhist shrines. Under his rule, the state supported 300,000 monks and priests. Pouring resources into religious monuments strained the economy to the breaking point. Over the next two centuries, wars further weakened the Khmer Empire. In 1431, a Thai army seized Angkor itself. Though the empire shifted south, its power declined and its capital was abandoned.

A farmer in Cambodia harvests rice by hand.

REVIEW & ASSESS

1. **READING CHECK** How did rice agriculture lead to prosperity and power for the Khmer Empire?

2. **ANALYZE CAUSE AND EFFECT** How did India influence the culture of the Khmer?

3. **IDENTIFY MAIN IDEAS AND DETAILS** What two factors led to the downfall of the Khmer Empire?

2.5

Angkor Wat

With its dramatic jungle setting and fantastic architecture, the temple city of Angkor Wat is the classic image of a lost city. Remote and mysterious, it has been the spectacular backdrop for many Hollywood movies.

MAIN IDEA

Khmer culture peaked with the building of Angkor Wat.

A GREAT TEMPLE COMPLEX

The Khmer capital city of Angkor is actually a series of cities and temples spread over more than 300 square miles. For almost 500 years, Angkor was the political and religious heart of the Khmer Empire and the largest city in the world. Each king added to its glory by building beautiful temples and even a whole new city within the city. In the 1100s, however, King Suryavarman II built Angkor's most celebrated addition—the temple complex of **Angkor Wat**.

Angkor Wat means "city that is a temple." Its complex of interconnected buildings covers 244 acres, making it the largest religious monument in the world. Built to honor the Hindu God Vishnu, the temple has at its center a vast five-towered pyramid. Each tower is shaped like a lotus bud. In Hinduism, the lotus flower represents beauty and purity while the tower symbolizes the home of the Hindu Gods. An outer wall and a wide moat represent mountains at the edge of the world and the ocean that lies beyond. Indeed, every feature of Angkor Wat has a symbolic meaning.

The temple represents the peak of Khmer artistic achievement. Among its most admired features are its extraordinarily intricate carvings. These include hundreds of dancers, each one unique. Another outstanding feature is a 1,970-foot stretch of **bas-reliefs** (slightly raised figures on a flat background) that show scenes from Hindu legends.

Angkor Wat was also built to be Suryavarman's tomb and possibly an astronomical observatory as well. There is some evidence that it is oriented to align with certain stars. Unlike most other Khmer temples, Angkor Wat faces west, toward the setting sun, which symbolizes death.

CHANGES AND RESTORATION

After the Khmer's switch to Buddhism, Angkor Wat became a Buddhist shrine. When the Khmer Empire collapsed, Angkor fell to its enemies. By the 1600s, it was largely abandoned. The jungle quickly consumed its wooden structures and covered its stone buildings.

Then, in 1860, the French explorer Henri Mouhot encountered the "lost" world of Angkor and Angkor Wat. Mouhot brought the site to the attention of westerners. Sadly, visitors and thieves began removing its treasures. Indeed, Angkor Wat has suffered terribly from looters, uncontrolled tourism, and even poorly performed restoration.

Fortunately, in 1992, it became a UNESCO World Heritage Site with carefully planned measures to protect it for future generations. Today Angkor Wat is Cambodia's main tourist attraction with over 2 million visitors every year. It is so important to the country that it forms the centerpiece of the Cambodian flag.

REVIEW & ASSESS

1. **READING CHECK** Why was Angkor Wat built?

2. **IDENTIFY MAIN IDEAS AND DETAILS** Why is Angkor Wat often thought of as representing the peak of Khmer artistic achievement?

3. **SEQUENCE EVENTS** What changes did Angkor Wat undergo during its long history?

VOCABULARY

On your paper, write the vocabulary word that best completes each of the following sentences.

1. Korea's three early kingdoms had a bitter _____, so they fought one another for control of Korea.

2. Korean potters developed _____, which was known for its bluish-green color.

3. The Korean national dish is called _____, which is made with spicy pickled cabbage and other vegetables.

4. For centuries, the traditional _____ worn by Korean men included full-length pants and a long jacket with wide sleeves.

5. Early Koreans invented a unique system of heating called _____, which is still used in Korean homes today.

6. As Chinese rulers tried to _____ Chinese culture on the people of Nam Viet, violent uprisings occurred.

7. The Khmer took advantage of the wet and fertile river deltas to _____ rice successfully, which led to their prosperity.

READING STRATEGY

8. **DETERMINE WORD MEANINGS** If you haven't already, complete the chart for at least three vocabulary words. Then use each word in a paragraph about the history of Korea, India, or Southeast Asia.

Word	Definition	Example from My Life
rivalry	competition	

MAIN IDEAS

Answer the following questions. Support your answers with evidence from the chapter.

9. How did the Silla kingdom triumph to unify Korea? **LESSON 1.1**

10. What borrowed aspects of Chinese culture helped the Koryo and Choson dynasties rule Korea for nearly a thousand years? **LESSON 1.3**

11. Despite strong Chinese influences, how did Korea develop a distinct culture? **LESSON 1.4**

12. Why did the Han Chinese want to occupy and control Nam Viet? **LESSON 2.3**

13. Why was rice farming important to the Khmer people? **LESSON 2.4**

14. What purposes did Angkor Wat serve? **LESSON 2.5**

CRITICAL THINKING

Answer the following questions. Support your answers with evidence from the chapter.

15. **ESSENTIAL QUESTION** How did civilizations in China and India influence civilizations in Korea and Southeast Asia? **HSS HI 2**

16. **COMPARE AND CONTRAST** How were the cultures of the three early Korean kingdoms—Silla, Koguryo, and Paekche—alike? **HSS HI 2**

17. **ANALYZE CAUSE AND EFFECT** What effect did the Japanese occupation have on Korea? **HSS HI 2**

18. **DRAW CONCLUSIONS** Why was the Korean invention of movable metal type a pioneering breakthrough in printing? **HSS HI 3**

19. **MAKE INFERENCES** How did the Khmer's hierarchical society reflect the influence of ancient Indian culture? **HSS HI 2**

20. **YOU DECIDE** Which do you think was the greater Korean cultural achievement, the development of celadon or the creation of the Tripitaka Koreana? Support your opinion with evidence from the chapter. **HSS REP 1**

INTERPRET MAPS

Study the map of Southeast Asia as it was in 1895. Then answer the questions that follow.

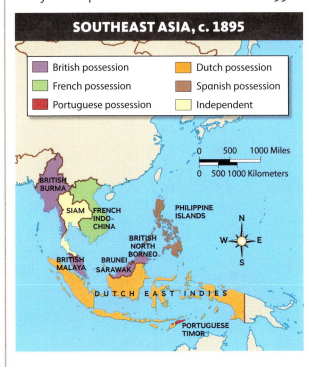

SOUTHEAST ASIA, c. 1895

- British possession
- French possession
- Portuguese possession
- Dutch possession
- Spanish possession
- Independent

0   500   1000 Miles
0   500 1000 Kilometers

BRITISH BURMA
SIAM
FRENCH INDO-CHINA
PHILIPPINE ISLANDS
BRITISH NORTH BORNEO
BRITISH MALAYA
BRUNEI SARAWAK
DUTCH EAST INDIES
PORTUGUESE TIMOR

N W E S

21. Based on the map, how would you describe foreign rule of Southeast Asia around 1895? **HSS CST 3**

22. Which European countries held the most territory in Southeast Asia around 1895? **HSS CST 3**

23. **MAP ACTIVITY** Sketch a map of Southeast Asia as it is today. Then compare it with Southeast Asia as it appeared in 1895. What similarities and diferences do you notice between borders of territories in 1895 and countries in the present day? **HSS CST 3**

ANALYZE SOURCES

Read the following paragraph about the Trung sisters. Then answer the question that follows.

> In A.D. 40, the Trung sisters set up an army with the aid of the Vietnamese lords. Fighting fearlessly, they expelled the Chinese and established their own kingdom. In A.D. 43, however, the Chinese quelled [put down] the rebellion. To avoid capture, the sisters committed suicide by jumping into the Hat River. Centuries later, stone figures of two women washed up on a sandbank in the Red River. Believed to be the earthly remains of the Trung Sisters, petrified and turned into statues, they were taken to Dong Nhan village and installed in a temple there.

24. The Trung sisters are still honored today in Vietnam. What qualities do you think the Vietnamese admire in the two sisters? **HSS REP 4**

WRITE ABOUT HISTORY

25. **INFORMATIVE** Suppose you are taking tourists on a tour of Angkor Wat. Write a paragraph in which you explain to them how Angkor Wat represents the peak of Khmer artistic achievement. Use the tips below to help you plan, organize, and revise your paragraph. **HSS HI 1**

TIPS

- Take notes from the lesson about Angkor Wat.
- Introduce the topic clearly.
- Develop the topic with supporting details about the temple and its relationship to Hinduism, artistic features, and symbolic meanings.
- Use two or three vocabulary terms from the chapter.
- Provide a concluding statement that summarizes the significance of the temple.
- Use word-processing software to produce and publish your final paragraph.

ON **LOCATION** WITH

Albert Lin

NATIONAL GEOGRAPHIC EMERGING EXPLORER

▶ Check out more at NGLSync.Cengage.com

Albert Lin, pictured here in the forests of Mongolia, teams up with other National Geographic Explorers as part of the Valley of the Khans Project to hunt for the tomb of Genghis Khan.

TWO PATHS

Society often encourages us to choose a single path in life, but I've always been interested both in the sciences and the humanities. Turning my education in engineering into one of the greatest adventures of my life has been a huge journey. The idea to search for the tomb of Genghis Khan occurred to me while backpacking in Mongolia. I wanted to do something that everyone thought was impossible.

Genghis Khan united Mongolia's feuding tribes and led them on a campaign of conquest unequalled in world history. He died in 1227, but the location of his tomb remains a mystery. In fact, Mongolian custom warns that disturbing Genghis Khan's burial site will unleash a curse that could end the world. With a cultural taboo as strong as that, you can't just start digging—you have to get smart.

Albert Lin examines a digital projection of northern Mongolia from inside the StarCAVE, a 3-D virtual environment.

USING TECHNOLOGY

There are many ways to look under the ground without having to touch it. I use non-invasive computer-based technologies to gather, synthesize, and visualize data without ever digging a hole. Satellite imagery, ground-penetrating radar, and remote sensors let me explore places and make archaeological discoveries while respecting the traditional beliefs of indigenous people.

The real trick is synthesizing the vast amounts of information we collect into something that can be understood. We program billions of individual data bits into a file that allows us to re-render it into a digital 3-D world. And then we have some fun in the StarCAVE, a virtual reality room that lets us manipulate our way through images projected on the ground, walls, and on every surface. Special glasses create the 3-D effect so we can "fly" over the landscape. For example if a mountain is described in an old text, I can go into the StarCAVE and travel around that region to see if it actually exists. Technology like this lets us conduct a non-invasive search for Genghis Khan in a way that is respectful to the Mongolians. We can try to solve this ancient mystery without overstepping cultural barriers.

WHY STUDY HISTORY ?

"The Mongols created a lot of what we know of as our modern history, but their story hasn't been fully told and their contributions have been underestimated. *Sharing the true history of the foundation of our cultural past is crucial.* **"** —Albert Lin

NATIONAL GEOGRAPHIC

Divining Angkor

BY RICHARD STONE

Adapted from "Divining Angkor," by Richard Stone, in *National Geographic*, July 2009

The Khmer kingdom lasted from the 9th to the 15th centuries. At its height it dominated a wide swath of Southeast Asia. Angkor, its capital, was the most extensive urban complex of the preindustrial world. As many as 750,000 people lived there. By the late 16th century, the once-magnificent capital was in decline.

Angkor became a powerhouse thanks to a sophisticated system of canals and reservoirs. Over several centuries, teams of laborers constructed hundreds of miles of canals and dikes. The city could hoard water in dry months and get rid of excess water during the rainy season.

The ability to divert and collect water would have afforded a measure of protection from floods, as well as a steady water supply. But forces beyond Angkor's control threw this system into disarray. Archaeologist Roland Fletcher was baffled when his team unearthed a vast structure in the waterworks and found that it had been destroyed, apparently by Angkor's own engineers.

These ruins are a vital clue to an epic struggle that unfolded as generations of Khmer engineers coped with an increasingly complex water system. "They probably spent vast portions of their lives fixing it," says Fletcher. Any deterioration of the waterworks would have left Angkor vulnerable to a natural disaster.

Starting in the 1300s, Europe endured a few centuries of unpredictable weather marked by harsh winters and chilly summers. Now it appears that Southeast Asia, too, experienced climatic upheaval. Extreme weather could have been the final blow to a vulnerable civilization. Prolonged and severe droughts, punctuated by torrential downpours, "would have ruined the water system," says Fletcher.

Angkor's end is a sobering lesson in the limits of human ingenuity. "Angkor's hydraulic system was an amazing machine," Fletcher says. Its engineers managed to keep the civilization's signal achievement running for six centuries—until, in the end, a greater force overwhelmed them.

For more from National Geographic
Check out "The Forgotten Road" at NGLSync.Cengage.com

UNIT INQUIRY: LEAVE A LEGACY OF INNOVATION

In this unit, you learned about Chinese, Japanese, Korean, and Indian civilizations. Based on your understanding of the text, what new products, methods, and ideas did these civilizations invent or develop? Which of these innovations do you think has made a lasting legacy on the modern world?

ASSIGNMENT Choose an innovation that you think our modern civilization will leave as a legacy for a future civilization. The innovation you choose should come from the 20th or 21st century. Be prepared to present your legacy to the class and explain why you chose it.

Plan As you choose your innovation, think about how other innovations—such as the Chinese invention of paper—dramatically changed and influenced many civilizations past and present. Make a list of the ways in which the innovation you selected has affected or changed the modern world. You might want to use a graphic organizer to help organize your thoughts. ▶

Produce Use your notes to produce detailed descriptions of the impact your innovation has made on modern civilization and what impact you envision it having on a future civilization. You might want to write your descriptions in outline or paragraph form.

Present Choose a creative way to present your innovation to the class. Consider one of these options:

- Create a multimedia presentation using photos to illustrate different ways your innovation has affected or changed modern civilization.

- Design an advertisement for your innovation, providing a "before" and "after" view of our civilization with and without the innovation.

- Write a paragraph describing how you envision this innovation will impact a future civilization and why.

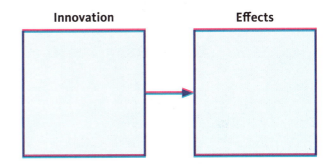

Innovation → Effects

MEDIEVAL, RENAISSANCE, AND REVOLUTIONARY EUROPE

NATIONAL GEOGRAPHIC

ON **LOCATION** WITH

Maurizio Seracini
Cultural Heritage Engineer

Europe experienced a "rebirth" around the 1300s, a time when writing, thinking, and the arts flourished. This movement, known as the Renaissance, began in Italy, and artists like Leonardo da Vinci, Raphael, and Michelangelo were hugely influential. I'm Maurizio Seracini, and I use technology to study priceless European works of art—and seek out ones that haven't been seen for centuries. Join me on an exploration of medieval and early modern Europe.

< **CRITICAL VIEWING** The Baptistery of Saint John in Florence, Italy, dazzles visitors with its mosaics and fine artwork. What types of imagery can you identify and what does it reveal about this time period?

Medieval, Renaissance, and Revolutionary Europe

768
Charlemagne becomes king of the Franks and, in time, unites much of Western Europe. *(bust of Charlemagne)*

1096
The Crusades begin. *(illustration of Crusaders in Jerusalem)*

1215
King John seals the Magna Carta.

c. 1300
The Renaissance begins in Italy.

1200

700

**1192
ASIA**
Military rule under leaders called shoguns begins in Japan.

**1325
THE AMERICAS**
The Aztec establish their capital in Tenochtitlán, present-day Mexico City. *(Aztec calendar)*

**610
ASIA**
Muhammad begins to spread Islam.

The World

CST 1 Students explain how major events are related to one another in time.

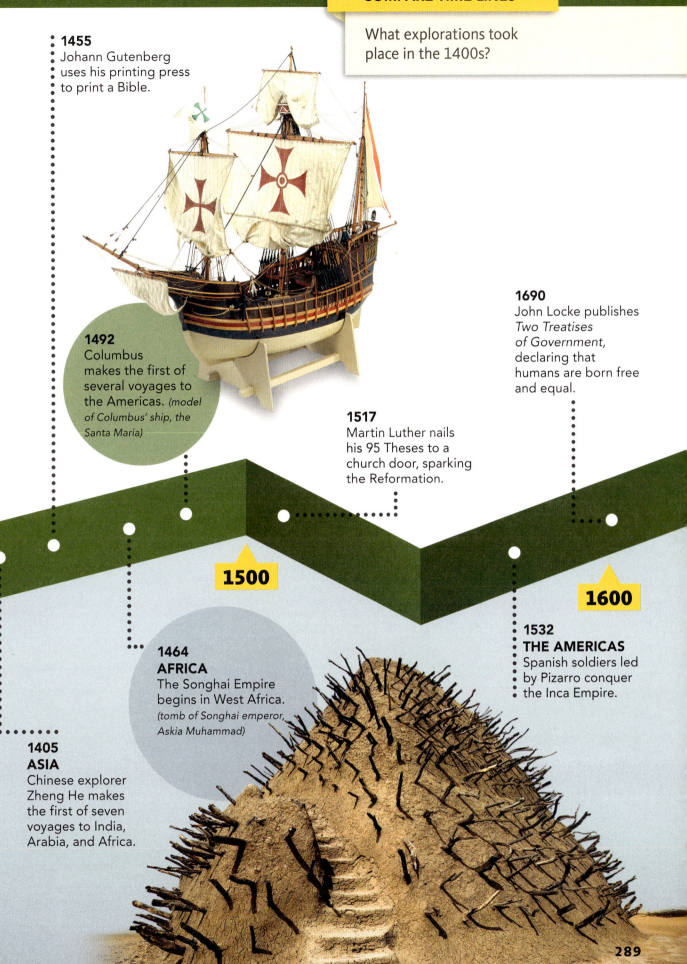

What explorations took place in the 1400s?

1455
Johann Gutenberg uses his printing press to print a Bible.

1492
Columbus makes the first of several voyages to the Americas. *(model of Columbus' ship, the Santa Maria)*

1690
John Locke publishes *Two Treatises of Government*, declaring that humans are born free and equal.

1517
Martin Luther nails his 95 Theses to a church door, sparking the Reformation.

1500

1600

1464
AFRICA
The Songhai Empire begins in West Africa. *(tomb of Songhai emperor, Askia Muhammad)*

1532
THE AMERICAS
Spanish soldiers led by Pizarro conquer the Inca Empire.

1405
ASIA
Chinese explorer Zheng He makes the first of seven voyages to India, Arabia, and Africa.

Europe
c. 1600

By the 1600s, Europe was divided into many states. One of these, the Holy Roman Empire, began in the 800s, when a Germanic king named Charlemagne united many other kingdoms under his rule. Charlemagne was a Christian and a strong supporter of the pope in Rome. He spread his faith throughout his empire.

However, over time, a revolution in thought led people to question the Roman Catholic Church. Some Europeans broke away from the Church and developed their own Christian religions, which soon spread over Europe.

What religions were practiced in the Holy Roman Empire?

EUROPEAN STATES

Europe, c. 1600
- Austrian-Habsburg possessions
- Spanish-Habsburg possessions
- Papal states
- Holy Roman Empire

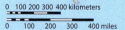
0   100 200 300 400 kilometers
0   100   200   300   400 miles

Renaissance Gallery

In the 1300s, an explosion in art called the Renaissance began in Italy and spread through Europe. Some of the greatest Renaissance artists created the works shown here.

Giotto: The Mourning of Christ (c. 1305)

Jan van Eyck: The Arnolfini Portrait (c. 1434)

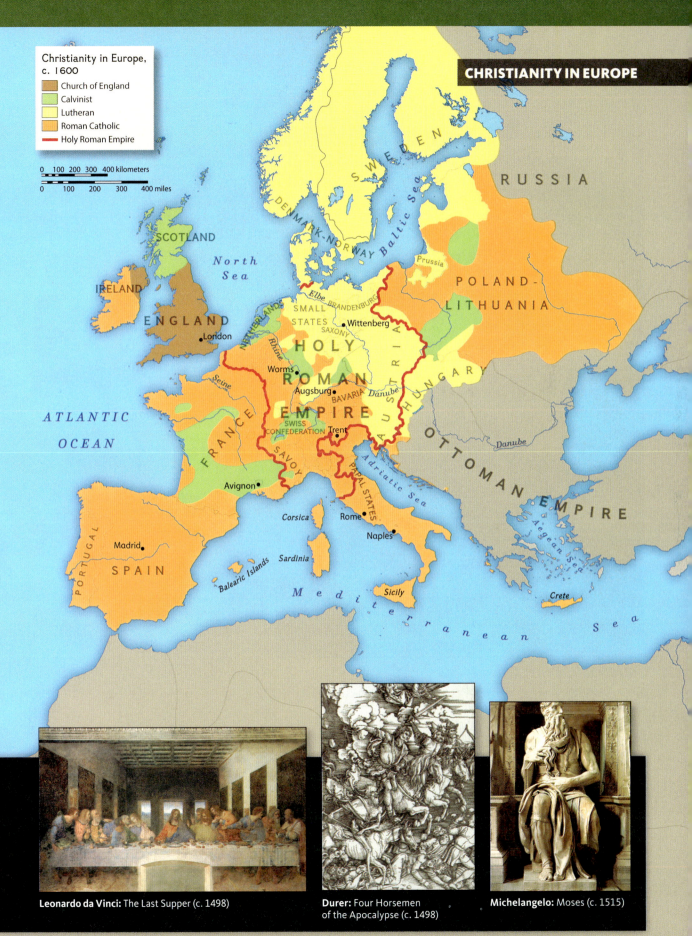

**Christianity in Europe,
c. 1600**

- ▨ Church of England
- ▧ Calvinist
- ▨ Lutheran
- ▧ Roman Catholic
- ▬ Holy Roman Empire

0 100 200 300 400 kilometers

0   100   200   300   400 miles

RUSSIA

SWEDEN

North
Sea

Baltic Sea

SCOTLAND

IRELAND

ENGLAND

London

NETHERLANDS

Prussia

POLAND-
LITHUANIA

Elbe

BRANDENBURG

SMALL
STATES

SAXONY

Wittenberg

HOLY

Rhine

Seine

ROMAN

Worms

Augsburg

EMPIRE

BAVARIA

Danube

AUSTRIA

HUNGARY

FRANCE

SWISS
CONFEDERATION

Trent

SAVOY

ATLANTIC

OCEAN

Avignon

Adriatic Sea

PAPAL
STATES

Corsica

Rome

Naples

OTTOMAN EMPIRE

Danube

Aegean Sea

PORTUGAL

Madrid

SPAIN

Balearic Islands

Sardinia

Sicily

Crete

M e d i t e r r a n e a n   S e a

Leonardo da Vinci: The Last Supper (c. 1498)

Durer: Four Horsemen
of the Apocalypse (c. 1498)

Michelangelo: Moses (c. 1515)

7.9.4 Identify and locate the European regions that remained Catholic and those that became Protestant and explain how the division affected the distribution of religions in the New World; CST 3 Students use a variety of maps and documents to identify physical and cultural features of neighborhoods, cities, states, and countries and to explain the historical migration of people, expansion and disintegration of empires, and the growth of economic systems.

11 FEUDALISM AND THE MIDDLE AGES

500 – 1453

ESSENTIAL QUESTION How did Europe change during the Middle Ages?

SECTION 1 FEUDALISM DEVELOPS

KEY VOCABULARY

chivalry
convert
feudalism
knight
lord
manor
medieval
serf
vassal

NAMES & PLACES

Charlemagne
Franks
Middle Ages

SECTION 2 POLITICAL AND SOCIAL CHANGE

KEY VOCABULARY

bubonic plague
burgher
cathedral
clergy
common law
guild
longbow
monastery
parliament

NAMES & PLACES

Crusades
Hundred Years' War
Inquisition
Joan of Arc
King John
Magna Carta
Reconquista

READING STRATEGY

DRAW CONCLUSIONS Drawing conclusions means using the facts in a text to make educated guesses. Use a chart like this one to jot down your conclusions about how feudalism and Christianity affected people during the Middle Ages.

Middle Ages

Feudalism	Christianity

During the Middle Ages, kings and nobles built thick-walled castles to keep out invaders. Some castles, like this one in England, were also surrounded by a moat to discourage the enemy.

Medieval Europe

The Germanic tribes that caused the fall of the Western Roman Empire in A.D. 476 didn't just devastate towns and kill many of their inhabitants. They destroyed a way of life. For hundreds of years, the Roman Empire had united much of Europe. With the empire no longer in control, "Now what?" could well have been the question on almost everyone's mind.

MAIN IDEA

After Rome fell, Western Europe underwent many political and cultural changes.

AFTER THE FALL OF ROME

What came next is a period historians call the **Middle Ages**. This era lasted from about 500 to 1450 in Western Europe and is also called the medieval period. **Medieval** comes from the Latin words *medium*, meaning "middle," and *aevum*, meaning "age."

During the early part of this period, Western Europe was very different from what it had been under Rome's strong central government and powerful army. After Rome fell, Germanic leaders seized power, and much of the region became divided into small kingdoms that were almost constantly at war. As a result of this widespread warfare, one of the greatest challenges facing leaders was to keep their people safe and secure. This challenge would help shape stronger governments over time.

It was a violent time, yet many kingdoms thrived. Thanks to the region's mostly moderate climate and rich soil, farmers could grow crops and feed themselves and their livestock. Abundant forestland provided wood for building, and mountains containing a wealth of minerals—particularly iron—allowed the Germanic peoples to make all the weapons they needed to fight their foes. In addition, Western Europe's long coastline and major rivers gave people access to the sea and plentiful supplies of fish.

POLITICAL AND CULTURAL CHANGES

The region's many waterways offered ideal routes and networks for trading. However, unlike the Romans, the Germanic peoples who migrated to Western Europe were not interested in trade. The tribes that settled in Roman lands in the early part of the Middle Ages preferred their own traditions to Roman ways.

For example, the new settlers had their own ideas about government. Tribes such as the **Franks** united to form powerful kingdoms but didn't create large centralized governments or write down their laws, as the Romans had. Instead, the people obeyed the unwritten rules and traditions of their king. They lived in small villages where they worked the land and tended their herds. As trade began to disappear in the region, so did many cities.

Just about the only force that helped unite Western Europe in the early Middle Ages was Christianity, which survived the fall of Rome. Before the 500s, most Germanic peoples, including the Angles, Jutes, and Saxons, practiced their traditional religions and worshipped many gods. After the Germanic leaders came to power, however, many of them **converted**, or changed their religion, to Christianity.

SAXONS, ANGLES, etc. Major tribe

| 0 | 200 | 400 Miles |
| 0 | 200 | 400 Kilometers |

North Sea

Baltic Sea

ATLANTIC OCEAN

PICTS

SCOTS

ANGLES

BRITONS

SAXONS

JUTES

ANGLES

SAXONS

FRISIANS

THURINGIANS

SLAVS

Seine R.

Rhine R.

KINGDOM OF THE FRANKS

BURGUNDIAN KINGDOM

BAVARIANS

LOMBARDS

KINGDOM OF THE OSTROGOTHS

GEPIDS

Rhône R.

Danube R.

Black Sea

KINGDOM OF THE SUEVES

BASQUES

Corsica

Adriatic Sea

Constantinople

KINGDOM OF THE VISIGOTHS

Rome

Sardinia

EASTERN ROMAN EMPIRE

Balearic Islands

Cyprus

Mediterranean Sea

Sicily

Crete

BERBERS

KINGDOM OF THE VANDALS

The first leader to convert was Clovis, who ruled the Franks. After Clovis defeated Roman Gaul (now France) in 486, he went on to conquer other weaker kingdoms. When he converted to Christianity, many of his subjects did, too. As a result of his conversion and that of other rulers, Christianity spread and increased in influence. Even though the Western Roman Empire had disappeared, the city of Rome itself retained a certain amount of power and strength. It remained the home of the pope as well as the center of Christianity.

REVIEW & ASSESS

1. READING CHECK How did government change in Western Europe after the fall of Rome?

2. INTERPRET MAPS Which of the six kingdoms labeled on the map might have been most exposed to attack from other kingdoms? Explain why.

3. COMPARE AND CONTRAST How did Western European culture in the early Middle Ages differ from culture during the Roman Empire?

7.6.1 Study the geography of the Europe and the Eurasian land mass, including its location, topography, waterways, vegetation, and climate and their relationship to ways of life in Medieval Europe; 7.6.2 Describe the spread of Christianity north of the Alps and the roles played by the early church and by monasteries in its diffusion after the fall of the western half of the Roman Empire; CST 3 Students use a variety of maps and documents to identify physical and cultural features of neighborhoods, cities, states, and countries and to explain the historical migration of people, expansion and disintegration of empires, and the growth of economic systems.

CHARLEMAGNE c. 742 – 814

He was a man of contrasts. He ruthlessly destroyed his enemies but loved learning. He was a tall, commanding figure but usually wore simple clothing. He received fabulous gifts from foreign kings but collected songs of ancient Germanic heroes. In spite of—or maybe because of—these contradictions, he became the first emperor in Western Europe since the fall of the Western Roman Empire. They didn't call this king of the Franks Charlemagne—or Charles the Great—for nothing.

Job: First emperor of the Holy Roman Empire

Home: Kingdom of the Franks

FINEST HOUR

After Charlemagne conquered and united the Germanic kingdoms of Western Europe, the pope placed a crown on Charlemagne's head, proclaiming him emperor of the Romans.

HOBBIES

He enjoyed hunting and swimming and often made his friends and nobles swim with him.

TRIVIA

He could get by on little sleep and sometimes woke his officials to hear the latest report or charge them with a new task.

DEATH

After swimming in one of his favorite springs, he came down with a fever and died a week later.

A MIGHTY RULER

More than 200 years after Clovis died, **Charlemagne** (SHAHR-luh-mayn) became the Frankish king in 768 and proved to be a natural leader. He had a vision for his reign. Charlemagne wanted to unite under his rule all of the Germanic kingdoms shown on the map in the previous lesson. To achieve that goal, the Frankish king battled such tribes as the Slavs, the Lombards, and the Saxons, who reigned in what is now Germany. In the end, Charlemagne succeeded. He brought many of the Germanic tribes together as one people and became the strongest leader in Western Europe.

While Charlemagne was doing battle with the Saxons and other powerful Germanic tribes, he ably administered his kingdom. He established new laws to keep order and appointed officials to run faraway regions of his realm. Each year, Charlemagne called the officials to his court to keep tabs on them. He also took care of his subjects. He founded

In this painting, Pope Leo III crowns Charlemagne emperor of the Romans before an audience of Church officials.

schools and protected the weak against injustice. Above all, he wanted to strengthen Christianity throughout his kingdom.

A CHRISTIAN EMPIRE

Like all Frankish kings since the 500s, Charlemagne was a Christian. In fact, his wars against the Germanic tribes had been fought not only to unite the tribes but also to spread his faith. After he conquered the Saxons, he declared that he would put to death anyone who refused to convert to Christianity. Since Charlemagne had already proved how ruthless he could be by slaughtering more than 4,000 Saxons who had fought against him, those who remained offered no further resistance.

Charlemagne was also a loyal defender of the pope at the time, Pope Leo III. After the pope passed laws that chipped away at the power of the nobles of Rome, they rebelled against him in 800. Leo asked for Charlemagne's help, and the king put the uprising down.

To express his gratitude, Leo crowned Charlemagne emperor of the Romans during a Christmas service in Rome. Charlemagne became the first German emperor of what would later be called the Holy Roman Empire. The title recognized Charlemagne as a guardian of Christianity. It also fueled his passion to strengthen the Church. By the time Charlemagne died in 814, he had created a strong Christian empire.

REVIEW & ASSESS

1. **READING CHECK** What were Charlemagne's two main goals during his reign?

2. **SEQUENCE EVENTS** What happened after Charlemagne put down the uprising in Rome?

3. **MAKE INFERENCES** How was Charlemagne a stabilizing, or steadying, force in Western Europe?

7.6.2 Describe the spread of Christianity north of the Alps and the roles played by the early church and by monasteries in its diffusion after the fall of the western half of the Roman Empire; 7.6.4 Demonstrate an understanding of the conflict and cooperation between the Papacy and European monarchs (e.g., Charlemagne, Gregory VII, Emperor Henry IV); CST 1 Students explain how major events are related to one another in time.

Investigating a Mysterious Treasure

People carefully combing every inch of a stretch of beach with a metal detector may dream of striking it rich, but they usually just find a few dollars in change. Who knows what Terry Herbert dreamed of finding with his metal detector as he searched a field in the English county of Staffordshire in 2009? The farmer who owned the land hoped Herbert would uncover his missing wrench. Instead, as **Caroline Alexander** has reported, he found a mysterious stash of long-ago buried treasure.

^
This gold sword hilt, or handle, was among the treasure found in Staffordshire. The hilt is inlaid with red gemstones called garnets. If you look closely, you can see traces of soil on the gems.

Archaeologists are trying to figure out who buried a great treasure in England in the late 600s and why.

BURIED TREASURE

Remember reading about the Angles and Saxons in the first two lessons of this chapter? Not all members of these powerful tribes lived in Germany. The Anglo-Saxons—made up mostly of Angles, Saxons, and Jutes—settled in England in the 400s and ruled there for about 600 years. Archaeologists know that the treasure Herbert uncovered in Staffordshire was buried during the Anglo-Saxons' rule. They have also determined that most of the Staffordshire Hoard, as it came to be called, consists of military items. (*Hoard* is just another word for a mass or collection of something.) The only nonmilitary items are a quotation from the Bible, inscribed on a thin strip of gold, and two golden crosses.

STAFFORDSHIRE, ENGLAND

What archaeologists don't know is who hid the hoard and why. Was the treasure buried by Anglo-Saxon soldiers or thieves? Did those who hid the treasure want to keep it safe from enemy hands? Did they plan to come back for it? Questions like these captured the imagination of National Geographic writer Caroline Alexander. As she points out in a 2011 issue of *National Geographic* magazine, "The Staffordshire Hoard was thrilling and historic—but above all it was enigmatic [mysterious]."

MYSTERIES AND MAGIC

Alexander believes the key to understanding the mystery of the hoard lies in understanding the importance of magic at that time. The Anglo-Saxons deeply believed in magic and certain supernatural creatures. For example, as Alexander writes, "Misfortune was commonly attributed to tiny darts fired by elves." Gold was thought to have magical properties that could please these creatures. So the hoard might also have been meant to ward off misfortune—particularly in battle.

But what about the Christian items? You've learned that many Germanic peoples converted to Christianity after the fall of Rome. This may explain the quotation from the Bible on the strip of gold and the two crosses. However, many of the new converts blended Christianity with their traditional beliefs. Some early Germanic Christian kings called on God to help them in battle. They also believed that biblical quotations could give them magical power in battle.

So was the hoard buried as an offering for the gods, the Christian God, or supernatural creatures? Perhaps it was a combination of all three. Or maybe it was none of the above. As Alexander admits, "Odds are we will never know the story behind the Staffordshire Hoard, but in a world without magic spells or dragons, would we understand it if we did?"

7.6.2 Describe the spread of Christianity north of the Alps and the roles played by the early church and by monasteries in its diffusion after the fall of the western half of the Roman Empire.

FEUDAL SOCIETY

In feudal society, everyone knew his or her place. Feudalism created an economy based on the possession of land. The upper three classes held all the power, and peasants and serfs had few rights.

King
Most kings inherited their position, but none could rule without the support of the noblemen.

Church Officials and Noblemen
Church officials and high-ranking nobles often exercised more power than the king.

Knights
Knights guarded their lord's castle and fought for him according to a strict code of conduct.

Peasants and Serfs
Peasants and serfs both worked the land, but serfs needed their lord's permission to travel, marry, or own property.

Feudal Society

The united Europe that Charlemagne had fought so hard to establish didn't last very long. About 30 years after his death in 814, his empire was divided into three kingdoms. Frankish rule grew weak, and Western Europe fell back into disorder. Once again, the Germanic kingdoms competed for power.

MAIN IDEA

In the Middle Ages, feudalism grew out of the need to provide security and defense.

A NEW SYSTEM

Kings in Western Europe and England could not defend their vast kingdoms on their own. To help them hold on to their land and protect their subjects, a political and social system called **feudalism** developed by the 800s. In this system, kings gave pieces of their land to noblemen known as **lords**. A lord, in turn, granted parts of this land, called fiefs (feefs), to lesser noblemen called **vassals**. The vassals paid taxes on the land and pledged their military service to the lord. This meant that a vassal had to organize his own army of fighting men. Many vassals were themselves soldiers in the army and served as **knights**, who were warriors on horseback. The lord protected his vassals in exchange for their service.

Vassals were supposed to be loyal to the king, but many vassals switched their allegiance to their lord. This was the man who guarded their families, after all. As a result, lords were supreme rulers in their own territory.

A NEW SOCIAL ORDER

The new system created a social order that was as tightly structured as a pyramid. At the very top sat the king. Next came the church officials and noblemen, who included lords and some vassals. Lords lived in fortified castles that were guarded by knights, the third class in feudal society.

Relatively few people belonged to the upper three classes. The great majority of people in the Middle Ages found themselves at the bottom of the social heap. This class included peasants and serfs. Although some peasants worked as artisans and merchants, most were farmers and laborers. **Serfs**, however, were tied to the land and gave their lord most of whatever they produced. In return, their lord gave them shelter and protection. Serfs weren't quite slaves. They were allowed to buy their freedom. Yet with no skills or education to help them earn money, they were basically powerless to change their condition.

REVIEW & ASSESS

1. **READING CHECK** What role did vassals play in the feudal system?

2. **INTERPRET VISUALS** How does the illustration show that peasants and serfs made up the largest class in society and had little power?

3. **MAKE INFERENCES** How did the relationship between a lord and his vassals affect that between vassals and the king?

7.6.3 Understand the development of feudalism, its role in the medieval European economy, the way in which it was influenced by physical geography (the role of the manor and the growth of towns), and how feudal relationships provided the foundation of political order.

1.5

MEDIEVAL KNIGHTS

Knights galloped into battle, striking terror into the hearts of enemy foot soldiers.

But a knight not only learned how to ride and fight. He also learned to live by a code of chivalry. This code of conduct demanded that a knight be brave and courteous and never shrink from a challenge. Around the 1400s, warfare began to change.

But before that, here's what the best-dressed knight wore and carried into battle.

What might have been a drawback of wearing this armor?

Helmet
Helmets had air holes and eye slits that provided a very narrow field of vision.

Pauldron
This shoulder armor helped protect the knight's head from sword strikes.

Breastplate
This chest armor was often flared at the bottom for greater flexibility.

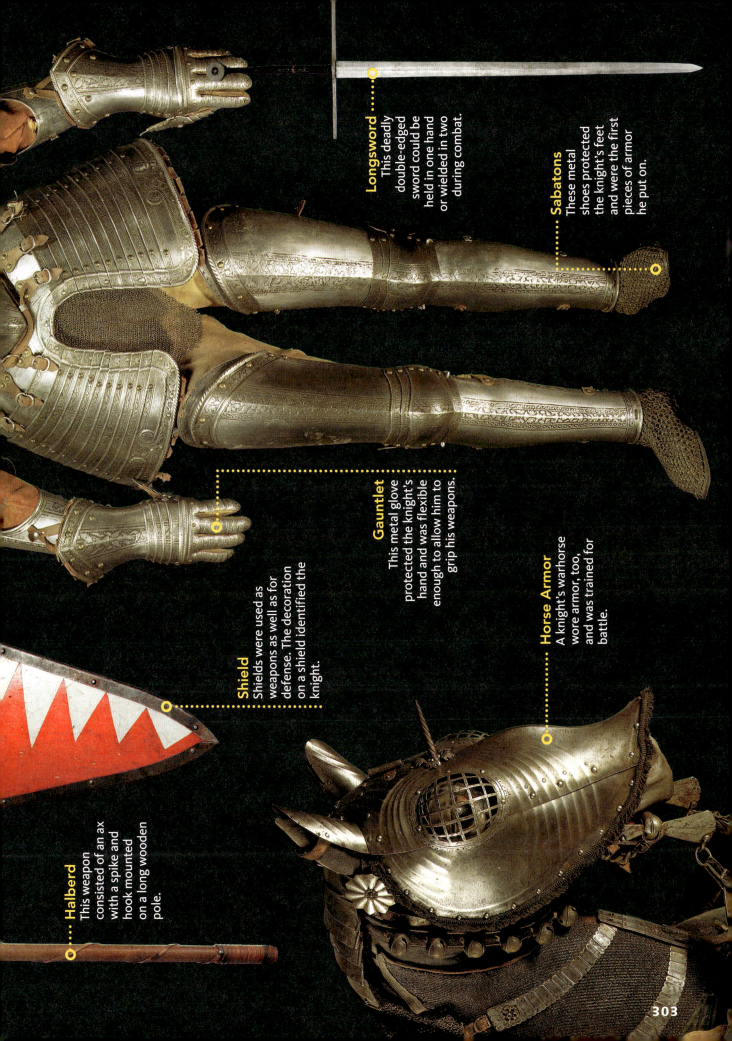

Longsword
This deadly double-edged sword could be held in one hand or wielded in two during combat.

Sabatons
These metal shoes protected the knight's feet and were the first pieces of armor he put on.

Gauntlet
This metal glove protected the knight's hand and was flexible enough to allow him to grip his weapons.

Shield
Shields were used as weapons as well as for defense. The decoration on a shield identified the knight.

Horse Armor
A knight's warhorse wore armor, too, and was trained for battle.

Halberd
This weapon consisted of an ax with a spike and hook mounted on a long wooden pole.

1.6 The **Manor System**

You're cold, tired, hungry, and dirty before you even start work. And no wonder. You get up before dawn to work the land, haul rocks, or do whatever your lord tells you to do. About 16 hours later, you retire to the comforts of your one-room home and huddle with your family around a smoky fire pit. Finally, you call it a night and fall asleep on the floor. At least you've got a sack for a blanket.

MAIN IDEA

Life on the manor was hard for most people but provided nearly everything they needed, including security.

A SELF-CONTAINED WORLD

The rough accommodations of peasants and serfs were part of everyday life in Europe's feudal society. The homes were part of the manor system, which tied the lowest class of people to the land and their lord. The **manor** was the system's basic unit, a walled-in, self-contained world located on land belonging to a lord.

A typical manor included a manor house, a church, a village, and lands with meadows, forests, pastures, and farms. The village provided such necessary businesses as a a mill, bakery, and forge where metal was worked into tools. The manor's farmland was divided into strips: one for the lord, one for the church, and the rest for the peasants and serfs. These laborers farmed the lord's lands as well as their own. They paid the lord rent for their land and fees for almost everything they used on the manor, including the woods and meadows.

LIFE ON THE MANOR

Life for peasants and serfs on the manor was hard. Their average lifespan was 30 years, and that was if they survived infancy. One out of six children did not. Those who grew into adulthood spent their lives performing hard physical labor and got by on a diet of bread, cheese, and vegetables. Peasants and serfs did get time off, though, on Sundays and religious holidays. With the lord's permission, they could even attend nearby fairs and markets.

While workers lived in one-room huts with dirt floors, the lord and his family lived much more comfortably in the manor house. The rooms in this fortified stone house had tiled floors, tapestries on the walls, and fine furnishings. After managing his lands, judging court cases, or hunting wild game, the lord would feast on meat, fish, bread, cheese, and fruit in his large dining room.

Peasants and serfs were sometimes admitted to the manor house on holidays or when the estate was under attack, but the church was the center of life on the manor. Church officials conducted religious services and also cared for the sick and needy. Some educated priests even instructed children in the Bible. The church required peasants and serfs to work its land for free and give one-tenth of their produce to the church, but workers did this willingly. They believed that doing these things was the key to escaping eternal punishment and attaining a better life after death.

MANOR IN THE MIDDLE AGES

This illustration shows a simplified view of a feudal manor in the 800s. Meadows, forests, pastures, and farmland lay outside the manor's walls.

A castle often served as the manor house.

Peasants, serfs, and the lord and his family regularly attended church.

Windows in the huts were so small that little natural light could enter the dwellings.

Guards were positioned along the wall to protect the manor from rival lords and invaders.

7.6.3 Understand the development of feudalism, its role in the medieval European economy, the way in which it was influenced by physical geography (the role of the manor and the growth of towns), and how feudal relationships provided the foundation of political order.

305

Church and Crown

Light streams through stained-glass windows in the great church, inspiring worship. The ceiling seems to rise to heaven. It took decades and even centuries to construct cathedrals in the Middle Ages—some bigger than a king's castle. They were built for the greater glory of God. But they were also meant to inspire awe in the wealth and power of the Church.

MAIN IDEA

In the Middle Ages, the Church controlled lives and challenged the authority of kings.

THE ROLE OF THE CHURCH

It is hard for people today to understand the extraordinary power Christianity had in the Middle Ages. The Roman Catholic Church dominated people's lives from the cradle to the grave. It was the strongest unifying force in medieval Europe. The Church baptized, married, pardoned, and buried everyone from serfs to kings. It promised that good people would go to heaven and the wicked would be punished after death.

The religious leaders who oversaw these ceremonies and delivered the teachings formed the **clergy**. The pope led this group, which included bishops and priests. While a priest was in charge of a single church,

a bishop oversaw a group of churches. Bishops exercised their authority from towering churches called **cathedrals**, the skyscrapers of their day.

Some Christians withdrew from medieval society to live in religious communities called **monasteries**. Monks, the people who lived in a monastery, spent much of their day praying, reading the Bible, and meditating. In addition, rulers and high-ranking clergy sometimes had monks make copies of ancient Greek and Roman texts. As a result, monks helped keep knowledge alive, and monasteries became centers of learning.

STRUGGLE FOR POWER

If anything, the power and wealth of the Church began increasing in the 1000s—in part because it received free land from nobles. At the same time, however, kings began to regain their former authority. The kings' return to power was largely because of the growth of towns and trade, which you will learn more about later. The kings' rise weakened the feudal structure, but it also led to a power struggle between kings and the Church.

The struggle came to a head in 1075. The German king Henry IV was next in line to become Holy Roman Emperor. Like Charlemagne, the first Holy Roman Emperor, Henry ruled over a multi-ethnic group of territories in central Europe, an empire that would continue until it dissolved in 1806. Henry had appointed his own priests to become bishops, but Pope Gregory VII claimed that these were religious appointments and should be his decision.

The conflict raged until Gregory shut Henry out of the Church, forcing the king to back down. Henry knew that if he did not, he would lose his throne. In those days, no one would have anything to do with a king who had been banished from the Church. Gregory got his way and lifted the ban. He then regained full control of religious appointments.

Critical Viewing Exterior supports allowed the construction of these high walls in Notre Dame Cathedral of Paris. Why do you think the stained-glass windows were placed near the ceiling?

REVIEW & ASSESS

1. **READING CHECK** How did Christianity unify the people of medieval Europe?

2. **ANALYZE LANGUAGE USE** What does the sentence "the Church dominated people's lives from the cradle to the grave" mean?

3. **DRAW CONCLUSIONS** Why was the conflict between King Henry IV and Pope Gregory VII important?

7.6.4 Demonstrate an understanding of the conflict and cooperation between the Papacy and European monarchs (e.g., Charlemagne, Gregory VII, Emperor Henry IV); 7.6.8 Understand the importance of the Catholic church as a political, intellectual, and aesthetic institution (e.g., founding of universities, political and spiritual roles of the clergy, creation of monastic and mendicant religious orders, preservation of the Latin language and religious texts, St. Thomas Aquinas's synthesis of classical philosophy with Christian theology, and the concept of "natural law").

King John and the Magna Carta

Here's a joke told by English schoolchildren: Where did King John sign the Magna Carta? At the bottom. Actually, he was in a meadow called Runnymede, and he didn't sign it—he placed his seal on it. And it was called the Articles of the Barons then. The barons—a group of noblemen—were not amused by the growing authority of the king.

MAIN IDEA

The Magna Carta marked a major step toward democratic government in Western Europe.

THE GREAT CHARTER

In the last lesson, you read that kings were regaining their power. **King John** was one in a long line of powerful English kings that began in 1066. In that year, William, Duke of Normandy—a region in France— invaded England and established a strong, centralized monarchy there. When John rose to the throne in 1199, he ruled England and half of present-day France. However, the king soon weakened his position by waging a series of failed, expensive wars.

A group of local barons took advantage of John's decreased power to stage a rebellion. The barons believed that by raising their taxes the king had violated common law. This was a system of law established in the 1100s that sought to ensure that people throughout England received equal treatment.

So, in 1215, the barons forced John to place his seal on their document, which came to be known as the **Magna Carta**, or "Great Charter." It was meant to be just a contract between the king and his nobles. However, the Magna Carta made the king subject to the law of the land and limited his authority.

A STEP TOWARD DEMOCRACY

Although the Magna Carta didn't benefit ordinary English people at the time, its guarantee of certain individual rights would have a great impact on the development of democracy. The document is recognized as the foundation of English law.

Since the 1200s and the sealing of the Magna Carta, Britain's Parliament has met on this site on the Thames River in London. Today, representatives meet in the Houses of Parliament, shown here, next to the clock tower called Big Ben.

A further step toward democracy—in the form of representative government—took place in 1258. Henry III, John's son, was king of England at the time. Like his father, he had angered a group of nobles. The nobles overruled Henry's authority and put together a council of 15 men to advise the king and limit his power. This group of representatives would come to be called a **parliament**.

After King Henry died in 1272, his son Edward I rose to the throne. In 1295, Edward assembled what is considered the first truly representative parliament. The group included two knights from every county and two residents from each town. They passed laws, imposed taxes, and discussed political and judicial matters. From that point on, English kings would have to share their power—whether they liked it or not.

REVIEW & ASSESS

1. **READING CHECK** In what way did the Magna Carta limit the king's authority?

2. **ANALYZE CAUSE AND EFFECT** How did the establishment of a parliament change the government of England?

3. **MAKE INFERENCES** Do you think the Magna Carta affected the lives of ordinary people? Why or why not?

7.6.5 Know the significance of developments in medieval English legal and constitutional practices and their importance in the rise of modern democratic thought and representative institutions (e.g., Magna Carta, parliament, development of habeas corpus, an independent judiciary in England); HI 2 Students understand and distinguish cause, effect, sequence, and correlation in historical events, including the long- and short-term causal relations.

DOCUMENT-BASED QUESTION

Charters of Freedom

By setting down individual rights in the Magna Carta, the barons—unknowingly—laid the groundwork for the development of democracy. The Parliament members who penned the English Bill of Rights and the American Founders who wrote the U.S. Bill of Rights found inspiration in the Great Charter. So the next time you speak your mind or celebrate a religious holiday, you might remember the documents on the next page. They helped make such freedoms possible.

This painting, like many others that illustrate the event, mistakenly shows King John signing the Magna Carta rather than setting his seal to it.

King John Signs the Magna Carta, A.C. Michael, 1903–1928

from the Magna Carta

Most of the Magna Carta's 63 articles deal with the relationships among the king, nobles, and clergy and largely ignore the rights of the lower classes. However, the principles expressed in the following article are significant today for all free men—and women.

CONSTRUCTED RESPONSE What individual rights are protected in this article from the Magna Carta?

> 39. No freeman shall be taken, imprisoned, disseised [stripped of property], outlawed, banished, or in any way destroyed, nor will We proceed against or prosecute him [put him on trial], except by the lawful judgment of his peers [equals] or by the law of the land.

from the English Bill of Rights

Concern over the increasing power of monarchs led Parliament to pass the English Bill of Rights in 1689. However, instead of focusing on the rights of nobles, the English Bill of Rights focuses on the rights of Parliament.

CONSTRUCTED RESPONSE Why do you think Parliament insisted on the free election and free speech of its members?

> 8. That election of members of Parliament ought to be free.
>
> 9. That the freedom of speech, and debates or proceedings in Parliament, ought not to be impeached [charged as a crime] or questioned in any court or place out of Parliament.

from the U.S. Bill of Rights

The U.S. Bill of Rights took the documents above a step or two further. Adopted in 1791, the Bill of Rights—the first ten amendments to the Constitution—guarantees personal freedoms, like these, that had previously not been clearly stated.

CONSTRUCTED RESPONSE Why do you think the American Founders insisted on having these freedoms clearly stated in the Bill of Rights?

> 4. The right of the people to be secure in their persons, houses, papers, and effects, against unreasonable searches and seizures, shall not be violated . . .
>
> 6. In all criminal prosecutions, the accused shall enjoy the right to a speedy and public trial, by an impartial [fair to both sides] jury. . . .

SYNTHESIZE & WRITE

1. **REVIEW** Review what you have learned about the Magna Carta and the development of democratic ideas in England.

2. **RECALL** On your own paper, write down the main idea expressed in each document.

3. **CONSTRUCT** Write a topic sentence that answers this question: How do the Magna Carta, English Bill of Rights, and U.S. Bill of Rights promote democratic ideas?

4. **WRITE** Using evidence from the documents, write a short essay to support your answer to the question in Step 3.

7.6.5 Know the significance of developments in medieval English legal and constitutional practices and their importance in the rise of modern democratic thought and representative institutions (e.g., Magna Carta, parliament, development of habeas corpus, an independent judiciary in England); 7.11.6 Discuss how the principles in the Magna Carta were embodied in such documents as the English Bill of Rights and the American Declaration of Independence; REP 4 Students assess the credibility of primary and secondary sources and draw sound conclusions from them.

The Crusades

In 1095, Pope Urban II condemned a group of people who had "invaded the lands of the Christians." The people Urban referred to were Muslims, and he called on Christians to wage war against them. Kings had regained a good bit of their authority, but the Church and the pope still had plenty of power—certainly enough for the pope to gather armies to fight the spread of Islam.

MAIN IDEA

Christians in Europe fought non-Christians to conquer Palestine and retake Spain.

BATTLE FOR PALESTINE

Specifically, the people Urban had condemned were Seljuk Turks, Muslim rulers who had seized control of Jerusalem in 1071. Their takeover had made Christian pilgrimages to the Holy Land—also called Palestine—almost impossible. The Holy Land included Jerusalem and the area around the city, sites that were sacred to Christians, Jews, and Muslims.

The Seljuks had also begun to attack the Christian Byzantine Empire, once the eastern half of the Roman Empire. When the Byzantine emperor asked for help, Pope Urban seized his chance to rally Christians against the growing power of Islam. His words had the desired effect. In 1096, Christian armies set off to fight a series of wars called the **Crusades** to reclaim the Holy Land. Christian leaders and soldiers were motivated by a desire to protect Christians and to slow the spread of Islam.

Peasants, knights, and foot soldiers joined the fight, and they achieved victory. In 1099, the army retook Jerusalem and divided the Holy Land into four Crusader states. But the triumph was short-lived. In 1144, the Muslims fought back and conquered Edessa, one of the Crusader states. Soon after, a new pope launched the Second Crusade, but this ended in disaster for the Europeans. A Third and Fourth Crusade were fought, but these also failed to defeat the enemy. By 1291, the Muslims had defeated the Crusaders and taken control of Palestine. The Crusades were over.

A SPANISH CRUSADE

The Crusades had an unexpected impact on Europe. During the wars, trade between Europe and the eastern Mediterranean region greatly increased because of greater contact between the two regions. After the wars, ideas as well as goods were exchanged. The trade led to the rise of a merchant class in Europe and the further decline of feudalism.

Still, crusading fever didn't die, and hostility toward any non-Christians increased. As soldiers galloped toward the Holy Land, they killed Jews in Europe as well as those in Palestine. After the Crusades, many Jews were expelled from England and France. The greatest expulsion effort, however, took place on the Iberian Peninsula, which includes present-day Spain and Portugal. In the 700s, Muslims had conquered almost the entire peninsula. When Islamic rule weakened in the 1000s, Christian kings began a long war, called the **Reconquista** (ray-cone-KEY-stah), to drive the Muslims off the peninsula.

7.6.6 Discuss the causes and course of the religious Crusades and their effects on the Christian, Muslim, and Jewish populations in Europe, with emphasis on the increasing contact by Europeans with cultures of the Eastern Mediterranean world; 7.6.9 Know the history of the decline of Muslim rule in the Iberian Peninsula that culminated in

THE CRUSADES, 1096–1204

ATLANTIC OCEAN

North Sea

Baltic Sea

ENGLAND

HOLY ROMAN EMPIRE

Bruges

Regensburg

Paris

Vienna

Vézeley

FRANCE Lyon

Venice

Belgrade

Toulouse

Zara

Black Sea

Marseille

Constantinople

Rome

Lisbon

SPAIN

Bari

BYZANTINE EMPIRE

Edessa

Antioch

Adriatic Sea

Damascus

Acre

Mediterranean Sea

Jerusalem

	Christian lands
	Muslim lands
←	First Crusade, 1096–1099
←	Second Crusade, 1147–1149
←	Third Crusade, 1189–1191
←	Fourth Crusade, 1202–1204

0   250   500 Miles
0   250   500 Kilometers

King Ferdinand and Queen Isabella of Spain stepped up the war. They used a powerful court known as the **Inquisition** to punish non-Christians. The court ordered the torture and execution of many Muslims and Jews who would not convert or who had converted but secretly practiced their former religion. In 1492, Ferdinand and Isabella finally defeated and expelled the last of the Muslim rulers and their followers from Spain and Portugal. They also drove out about 200,000 Jews. Unlike the Crusades, the Reconquista had achieved its goal— but at the cost of many human lives.

FERDINAND AND ISABELLA

The Reconquista ended when the Spanish army conquered Granada, a city in Spain. When the Muslim ruler handed over the keys to his palace, the Alhambra, Ferdinand and Isabella swore that Muslims would always be able to follow their faith in Spain. They broke that promise a few years later when they ordered Muslims to convert to Christianity or leave the country.

REVIEW & ASSESS

1. **READING CHECK** Why did Pope Urban II encourage Christians to begin a series of wars against Muslims?

2. **INTERPRET MAPS** Which Crusade involved much of Western Europe?

3. **SEQUENCE EVENTS** What efforts to drive Muslims from Europe were undertaken after the Crusades ended?

the Reconquista and the rise of Spanish and Portuguese kingdoms; 7.9.7 Describe the Golden Age of cooperation between Jews and Muslims in medieval Spain that promoted creativity in art, literature, and science, including how that cooperation was terminated by the religious persecution of individuals and groups (e.g., the Spanish Inquisition and the expulsion of Jews and Muslims from Spain in 1492); CST 3 Students use a variety of maps and documents to identify physical and cultural features of neighborhoods, cities, states, and countries and to explain the historical migration of people, expansion and disintegration of empires, and the growth of economic systems.

2.5 War and Plague

Shattered buildings and churches, deserted villages, and abandoned fields—these formed the landscape of Europe after war and disease swept through the continent in the 1300s. Both catastrophes brought suffering and death to millions and, like the Crusades, greatly weakened the feudal way of life.

MAIN IDEA

War and disease devastated Europe in the 1300s and brought about fundamental changes to society.

WAR BETWEEN ENGLAND AND FRANCE

The roots of the war were established long before the 1300s. As you may remember, William, Duke of Normandy, conquered England in 1066 and became its king. William and the Norman kings who came after him were vassals to the French kings. However, they also ruled over England in their own right. This created a tense relationship between England and France. Kings from both countries were very powerful and competed for territory in France. In time, they also competed over who would be king of France.

The situation came to a head in 1328 when the king of France died. Edward III of England believed he should succeed him, but French nobles crowned a Frenchman instead. In 1337, Edward invaded France to claim the throne. His actions began the **Hundred Years' War** between England and France. This was not a continuous conflict but rather a series of wars that dragged on for 116 years.

Between the beginning of the war in 1337 and its end in 1453, the English won many important victories. The French cause seemed hopeless until rescue came from an unexpected source. A French peasant girl called **Joan of Arc** claimed that Christian saints had told her to save her country. She impressed Charles, the ruler of France, and was given command of his army in 1429. Her religious and patriotic passion inspired her soldiers to win a battle that turned the tide of the war. The English captured and executed Joan, but they had lost the war. By 1453, the French had driven the English out of their lands.

Both sides were aided in their fight by deadly new weapons. The powerful **longbow** allowed archers to fire arrows with enough force to pierce a knight's armor. Cannons, made possible by the invention of gunpowder, could blast through castle walls. These weapons changed the nature of European warfare and made knights and castles, the symbols of feudalism, almost powerless.

DISEASE SPREADS OVER THE WORLD

As if war and its new weapons weren't enough, medieval Europeans suffered from widespread disease. Poor diet, filthy living conditions, and a lack of medicine made sickness common.

In 1347, however, a devastating disease known as the **bubonic plague** swept through Europe. Infected rats carried fleas that spread the disease to humans along land and sea trade routes from Asia to Europe and Africa. Unfortunately, no one at the time understood that the plague was caused by bites from these fleas.

Death of Bertrand du Guesclin, Chronique d'Angleterre, late 15th century

Critical Viewing In this 15th-century painting, English soldiers use longbows and cannon fire to fight for control of a French castle during the Hundred Years' War. What different actions does the painting illustrate?

Instead, many people believed the plague was a punishment from God. Some Christians believed the Jews had caused the plague by poisoning town wells. As a result, they destroyed entire Jewish communities. By the early 1350s, the worst of the plague was over in Europe, but by then it had killed about one-third of the continent's population. The deaths of so many people—from disease and war—led to major social and economic changes that would finally bring an end to feudalism.

JOAN OF ARC

After the English captured Joan of Arc, she was tried by the Inquisition and found guilty of being a witch. The court believed that the voices she claimed to hear were those of the devil. In 1431, Joan was burned at the stake. She was about 19 years old. Twenty-five years later, another court pardoned her. In 1920, the Catholic Church declared Joan a saint.

REVIEW & ASSESS

1. **READING CHECK** What impact did the Hundred Years' War and the bubonic plague have on medieval Europe?

2. **ANALYZE CAUSE AND EFFECT** How did events in 1066 lead to the Hundred Years' War?

3. **MAKE INFERENCES** How did the rats that carried plague-infected fleas probably travel along the trade routes?

7.6.7 Map the spread of the bubonic plague from Central Asia to China, the Middle East, and Europe and describe its impact on global population; HI 2 Students understand and distinguish cause, effect, sequence, and correlation in historical events, including the long- and short-term causal relations.

OCTOBER 1347

In a port in Italy, workers unload a ship's cargo and also release rats covered in fleas carrying the bubonic plague. According to an old legend, a childhood rhyme was said to describe the plague. The rhyme begins with "Ring around the rosie," which may refer to the red blisters caused when the fleas bit their victims. "A pocket full of posies" was said to be the flowers people carried to ward off the disease. When the flowers failed as a cure, "we all fall down," or die. In this painting, called *The Triumph of Death*, death is represented by skeleton figures. What generalization can you make about death's victims?

Growth of Towns

In the late Middle Ages, a saying started making the rounds: Town air makes you free. In the towns, you could work at a job and keep all your wages. You could go where you wanted without having to ask anyone's permission because you were no longer bound to a landowning lord or vassal. In fact, you answered to no one but the king.

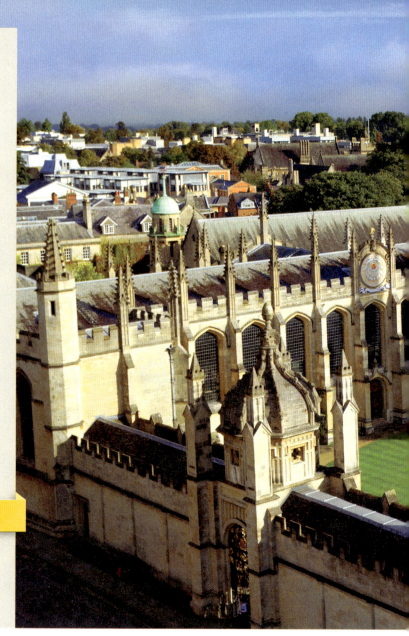

MAIN IDEA

The growth of towns and trade led to economic, political, and cultural changes that brought the Middle Ages to an end.

ECONOMIC OPPORTUNITIES ARISE

People had been moving to towns since about 1000, but the bubonic plague greatly accelerated this movement. With about a third of the workforce wiped out by the disease, employers desperate for help increased wages to attract workers. Many peasants, and many serfs as well, left the manor to apply for jobs in the towns. As a result, the manor system began to fall apart.

After life on the manor, the bustling, exciting towns might have made a welcome change. Towns held weekly markets where local produce was sold, while town fairs brought in trade goods from other places.

In time, a merchant class composed of traders and craftspeople arose. Wealthy town-dwelling merchants, known as **burghers**, could be elected to sit on governing councils. Groups of craftspeople, such as shoemakers or silversmiths, joined together to form **guilds**, which helped protect and improve the working conditions of their members.

THE MIDDLE AGES END

The growth of towns and their prosperous trade further helped kings regain their authority. By taxing the towns within his realm, a king earned money to pay for his army. A strong army brought peace

All Souls College, at England's University of Oxford, was founded in the 1400s during Europe's revival of learning.

and stability to his land. Increasingly, power and people's loyalty shifted from local lords to their king.

Europe experienced cultural changes as well as economic and political ones. You may remember that the Crusades brought European traders into contact with the civilizations of Islam and Byzantium. These civilizations had preserved the writings of ancient Greek and Roman philosophers in their libraries. As the Middle Ages came to a close, people became eager to gain knowledge. Universities were founded to satisfy this desire for learning. Monasteries were no longer the only centers of education. After centuries of war, instability, and fear, Europe was more than ready to embark on a new age of creativity.

REVIEW & ASSESS

1. **READING CHECK** What economic opportunities did towns offer ordinary people?

2. **ANALYZE CAUSE AND EFFECT** How did the growth of towns affect monarchs?

3. **MAKE INFERENCES** Why do you think learning was revived at the end of the Middle Ages?

7.6.3 Understand the development of feudalism, its role in the medieval European economy, the way in which it was influenced by physical geography (the role of the manor and the growth of towns), and how feudal relationships provided the foundation of political order; HI 2 Students understand and distinguish cause, effect, sequence, and correlation in historical events, including the long- and short-term causal relations.

VOCABULARY

Use each of the following vocabulary words in a sentence that shows an understanding of the word's meaning.

1. **medieval** (HSS 7.6)
   The Middle Ages is also known as the medieval period, which was a time of many political, economic, and cultural changes in Western Europe.

2. **monastery** (HSS 7.6.2)

3. **feudalism** (HSS 7.6.3)

4. **manor** (HSS 7.6.3)

5. **serf** (HSS 7.6.3)

6. **parliament** (HSS 7.6.5)

7. **cathedral** (HSS 7.6.8)

8. **longbow** (HSS 7.6.3)

9. **bubonic plague** (HSS 7.6.7)

10. **guild** (HSS 7.6.3)

READING STRATEGY

11. **DRAW CONCLUSIONS** If you haven't already, complete your chart to draw conclusions about how feudalism and Christianity affected people during the Middle Ages. Then answer the question.

Middle Ages

Feudalism	Christianity
People's loyalties were divided between their king and their lord.	The Church dominated people's lives.

What impact did the power struggles between kings and lords and between kings and the Church have on people during the Middle Ages? (HSS HI 2)

MAIN IDEAS

Answer the following questions. Support your answers with evidence from the chapter.

12. What helped many small kingdoms thrive after the fall of Rome? **LESSON 1.1** (HSS 7.6.1)

13. Why did the pope crown Charlemagne emperor of the Romans? **LESSON 1.2** (HSS 7.6.4)

14. What led to the emergence of feudalism in Europe? **LESSON 1.4** (HSS 7.6.3)

15. What did a typical manor include? **LESSON 1.6** (HSS 7.6.3)

16. How did the Church become more powerful and wealthy in the 1000s? **LESSON 2.1** (HSS 7.6.8)

17. How did the Magna Carta affect the development of democracy in Western Europe? **LESSON 2.2** (HSS 7.6.5)

18. In what way did the Crusades help weaken feudalism? **LESSON 2.4** (HSS 7.6.6)

19. How did the bubonic plague contribute to the growth of towns? **LESSON 2.7** (HSS 7.6.7)

CRITICAL THINKING

Answer the following questions. Support your answers with evidence from the chapter.

20. **ESSENTIAL QUESTION** How did Europe change over the course of the Middle Ages? (HSS HI 1)

21. **EVALUATE** How did a code of conduct help the knights do their job? (HSS 7.6.3)

22. **COMPARE AND CONTRAST** How did manor life differ for workers and the lord of the manor? (HSS 7.6.3)

23. **ANALYZE CAUSE AND EFFECT** What happened as a result of King John's weakened power? (HSS 7.6.5)

24. **YOU DECIDE** Do you think feudalism benefited the lives of ordinary people or made them worse? Support your opinion with evidence from the chapter. (HSS REP 1)

INTERPRET CHARTS

Study this chart, which compares the feudal structure in medieval Europe with that in medieval Japan. Then answer the questions that follow.

Feudal Structure in Europe and Japan	Europe	Japan
Ruler	King	Emperor
Landowners	Nobles and Church	Daimyo
Warriors	Knights	Samurai
Lower Classes	Peasants and serfs	Peasants, artisans, and merchants

25. How was the feudal structure in Europe similar to that in Japan? (HSS HI 2)

26. How did the makeup of the lower classes in the two regions differ? (HSS HI 2)

ANALYZE SOURCES

A Frankish scholar named Einhard was a trusted friend and adviser of Charlemagne and wrote a biography about his king. Read this excerpt from Einhard's biography of Charlemagne. Then answer the question that follows.

> He cherished the Church of St. Peter the Apostle at Rome above all other holy and sacred places, and heaped its treasury with a vast wealth of gold, silver, and precious stones . . .
> [T]hroughout his whole reign the wish that he had nearest at heart was to re-establish the ancient authority of the city of Rome . . . and protect the Church of St. Peter.

27. What does the excerpt suggest about Charlemagne's feelings toward the Church? (HSS REP 4)

WRITE ABOUT HISTORY

28. INFORMATIVE What events brought about the downfall of feudalism and ended the Middle Ages? Write a paragraph for a children's encyclopedia, summarizing these events and explaining how they brought about the end of feudalism and the Middle Ages. You might create a chart or web diagram to organize your ideas and details. (HSS HI 2)

TIPS

- Take notes from the lessons on the Crusades, the increasing power of the Church, the Hundred Years' War, and the growth of towns.
- State your main idea clearly at the beginning of the paragraph.
- Support your main idea with relevant facts, details, and examples.
- Use vocabulary from the chapter.
- Provide a concluding statement about the end of feudalism and the Middle Ages.

12

RENAISSANCE AND REFORMATION
1300 – 1600

ESSENTIAL QUESTION How did new ways of thinking transform European culture?

SECTION 1 THE ITALIAN RENAISSANCE

KEY VOCABULARY
classical
humanism
patron
perspective
Renaissance man
secular
vernacular

NAMES & PLACES
Borgias
Leonardo da Vinci
Medici
Michelangelo
Renaissance

SECTION 2 THE NORTHERN RENAISSANCE

KEY VOCABULARY
cartography
printing press
woodcut

NAMES & PLACES
Elizabethan Age
Johann Gutenberg
William Shakespeare

SECTION 3 THE REFORMATION

KEY VOCABULARY
denomination
heresy
indulgence
missionary
nation-state

NAMES & PLACES
Council of Trent
Counter Reformation
Great Schism
Jesuits
Martin Luther
Protestant
Reformation

READING STRATEGY

ANALYZE LANGUAGE USE
When you analyze language use, you note how word choices indicate the author's purpose. Some word choices involve figurative language, such as personification. As you read the chapter, use a concept cluster like this one to help you analyze figurative language.

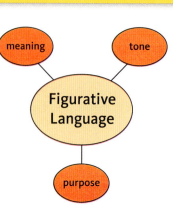

Construction of the Duomo, or cathedral, of Florence, Italy—shown here— began in 1296. Its dome came to symbolize the Renaissance.

Rise of the Individual

In the 1300s, a revolution began to brew in Europe. But this revolution didn't involve weapons and war. This was a movement of ideas. People decided they wanted to enjoy life on Earth—and not just look forward to their reward in heaven. They focused on the individual and believed every person had unlimited possibilities. This was not what the Church had taught in the Middle Ages. The movement was, indeed, revolutionary.

MAIN IDEA

The growth of humanism, with its emphasis on the individual, led to a rebirth of the arts and learning.

THE GROWTH OF HUMANISM

The new movement was called **humanism**. Instead of blindly obeying the authority of a king or the teachings of the Church, the followers of this movement wanted to be independent and think for themselves. Humanists stressed living a Christian life but also sought to explore a new understanding of the individual in relation to God. Humanism inspired a new sense of possibility. People suddenly felt as if they could do anything they chose.

The movement's followers found inspiration in **classical**, or ancient Greek and Roman, writings. Scholars in the Muslim empires had obtained and preserved many classical writings. Growing trade with these empires brought Europeans into greater contact with the texts. Humanists admired what the people of those ancient times had done and said and built.

An Italian poet named Petrarch became an early humanist leader and collected around 200 classical manuscripts. Some of these manuscripts had been hidden away in monastery libraries for centuries. People learned Greek just so they could read them. They began to forget about Charlemagne and wanted to learn more about the great leaders of ancient Greece and Rome.

REBIRTH OF THE ARTS

This rebirth of classical learning led to a movement of great creativity in the arts, writing, and thinking. Historians call the movement the **Renaissance**, which actually means "rebirth" in French. The Renaissance lasted from about 1300 to 1600 and began in Italy.

As the center of the ancient Roman Empire, Italy was well positioned to become the movement's birthplace. In addition, many of its cities—including Florence, Venice, Rome, and Milan—had become wealthy from trade. Ideas as well as goods were traded in these cities, which attracted artists, writers, and scientists.

Italian cities particularly benefited from the reopening of the ancient trade routes of the Silk Roads between Europe and China. Interest in Asian markets had been sparked, in part, by Venetian merchant Marco Polo. He wrote about the wonders he saw as he traveled the Silk Roads from Europe to Central Asia, China, and India.

7.8.1 Describe the way in which the revival of classical learning and the arts fostered a new interest in humanism (i.e., a balance between intellect and religious faith); 7.8.2 Explain the importance of Florence in the early stages of the Renaissance and the growth of independent trading cities (e.g., Venice), with emphasis on the cities' importance in the

No city in Italy was more influential during the Renaissance than Florence. Artists like **Leonardo da Vinci**, Raphael, and **Michelangelo** came to Florence hoping to make a name for themselves—and they certainly did. Leonardo excelled as a painter, an inventor, and a scientist. You'll read more about the genius of Leonardo later in the chapter. Raphael came to Florence to study the great masters, including Leonardo, and created his own masterpieces. Michelangelo was a painter and sculptor whose muscular subjects convey great intensity and power. These artists and many, many others are counted among the greats of the Italian Renaissance. They were all part of an earthshaking cultural shift that transformed Europe.

REVIEW & ASSESS

1. **READING CHECK** What inspired the development of humanism?

2. **IDENTIFY MAIN IDEAS AND DETAILS** Why did the Renaissance begin in Italy?

3. **ANALYZE LANGUAGE USE** What does the phrase "an earthshaking cultural shift" suggest about the impact of the Renaissance in Europe?

spread of Renaissance ideas; 7.8.3 Understand the effects of the reopening of the ancient "Silk Road" between Europe and China, including Marco Polo's travels and the location of his routes; 7.8.5 Detail advances made in literature, the arts, science, mathematics, cartography, engineering, and the understanding of human anatomy and astronomy (e.g., by Dante Alighieri, Leonardo da Vinci, Michelangelo di Buonarroti Simoni, Johann Gutenberg, William Shakespeare).

New Styles and Techniques

Remember reading in the last chapter about the great stained-glass-filled cathedrals built during the Middle Ages? The walls of these churches seemed to stretch to the sky. But heavy brick blocks were often placed on the outside of a cathedral to support its soaring walls. As you'll see, Renaissance architects would try to find another, less visible means of support.

MAIN IDEA

The Renaissance inspired new forms of expression in art, literature, and architecture.

ART AND LITERATURE

Renaissance architects came up with new building strategies. However, the movement demanded new forms of expression from artists as well. For example, they found ways to show landscapes in a realistic manner by developing a technique called **perspective**

to produce an impression of depth and distance. While art during the Middle Ages appeared flat, perspective allowed Renaissance artists to produce works that looked three-dimensional.

The subjects of the artwork changed, too. Artists including Titian (TIH-shun), a great painter in Venice, still drew inspiration from religious subjects. But **secular**, or nonreligious, subjects also became popular. For example, Sandro Botticelli of Florence painted *La Primavera*, which celebrates the arrival of spring.

New styles in the arts weren't limited to painters and sculptors. Renaissance writers got in on the act as well. Instead of using Latin, the language of the Church, many wrote in the **vernacular**, or their native language. One of the first to do so was the poet Dante, who wrote his masterpiece, *The Divine Comedy*, in Italian in the early 1300s. The work describes Dante's long journey led in part by the ancient Roman poet Virgil.

ARCHITECTURE

During the Renaissance, architects found inspiration by studying the buildings of ancient Rome. They incorporated classical Roman engineering features such as arches and domes in their own creations. One of the greatest of these architects was Filippo Brunelleschi (brew-nuhl-LESS-key) of Florence, whose impressive dome is illustrated on the opposite page.

It all began with a contest. In 1418, architects were challenged to build a self-supporting dome for the cathedral of

PERSPECTIVE

Renaissance artists often included perfectly proportioned buildings in their paintings. As you can see in this painting, *The Ideal City* by Piero della Francesca, the larger buildings in the foreground and the smaller ones in the background provide the illusion of depth and distance.

BRUNELLESCHI'S DOME

When the dome was completed in 1436, it soared to a height of about 374 feet. Engineers today still do not fully understand how Brunelleschi constructed his masterpiece. It remains the largest brick dome ever built.

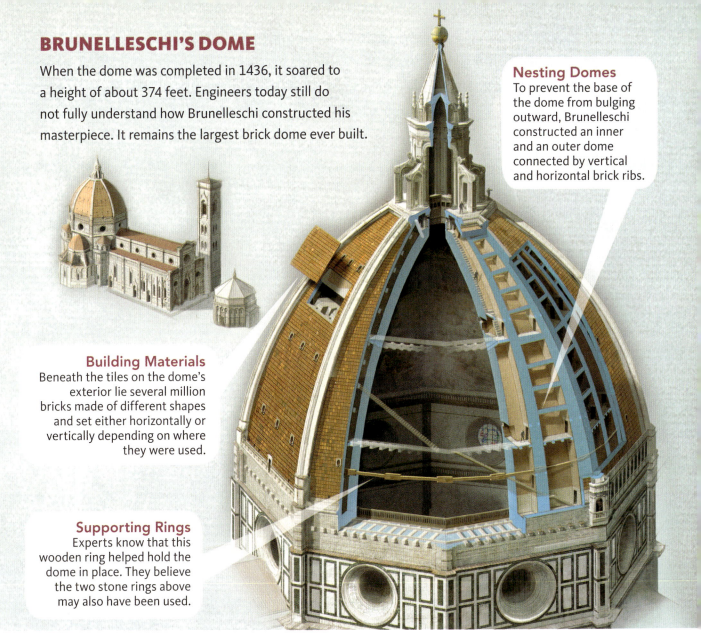

Nesting Domes
To prevent the base of the dome from bulging outward, Brunelleschi constructed an inner and an outer dome connected by vertical and horizontal brick ribs.

Building Materials
Beneath the tiles on the dome's exterior lie several million bricks made of different shapes and set either horizontally or vertically depending on where they were used.

Supporting Rings
Experts know that this wooden ring helped hold the dome in place. They believe the two stone rings above may also have been used.

Florence. Brunelleschi won the competition, but at first even he wasn't sure how to build the dome, which had to sit on a base that was about 150 feet wide. Without internal support, how could the dome be prevented from sagging and collapsing? Eventually, inspiration struck. Instead of constructing massive visible supports, Brunelleschi proposed building two domes, one nested inside the other. The effect would be of a dome rising effortlessly in the air. The dome would come to symbolize the freedom of the Renaissance and of the human spirit. It also inspired other architects and helped make Florence the center of the Renaissance.

REVIEW & ASSESS

1. **READING CHECK** What new techniques did Renaissance artists use?

2. **MAKE INFERENCES** Why do you think some Renaissance writers began expressing themselves in the vernacular?

3. **INTERPRET VISUALS** What difficulties do you think the builders of the dome encountered during its construction?

7.8.5 Detail advances made in literature, the arts, science, mathematics, cartography, engineering, and the understanding of human anatomy and astronomy (e.g., by Dante Alighieri, Leonardo da Vinci, Michelangelo di Buonarroti Simoni, Johann Gutenberg, William Shakespeare).

School of Athens, Raphael Sanzio, 1511

A.D. 1511

Raphael, who was only 27 when he completed this fresco, celebrated the classical period by peopling his painting with ancient Greek philosophers and scientists. The figures at its center are the philosopher Plato on the left and his star student, Aristotle, on the right. Raphael merges the Renaissance with the classical period by using Leonardo da Vinci as the model for Plato. Other Renaissance artists, including Michelangelo and Raphael himself, also appear in the painting. How does *School of Athens* express the spirit of the Renaissance?

7.8.5 Detail advances made in literature, the arts, science, mathematics, cartography, engineering, and the understanding of human anatomy and astronomy (e.g., by Dante Alighieri, Leonardo da Vinci, Michelangelo di Buonarroti Simoni, Johann Gutenberg, William Shakespeare).

329

The Medici and the Borgias

The Medici were like the godfathers, or crime bosses, of the Renaissance. They defeated their rivals by whatever means necessary—including murder. But the Medici family used its wealth and power to support some of the greatest artists in Florence.

MAIN IDEA

Wealthy and powerful families supported Renaissance artists and thinkers in many Italian cities.

WEALTHY FLORENCE

There were other rich families in Florence, but it was the **Medici** (MEH-dee-chee) who clawed their way to the top. Like other great families in the city, the Medici built their fortune as bankers and textile merchants. They were part of a wealthy merchant class that had developed in Italy and gained great power. The family's money bought them so much political power that the Medici ruled Florence during the Renaissance.

But the Medici weren't all about money and political gain. The Renaissance had brought about a renewed sense of pride throughout Italy. Rich families competed to restore the glory of ancient Rome's civilization to their cities and so became patrons of the arts. **Patrons** used some of their wealth to encourage and support artists. This support allowed the artists to create and work full-time on their masterpieces.

The Medici family made sure that Florence became the place to be for the great artists and scholars of the day. They spent fortunes attracting the best and brightest to their city. No member of the Medici family was more successful at bringing artists and scholars to Florence than Lorenzo de Medici, also known as Lorenzo the Magnificent. A poet himself, Lorenzo supported some of the most important artists of the Renaissance, including Leonardo da Vinci and Michelangelo.

POWERFUL ROME

Florence got a head start, but eventually Renaissance ideas and a new flood of people made their way to Rome. The pope, who ruled both Rome and the Catholic Church, rebuilt the city and brought back its authority and importance. In time, Rome became almost as powerful as Florence, and the two cities competed for dominance. When Michelangelo created his statue of the biblical hero David, it was originally placed outside the center of Florence's government. The towering, muscular David stood there, tense and ready for battle, with his eyes looking warningly in the direction of Rome.

The pope had authority over Rome, but the city, like Florence, had its share of patrons. The **Borgia** (BOR-gee-ah) family, originally from Spain, was the most powerful group of patrons in Rome. The Borgias were even more ruthless than the Medici. Since the Church controlled Rome, the Borgias attempted to control the Church. In the 1400s, two members of the family became popes. Another Borgia named Cesare (CHAY-suh-ray) was made a cardinal, a high-ranking member of the clergy, at the age of 17. Like many of the Borgias, Cesare used political methods that were less than honest. However, he did do one thing right: He briefly brought Leonardo da Vinci to Rome.

This museum in Florence, called the Pitti Palace, was built in 1472 for Luca Pitti. However, the palace became the official residence of the Medici in 1550.

REVIEW & ASSESS

1. **READING CHECK** What roles did the Medici play in Florence?

2. **ANALYZE CAUSE AND EFFECT** How did the Medici family become wealthy?

3. **MAKE INFERENCES** Why did some members of the Borgia family want to join the clergy?

LEONARDO
DA VINCI 1452–1519

According to legend, Leonardo's father asked his teenage son to paint a wooden shield. The boy decided to paint a face on the shield—but not a human face. Instead, he collected an assortment of dead animals, including maggots, bats, and lizards, to create the head of a monster belching smoke. When Leonardo's father saw the painting, he was so stunned by its realism that he knew his son would be a painter. He was right. But Leonardo would be so much more.

Jobs: Painter, sculptor, engineer, scientist, and inventor

Home: He was born near Vinci but made his home wherever he found work—mostly Florence and Milan.

FINEST HOUR

Perhaps the acclaim received by his great painting, the *Mona Lisa*

WORST MOMENT

Seeing his bitter rival, Michelangelo, given the honor of decorating the Vatican, the palace of the pope in Rome

TRIVIA

He was left-handed and wrote backward, either because it was easier or to prevent the curious from reading his notebooks. His writing had to be held up to a mirror to be read.

LEONARDO THE ARTIST

Because of Leonardo da Vinci's obvious talent, he was sent to apprentice under Andrea del Verrocchio (vehr-OAK-ee-oh), a great painter in Florence. Eventually, Leonardo was given the honor of painting an angel in one of his teacher's paintings. It turned out to be the best part of the painting. Soon after, Leonardo left his teacher's studio to strike out on his own.

Word quickly spread about the young painter. Soon, nobles, patrons, and popes engaged Leonardo's services. He would produce several great works, including two very celebrated paintings. One is the *Mona Lisa*, shown here and arguably the most famous painting in the world. The other is *The Last Supper*, one of the best-known frescoes in history. The fresco depicts the final meal that, according to Christian belief, Jesus and his followers ate together. It is admired for the different emotions expressed by the followers and for the use of light and angles to draw attention to Jesus, the central figure.

LEONARDO'S *MONA LISA*

Many mysteries surround the *Mona Lisa*. For one thing, no one really knows the subject's identity, although she is believed to be Lisa Gherardini (gehr-ahr-DEE-nee), the wife of a merchant. (*Mona* means "madame.") But it is her mysterious smile that has captured people's imagination for centuries. What is she smiling about? And what's going on behind those eyes? Leonardo never gave the painting to whoever commissioned it. Instead, he kept it with him all his life. Today the painting hangs in the Louvre, a museum in Paris.

Mona Lisa, Leonardo da Vinci, 1503–1506

ULTIMATE RENAISSANCE MAN

Unfortunately for the world, Leonardo produced relatively few paintings—only about 17. He began many other paintings and other works of art but failed to finish them. This failure was probably due to his interest in so many other fields, including engineering and anatomy, or the study of the human body. Leonardo dissected, or cut up, the bodies of dead people, and used what he learned to make remarkably accurate anatomical sketches. These sketches helped him portray people more realistically. He also designed machines, including early forms of a flying machine and a submarine.

Leonardo studied whatever interested him and recorded his observations and sketches in a collection of notebooks. These are works of art themselves but were not widely known until more than 100 years after his death. Many people had considered Leonardo to be solely an artist and so were amazed at the breadth of his knowledge. In fact, with all his talents, Leonardo embodied the well-rounded ideal of Renaissance and humanist thinking. He could do it all. He was a painter, an architect, an inventor, an engineer, and a scientist. All these qualities and many more made Leonardo the ultimate **Renaissance man**.

REVIEW & ASSESS

1. **READING CHECK** Why is Leonardo da Vinci considered a true Renaissance man?

2. **INTERPRET VISUALS** The *Mona Lisa* is said to represent the idea of happiness. What details in the painting do you think make Mona Lisa appear happy?

3. **MAKE INFERENCES** Why do you think Leonardo decided to keep the *Mona Lisa* for himself?

7.8.5 Detail advances made in literature, the arts, science, mathematics, cartography, engineering, and the understanding of human anatomy and astronomy (e.g., by Dante Alighieri, Leonardo da Vinci, Michelangelo di Buonarroti Simoni, Johann Gutenberg, William Shakespeare).

333

Searching for a Lost da Vinci

What if there were a painting by Leonardo that was just waiting to be uncovered? Italian engineer Maurizio Seracini is convinced one exists, and he thinks he knows where it is. His obsession has taken him to Florence, where he has conducted extensive research and experienced both triumphs and defeats. Seracini has also gathered a team, including photographer Dave Yoder, to help him find the hidden masterpiece. The question is: Will they find the lost da Vinci?

^
A member of Seracini's team looks on nervously as a probe is inserted in this painting by Giorgio Vasari. Seracini believes Leonardo's missing painting lies hidden behind Vasari's work.

Researchers are trying to find a long-lost painting by Leonardo da Vinci.

A CENTURIES-OLD MYSTERY

The object of Seracini's search dates back about 500 years. Around 1505, Leonardo painted a fresco called *The Battle of Anghiari* (ahn-ghee-AHR-ee) on the wall of a room in the Palazzo Vecchio, the town hall of Florence. The fresco depicts four men on horseback, engaged in an intense battle. Leonardo had completed the *Mona Lisa*, but it was *The Battle of Anghiari* that other artists came to admire and copy.

Photographer Dave Yoder

About 50 years later, a Renaissance artist and writer named Giorgio Vasari was asked to redecorate the town hall. However, legend has it that rather than destroy Leonardo's fresco, Vasari built a wall over the painting. He then painted his own battle scene on the new wall. Vasari had preserved other great works in a similar way.

An expert on Leonardo first told Seracini about the lost painting and suggested that he gather a team to look for it. As part of the team, National Geographic photographer Dave Yoder said his challenge was "to find things to photograph about a painting that might or might not be behind a wall." They also weren't sure which wall to look behind.

CLUES AND FINDINGS

But Seracini believes Vasari provided a clue to the painting's whereabouts. On a small flag in his painting, the artist wrote in tiny letters the Italian words *Cerca trova*, which mean "Seek and you shall find." At first Seracini used noninvasive methods to reveal what he called "a subtle gap behind the wall on which Vasari painted, which could have been constructed by Vasari himself to protect Leonardo's masterpiece."

Soon after this discovery, however, officials in Florence had Seracini's team use an endoscope, a more invasive method, to explore the painting. An endoscope is a lighted instrument that can be inserted inside an object to examine it. To reduce the damage, Seracini mostly inserted the endoscope into holes that had already opened in Vasari's painting. Material taken from one hole revealed traces of colors that only Leonardo had used. One black pigment was believed to be the same type used in painting the *Mona Lisa*.

Despite this promising finding, Italian authorities called a halt to further exploration in 2012. Restorers protested the invasion of Vasari's masterpiece. They also didn't believe Seracini's theory. As a result, the holes were filled in, and the scaffolding was taken down. So, is the lost da Vinci lost for good? Both Seracini and Yoder hope not. "I think it's likely that there is at least part of Leonardo's fresco somewhere in the room," says Yoder. "But given the technology we're limited to, we could easily miss it by a few inches, and then the world would never know."

1. **READING CHECK** What does Seracini think is hidden behind Vasari's fresco?

2. **ANALYZE CAUSE AND EFFECT** What event brought the search to a halt?

3. **FORM AND SUPPORT OPINIONS** Do you think the search for the lost da Vinci should continue? Explain why or why not.

The Renaissance Moves North

You've heard about the wonders in Italy, but you still can't believe your eyes and ears. In Florence, you marvel at the lifelike, muscular statue of David. You stop on the street in Rome to listen to people discuss the limitless possibility of the individual. In Milan, you gaze at *The Last Supper* and admire its depth and emotional power. You can't wait to get back home to northern Europe and tell everyone what you've seen and heard.

MAIN IDEA

Renaissance ideas spread from Italy and influenced art and literature across northern Europe.

ARTISTIC STYLES

Great ideas cannot be contained. This was true even in the 1400s and 1500s. In time, Italian Renaissance ideas began to influence northern Europe. Trade and the growth of cities spread the ideas to countries such as France, Belgium, the Netherlands, Germany, Spain, and England.

Artists from these countries visited Italy's cities to soak up their rebirth of culture firsthand. Powerful rulers in countries like France and England brought Italian artists to their courts. The kings and queens became the artists' patrons and paid them to create works that became a source of national pride.

While northern European artists were inspired by the Italian Renaissance, many put their own spin on artistic styles. For instance, instead of focusing on classical subjects, artists of the Northern Renaissance often painted scenes of everyday life. A Flemish artist named Pieter Bruegel (BROY-guhl) the Elder demonstrated this style. (*Flemish* refers to people from a region called Flanders, which is in present-day Belgium.) As the painting on the opposite page illustrates, Bruegel often depicted the lives of peasants with remarkable realism.

Another Flemish artist, Jan van Eyck (yahn van EHK), painted detailed, colorful portraits and images of religious subjects. The rich color in his paintings was largely due to his use of oil paint. Artists of the Italian Renaissance had mostly used water-based paints that often faded quickly. When Italian artists visited northern Europe, they eagerly adopted van Eyck's use of oils and brought the style back to Italy. The trade of ideas didn't go in only one direction.

The German artist Albrecht Dürer (DYUR-uhr) is often considered to be the greatest artist of the Northern Renaissance. Dürer had visited Italy and absorbed the styles there. He combined classical ideas, perspective, and great attention to detail to create realistic paintings and **woodcuts**, or images carved on blocks of wood.

SCHOLARS AND WRITERS

The Italian Renaissance and its humanist ideals also influenced the intellectual thinking of northern Europe. As you may recall, Petrarch was an early humanist leader of the Italian Renaissance. The Dutch scholar and priest Desiderius Erasmus (dehz-ih-DEHR-ee-uhs ir-RAZ-muhs) was a key humanist leader of the Northern

The Peasant Dance, Pieter Bruegel the Elder, 1567

Critical Viewing In this painting by Bruegel, peasants dance in a village square. What can you learn about the peasants' way of life from the painting?

Renaissance. Erasmus focused on making classical works and Christian texts more accessible to ordinary people. He also criticized some Church practices and called for reform. As you will see later in the chapter, the writings of Erasmus and others would have a big impact on the Church. Another humanist, the English statesman Thomas More, promoted free education for men and women, which was a radical idea at the time.

Unlike Erasmus and More, the best-known writer of the Northern Renaissance did not try to reform society. This author wrote tragic, comic, and historical plays filled with characters that spring to life off the page. Their passions, humor, personalities, and conflicts still capture our imagination today. Many people believe that the man who created these characters—William Shakespeare—is the greatest writer in the English language.

REVIEW & ASSESS

1. **READING CHECK** How did Renaissance ideas spread from Italy to northern Europe?

2. **COMPARE AND CONTRAST** In what ways did the artistic styles of the Northern Renaissance differ from those of the Italian Renaissance?

3. **SYNTHESIZE** Based on what you have learned about humanism, how did the scholars and writers of the Northern Renaissance reflect its ideals?

7.8.2 Explain the importance of Florence in the early stages of the Renaissance and the growth of independent trading cities (e.g., Venice), with emphasis on the cities' importance in the spread of Renaissance ideas; 7.8.4 Describe the growth and effects of new ways of disseminating information (e.g., the ability to manufacture paper, translation of the Bible into the vernacular, printing); 7.8.5 Detail advances made in literature, the arts, science, mathematics, cartography, engineering, and the understanding of human anatomy and astronomy (e.g., by Dante Alighieri, Leonardo da Vinci, Michelangelo di Buonarroti Simoni, Johann Gutenberg, William Shakespeare); 7.9.2 Describe the theological, political, and economic ideas of the major figures during the Reformation (e.g., Desiderius Erasmus, Martin Luther, John Calvin, William Tyndale).

WILLIAM SHAKESPEARE

1564–1616

Some people don't believe William Shakespeare wrote the works credited to him, in part because he didn't have a university education. These doubters have identified other writers of the time as the authors of Shakespeare's work, but they've never been able to prove their theories. Maybe some people can't believe that a man of humble background could pen some of the greatest plays ever written. But that seems to have been exactly what happened.

Jobs: Playwright, poet, actor

Home: Stratford upon Avon; married to Anne Hathaway, with whom he had three children

FINEST HOUR

Writing and performing for his patrons—first Queen Elizabeth I and later King James I of England

WORST MOMENT

Perhaps the death of his son, Hamnet, at age 11

DEATH

Unlike many writers of his day, he died a rich man and left most of his possessions to his daughter Susanna.

TRIVIA

Some of the writers of his time didn't respect him and referred to him as an "upstart crow."

THE BARD

The Northern Renaissance was well established in England by the time **William Shakespeare** went to seek his fortune in London around 1585. He began as an actor and apparently had a successful career. In time, he became part owner of a theatrical company known as the Lord Chamberlain's Men and began writing his own plays. By around 1594, the company was mainly performing only Shakespeare's plays, and the playwright acted in many of them himself.

The Bard—or poet—as he is often called, wrote more than 150 poems and 37 plays, including tragedies such as *Romeo and Juliet* and comedies such as *A Midsummer Night's Dream*. Shakespeare's plays have stood the test of time largely because of their insight into human nature. Shakespeare created complex characters with deep emotions and used clever wordplay to make his audience laugh or cry. The plays also reflected the Renaissance mindset.

Romeo and Juliet is a timeless work. Its themes can be interpreted and expressed in many ways, and the story can be set in many different eras. This film version takes place in the present day and features actors Leonardo DiCaprio and Claire Danes.

They dealt with human life rather than religious themes. And many of the plays were based on stories and characters from classical Greek and Latin works.

THE ELIZABETHAN AGE

Most of Shakespeare's plays were written during the **Elizabethan Age**, or the reign of Queen Elizabeth I, which lasted from 1558 to 1603. Elizabeth spoke many languages, wrote poetry, and was a gifted musician. The queen supported the Globe Theater, where many of Shakespeare's plays were performed before people from all walks of life. After Elizabeth died, her cousin James I rose to the throne. James soon became the patron of Shakespeare's theatrical company, which then changed its name to the King's Men. Shakespeare wrote some of his greatest plays, including *Macbeth*, under the king's patronage.

Shakespeare retired from the theater when he was 49 and died three years later. Several years after his death, his plays were collected in a volume. The English playwright Ben Jonson, who had known Shakespeare, understood his friend's genius. In an introduction to the volume, Jonson wrote that Shakespeare "was not of an age, but for all time."

REVIEW & ASSESS

1. **READING CHECK** How did Shakespeare's plays reflect Renaissance ideas?

2. **MAKE INFERENCES** Why do you think Shakespeare's plays appealed to all people, from the very wealthy to the very poor?

3. **ANALYZE LANGUAGE USE** What does the phrase "not of an age, but for all time" suggest about Shakespeare's legacy?

7.8.5 Detail advances made in literature, the arts, science, mathematics, cartography, engineering, and the understanding of human anatomy and astronomy (e.g., by Dante Alighieri, Leonardo da Vinci, Michelangelo di Buonarroti Simoni, Johann Gutenberg, William Shakespeare).

The Printing Press

Today, ideas can fly around the world at the push of a button or the click of a mouse. In the early days of the Renaissance, however, ideas mostly spread by word of mouth as traders and travelers made their slow way from place to place. But then a German printer came up with an invention that sped up the exchange of ideas. In many ways, it was the Internet of its day.

MAIN IDEA

The printing press greatly quickened the spread of Renaissance ideas and information.

TECHNOLOGICAL ADVANCE

The invention was the **printing press**, and it was developed around 1450 by the German blacksmith, goldsmith, publisher, and printer **Johann Gutenberg**. He developed the press by improving on the Chinese technology of woodblock printing. Chinese printers had carved text onto a wooden block, inked the block, and then pressed it onto paper. Gutenberg developed movable metal type, with a separate piece of type for each letter. Using this technology, printers could arrange the letters any way they liked. They could also use and reuse the pieces. The diagram on the opposite page shows how the printing press worked.

Around the same time, a new technique for making paper was developed, which made paper easier to manufacture. Gutenberg used this paper and his new press to print a Latin Bible in 1455. He tried to keep his printing technique a secret, but his beautiful Bible caught people's attention. Like Renaissance culture, the technology of the new printing press spread quickly.

IMPACT OF PRINTING

It's hard to overestimate the impact of the printing press. It resulted in an information explosion throughout Europe. Before the press, most printers made every copy of a book by hand, which could take a full month. In the same amount of time, Gutenberg's press could produce 500 books. These books were far cheaper than the handmade copies. They also spread ideas much more quickly.

As you know, people had become eager for knowledge by the time of the Renaissance. The printing press only fueled this demand. As more books became available, more people learned to read, and more universities were founded. In addition, libraries became better stocked with reliable information, which helped in the advancement of science, technology, and scholarship.

Many of the first printed books were religious and classical works, but a demand for less scholarly reading soon grew. In response, publishers printed poetry, plays, travel books, and histories. People also wanted to read books in their native language, instead of Latin. Remember that Dante began this trend when he wrote *The Divine Comedy* in Italian. As a result, books began to be printed in the vernacular—even the Bible. This allowed many more people to read the Bible and interpret its teachings for themselves for the first time. As you'll see in the next section, this trend would cause trouble for the Catholic Church. Soon Gutenberg's invention would be printing pamphlets that would question the authority of the pope himself.

PRINTING ON GUTENBERG'S PRESS, STEP BY STEP

4. Press
The printer rolls the type box under the press and uses the handle to imprint letters onto the paper.

2. Ink Ball
The printer uses the ink ball to apply an oil-based ink onto the type.

1. Type Box
The printer arranges the letters in the type box.

3. Paper Holder
The printer inserts paper in the holder and folds it onto the inked type.

GUTENBERG'S BIBLE

The Gutenberg Bible, as it came to be called, contained 1,286 pages with about 42 lines on each page. It was remarkable for its neat, even letters and hand-painted illustrations of nature. Gutenberg printed 200 copies of his Bible, of which about 50 survive today.

REVIEW & ASSESS

1. **READING CHECK** How did the printing press help spread information?

2. **INTEGRATE VISUALS** Based on the diagram and what you have learned about the printing press, how do you think the new invention improved printers' lives?

3. **ANALYZE CAUSE AND EFFECT** What happened once the printing press made books more widely available?

7.8.4 Describe the growth and effects of new ways of disseminating information (e.g., the ability to manufacture paper, translation of the Bible into the vernacular, printing); HI 2 Students understand and distinguish cause, effect, sequence, and correlation in historical events, including the long- and short-term causal relations.

2.4 Legacy in the Arts and Sciences

 Did you know that the Renaissance influenced many modern developments? GPS technology owes a debt to the advances Renaissance scientists made in mapmaking. Studies of the human body in the 1500s paved the way for today's medical-imaging techniques. As for the arts, if you travel to almost any state capitol, you'll see a dome that resembles Brunelleschi's. The Renaissance left us a living legacy.

MAIN IDEA

Renaissance advances in the arts and sciences continue to influence thinking today.

THE ARTS AND ARCHITECTURE

As you have learned, Renaissance architects revived ancient Greek and Roman ideas to build and perfect such structures as domes, arches, and columns. These structures continue to be important elements in architecture today. Similarly, Renaissance artists' realistic portrayal of individuals and use of perspective have influenced modern and contemporary artists.

You've read about William Shakespeare, but the Renaissance also produced such literary figures as Spanish writer Miguel de Cervantes (sehr-VAHN-tez) and Italian historian Niccolò Machiavelli. In Cervantes' masterpiece, the novel *Don Quixote* (key-HOE-tay), the author used humor and insight to tell his tale. The novel has influenced other writers since its publication about 400 years ago. Machiavelli wrote a book on effective leadership called *The Prince*. The book continues to influence leaders—and would-be leaders—today.

IMPACT OF SCIENTIFIC ADVANCES

The Renaissance made its mark on the sciences, too. Some historians say that Gutenberg's printing press is the greatest invention of the past 1,000 years—more significant than the computer or the Internet. The printing press made it possible for people all around the world to share, study, and challenge others' ideas.

In mathematics, Renaissance scholars came up with the idea of using letters in algebraic equations; for example, $x + y = 5$. Renaissance thinkers also became interested in the natural world. Some scientists learned about the metals and minerals that make up Earth's surface. Others studied astronomy and gained new understanding of the wider universe and Earth's place in it.

You've learned about Leonardo da Vinci's anatomical sketches. In 1543, the Belgian physician Andreas Vesalius (vuh-SAHL-ee-us) dissected the bodies of executed criminals and published his findings. As a result of his accurate drawings of the human body, anatomy became a scientific discipline.

Scientific ideas were also applied to **cartography**, or mapmaking, during the Renaissance. Using these new ideas, exploration by men such as Christopher Columbus continued to improve the accuracy of maps. Exploration also opened up new lands to colonization and settlement. The legacy of these events is still felt today.

Statue of Martin Luther King, Jr., at his memorial

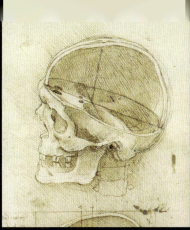

Drawing of the skull by Leonardo

Michelangelo's *David*

THEN AND NOW

These images demonstrate the legacy of the Renaissance. Find each work created during the Renaissance and compare it to its modern counterpart. What similarities and differences do you see in each pair?

Dome of St. Peter's Basilica in Rome

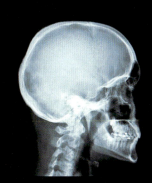

X-ray of the skull

Capitol Building dome in Washington, D.C.

1. **READING CHECK** What were some of the important scientific advances made during the Renaissance?

2. **COMPARE AND CONTRAST** In what way was the impact of Gutenberg's printing press similar to that of the Internet?

3. **MAKE CONNECTIONS** How have Renaissance advances in cartography affected modern life?

7.8.5 Detail advances made in literature, the arts, science, mathematics, cartography, engineering, and the understanding of human anatomy and astronomy (e.g., by Dante Alighieri, Leonardo da Vinci, Michelangelo di Buonarroti Simoni, Johann Gutenberg, William Shakespeare); HI 3 Students explain the sources of historical continuity and how the combination of ideas and events explains the emergence of new patterns.

Protests
Against the
Catholic Church

Thanks to Gutenberg's new printing press, the printers quickly finish making copies of the pamphlet a customer brought in. But they're a bit nervous about its contents. The pamphlet, by Martin Luther, contains a list of items criticizing the Church. The printers are used to seeing old ideas challenged, but this list seems to go too far.

MAIN IDEA

In the 1500s, Martin Luther's protests against the Roman Catholic Church led to the Reformation.

HENRY VIII

King Henry VIII of England formed a new branch of Protestantism when the Church refused to grant him a divorce. The king wanted to divorce and marry a woman he hoped would give him a son.

MARTIN LUTHER

As you know, some people had begun to criticize the Church and call for reforms during the Renaissance. In the last chapter, you also learned that the Church became weaker as the authority of kings increased. In 1305, a powerful French king moved the center of the Church from Rome to Avignon (ah-veen-YOHN), in France, and appointed a French pope. Following a struggle for power, two popes were elected in 1378: one in Rome and the other in Avignon. This split in the Church is known as the **Great Schism** (*schism* means "split"). Although the Church was unified once again in 1417 and Rome restored as the center of Christianity, the Church had been weakened even further.

The Church needed money to regain its former strength, but some people believed the Church used questionable practices to obtain it. For example, Church officials sold **indulgences**, which relaxed the punishment for a sin. However, sometimes the officials sold an indulgence as forgiveness for a sin, with no punishment imposed. Many people, though, believed that only God could forgive sins. People also objected to paying one-tenth of their income to the Church every year in taxes.

A German monk named **Martin Luther** actively protested against these practices. On October 31, 1517, Luther nailed a list of protests, known as the 95 Theses, to a church door in Wittenberg, Germany. The list included the idea that the Bible was the only source of religious truth and that priests were not needed to interpret its words. Luther further suggested that salvation came through faith in Christ alone. Those who supported Luther's ideas would be called **Protestants**, which comes from the word *protest*. The reform movement Luther began is known as the **Reformation**.

PROTESTANTISM GROWS

After Luther made the 95 Theses public, Pope Leo X demanded that the monk take back his statements. Luther refused and was excommunicated, or cut off, from the Church. Nevertheless, pamphlets containing Luther's theses were soon printed, and his ideas spread rapidly.

ATLANTIC OCEAN

SCOTLAND

North Sea

SWEDEN

DENMARK

IRELAND

ENGLAND

London

Wittenberg

POLAND-LITHUANIA

HOLY ROMAN EMPIRE

SWISS CONFEDERATION

AUSTRIA

FRANCE

Geneva

HUNGARY

ITALIAN STATES

OTTOMAN EMPIRE

PAPAL STATES

Adriatic Sea

Black Sea

SPAIN

Mediterranean Sea

Anglican
Calvinist
Lutheran

0   200   400 Miles
0   200   400 Kilometers

In response, peasants throughout Europe used Luther's teachings to stage revolts for better wages and living conditions.

Luther's teachings also had a great impact on Christianity. As people interpreted the Bible for themselves, their differing beliefs led to the development of many branches, or **denominations**, of Protestant religions. One branch, called Lutheranism, was inspired by Luther's teachings. Another, called Calvinism, was led by a French reformer named John Calvin who believed that God chose people for salvation. They could do nothing to earn it. A third branch, called Anglicanism or the Church of England, was begun in England by King Henry VIII. Protestantism would have a lasting impact on Europe. But in the meantime, the Catholic Church began to look for ways to stop its spread.

REVIEW & ASSESS

1. **READING CHECK** What Church practices did Martin Luther protest against?

2. **INTERPRET MAPS** How did the spread of the Lutheran and Calvinist branches of Protestantism differ from that of the Anglican branch?

3. **IDENTIFY MAIN IDEAS** Why did many branches of Protestantism develop?

 7.9.1 List the causes for the internal turmoil in and weakening of the Catholic church (e.g., tax policies, selling of indulgences); 7.9.2 Describe the theological, political, and economic ideas of the major figures during the Reformation (e.g., Desiderius Erasmus, Martin Luther, John Calvin, William Tyndale); CST 3 Students use a variety of maps and documents to identify physical and cultural features of neighborhoods, cities, states, and countries and to explain the historical migration of people, expansion and disintegration of empires, and the growth of economic systems.

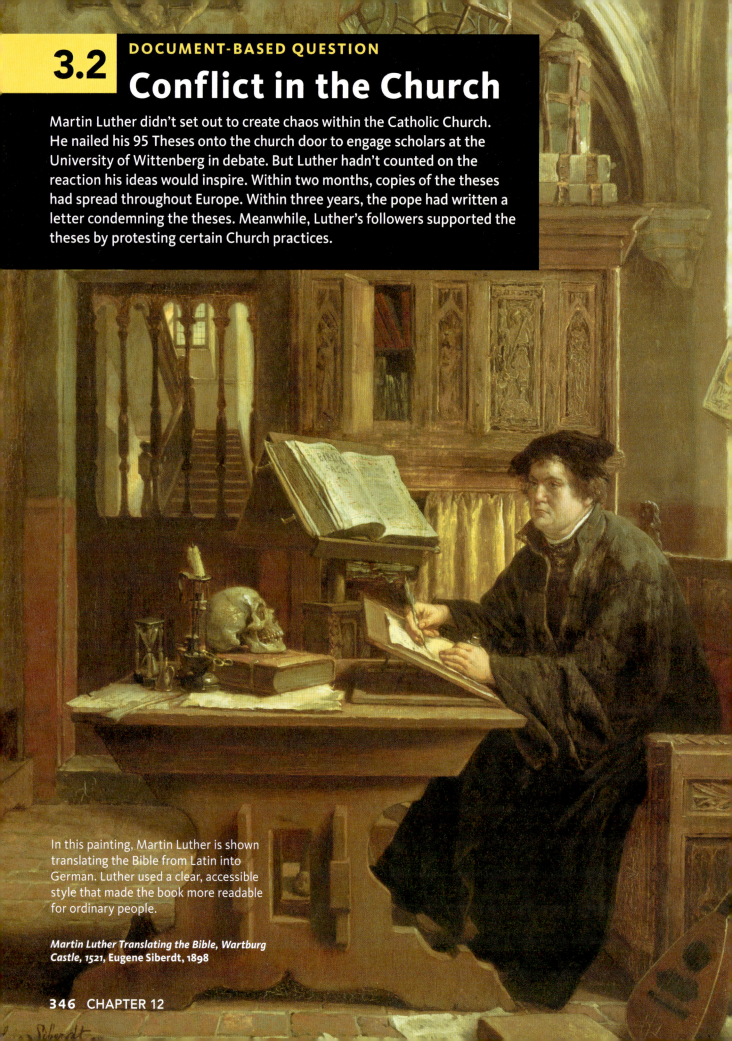

Martin Luther didn't set out to create chaos within the Catholic Church. He nailed his 95 Theses onto the church door to engage scholars at the University of Wittenberg in debate. But Luther hadn't counted on the reaction his ideas would inspire. Within two months, copies of the theses had spread throughout Europe. Within three years, the pope had written a letter condemning the theses. Meanwhile, Luther's followers supported the theses by protesting certain Church practices.

In this painting, Martin Luther is shown translating the Bible from Latin into German. Luther used a clear, accessible style that made the book more readable for ordinary people.

Martin Luther Translating the Bible, Wartburg Castle, 1521, Eugene Siberdt, 1898

DOCUMENT ONE

Primary Source: Pamphlet

from the 95 Theses

In his 95 Theses, Luther expresses his criticism of the Church in statements that sum up his interpretation of teaching found in the Bible. In the following two theses, Luther presents his idea that letters of pardon, or indulgences, do not make people better and cannot ensure salvation.

CONSTRUCTED RESPONSE Why might the Church have taken offense at these statements?

> 44. . . . Love grows by works of love, and man becomes better; but by pardons man does not grow better, only more free from penalty.
>
> 52. The assurance of salvation by letters of pardon is vain [useless], even though . . . the pope himself were to stake his soul upon it.

DOCUMENT TWO

Primary Source: Letter

from the Papal Bull of Pope Leo X

In 1520, Pope Leo X issued a papal bull, or official letter, giving Luther 60 days to take back his theses. In the following excerpt from the bull, Leo condemns Luther's ideas and tells followers of Catholicism ("the faithful") how to handle them.

CONSTRUCTED RESPONSE According to the pope, how should Catholics deal with Luther's ideas?

> With the advice and consent of these our venerable [respected] brothers, . . . we condemn, reprobate [disapprove], and reject completely each of these theses. . . . We forbid each and every one of the faithful . . . to read, assert, preach, praise, print, publish, or defend them.

DOCUMENT THREE

Primary Source: Leaflet

Leaflet Against Johann Tetzel

Luther's followers distributed this leaflet to protest against the practices of Johann Tetzel, a monk who sold indulgences. Tetzel is said to have written the last two lines in the leaflet:
"As soon as gold in the cashbox rings,
The rescued soul to heaven springs."

CONSTRUCTED RESPONSE Why do you think the people shown in the leaflet are happy to see Tetzel?

SYNTHESIZE & WRITE

1. **REVIEW** Review what you have learned about the Reformation and protests against the Catholic Church.

2. **RECALL** On your own paper, write down the main idea expressed in each document.

3. **CONSTRUCT** Write a topic sentence that answers this question: How did the Church and Luther's followers react to the 95 Theses?

4. **WRITE** Using evidence from the documents, write a short paragraph to support your answer to the question in Step 3.

 7.9.1 List the causes for the internal turmoil in and weakening of the Catholic church (e.g., tax policies, selling of indulgences); 7.9.2 Describe the theological, political, and economic ideas of the major figures during the Reformation (e.g., Desiderius Erasmus, Martin Luther, John Calvin, William Tyndale); REP 2 Students distinguish fact from opinion in historical narratives and stories; REP 4 Students assess the credibility of primary and secondary sources and draw sound conclusions from them; REP 5 Students detect the different historical points of view on historical events and determine the context in which the historical statements were made (the questions asked, sources used, author's perspectives).

The Counter Reformation

After the Reformation, the Catholic Church was down but certainly not out. Millions of faithful followers remained loyal. They continued to recognize the pope as their leader and trusted their priests' interpretation of the Bible. But Church officials knew that to keep their members and bring Protestants back to the fold, they had to stop the spread of Protestantism. To do that, they had to make some changes.

MAIN IDEA

Reforms and a new religious order established during the Counter Reformation helped strengthen Catholicism.

REFORM FROM WITHIN

The changes the Catholic Church made were part of a movement called the Catholic Reformation—sometimes also called the **Counter Reformation**. (In this use of the word, *counter* means "against.") A meeting of Church officials and scholars summoned by the pope in 1545 was a key element of the movement.

The meeting, which came to be known as the **Council of Trent**, met for 26 sessions over 18 years, mostly in the northern Italian city of Trent. During that time, the council worked to define Catholic beliefs and practices and determine how the Church needed to change. Council members also sought to clarify how Catholicism differed from Protestantism. For example, while Protestants believed that the Bible could be understood directly by individuals, the Church taught that it must be interpreted and understood in light of tradition.

To make sure Catholics didn't stray from their faith, the Church also established a Roman Inquisition. Like the Spanish Inquisition discussed in the previous chapter, the Roman Inquisition used harsh methods, including torture, to force a confession and punish heresy, or a denial of Church teachings. Protestants were, of course, considered to be guilty of heresy.

In addition, Church officials created a list of books they objected to. Followers of Catholicism were forbidden to read the books, which included Bibles in the vernacular as well as most anything written by Luther, Calvin, and Erasmus. The books were collected by Church clergy and burned.

On the other hand, the Church also applied gentler methods to broaden its appeal. It built new, larger churches to hold more worshippers. In addition, priests sometimes delivered sermons in the vernacular.

A NEW RELIGIOUS ORDER

The struggle to revive Catholicism was aided by the development of a new religious order called the Society of Jesus, whose followers were known as **Jesuits** (JEHZH-oo-ihts). A former Spanish knight named Ignatius of Loyola formed the order, and he insisted on strict obedience.

Beginning in 1540, Ignatius commanded his followers as their "Superior General," and the Jesuits carried out their duties with great discipline. They also took vows of poverty and obedience, promising to fight "for the greater glory of God."

Christian missions

From the start, the Jesuits' purpose was to obey the pope and go wherever he thought they were most needed. In time, this meant establishing schools and universities throughout Europe and the world. The Jesuits provided a good education to thousands of men and inspired many to dedicate their lives to the Church.

The Jesuits also worked as **missionaries** by spreading Catholicism to people in Africa, Asia, and the Americas.

To prepare for this task and enable them to communicate their faith to people in other parts of the world, Jesuit priests studied many different languages.

Through their support of the Counter Reformation, the Jesuits and other Catholic reformers helped revitalize the Church. By the end of the 1500s, the Church had regained much of its power. The Church was ready to play an important role in the coming century.

REVIEW & ASSESS

1. **READING CHECK** What were some of the methods used during the Counter Reformation to stop the spread of Protestantism?

2. **MAKE INFERENCES** Why do you think the Church burned certain books?

3. **DRAW CONCLUSIONS** Why was it important to the Catholic Church to establish its own schools and universities?

7.9.5 Analyze how the Counter-Reformation revitalized the Catholic church and the forces that fostered the movement (e.g., St. Ignatius of Loyola and the Jesuits, the Council of Trent); 7.9.6 Understand the institution and impact of missionaries on Christianity and the diffusion of Christianity from Europe to other parts of the world in the medieval and early modern periods; locate missions on a world map.

The Impact of the Reformation

The Reformation resulted in a cultural shift. Once people could interpret the Bible for themselves, they formed new ideas about the Christian religion. More Protestant denominations formed as differences in beliefs developed, and new Protestant churches sprang up. Europe would never be the same.

MAIN IDEA

The Reformation had a long-lasting religious, social, and political impact on Europe.

RELIGIOUS EFFECTS

Protestantism flourished. Like Catholics, Protestants founded universities and parish schools to teach their beliefs and gain new followers. As a result, because both Protestants and Catholics wanted to read the Bible, the Reformation increased literacy.

In England, many Anglicans learned to read the Bible but not in the vernacular. They followed the Catholic belief that prohibited reading the Bible in translation. However, reformer William Tyndale believed that Anglicans should reject all Catholic beliefs and practices and so began to prepare an English translation of the New Testament.

Tyndale completed his work in Germany. In time, however, Catholic officials there arrested and executed him for his beliefs.

POLITICAL EFFECTS

The Reformation had both positive and negative political effects. On the positive side, the Reformation influenced the development of democracy and federalism. Protestants who formed a church sometimes governed it themselves. This practice would later encourage religious groups immigrating to the English colonies to form a government with equal and fair laws—an early step toward democracy. In addition, Calvinist churches sometimes allowed church members to share power with the clergy. This practice represented an early form of federalism in which power is shared, like that between a national government and state governments.

On the negative side, the Reformation led to widespread warfare in Europe. In the years after Luther published the 95 Theses, religious wars erupted within countries and between them. The Thirty Years' War, for example, started as a conflict between Catholics and Protestants in Central Europe. The war, which lasted from 1618 to 1648, devastated the German states, killing an estimated seven million people.

Although the Catholic Church had partly recovered from the Reformation, its power in Europe would come to be challenged by powerful kings. These kings worked to bring all of the people within their territory under a unified rule. As a result, powerful modern **nation-states** began to emerge, with their own independent governments and populations united by a shared culture, language, and national pride.

The Catholic Church would also face challenges from another source. Scientists influenced by humanism would begin to question accepted views—including those of the Church. Their discoveries would change the way people looked at the world.

Church towers in the northern European country of Latvia represent three different Christian denominations: (from left to right) Lutheranism, Catholicism, and Anglicanism.

REVIEW & ASSESS

1. **READING CHECK** What were some of the religious effects of the Reformation?

2. **DETERMINE WORD MEANINGS** In the sentence "Because more people wanted to read the Bible, the Reformation also increased literacy," what does *literacy* mean?

3. **ANALYZE CAUSE AND EFFECT** What led to the rise of nation-states?

7.9.3 Explain Protestants' new practices of church self-government and the influence of those practices on the development of democratic practices and ideas of federalism; HI 2 Students understand and distinguish cause, effect, sequence, and correlation in historical events, including the long- and short-term causal relations.

Complete each of the following sentences using one of the vocabulary words from the chapter.

1. A movement called _____ focused on the potential of the individual. **HSS 7.8.1**

2. During the Renaissance, artists often painted nonreligious, or _____, subjects. **HSS 7.8.1**

3. Artists use _____ to produce an impression of depth and distance. **HSS 7.8.5**

4. Instead of Latin, some Renaissance writers wrote in the _____. **HSS 7.8.4**

5. Wealthy _____ often supported artists during the Renaissance. **HSS 7.8.2**

6. Gutenberg's development of the _____ helped spread ideas quickly. **HSS 7.8.4**

7. The Roman Inquisition punished _____, or a denial of Church policy. **HSS 7.9.5**

READING STRATEGY

8. **ANALYZE LANGUAGE USE** If you haven't already, complete at least three concept clusters that analyze figurative language. Then use each example of the language in a sentence of your own. **HSS REP 5**

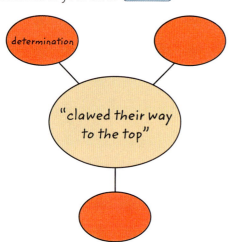

determination

"clawed their way to the top"

MAIN IDEAS

Answer the following questions. Support your answers with evidence from the chapter.

9. What was the Renaissance? **LESSON 1.1** **HSS 7.8**

10. What artistic subjects became popular during the Renaissance? **LESSON 1.2** **HSS 7.8.1**

11. Why were the best artists and scholars attracted to Florence during the Renaissance? **LESSON 1.4** **HSS 7.8.2**

12. Who often served as patrons of Northern Renaissance artists? **LESSON 2.1** **HSS 7.8**

13. How did Gutenberg's printing press improve on Chinese woodblock printing? **LESSON 2.3** **HSS HI 3**

14. Which event triggered the Reformation? **LESSON 3.1** **HSS 7.9.2**

15. What was the purpose of the Counter Reformation? **LESSON 3.3** **HSS 7.9.5**

CRITICAL THINKING

Answer the following questions. Support your answers with evidence from the chapter.

16. **ESSENTIAL QUESTION** How did the ideas of humanism differ from those of the Middle Ages? **HSS 7.8.1**

17. **MAKE PREDICTIONS** What might have happened if wealthy patrons had not supported Renaissance artists? **HSS HI 2**

18. **MAKE INFERENCES** Why do you think art experts become so excited over the prospect of finding a new painting by Leonardo da Vinci? **HSS 7.8.5**

19. **DRAW CONCLUSIONS** What conclusions can you draw about Shakespeare's career based on the fact that he died a rich man? **HSS 7.8.5**

20. **SEQUENCE EVENTS** What events followed Martin Luther's publication of his 95 Theses? **HSS CST 1**

21. **YOU DECIDE** What was the most important achievement of the Renaissance? Support your opinion with evidence from the chapter. **HSS REP 1**

INTERPRET VISUALS

Study the paintings below from the Middle Ages and the Renaissance. Then answer the questions that follow.

Medieval painting from Catalan School, Spain

Renaissance painting by Raphael

22. In what ways are the two paintings alike? HSS 7.8.5

23. How do the artistic styles differ in the two paintings? HSS 7.8.5

ANALYZE SOURCES

In 1568, Giorgio Vasari wrote a collection of biographies about the great artists of his day, including Michelangelo. In this excerpt, a high-ranking government official named Piero Soderini has a suggestion for improving Michelangelo's famous sculpture of David.

> While Michelangelo was giving it the finishing touches, [Soderini] told Michelangelo that he thought the nose of the figure was too large. Michelangelo, . . . having quickly grabbed his chisel in his left hand along with a little marble dust, . . . began to tap lightly with the chisel, allowing the dust to fall little by little without retouching the nose from the way it was. Then, looking down at [Soderini] who stood there watching, he ordered: "Look at it now." "I like it better," replied [Soderini]: "you've made it come alive."

24. Based on this story, what were some of Michelangelo's personality traits? HSS REP 4

WRITE ABOUT HISTORY

25. EXPLANATORY How did the Renaissance affect Europe? Write a paragraph designed to inform museumgoers about the ways in which Renaissance ideas about art, literature, and thinking changed Europe. Use the tips below to help you plan, organize, and revise your paragraph. HSS HI 2

TIPS

- Take notes from the lessons on how the Renaissance affected people and events in Europe. You might use a web diagram to organize your notes.

- State your main idea clearly at the beginning of the paragraph.

- Support your main idea with relevant facts, details, and examples.

- Use two or three vocabulary terms from the chapter.

- Provide a concluding statement about the ways in which the Renaissance changed Europe.

- Use word-processing software to produce and publish your final paragraph.

13

THE AGE OF
SCIENCE AND EXPLORATION
1400 – 1700

ESSENTIAL QUESTION How did new ideas affect Europeans' views of the world?

SECTION 1 THE SCIENTIFIC REVOLUTION

KEY VOCABULARY	NAMES & PLACES
elliptical	Galileo Galilei
geocentric theory	Isaac Newton
heliocentric theory	Nicolaus Copernicus
hypothesis	René Descartes
scientific method	Robert Hooke
scientific rationalism	Scientific Revolution
theory	Sir Francis Bacon

SECTION 2 THE AGE OF EXPLORATION

KEY VOCABULARY	NAMES & PLACES
caravel	Christopher Columbus
colony	Columbian Exchange
exploit	Dutch East India Company
quinine	Ferdinand and Isabella
rivalry	Prince Henry the Navigator
smallpox	

SECTION 3 EUROPEAN EMPIRES

KEY VOCABULARY	NAMES & PLACES
conquistador	Atahualpa
cottage industry	Francisco Pizarro
mercantilism	Hernán Cortés
plantation	Middle Passage
racism	Pedro Álvares Cabral
triangular trade	Tenochtitlán

READING STRATEGY

MAKE INFERENCES
When you make inferences, you "read between the lines" to find information that isn't stated directly. As you read the chapter, use a chart like this one to make inferences about the relationship between the Scientific Revolution and European exploration.

I Learned	My Inference

A giant collection of telescopes in Chile scans the night sky. During the Age of Exploration, observations of the stars and planets led to changes in scientific views of the universe.

Roots of the Revolution

The period following the Middle Ages was one of major changes in Europe. The Renaissance brought an explosion of creativity in art, literature, and architecture. The Reformation transformed people's religious ideas. Another important movement introduced great advances in science. This movement is called the **Scientific Revolution**, and it began in Europe around the mid-1500s.

MAIN IDEA

Before the Scientific Revolution, Europeans generally relied on the works of ancient Greek thinkers and medieval Muslim scholars to answer scientific questions.

ANCIENT GREEK SCIENTISTS

Since earliest times, people have attempted to understand and explain the natural world—sometimes through religion, sometimes through science, and sometimes by combining the two. Early scientists called themselves "natural philosophers," and their methods differed greatly from those of modern scientists.

The ancient Greeks were great thinkers, and they often based their scientific explanations on reasoning rather than evidence. Indeed, some famous Greek philosophers rejected the need for scientific experiments. They believed that if enough clever men thought for long enough, they would discover the truth. This belief led to some incorrect theories. A **theory** is a proposed explanation for a set of facts.

Two ancient Greek thinkers, Aristotle and Ptolemy, promoted the **geocentric theory**, which placed Earth at the center of the universe. According to this theory, the sun, moon, and planets all moved in a circular path around Earth. This theory later supported the Christian belief that God had created Earth at the center of the universe. Even though the theory was wrong, it influenced scientific ideas about the universe for hundreds of years.

In other areas, however, the ancient Greeks made some valuable contributions to scientific knowledge. For example, the Greek mathematicians Pythagoras, Euclid, and Archimedes (ahr-kuh-MEE-deez) developed theories on which modern mathematics is based.

MEDIEVAL MUSLIM SCHOLARS

After the collapse of the Roman Empire in A.D. 476, most classical knowledge was lost to western Europe. However, it survived in the Muslim empire. Between the 600s and 1100s, Muslim scholars studied Greek scientific theories and combined them with ideas from other regions. From India, for example, they adopted such mathematical concepts as the decimal system, the number zero, and the ten Arabic numerals commonly used today. By bringing together learning from different cultures, Muslim scholars advanced mathematical understanding.

Muslim scholars also made significant advances in astronomy. They developed special buildings called observatories for studying the stars. These buildings had scientific instruments that allowed astronomers to accurately plot the locations of stars. As a result, scientists

Scenographia Systematis Mundani (Harmonia Macrocosmica or Atlas Coelestis), 1660

were able to develop more accurate calendars and methods of navigation.

The advanced knowledge of the Muslims spread throughout their vast empire and beyond, eventually reaching western Europe after the 1200s. Beginning in the 1500s, European scientists combined this knowledge with new technology and a willingness to challenge long-accepted ideas. These actions sparked a revolution in scientific thinking.

GEOCENTRIC THEORY ^

This illustration from the 1600s depicts the geocentric theory, which incorrectly placed Earth at the center of the universe. The illustration shows the sun, moon, and other planets revolving around a much larger Earth. The surrounding band shows the signs of the zodiac, an imaginary belt in the heavens that encircles the orbits of the planets. The zodiac plays a major role in astrology, the study of how the stars and planets supposedly influence people's lives and events on Earth. In the Middle Ages, astronomy and astrology were closely linked.

REVIEW & ASSESS

1. **READING CHECK** What sources of knowledge did scholars turn to before the Scientific Revolution?

2. **DETERMINE WORD MEANINGS** How do the roots of the words *geocentric* and *observatory* help clarify their meanings?

3. **ANALYZE CAUSE AND EFFECT** How did medieval Muslim scholars help advance the field of mathematics?

7.10.1 Discuss the roots of the Scientific Revolution (e.g., Greek rationalism; Jewish, Christian, and Muslim science; Renaissance humanism; new knowledge from global exploration).

1.2 Discoveries and Inventions

You are a scientist living in the early 1600s. You spend many hours looking through a telescope, studying the stars and planets. Your observations lead you to believe the planets revolve around the sun. But you are afraid to publicly state this view because it conflicts with the teachings of the powerful Catholic Church. There could be serious consequences if you publish your findings.

MAIN IDEA

Improved technology and a focus on direct observation led to important scientific discoveries from the 1500s through the 1600s.

STRUCTURE OF THE UNIVERSE

The geocentric theory placed Earth at the center of the universe. According to this theory, the sun, planets, and stars revolved around Earth in perfect circles. Some scientists began to doubt this theory, however.

In the early 1500s, a Polish scientist named **Nicolaus Copernicus** was studying the locations of the stars to create a more accurate calendar. He noticed that his mathematical calculations worked better if he assumed that Earth revolved around the sun. He proposed the **heliocentric theory**, stating that the sun was the center of the universe. Copernicus published his theory in 1543, the year he died. His theory challenged the long-held view of Earth as the center of the universe.

The research of other scientists supported the heliocentric theory. The German scientist Johannes Kepler concluded that Copernicus's basic ideas were correct. Kepler added that the planets had **elliptical**, or oval, orbits rather than perfect circular ones.

Using more powerful telescopes, the Italian scientist **Galileo Galilei** (gal-uh-LAY-oh gal-uh-LAY-ee) made observations that further supported Copernicus's theory. In 1633, the Catholic Church condemned Galileo's discoveries and put him on trial. The church required Galileo to deny support for Copernicus's theory and kept Galileo under house arrest for the rest of his life. Over time, however, the heliocentric theory gained acceptance.

The English scientist **Isaac Newton** further expanded scientific understanding of the universe in the 1600s. He proposed the law of universal gravitation, which holds that all objects in the universe attract one another. With this law and his three laws of motion, Newton created a complete mechanical explanation of motion in the universe. The Royal Society of London, an organization dedicated to advancing and sharing scientific knowledge, helped spread Newton's ideas. His work would provide the foundation of modern physics and lead to scientific advances ranging from steam engines to space rockets.

BIOLOGY AND CHEMISTRY

While some scientists explored the universe, others focused on life on Earth. The invention of the microscope around 1590 allowed biologists to explore a new microscopic world and to observe things that had previously been invisible to them.

TECHNOLOGY OF THE 1600s

Scientists developed new tools and instruments as the Scientific Revolution spread in the 1600s.

Galileo's Pendulum Clock
Galileo Galilei designed a clock operated by a pendulum. This model of Galileo's design was built in the 1800s.

Newton's Color Wheel
Isaac Newton experimented with light and invented the first color wheel.

Hooke's Microscope
Robert Hooke was among the first to build a practical compound microscope, which had more than one lens.

The English scientist **Robert Hooke** used his microscope to produce detailed drawings of tiny creatures, such as fleas. In 1665, Hooke coined the word *cell* to name the microscopic structures he observed in thin slices of cork. Hooke was the first scientist to describe cells.

Hooke worked closely with Irish scientist Robert Boyle. Together, they discovered that air is made up of gases and determined how changes in the volume of a gas affect the gas's pressure. They formed Boyle's Law to describe this relationship. Boyle's work with gases led him to propose that all matter is made up of smaller particles that join together in different ways. Boyle's theory challenged the ideas of Aristotle, who stated that the physical world consisted of the four elements of earth, fire, air, and water. The experimental work and writings of Hooke and Boyle greatly advanced the fields of biology and chemistry.

REVIEW & ASSESS

1. **READING CHECK** How did technology and direct observation help advance science in the 1500s and 1600s?

2. **MAKE INFERENCES** Why did the Catholic Church condemn Galileo's ideas?

3. **DRAW CONCLUSIONS** How did Robert Hooke advance the field of biology?

7.10.2 Understand the significance of the new scientific theories (e.g., those of Copernicus, Galileo, Kepler, Newton) and the significance of new inventions (e.g., the telescope, microscope, thermometer, barometer).

359

The Scientific Method

For more than 2,000 years, European scientists believed that a person's health depended on a balance of four body fluids called *humors*. They thought diseases were caused by an imbalance in these fluids. Even though no evidence supported the theory, European scientists did not question it.

MAIN IDEA

Two European philosophers, Sir Francis Bacon and René Descartes, helped advance a new approach to science in the 1600s.

SIR FRANCIS BACON

How do scientists develop knowledge? Most people would answer that scientists make observations and conduct experiments. But, surprisingly, that approach is relatively new. Before the 1600s, European scholars mainly referred to ancient Greek or Roman writers or to the Bible to decide what to believe. They did not seek answers by carefully observing nature themselves. The Scientific Revolution changed that approach. Scholars began to rely on observations, experiments, evidence, and reasoning in order to understand the natural world.

Galileo was one of the first scientists to actually test scientific ideas through experiments. Along with Copernicus and Kepler, he started a revolution in scientific thinking.

Two important thinkers of the 1600s—**Sir Francis Bacon** and **René Descartes** (reh-NAY day-KAHRT)—promoted ideas that eventually led to an entirely new approach to science. This approach, called the **scientific method**, is a logical procedure for developing and testing ideas. One of the key steps in the procedure is forming a **hypothesis**, an explanation that can be tested.

Sir Francis Bacon was an English philosopher, politician, and writer who had a strong interest in science. He pioneered a different approach to science in 1620 in the book *New Instrument*. Bacon urged scientists to gather data by following specific steps. Bacon's insistence on observation and experimentation as the keys to scientific accuracy became the cornerstone of modern science.

RENÉ DESCARTES

René Descartes was a brilliant French philosopher who shared Bacon's interest in science. But instead of emphasizing experimentation, Descartes relied on logic and mathematics to learn about the world. He agreed with Bacon on the need for proof in answering questions. In fact, Descartes believed that everything should be doubted until it was proved by reason.

Descartes went so far as to declare that the only thing he knew for certain was that he existed. He reasoned, "I think, therefore I am." From this starting point, Descartes used mathematical reasoning and logic to establish other certainties. Descartes argued that in mathematics, the answers were always correct because you began with simple, provable principles and then used logic to gradually build on them.

This painting shows Galileo Galilei explaining his theories at the University of Padua in Italy.

Portrait of Galileo Galilei, **Félix Parra, 1873**

THE SCIENTIFIC METHOD

The scientific method is a logical approach for forming and testing ideas. The steps shown here describe the general approach. However, not all scientific inquiries follow the steps in this exact order.

Step One: Observe and Question

A scientist makes observations and gathers information on a subject. The scientist forms a question about the subject.

Step Two: Hypothesize

The scientist proposes a hypothesis, an idea or explanation that answers the question.

Step Three: Experiment

The scientist designs and conducts an experiment to test the hypothesis.

Step Four: Analyze Data

The scientist records and carefully examines the data from the experiment.

Step Five: Evaluate and Share Results

The scientist judges whether the data do or do not support the hypothesis and publishes an article describing the experiment and results.

The ideas of Bacon and Descartes became known as **scientific rationalism**. In this school of thought, observation, experimentation, and mathematical reasoning replaced ancient wisdom and church teachings as the source of scientific knowledge. Scientific rationalism provided a procedure for establishing proof for scientific theories. It laid a foundation for formulating theories on which other scientists could build.

The influence of scientific rationalism extended beyond science. Bacon was active in politics and government, and he applied the principles of scientific rationalism to government. He argued that the direction of government should be based on actual experience.

Other writers argued that scientific rationalism encouraged people to think for themselves, so people should be allowed to take more control of their own lives. This thinking undermined the authority of the Catholic Church and contributed to the development of democratic government.

REVIEW & ASSESS

1. **READING CHECK** According to Bacon and Descartes, what are the best ways to build knowledge?

2. **EVALUATE** Why is it important to share the results of experiments?

3. **MAKE CONNECTIONS** How has the development of the scientific method affected your life?

7.10.3 Understand the scientific method advanced by Bacon and Descartes, the influence of new scientific rationalism on the growth of democratic ideas, and the coexistence of science with traditional religious beliefs; HI 3 Students explain the sources of historical continuity and how the combination of ideas and events explains the emergence of new patterns.

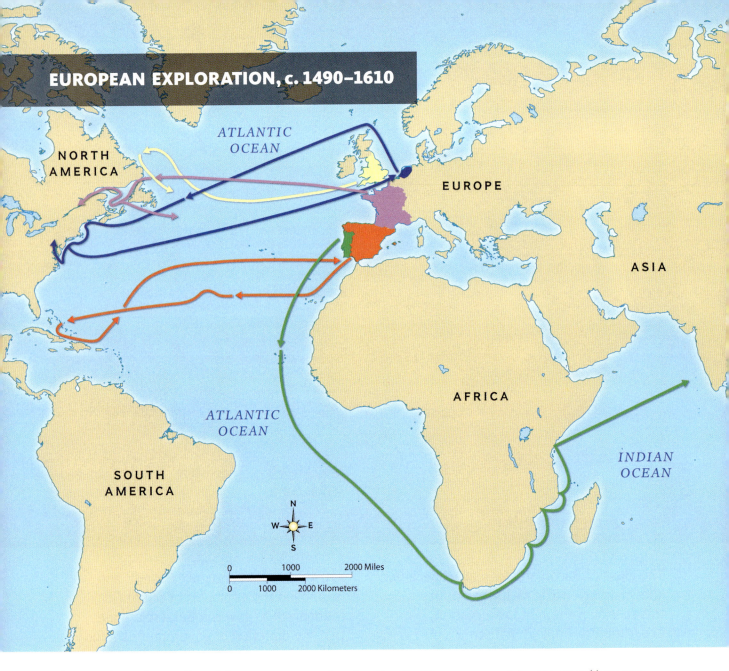

EUROPEAN EXPLORATION, c. 1490–1610

NORTH AMERICA

ATLANTIC OCEAN

EUROPE

ASIA

ATLANTIC OCEAN

AFRICA

INDIAN OCEAN

SOUTH AMERICA

N W E S

| 0 | 1000 | 2000 Miles |
| 0 | 1000 | 2000 Kilometers |

The map above shows a few of the many voyages of exploration that European countries sponsored between the 1400s and 1700s. The chart below describes the voyages shown on the map.

Sponsoring Country	Voyage
Spain	**1492** Italian navigator Christopher Columbus lands in the Americas while searching for a western sea route to Asia.
Portugal	**1497–1498** Portuguese explorer Vasco da Gama sails to India, establishing a direct sea route to Asia.
England	**1497** Italian explorer John Cabot tries to find a northwest passage through North America to Asia. He paves the way for England's colonization of North America.
France	**1535** French navigator Jacques Cartier explores the St. Lawrence River, in what is now Canada, hoping it will lead to Asia.
Netherlands	**1609** English explorer Henry Hudson sails to the New World and explores the river that will later be named after him.

An **Expanding World**

The key to successful trading is being able to supply what people want. In the 1400s, Europeans wanted Asian spices. But Ottoman Turks controlled the trade routes to Asia, and they charged high prices. European rulers and merchants knew that whoever found an alternative sea route to Asia would become fabulously wealthy.

MAIN IDEA

The desire to control trade encouraged Europeans to explore the world.

THE PUSH TO EXPLORE

For about a thousand years after the fall of the Roman Empire, western Europeans tended to view the rest of the world with hostility and fear. By about 1450, however, the time was right for change. The Renaissance encouraged a spirit of adventure and inspired curiosity about the world. Western Europe's population was booming. Above all, merchants were impatient to find new trading opportunities—and new markets.

In the 1400s, many of Europe's most valuable luxuries, including silk and spices, came from Asia. However, the Ottoman Empire controlled the trade routes. Europe's leaders and merchants wanted a share of this profitable trade, so they sponsored numerous sailing expeditions to search for an alternative sea route to Asia.

AIDS TO EXPLORATION

By 1450, important advances in shipbuilding had made longer sea journeys possible. The Portuguese had pioneered ocean-going ships called **caravels**, which were fast, sturdy, and easy to maneuver. The caravel had triangular sails that enabled it to sail effectively against the wind, which earlier sailing ships could not do.

Along with advances in shipbuilding came improvements in navigational techniques. Greater knowledge of astronomy allowed sailors to steer a course by the stars. In addition, such technological tools as the astrolabe, quadrant, and magnetic compass further improved navigation. These tools also helped explorers draw more accurate maps of their travels.

With the new ability to travel to distant parts of the world, European explorers undertook numerous expeditions in a period of time that came to be known as the Age of Exploration. In less than a century, Europeans greatly extended their geographic knowledge of the continents of Europe, Africa, and Asia—and then North and South America. Their travels brought together the people of many different lands.

REVIEW & ASSESS

1. **READING CHECK** Why did Europeans want to find a sea route from Europe to Asia?

2. **IDENTIFY MAIN IDEAS AND DETAILS** What advances made long sea voyages possible in the 1400s?

3. **INTERPRET MAPS** Which explorer found a direct sea route to Asia? Describe the route.

 7.11.1 Know the great voyages of discovery, the locations of the routes, and the influence of cartography in the development of a new European worldview; CST 3 Students use a variety of maps and documents to identify physical and cultural features of neighborhoods, cities, states, and countries and to explain the historical migration of people, expansion and disintegration of empires, and the growth of economic systems.

2.2 Exploration and Colonization

Pedro is just 16 years old when he joins an expedition to sail across the Atlantic Ocean. Bringing just the clothes he's wearing, he climbs aboard a wooden ship to sail off to . . . he's not sure exactly where. He has no idea when he will return. He's excited—and scared, much like the other sailors on European expeditions.

MAIN IDEA

During the Age of Exploration, five western European nations competed for trade, land, and riches.

COMPETITION AMONG NATIONS

Portugal, a great seafaring nation, took the lead in European exploration. In 1419, **Prince Henry the Navigator**, the son of Portugal's king, established a navigation school in Portugal. He began encouraging sailors to explore Africa's western coast, where they soon established trading posts. The Portuguese discovered an eastern sea route to India in 1498 and eventually established a profitable Asian trade.

In 1492, Spain's monarchs **Ferdinand and Isabella** funded an expedition, led by the Italian navigator **Christopher Columbus,** to find a sea route to Asia by sailing west across the Atlantic Ocean. Although the expedition failed to achieve its goal, reaching the Americas proved to be of great benefit to Spain. The Spanish established colonies in the Caribbean and conquered large areas of the Americas. As you know, a **colony** is a group of people who settle in a new land but keep ties to their native country.

Portugal and Spain developed a heated **rivalry**, or competition, over who would control the newly encountered lands. In 1494, Portugal and Spain agreed to the Treaty of Tordesillas (tawr-day-SEE-yahs) to settle their dispute. The treaty drew an imaginary line through the Atlantic Ocean from north to south. Portugal received the easterly lands, including Brazil, while Spain would receive any newly encountered lands to the west.

The English, Dutch, and French entered the competition for trade and new lands later. The English formed the East India Company in 1600 and established trading posts in India. They established colonies in North America as well. In 1602, the Dutch founded the **Dutch East India Company** to compete for trade in the Indian Ocean. The French joined the exploration race largely to compete with their English rivals.

IMPACT OF EXPLORATION

European exploration changed the world. Trade increased greatly. At trading posts, both goods and ideas were readily exchanged. As trading posts developed into colonies, more and more people moved from Europe to establish farms, towns, and cities in Asia, Africa, and the Americas. These colonies enriched the mother countries, which claimed land and **exploited**, or used to their own advantage, local resources and native people. The colonists brought European culture to places all over the world. As the Age of Exploration turned into a competition for land and riches, Europeans ended up controlling much of the world.

SAILING ON A CARAVEL

The caravel was one kind of ship used by early explorers, including Christopher Columbus. The ship was small, fast, and easy to maneuver. It could sail about 100 miles a day and held a crew of about 20 sailors.

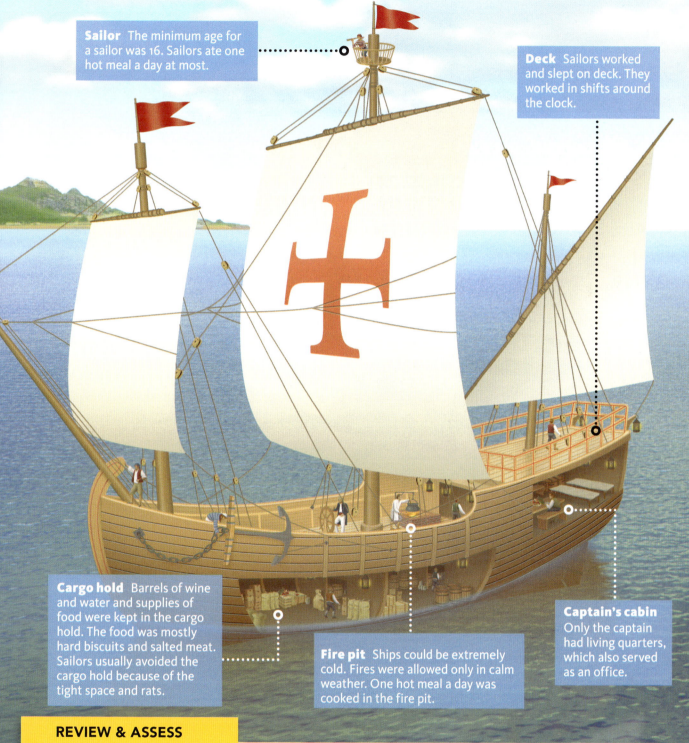

Sailor The minimum age for a sailor was 16. Sailors ate one hot meal a day at most.

Deck Sailors worked and slept on deck. They worked in shifts around the clock.

Cargo hold Barrels of wine and water and supplies of food were kept in the cargo hold. The food was mostly hard biscuits and salted meat. Sailors usually avoided the cargo hold because of the tight space and rats.

Fire pit Ships could be extremely cold. Fires were allowed only in calm weather. One hot meal a day was cooked in the fire pit.

Captain's cabin Only the captain had living quarters, which also served as an office.

REVIEW & ASSESS

1. **READING CHECK** How did the reasons for European exploration change over time?

2. **ANALYZE CAUSE AND EFFECT** What were some major effects of European exploration?

3. **INTERPRET VISUALS** What do you think were the best and worst parts of a sailor's life on a caravel?

7.11.1 Know the great voyages of discovery, the locations of the routes, and the influence of cartography in the development of a new European worldview; HI 2 Students understand and distinguish cause, effect, sequence, and correlation in historical events, including the long- and

OCTOBER 12, 1492

Around 2:00 a.m. on a moonlit night, the Spanish sailor Rodrigo de Triana yelled out the words his fellow sailors were so desperate to hear: "Land! Land!" The three small ships of Christopher Columbus's fleet had finally reached land. But what land? Columbus was aiming for Asia. Convinced that he'd reached it, he called the lands the West Indies and the natives Indians. In fact, Columbus had massively underestimated the size of the planet. He had unexpectedly found an area unknown to Europeans: the Americas or New World. The precise location of this landfall remains a mystery. One possibility is an island in the Bahamas called Samana Cay, which is shown above.

DOCUMENT-BASED QUESTION

A New World

During the European Age of Exploration, the leaders of many expeditions kept journals, in which they wrote detailed accounts of their voyages. Christopher Columbus kept such a journal. The voyages of Columbus and other explorers changed Europeans' view of the world—and their maps.

These ships are replicas of the *Pinta*, the *Santa María*, and the *Niña*, the three ships that made up Columbus's expedition in 1492.

from *The Journal of Christopher Columbus*

Christopher Columbus's original journal from his historic voyage in 1492 was lost. Then, in 1790, a full copy was found in the writings of the Spanish historian Bartolomé de Las Casas. In this excerpt from the journal, Columbus addresses his sponsors, the Spanish monarchs Ferdinand and Isabella. He discusses the direction of his voyage and how he intends to record the voyage.

CONSTRUCTED RESPONSE What land was Columbus trying to reach, and what was unusual about his route?

Your Highnesses ... determined to send me, Christopher Columbus, to the above-mentioned countries of India ... and furthermore directed that I should not proceed by land to the East, as is customary, but by a Westerly route, in which direction we have hitherto no certain evidence that any one has gone ... Moreover, Sovereign Princes, besides describing every night the occurrences of the day, and every day those of the preceding night, I intend to draw up a nautical chart, which shall contain the several parts of the ocean and land in their proper situations; and also to compose a book to represent the whole by picture with latitudes and longitudes.

Map from 1513

This map by the German mapmaker Martin Waldseemüller was published in 1513. It was the first printed map to include a part of the New World. It highlights the importance of the islands of the Caribbean. The area labeled with the Latin words *terra incognita*, meaning "unknown land," is present-day Brazil.

CONSTRUCTED RESPONSE What does this map demonstrate about European knowledge of the Western Hemisphere in 1513?

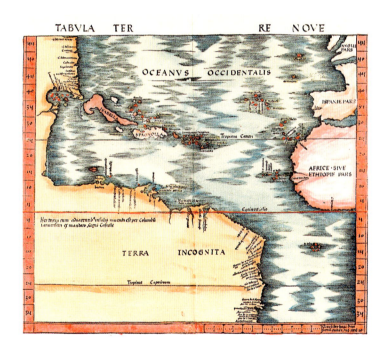

SYNTHESIZE & WRITE

1. **REVIEW** Review what you have learned about the Age of Exploration.

2. **RECALL** Think about your responses to the constructed response questions above.

3. **CONSTRUCT** Write a topic sentence that answers this question: How did European voyages lead to unexpected results?

4. **WRITE** Using evidence from the documents, write an informative paragraph that supports your topic sentence.

7.11.1 Know the great voyages of discovery, the locations of the routes, and the influence of cartography in the development of a new European worldview; REP 4 Students assess the credibility of primary and secondary sources and draw sound conclusions from them; HI 4 Students recognize the role of chance, oversight, and error in history.

The Columbian Exchange

For lunch, a girl in the United States eats an apple and a roast beef sandwich on wheat bread. A boy in Ireland chows down on a turkey-and-tomato sandwich and some french fries. In 1500, neither person could have eaten this lunch. The two meals are a result of the **Columbian Exchange**—a transfer of foods, plants, animals, and diseases between the Old and New Worlds.

MAIN IDEA

A global exchange of foods, plants, animals, and diseases occurred in the period after Columbus arrived in the Americas, bringing both benefits and disaster.

EUROPEAN DISEASES

European diseases killed more Native Americans than warfare. The native population of Central America fell from about 25 million to 2.5 million between 1519 and 1565 due to disease.

FROM EAST TO WEST

The European encounter with the New World coincided with improved sea connections within the Old World of Europe, Africa, and Asia. The combined impact was enormous. Places and people that were once isolated from one another became part of a global exchange network. The contact and trade between these far-flung lands helped some people—and harmed others.

European explorers and colonists wanted to re-create their European lifestyles in the New World. They introduced such familiar foods as wheat, barley, oats, grapes, apples, citrus fruits, and olives. They also brought cattle, sheep, pigs, goats, chickens, and horses. These plants and animals flourished in the Americas. Wheat could be grown in places where native crops could not, and it became one of North America's most important crops. The use of horses changed warfare and transportation in the Americas, while other livestock provided new sources of food.

Europeans also brought crops from Africa and Asia to the Americas. These crops included bananas, coffee beans, and sugarcane. Sugarcane grew especially well in the Caribbean climate. Using slave labor, European growers were able to harvest the sugar and sell it at a huge profit in Europe.

Unfortunately, Europeans also introduced deadly new diseases to the Americas. Native people had no resistance against such diseases as measles, malaria, and smallpox. Smallpox proved to be especially deadly, killing millions of native people across the Americas. Caused by a virus, smallpox is highly contagious. It produces a high fever and small blisters on the skin that leave pitted scars. The virus would finally be eradicated, or eliminated, in the United States in the 1900s.

FROM WEST TO EAST

In the Columbian Exchange, animals and plants also traveled from the Americas to Europe and Africa. Explorers returned to Europe with such exotic foods as turkeys, peppers, corn, tomatoes, potatoes, beans, and squashes. Many of these foods eventually became

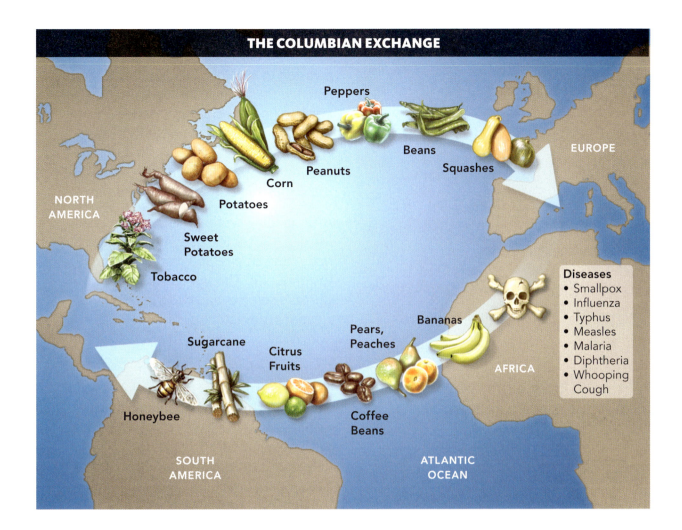

THE COLUMBIAN EXCHANGE

Peppers

Beans

Squashes

EUROPE

Corn

Peanuts

Potatoes

NORTH
AMERICA

Sweet
Potatoes

Tobacco

Diseases
• Smallpox
• Influenza
• Typhus
• Measles
• Malaria
• Diphtheria
• Whooping
  Cough

Bananas

Pears,
Peaches

AFRICA

Sugarcane

Citrus
Fruits

Honeybee

Coffee
Beans

SOUTH
AMERICA

ATLANTIC
OCEAN

a regular part of European diets. Other imports were considered luxuries, including tobacco, vanilla, and cacao beans. Vanilla was used as a flavoring, while cacao beans were used to make chocolate drinks, which were sweetened with imported sugar.

The New World also contributed an important medicine called **quinine** to the Old World. Europeans learned about quinine, which comes from the bark of a tree in South America, in the 1600s. For about 300 years, it served as the only effective remedy for malaria, which is carried by mosquitoes. Quinine's use as a treatment for malaria benefitted millions of people and allowed Europeans to colonize malaria-ridden areas of the world.

For better or worse, the Columbian Exchange affected the lives of people throughout the world. About 30 percent of the foods eaten today originated in the Americas. A greater variety of foods helped improve the nutrition of people around the world. However, the effect of the Columbian Exchange on native populations in the Americas was disastrous.

REVIEW & ASSESS

1. **READING CHECK** How did the Columbian Exchange benefit Europeans?

2. **ANALYZE CAUSE AND EFFECT** Why was the Columbian Exchange disastrous for Native Americans?

3. **INTERPRET MAPS** What foods do you eat that came to the Americas in the Columbian Exchange?

7.11.2 Discuss the exchanges of plants, animals, technology, culture, and ideas among Europe, Africa, Asia, and the Americas in the fifteenth and sixteenth centuries and the major economic and social effects on each continent; CST 3 Students use a variety of maps and documents to identify physical and cultural features of neighborhoods, cities, states, and countries and to explain the historical migration of people, expansion and disintegration of empires, and the growth of economic systems; HI 3 Students explain the sources of historical continuity and how the combination of ideas and events explains the emergence of new patterns.

The **Spanish Conquest**

Two Aztec messengers run to carry an important message to their king: Strangers have invaded their land. The invaders have white skin that looks like that of a ghost. They wear clothes that cover their entire bodies. They sit on deer that carry them wherever they want to go. They have a weapon that shoots a ball of stone, which comes out raining fire and shooting sparks. The messengers' report fills the Aztec king with terror.

MAIN IDEA

Spain created a large American empire that covered parts of the Caribbean and Central and South America by the mid-1500s.

CORTÉS AND THE AZTEC

As you learned earlier, the Treaty of Tordesillas divided the New World between Spain and Portugal. Spain was quick to explore and exploit its new territory. The Spanish established important colonies on several Caribbean islands, including what are now Haiti, the Dominican Republic, and Cuba. Although these islands provided valuable agricultural land, they did not supply the gold so coveted by the Europeans.

Seeking gold, in 1519 the Spanish launched their most daring conquest ever—the invasion of Mexico. The Spanish adventurers who led the conquest of the Americas became known as **conquistadors** (kahn-KEES-tuh-dawrs). A conquistador named **Hernán Cortés** led the invasion of Mexico with about 500 men who had come to the Caribbean to make their fortunes.

After landing on the uncharted coast of Mexico, Cortés learned of the fabulously rich Aztec Empire and marched inland to conquer it. Though outnumbered, Cortés's soldiers had superior steel weapons, devastating cannons, and horses, all unknown in the New World.

On his march to the Aztec capital of **Tenochtitlán** (tay-nohch-teet-LAHN), Cortés was joined by many native tribes who resented the harsh rule of the Aztec. With their support, Cortés fought and defeated the Aztec in a series of battles and a final dramatic siege that destroyed the magnificent city of Tenochtitlán. Its ruins lie buried under what is now Mexico City. The Spanish gained what they wanted—Aztec gold and silver—and they ruled Mexico for the next 300 years.

PIZARRO AND THE INCA

With Mexico conquered, the Spanish then pushed into South America. Sometime between 1530 and 1532, the conquistador **Francisco Pizarro** set off to invade the reportedly rich land of Biru, or what is now Peru. The huge and well-organized Inca Empire was based in Peru.

Pizarro's army had fewer than 200 men, but their steel weapons and horses gave them a deadly advantage. So did their cruelty. When Pizarro arrived, he found the Inca Empire weakened by smallpox and a bitter civil war. Pizarro arranged a meeting with the newly appointed Inca emperor, **Atahualpa** (ah-tah-WAHL-pah), but he had laid a dangerous trap.

Landing of the Spanish in Veracruz, Diego Rivera, 1951

Critical Viewing This mural by the Mexican artist Diego Rivera depicts the Spanish conquest of Mexico. How would you describe the Spaniards' treatment of the native people?

Although Atahualpa was accompanied by between 3,000 and 5,000 attendants, the Spanish cavalry cut a path to the Inca emperor and captured him. They then slaughtered many of his stunned and unarmed followers.

Atahualpa offered the Spanish a roomful of gold and two rooms of silver in exchange for his release. However, after obtaining the gold and silver, the Spanish killed the Inca ruler.

The Spanish went on to conquer much of the vast Inca Empire, which stretched from Ecuador into central Chile. The Inca continued to resist the Spanish until 1572, when the Spanish executed the last Inca ruler. Through military conquest, the Spanish built a large empire that helped make Spain the richest and most powerful country in the world in the 1500s. The Spanish continued to rule over much of South America for centuries.

REVIEW & ASSESS

1. **READING CHECK** What drove the Spanish to invade and conquer large areas of the Americas?

2. **COMPARE AND CONTRAST** How was Pizarro's conquest of the Inca similar to Cortés's conquest of the Aztec?

3. **MAKE INFERENCES** Why were small numbers of the Spanish able to conquer large areas of the Americas?

373

Portugal's Empire

On the sand of an African beach, your crew sets up a huge stone cross. Its design and words stake Portugal's claim to this land where your crew has arrived. Many crosses like the one you've just erected dot the coasts of Africa and other lands.

MAIN IDEA

Portugal built a powerful trading empire that extended along the coast of Africa and reached into areas of the Indian Ocean and South America.

A TRADE NETWORK

In the Age of Exploration, many European nations subscribed to an economic theory called **mercantilism**. This theory held that a nation's wealth and power depended on the possession of precious metals, such as gold and silver, and on profitable trade. European nations sought colonies to supply these precious metals as well as raw materials for **cottage industries**, in which artisans manufactured goods in their homes.

In the Middle Ages, Portugal was a relatively small and undeveloped country. Beginning in 1415, however, Portugal's kings encouraged seafarers to explore the west coast of Africa, hoping to find an easterly sea route to tap into the spice trade with Asia. Portuguese explorers systematically advanced along Africa's coastline. By 1460, they had established trading posts that were sending spices, gold, and slaves to European markets.

Portugal's explorers continued around the southern tip of Africa, along its eastern coast, and across the Indian Ocean. They reached India itself in 1498. The Portuguese built strongly fortified trading posts to control important areas, including Goa and Calicut in India and Macao in China. By the 1540s, the Portuguese had reached Japan and completely dominated the Indian Ocean trade. They were unrivaled until the Dutch and English muscled into the Indian Ocean trade in the early 1600s.

SUGAR, GOLD, AND DIAMONDS

The Portuguese stumbled across Brazil when they sailed too far west on a trip to India. In 1500, the Portuguese explorer **Pedro Álvares Cabral** sighted the coast of Brazil and landed for a short time to stake Portugal's claim to the area.

At first, Portugal had limited interest in Brazil, which provided little more than brazilwood, a source of red dye. But after the French began trading with Brazil's native people, Portugal decided to establish a colony to assert its authority over the area. Brazil's scattered tribes offered no organized resistance. Portugal established its first Brazilian colony in 1532 and divided the colony into administrative districts with a governor in charge.

The Portuguese kings encouraged Brazilian colonists to set up large farms, called **plantations**, for growing sugarcane, a plant used to make sugar. In the 1500s, sugar was a rare luxury in Europe, and Portugal expected to make huge profits from its import. However, growing and processing sugarcane was complex and labor-intensive. Sugarcane producers used

a huge number of slaves to perform the hard and often dangerous work. Over the course of 300 years, Brazil would import nearly 4 million slaves from West Africa.

Then, in 1695, huge quantities of gold were discovered in Brazil, sparking a gold rush. By 1760, gold rivaled sugar as Brazil's main export. The search for gold led to the discovery of diamonds in the 1720s, adding to the wealth that Portugal gained from Brazil. Almost all the wealth was made possible through a much bigger trade, however—the slave trade. You'll learn more about the Atlantic slave trade in the next lesson.

REVIEW & ASSESS

1. **READING CHECK** How was the relatively small country of Portugal able to build a powerful trading empire?

2. **DRAW CONCLUSIONS** Why did Portuguese kings encourage colonists in Brazil to establish plantations for growing sugarcane?

3. **ANALYZE CAUSE AND EFFECT** How did the sugar trade contribute to the development and growth of the slave trade?

7.11.3 Examine the origins of modern capitalism; the influence of mercantilism and cottage industry; the elements and importance of a market economy in a seventeenth-century Europe; the changing international trading and marketing patterns, including their locations on a world map; and the influence of explorers and map makers; HI 2 Students understand and distinguish cause, effect, sequence, and correlation in historical events, including the long- and short-term causal relations; HI 6 Students interpret basic indicators of economic performance and conduct cost-benefit analyses of economic and political issues.

The Atlantic Slave Trade

You are young and strong. You work more than 18 hours a day, chopping stalks of sugarcane with a machete and loading the stalks onto carts. If you stop to rest, you will be beaten. You're thirsty, but you cannot ask for water. All your muscles ache, and your hands are blistered. You are a slave on a sugarcane plantation in Brazil in 1588. You have no way to escape.

MAIN IDEA

To supply labor on plantations in the New World, Europeans imported and enslaved millions of Africans.

SLAVE LABOR

To increase their profits, the European plantations in the New World wanted a large supply of cheap workers. At first, Europeans believed they could use Native Americans to meet their labor needs. But disease and warfare killed millions of Native Americans, and many who were forced into labor easily escaped into the familiar countryside.

Beginning in the mid-1450s, the Portuguese and Spanish solved the labor-shortage problem by buying and transporting slaves from West Africa. The West Africans were more resistant to European diseases, and they could not easily escape into lands that were largely unknown to them.

Slavery was common in West Africa, and local rulers grew rich by kidnapping and selling their enemies to Europeans. In return for the captives, the rulers received gold, trinkets, and guns. By 1650, more than 40 trading posts on Africa's west coast were sending slaves to the New World.

These trading posts formed part of a transatlantic trading network known as the **triangular trade**. On the first leg of the triangle, European ships carried cheap manufactured goods to West Africa, where they were used to buy slaves. On the second or middle leg of the triangle, these slaves were brought to the Americas, where they were sold for a huge profit. On the third leg of the triangle, the slave ships returned to Europe laden with valuable sugar, tobacco, coffee, and cotton. The cotton was used in the cottage industry of making cloth.

The triangular trade was a massive moneymaking business for mercantilist countries. Major participating countries—such as Portugal, Spain, Great Britain, France, and the Netherlands—were prepared to fight wars to secure their share of the trade.

IMPACT OF THE SLAVE TRADE

Europeans treated African slaves as property, not people. The slaves had no rights, and their owners could treat them any way they wanted. This system of slavery was based on both custom and **racism**, the belief that some races are better than others. Europeans genuinely believed that they were superior and justified slavery as a way of civilizing Africans.

The conditions on the slave ships were especially brutal. Up to 600 slaves were chained together in dark, overcrowded holds, where it was impossible to move and difficult to even breathe. The crossing from Africa to the Americas took at least

THE MIDDLE PASSAGE

This illustration shows how enslaved Africans were transported from Africa to the Americas on a European slave ship. The journey could take up to 90 days, depending on the weather.

Chained below deck, slaves could not stand up or move. They were only taken above deck for brief periods.

three weeks and often as long as three months. The trip became known as the **Middle Passage** because it was considered the middle leg of the triangular trade. An estimated 13 to 20 percent of slaves died on the voyage from hunger, thirst, disease, suffocation, drowning, and abuse.

For many slaves, conditions in the colonies were little better than on the ships. Some slaveholders believed it was more cost-effective to replace overworked slaves who died than it was to improve conditions so that slaves lived and worked longer. On sugar plantations, death rates were especially high due to overwork, poor nutrition, harsh treatment, and disease. But colonists grew rich by using slaves to produce sugar, tobacco, coffee, and cotton and to mine gold, silver, and diamonds.

The number of people forced into slavery in the transatlantic slave trade is staggering. Slave traders took entire villages and ethnic groups in Africa, destroying whole communities and cultures. Over a period of about 360 years, from 1501 to 1867, more than 12 million Africans were forced into slavery. It was the largest forced migration of people in history.

REVIEW & ASSESS

1. **READING CHECK** How did the transatlantic slave trade affect Africans and Europeans?

2. **IDENTIFY PROBLEMS AND SOLUTIONS** Instead of using slaves, how might Europeans have solved their labor-shortage problem in the New World?

3. **ANALYZE VISUALS** What hardships did African slaves endure on the Middle Passage?

 7.11.3 Examine the origins of modern capitalism; the influence of mercantilism and cottage industry; the elements and importance of a market economy in a seventeenth-century Pausage; the changing international trading and marketing patterns, including their locations on a world map; and the influence of explorers and map makers; HI 4 Students recognize the role of chance, oversight, and error in history; HI 6 Students interpret basic indicators of economic performance and conduct cost-benefit analyses of economic and political issues.

VOCABULARY

Write the vocabulary word that completes each of the following sentences.

1. The _____ incorrectly states that Earth is at the center of the universe. HSS 7.10.1

2. In 1543, Copernicus published the controversial _____, which stated that the sun was the center of the universe. HSS 7.10.2

3. The purpose of an experiment is to test an explanation that is called a _____. HSS 7.10.3

4. Many European explorers sailed on fast, maneuverable ships called _____. HSS 7.11.1

5. Spanish _____ defeated the Aztec and Inca empires. HSS 7.7.3

6. Portuguese colonists in Brazil grew sugarcane on large farms called _____. HSS 7.11.3

7. In the _____, trade ships traveled from Europe to West Africa to the Americas and back to Europe. HSS 7.11.2

READING STRATEGY

8. **MAKE INFERENCES** Complete your chart to make inferences about the relationship between the Scientific Revolution and European exploration. Then answer the question.

I Learned	My Inference
Observatories helped astronomers accurately plot the locations of stars, which led to better navigation.	Better navigation made it easier for ships to travel far from home.

How did the Scientific Revolution influence European exploration? HSS 7.10.1

MAIN IDEAS

Answer the following questions. Support your answers with evidence from the chapter.

9. What were the scientific theories of the ancient Greeks based on? **LESSON 1.1** HSS 7.10.1

10. What impact did the invention of the microscope have on scientific discovery? **LESSON 1.2** HSS 7.10.2

11. How did the ideas of Sir Francis Bacon affect the practice of science? **LESSON 1.3** HSS 7.10.3

12. What motivated Europeans to explore the world in the mid-1400s? **LESSON 2.1** HSS 7.11.1

13. How did Prince Henry the Navigator promote exploration in the 1400s? **LESSON 2.2** HSS 7.11.1

14. What were some of the new foods introduced to Europe as part of the Columbian Exchange? **LESSON 2.5** HSS 7.11.2

15. Why did the Spanish invade and conquer large areas of Central and South America? **LESSON 3.1** HSS 7.7.3

16. Why did Europeans ship millions of enslaved Africans to the New World? **LESSON 3.3** HSS 7.11.2

CRITICAL THINKING

Answer the following questions. Support your answers with evidence from the chapter.

17. **ESSENTIAL QUESTION** How did scientific thought and voyages of exploration affect Europeans' views of the world? HSS HI 1

18. **MAKE INFERENCES** What did Descartes mean when he said, "I think, therefore I am"? HSS 7.10.3

19. **DRAW CONCLUSIONS** Why was the first voyage of Christopher Columbus important? HSS 7.11.1

20. **ANALYZE CAUSE AND EFFECT** How did the Atlantic slave trade affect African families, communities, and cultures? HSS HI 2

21. **YOU DECIDE** Was the Columbian Exchange mainly good or bad for the native people in the Americas? Explain your opinion. HSS 7.11.2

Look closely at the triangular trade map. Then answer the questions that follow.

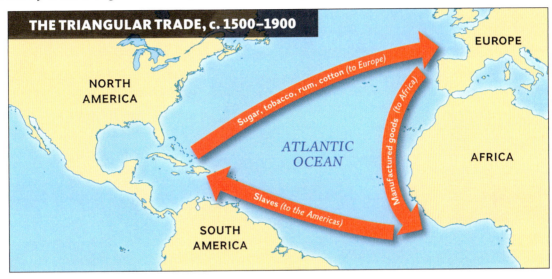

THE TRIANGULAR TRADE, c. 1500–1900

NORTH AMERICA

Sugar, tobacco, rum, cotton (to Europe)

Manufactured goods (to Africa)

ATLANTIC OCEAN

EUROPE

AFRICA

Slaves (to the Americas)

SOUTH AMERICA

22. What goods were shipped from Europe to Africa and exchanged for slaves? HSS CST 3

23. Why is the route shown on the map referred to as the triangular trade? HSS CST 3

ANALYZE SOURCES

Olaudah Equiano, the son of a village leader in the African kingdom of Benin, was captured and sold into slavery at the age of 11. He later gained his freedom and, in 1789, wrote his autobiography, *The Interesting Narrative of the Life of Olaudah Equiano*. In this excerpt from the autobiography, Equiano describes his voyage on the Middle Passage.

The closeness of the place, and the heat of the climate, added to the number in the ship, which was so crowded that each had scarcely room to turn himself, almost suffocated us. This produced copious perspirations [a lot of sweat], so that the air soon became unfit for respiration, from a variety of loathsome smells, and brought on a sickness among the slaves, of which many died.

24. How would you describe the treatment of enslaved Africans on the Middle Passage?
HSS REP 4

WRITE ABOUT HISTORY

25. INFORMATIVE Write an informative paragraph for other students explaining how scientific rationalism changed Europeans' basic approach to science. HSS 7.10.3

TIPS

- Take notes from Lessons 1.1, 1.2, and 1.3 on early Europeans' approach to science.

- State a main idea on how scientific rationalism affected Europeans' practice of science.

- Develop the paragraph with relevant, well-chosen facts, concrete details, or examples about early Europeans' approach to science.

- Use appropriate transitions, such as *because, in contrast*, or *as a result*, to clarify the relationships among ideas.

- Use at least two vocabulary terms from the chapter.

- Provide a concluding sentence that follows from and supports the information presented.

14

ENLIGHTENMENT AND REVOLUTION
1600 – 1815

ESSENTIAL QUESTION How did new ways of thinking about government and human rights lead to revolution?

SECTION 1 THE AGE OF REASON

KEY VOCABULARY
absolute monarch
contract
divine right
enlightened despot
free enterprise
laissez-faire
natural right
philosophe
reason

NAMES & PLACES
Adam Smith
Catherine the Great
Frederick the Great
Jean-Jacques Rousseau
John Locke
Joseph II
Louis XIV
Mary Wollstonecraft
Montesquieu
Voltaire

SECTION 2 TWO REVOLUTIONS

KEY VOCABULARY
bourgeoisie

NAMES & PLACES
Declaration of Independence
Declaration of the Rights of
  Man and of the Citizen
Jacobins
Louis XVI
Napoleon Bonaparte
Thomas Jefferson

READING STRATEGY

DETERMINE WORD MEANINGS When you determine the meaning of an unfamiliar word, you may think of similar words that you already know, such as *light*, to help you understand the word *Enlightenment*. As you read the chapter, use a word map like this one to help you remember the meaning of unfamiliar words.

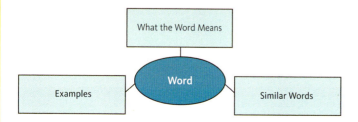

What the Word Means

Word

Examples

Similar Words

Several years after the French Revolution, the emperor Napoleon had this monument, the Arc de Triomphe, erected in Paris to celebrate his military victories.

The Enlightenment

It takes courage to oppose ideas that your rulers accept and enforce. But when you passionately believe you are right, it is possible to change the world. That's what a group of European thinkers did in the 1700s.

MAIN IDEA

Influential thinkers in the 1700s believed human reason was the best way to solve problems.

WHAT WAS THE ENLIGHTENMENT?

Starting in the late 1600s, Europe was swept by a cultural and intellectual movement that became known as the Enlightenment or the Age of Reason. (**Reason** is the power of the human mind to think and understand in a logical way.) As you've already learned, ancient Greek and Roman philosophers used logic and reason to explain the world around them. This way of thought was rediscovered during the Renaissance and was expanded on during the Scientific Revolution and the Enlightenment. The Reformation, which questioned the authority of the Catholic Church, also influenced the Enlightenment.

Enlightened thinkers were often known as **philosophes** (fee-loh-ZOHFS), the French word for "philosophers." They applied the logical thinking used in science to other areas, especially government and society. The name *Enlightenment* came from the philosophes' belief that the "light" of human reason would shatter the "darkness" of ignorance, superstition, and unfair authority.

At the heart of the Enlightenment was its open-mindedness and focus on what it means to be human, which was also a focus of the Renaissance. Enlightenment thinkers questioned and often opposed long-established institutions, beliefs, and social order. Philosophes also felt that the justice system was frequently unfair. Many claimed that rulers had too much power and that they kept their subjects uneducated and in poor conditions. By challenging established authority, the philosophes proved their courage as well as their independent thinking.

IDEAS AND INFLUENCES

The Enlightenment did not have a single set of clearly defined beliefs. Still, most philosophes shared some common ideas. Most important was the idea that human reason, not tradition or religious faith, should guide the actions of individuals and rulers. Philosophes argued that all knowledge should be based on reason. They also believed that civilization was becoming more and more advanced and that human reason could make further improvements.

A third common belief was that the "natural" state for any system was a rational and orderly arrangement, like the systems found in nature. This way of thinking extended to natural laws and **natural rights**, including life, liberty, and property. According to the philosophes, these laws and rights automatically applied to everyone and could be explained through reason.

Liberties such as freedom of speech were especially important to the philosophes. They held that people, regardless of class, have basic human rights. Some philosophes argued that natural rights applied to people who were often thought to be inferior. Slaves, they claimed, should be freed. Female thinkers argued that women should have equal rights with men. Further, the

Critical Viewing This painting depicts a *salon*. What does the image suggest about women's participation in Enlightenment discussions?

An Evening at Madame Geoffrin's, Anicet-Charles Lemonnier, 1812

philosophes reasoned that no person has the automatic right to rule others. They opposed rulers who did not respect or protect their subjects' natural rights.

The Enlightenment touched every area of people's lives, including politics, religion, society, science, culture, education, and economics. It influenced the way people were ruled and how they worshipped, interacted, and traded. Writers, poets, and artists all helped spread enlightened ideas east to Russia and west to the Americas.

Portrait of the Marquise de Pompadour, Maurice-Quentin Delatour, 1748–1755

SALONS

The Enlightenment *salons* were gatherings organized by wealthy women. Salon hostesses would invite thinkers, writers, and artists to discuss their opinions. These lively conversations helped the philosophes refine and spread their ideas. Madame de Pompadour (at left) was one of the best-known hostesses.

REVIEW & ASSESS

1. **READING CHECK** What was the Enlightenment?

2. **ANALYZE CAUSE AND EFFECT** How did the Renaissance, Reformation, and Scientific Revolution inspire the Enlightenment?

3. **IDENTIFY MAIN IDEAS AND DETAILS** What natural rights did the philosophes and other thinkers believe people had?

7.11.4 Explain how the main ideas of the Enlightenment can be traced back to such movements as the Renaissance, the Reformation, and the Scientific Revolution and to the Greeks, Romans, and Christianity; HI 2 Students understand and distinguish cause, effect, sequence, and correlation in historical events, including the long- and short-term causal relations.

Enlightenment
Thinkers

The enlightened thinkers of the 1700s helped develop and promote new ideas about government that involved both rulers and those they ruled. Thanks to these great minds, we enjoy the freedoms we have today.

MAIN IDEA

Enlightened ideas gave people a greater voice in government and society.

POLITICAL THINKERS

In 1690, an Englishman named **John Locke** published *Two Treatises of Government*. Locke asserted that humans were born free and equal with natural rights including life, liberty, and property. He also claimed that a leader could rule only with the consent of the people. As a result, Locke proposed the idea of a **contract**, or agreement, between rulers and the ruled with clearly defined rights and responsibilities for each. People, he believed, had the right to overthrow rulers who broke this contract. This idea would prove hugely influential in North America, France, and Latin America.

Like Locke, a Frenchman known as **Montesquieu** (mohn-tehs-KYOO) believed that liberty was a natural right. In 1748, he expressed his opposition to rule by a single all-powerful individual. Instead, he proposed the separation of government powers into three branches—legislative, judicial, and executive.

Montesquieu believed his plan would limit government power and preserve individual freedom. The ideas of these political thinkers helped form the foundations of the United States government.

SOCIAL THINKERS

During the same period, several European writers were proposing new ideas about humans and society. The popular French writer **Voltaire** used his books and plays to promote enlightened ideas of social reform. He was especially outspoken about limiting the power of the Church and encouraging tolerance of all religions.

The philosophe **Jean-Jacques Rousseau** (roo-SOH) believed that all people are born free and good. He stressed government's responsibility to protect both individual rights and society as a whole. He proposed a social contract between individuals and the society in which they live. In the contract, individuals would agree to work toward the good of the country rather than pursuing only their personal interests.

A few philosophes also supported equality for women. In 1792, an English writer and thinker named **Mary Wollstonecraft** published *A Vindication of the Rights of Woman*. Wollstonecraft argued that because women have the ability to reason, they deserve equal rights to men.

Enlightenment thinkers also influenced economics. At the time, most governments practiced mercantilism and closely controlled and regulated commerce. An enlightened Scottish economist named **Adam Smith** described a freer economy called **laissez-faire** (LEHS-ay FAYR), which is French for "leave it alone." He argued for a system of **free enterprise**, or a market economy. In this system, people selling and buying products in markets would determine what products were needed and what price should be paid for them. Smith's 1776 book, *The Wealth of Nations*, influenced ideas about the economy for the next hundred years.

KEY ENLIGHTENMENT THINKERS

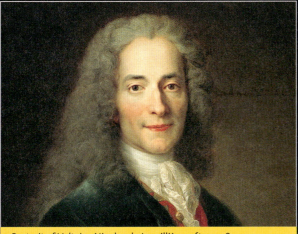

Portrait of Voltaire, Nicolas de Largillière, after 1718

Voltaire
- Outspoken social reformer and defender of civil liberties
- Proposed religious tolerance and limiting the power of the Catholic Church

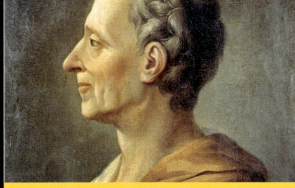

Portrait of Montesquieu, 1728

Montesquieu
- Believed the power of government should be limited
- Advocated the separation of government powers (legislative, judicial, and executive)

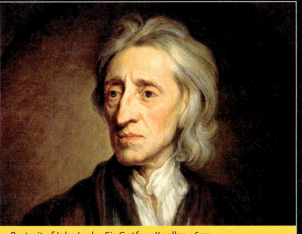

Portrait of John Locke, Sir Gotfrey Kneller, 1697

Locke
- Proposed the idea of a contract between the ruler and the ruled
- Believed governments that fail to uphold their subjects' natural rights should be overthrown
- Believed government power came only from the people

Portrait of Mary Wollstonecraft, John Opie, c. 1797

Wollstonecraft
- Stated that women are rational human beings
- Argued that natural rights extend to women as well as men
- Insisted women deserve equal rights in education and society

REVIEW & ASSESS

1. **READING CHECK** According to the philosophes, what right did the people have if rulers broke the social contract?

2. **COMPARE AND CONTRAST** What ideas did the political and social thinkers have in common?

3. **MAKE INFERENCES** How did Mary Wollstonecraft use reason to argue for women's equal rights?

7.11.3 Examine the origins of modern capitalism; the influence of mercantilism and cottage industry; the elements and importance of a market economy in a seventeenth-century Europe; the changing international trading and marketing patterns, including their locations on a world map; and the influence of explorers and map makers; 7.11.5 Describe how democratic thought and institutions were influenced by Enlightenment thinkers (e.g., John Locke, Charles-Louis Montesquieu, American founders).

1.3
Europe's Rulers and the Enlightenment

 Being an absolute ruler would be pretty tempting if you were a king or queen. You could keep all the government's wealth and power to yourself. In the 1600s and 1700s, many rulers did just that, but the Enlightenment influenced some kings and queens to try a new path.

MAIN IDEA

Enlightenment ideas changed the way Europe was ruled.

THE RISE OF ABSOLUTE MONARCHY

To understand why Enlightenment thinkers argued that people should have rights and freedoms, it is important to know how governments changed over time in Europe. In medieval Europe, influential groups such as the nobility and the Church limited the power of kings and queens. As medieval order broke down, however, monarchs took more power for themselves. By 1600, some ruled as **absolute monarchs**. They had unlimited authority and almost no legal limits. They claimed to rule by **divine right**, meaning that their power came directly from God.

During the 1600s and 1700s, absolute monarchs ruled the European kingdoms of Russia, Austria, and Prussia (part of what is now Germany). The greatest of all was **Louis XIV** of France. For most of his 72-year reign, Louis ignored all of France's traditional institutions. He excluded the nobles from government and enforced his will through government officials. At Versailles (vair-SY), near Paris, he built a massive palace to show off his power. Louis became known as the Sun King because he chose the sun as his symbol. Indeed, all France revolved around him, like the planets around the sun.

Yet at the same time, a growing middle class was pressing for a voice in the policies that affected them. In England, as you may recall, this trend led to the creation of the Magna Carta and a parliament made up of nobles and elected commoners. Attempts to restore absolute monarchy in England were defeated in England's civil war of 1642 to 1651 and by a revolution in 1688. The subsequent English Bill of Rights of 1689 guaranteed basic rights to English citizens.

ENLIGHTENED DESPOTS

As the ideas of the Enlightenment spread in the 1700s, some monarchs applied reforms in their countries. Because they never surrendered their complete authority, they became known as **enlightened despots**, absolute monarchs who applied certain Enlightenment ideas. One was **Frederick the Great**, who ruled Prussia from 1740 to 1786. He introduced religious tolerance and legal reforms. He also banned torture and helped peasants improve their farms. However, Frederick refused to change the social hierarchy in Prussia.

Joseph II of Austria oversaw enlightened reforms between 1780 and 1790. He introduced religious tolerance, freedom of the press, and various law reforms. Joseph firmly believed in social equality. He promoted elementary education for all children. He abolished serfdom and tried to introduce a new system of taxes on the land that would be more fair to different social classes.

Catherine the Great ruled Russia from 1762 to 1796. Although Catherine favored enlightened ideas, she struggled to introduce reforms. She considered freeing the serfs, but changed her mind when she realized she needed the support of serf-owning nobles to keep herself in power. Similarly, when Catherine called together elected representatives from all classes to suggest reforms, the meeting failed because of each group's self-interest. However, Catherine did succeed in expanding education, science, and the arts in Russia.

Louis XIV King of France, Andry (from a 1701 portrait by Hyacinthe Rigaud), 18th century

VERSAILLES

In modern numbers, Louis XIV's Versailles cost more than two billion dollars to build and involved more than 36,000 workers. It was the largest and most luxurious palace in Europe, with 700 rooms and 2,000 windows. Its rich decorations included 6,000 paintings, 2,000 sculptures, and the famous Hall of Mirrors, which was lit by 20,000 candles.

REVIEW & ASSESS

1. READING CHECK
How were absolute monarchs and enlightened despots similar and different?

2. MAKE CONNECTIONS
In what ways did the enlightened despots reflect the ideas of the philosophes? In what ways did they fail to reflect those ideas?

3. ANALYZE CAUSE AND EFFECT
What effect did the Enlightenment have on monarchs such as Frederick the Great, Joseph II, and Catherine the Great?

7.11.6 Discuss how the principles in the Magna Carta were embodied in such documents as the English Bill of Rights and the American Declaration of Independence; HI 2 Students understand and distinguish cause, effect, sequence, and correlation in historical events, including the long- and short-term causal relations.

The American Revolution

The Enlightenment lit a flame that could be seen not just in Europe, but across the Atlantic. Visions of liberty and equality would spark revolutions throughout the Americas and in France. The first to rebel were Britain's 13 colonies.

MAIN IDEA

The American Revolution followed the ideas of the Enlightenment and inspired other revolutions.

THE COLONIES REVOLT

The American Revolution was a key event for the development of the United States. It was also extremely influential in terms of world history.

Taxes were one important cause of the American Revolution. In the 1760s and 1770s, Britain's Parliament introduced a series of new taxes in its American colonies. The colonists protested that the British government could not tax them because they were not represented in Parliament. Tensions between Britain and the colonists grew. Then, on April 19, 1775, British soldiers and colonists exchanged shots at Lexington, Massachusetts. Parliament sent an army to North America to crush the rebellion against Britain.

On July 4, 1776, representatives of the 13 American colonies approved the **Declaration of Independence**. This document, written by **Thomas Jefferson**, drew on the Enlightenment ideas of John Locke and the basic concepts in the Magna Carta. It stated that rulers had a contract with their subjects to protect the people's natural rights. Jefferson listed all the ways in which Britain's king had broken this contract with the colonies.

After years of war against the British army, the colonists prevailed. In 1783, Britain officially recognized the independence of the United States of America. The country's first constitution was the Articles of Confederation. This document did not create a strong government, and in 1787, the country's leaders met in Philadelphia to revise it. Instead, they wound up writing a new Constitution. It went into effect in 1789.

Several Enlightenment ideas were reflected in the U.S. Constitution. For example, the executive, legislative, and judiciary branches were separated and assigned different powers. This measure ensured that no single person or government branch could achieve absolute control. A Bill of Rights listed individual rights that the government could not violate, such as freedom of speech and freedom of worship.

THE WORLD FOLLOWS

The American Revolution had an immediate effect in Europe. All people, not just the philosophes, could see the ideas of the Enlightenment turned into the reality of an elected government.

France had sent soldiers and aid to the colonists in fighting France's long-time enemy, Britain. Now French soldiers returned home and shared what they had learned about individual freedoms. These ideas helped sow the seeds of revolution in France. In the decades that followed, other European colonies also set out on the path to independence.

Critical Viewing Modern-day reenactors portray British troops in a battle from the American Revolution. Why do Americans commemorate the war with events like this one?

The French Revolution

Some events are so momentous that they can change the course of history. The French Revolution was one such turning point. It shattered established ideas about government and society and its effects were felt throughout Europe for the next 25 years.

MAIN IDEA

Long-oppressed French commoners seized power from the upper classes.

THE THREE ESTATES

In 1789, France exploded into revolution. The reasons were a mix of social and political problems that provoked people to action.

Prerevolutionary France suffered from inequality among its three main social classes, called estates. The First Estate was the Catholic clergy, who had significant powers and privileges such as paying very few taxes. The Second Estate was the nobility, who lived in privileged isolation at the king's court in Versailles. The nobles enjoyed lavish lifestyles and, like the members of the First Estate, were only lightly taxed.

The Third Estate was the common people, the vast majority of France. The Third Estate had its own hierarchy. At the top was the **bourgeoisie** (boor-jwah-ZEE), or middle class, made up of relatively prosperous and educated professionals and merchants. Beneath the bourgeoisie were the peasants, who made up the majority of the population. Hard work, hunger, and poverty were the norm for most of these people. The Third Estate paid the largest share of the nation's taxes but had no say in government.

At the top of society was the French king, **Louis XVI**. Louis ruled as an absolute monarch, but he was not an effective ruler. Instead, he was weak and manipulated by clever nobles and his unpopular Austrian wife, Marie Antoinette.

Louis lived in great splendor and did little to help his long-suffering subjects. In addition, a series of wars, including Louis's support of the American Revolution, had left the nation almost bankrupt. France's outdated economy favored the rich nobles, who prevented attempts at economic reform. The result was a major financial crisis and even higher taxes for the Third Estate. Making things still worse, France experienced a disastrous grain harvest in 1788. All across the country, the Third Estate was plunged into crippling poverty and deadly hunger.

THE END OF THE MONARCHY

To deal with the crisis, Louis was forced to summon a representative assembly called the Estates-General, which had not met since 1614. As the name implies, delegates to the Estates-General represented the estates to which they belonged.

At the meetings in the town of Versailles, the First and Second Estates combined had approximately the same number of delegates as the Third Estate. These wealthier estates worked to promote their own interests. Frustrated and angry, the Third Estate established a new representative body called the National Assembly. The National Assembly gave the Third Estate more power and was defended by armed mobs that were formed into a national guard.

All across France, peasants rose up in support of the National Assembly. Louis was forced to accept its authority. The National Assembly abolished the privileges of the nobles and effectively made Louis a prisoner. In August 1789, the assembly issued the **Declaration of the Rights of Man and of the Citizen**, which proclaimed the liberty and equality of all people. The assembly tried to form a new government in which Louis would share power with an elected legislature. However, the king refused to cooperate.

REVIEW & ASSESS

1. **READING CHECK** How did the revolution change relations among France's three estates?

2. **COMPARE AND CONTRAST** In what ways were conditions for the three estates similar and different?

3. **IDENTIFY PROBLEMS AND SOLUTIONS** How did the Third Estate seek to improve its conditions?

JULY 14, 1789

The Bastille, a fortress prison in Paris, was seen as a symbol of the royalist tyranny that the French revolutionaries wanted to overthrow. On the morning of July 14, revolutionary leaders tried to negotiate the surrender of the arms and ammunition stored in the Bastille. As the day went by, the crowd outside grew increasingly restless and finally surged into the fortress courtyard. This painting illustrates the violence that followed when the revolutionaries clashed with the prison officers. How are the revolutionaries and officers portrayed in the painting?

Storming of the Bastille, July 14, 1789, Charles Thévenin, c. 1790

From Republic to Empire

Imagine living in constant fear that your friends or even your family would accuse you of a crime. And what if the government would then torture and execute you, even if you were innocent? Revolutionary life was dangerous.

MAIN IDEA

Revolutionary France grew more and more unstable until Napoleon Bonaparte seized power.

THE GUILLOTINE

One of the most striking images of the French Revolution is the guillotine (GEE-yuh-teen), the machine used to execute thousands, including Louis XVI.

The guillotine had a blade that plunged down grooves in two upright posts to slice through the victim's neck, beheading him or her in one stroke.

REIGN OF TERROR

Louis XVI was forced to surrender most of his remaining powers in 1791. Then, in 1792, the absolute monarchs of Austria and Prussia invaded France, aiming to restore Louis to power. The French defeated the invasion, but it led to a drastic reaction from the new government. Thousands of suspected royalists were massacred. Then, in September 1792, France declared itself a republic. In 1793, Louis XVI and Marie Antoinette were publicly executed in Paris.

Their deaths did little to restore order. Rival political groups argued over how to run the country. Faced with internal disorder and threats from abroad, the revolutionary government grew more radical. Eventually, an extremist group called the **Jacobins** took control. The group was led by a former lawyer called Robespierre, who began a bloody period called the Reign of Terror.

Using the excuse of defending the republic, Robespierre's followers imprisoned, tortured, and murdered tens of thousands. Nobody was safe. In 1794, the mob turned against Robespierre himself and executed him.

NAPOLEON'S RISE TO POWER

Because of the chaos, France was ready for a strong leader—and one emerged. **Napoleon Bonaparte** was an ambitious and brilliant young military officer who rose to fame fighting the royalists in 1795. Napoleon's military successes and popularity gave him political influence, and, in 1799, he seized control of the government.

Napoleon was granted total control. With this power, he brought much-needed stability to the country. Although he ruthlessly crushed political opponents, Napoleon preserved revolutionary ideals and enlightened values, including equality, liberty, religious tolerance, and the rule of law. His most lasting contribution may be the Napoleonic Code, a clear and organized system of laws for France.

Napoleon defeated many other European nations in battle and crowned himself emperor in 1804. In 1814, however, Britain and its allies defeated France and restored the French monarchy. Just a year later, Napoleon returned and briefly retook power before being defeated at the Battle of Waterloo.

Critical Viewing This painting shows Napoleon crossing the Alps on his way to conquer Italy. Why would Napoleon choose to have himself portrayed in this way?

REVIEW & ASSESS

1. **READING CHECK** How was Napoleon able to seize control of France's government?

2. **ANALYZE CAUSE AND EFFECT** What were the effects of the invasion from Austria and Prussia?

3. **EVALUATE** Could Napoleon be described as an enlightened despot? Why or why not?

HI 2 Students understand and distinguish cause, effect, sequence, and correlation in historical events, including the long- and short-term causal relations.

395

Declarations of Freedom

Many Enlightenment thinkers were also gifted writers. Through books, essays, and other documents, they explained their ideas about rights and liberties to the world. These writings set the stage for revolution.

Declaration of Independence, July 4th, 1776, John Trumbull, 1817–1819

In this detail from a painting that hangs in the United States Capitol Building, Thomas Jefferson (in the red vest) presents the Declaration of Independence to committee members.

The Declaration of Independence (1776)

This famous document proclaims the independence of the British colonies and the founding of the United States of America. It was adopted by the Continental Congress on July 4, 1776. The declaration was largely created by Thomas Jefferson, a delegate from Virginia. He drew heavily on the political theories of John Locke. These ideas are most apparent in this passage asserting human equality and natural rights.

CONSTRUCTED RESPONSE How did the ideas of John Locke influence the creation of the Declaration of Independence?

We hold these truths to be self-evident, that all men are created equal, that they are endowed by their Creator with certain unalienable Rights, that among these are Life, Liberty, and the pursuit of Happiness.—That to secure these rights, Governments are instituted among Men, deriving their just powers from the consent of the governed,—That whenever any Form of Government becomes destructive of these ends, it is the Right of the People to alter or to abolish it, and to institute new Government.

The Declaration of the Rights of Man and of the Citizen (1789)

This French Revolutionary document is a basic charter of human liberties. Its 17 articles build on the idea of equality and rights for all. Article 6 emphasizes every citizen's equality before the law. This article reflects the ideas of French philosophe Jean-Jacques Rousseau by stating that laws should reflect the will of the people. It further stresses that every citizen has the right to take part in government.

CONSTRUCTED RESPONSE Why do you think the Declaration of the Rights of Man and of the Citizen emphasized the Enlightenment idea of equality?

Law is the expression of the general will. Every citizen has a right to participate personally, or through his representative, in its foundation. It must be the same for all, whether it protects or punishes. All citizens, being equal in the eyes of the law, are equally eligible to all dignities [high offices] and to all public positions and occupations, according to their abilities, and without distinction except that of their virtues and talents.

SYNTHESIZE & WRITE

1. **REVIEW** Review what you have learned about the Enlightenment and the influence of its ideas.

2. **RECALL** On your own paper, write down the main idea expressed in each document.

3. **CONSTRUCT** Write a topic sentence that answers this question: What basic human rights were claimed by people following the Enlightenment?

4. **WRITE** Using evidence from the documents, write an essay to support your answer to the question in Step 3.

7.11.5 Describe how democratic thought and institutions were influenced by Enlightenment thinkers (e.g., John Locke, Charles-Louis Montesquieu, American founders); REP 4 Students assess the credibility of primary and secondary sources and draw sound conclusions from them.

397

VOCABULARY

Use each of the following vocabulary words in a sentence that shows an understanding of the term's meaning.

1. contract (HSS 7.11.5)

Jefferson said Britain had broken the terms of the contract, or agreement, between the ruler and the people.

2. laissez-faire (HSS 7.11.3)

3. absolute monarch (HSS 7.11)

4. divine right (HSS 7.11)

5. enlightened despot (HSS 7.11)

6. reason (HSS 7.11.4)

7. bourgeoisie (HSS 7.11)

READING STRATEGY

8. DETERMINE WORD MEANINGS If you haven't already, complete at least three word maps for unfamiliar words from the chapter.

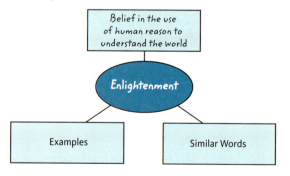

Belief in the use of human reason to understand the world

Enlightenment

Examples

Similar Words

Use each of the three words in a sentence that shows an understanding of the word's meaning. (HSS 7.11.4)

MAIN IDEAS

Answer the following questions. Support your answers with evidence from the chapter.

9. Why is the Enlightenment also referred to as the Age of Reason? **LESSON 1.1** (HSS 7.11)

10. Explain John Locke's idea about a contract between rulers and the ruled. **LESSON 1.2** (HSS 7.11.5)

11. Why did some absolute monarchs introduce reforms in their countries? **LESSON 1.3** (HSS 7.11)

12. Why did the American colonies rebel against Britain? **LESSON 2.1** (HSS 7.11.6)

13. What were living conditions like for the Third Estate in France before the French Revolution? **LESSON 2.2** (HSS 7.11)

14. What was the Reign of Terror? **LESSON 2.4** (HSS 7.11)

CRITICAL THINKING

Answer the following questions. Support your answers with evidence from the chapter.

15. **ESSENTIAL QUESTION** How did the ideas of the Enlightenment inspire revolutions in Britain's American colonies and in France? (HSS 7.11.6)

16. **SYNTHESIZE** Why would an absolute monarch like Louis XIV oppose the idea of natural rights? (HSS REP 5)

17. **COMPARE AND CONTRAST** In what ways were the American and French Revolutions the same and different? (HSS HI 2)

18. **MAKE INFERENCES** What did the Declaration of Independence do for the colonists of British North America? (HSS 7.11.5)

19. **DRAW CONCLUSIONS** Why was Napoleon granted absolute power as leader of the French Republic? (HSS 7.11)

20. **YOU DECIDE** Which of the Enlightenment thinkers do you think had the greatest impact on the American and French Revolutions? Explain your choice. (HSS 7.11.5)

INTERPRET MAPS

This map shows Napoleon's empire in 1812. Look closely at the map and answer the questions that follow.

NAPOLEON'S EMPIRE, 1812

Legend:
- French Empire
- Controlled by Napoleon
- Allies of Napoleon
- At war with Napoleon
- Neutral
- → Napoleon's route into Russia
- ◄-- Napoleon's route out of Russia

21. What European countries were under the influence of France in 1812? (HSS CST 3)

23. What challenges would Napoleon face in trying to conquer Russia? (HSS CST 3)

ANALYZE SOURCES

On the way to his inauguration in Washington, D.C., in 1861, Abraham Lincoln stopped in Philadelphia. While there, he gave a speech at Independence Hall, where the Declaration of Independence was signed in 1776. Read the following excerpt from that speech about the Declaration of Independence. Then answer the question.

> [The Declaration of Independence] gave liberty, not alone to the people of this country, but, I hope, to the world, for all future time.

22. Do you agree with Abraham Lincoln's assessment of the significance of the Declaration of Independence? Explain.
(HSS REP 4)

WRITE ABOUT HISTORY

24. EXPOSITORY Write a speech for an Independence Day celebration in your town. Your speech should explain the Enlightenment, its main ideas, and how it helped shape the government and society we have today.
(HSS 7.11.5)

TIPS

- Take notes from the lessons about the Enlightenment, its ideas, and its influences.
- Begin the speech with an introductory paragraph defining the Enlightenment.
- Develop the speech with ideas that were central to the Enlightenment.
- Use two or three vocabulary terms from the chapter in your speech.
- Conclude the speech by explaining how the Enlightenment influenced society and government.

NATIONAL GEOGRAPHIC

ON **LOCATION**
WITH **Maurizio**
SERACINI

NATIONAL GEOGRAPHIC FELLOW

▶ Check out more at NGLSync.Cengage.com

It's not just about the art in museums for Maurizio Seracini, an Italian art expert who uses technology to seek out long-hidden masterpieces no one has seen for centuries.

BELOW THE PAINT

I love the way that technology is helping to write new pages of our history, find hidden treasures, and prove or disprove theories. In art history, for example, new technology has shown that Leonardo da Vinci's acclaimed painting *The Adoration of the Magi* is much more than it appears. It proves that while Leonardo drew the painting's original design, it was actually painted much later by an unknown and inferior artist who changed Leonardo's layout considerably. Technology allows us to peer through the layers of brown paint to reveal over 70 wonderful new images sketched by Leonardo that have not been seen for centuries.

EVOLVING TECHNOLOGY

Momentous discoveries like this take time and patience. In 1975, I was asked to use technology to solve a 500-year-old mystery about a lost Leonardo da Vinci masterpiece, *The Battle of Anghiari*. This mural painting was supposed to have been painted on the wall of a hall in the Palazzo Vecchio in Florence, Italy. Decades later, the hall was rebuilt and redecorated by another artist, Vasari, and Leonardo's celebrated masterpiece disappeared. We wanted to know if it was gone or if some of it was still there, but the technology of the 1970s wasn't sophisticated enough to tell.

In 2000, we were able to use 3-D modeling and thermography to reconstruct the hall at the time of Leonardo. We also learned that in similar projects, Vasari had saved existing artworks by constructing a brick wall in front of them and leaving a small

Seracini carefully uses a scope with a tiny camera to examine the surface behind a fresco painted by Vasari.

air gap. Maybe Vasari had done the same thing for *The Battle of Anghiari*? We used sophisticated radio antennas to find air gaps in the area where we believed the mural was painted—directly behind a wall with a Vasari fresco on it. But the need to preserve Vasari's work stopped any further investigation.

We returned with new technology in 2011: an endoscope with a 4mm camera, to explore the wall behind the Vasari fresco. We found fragments of red, black, and beige paint. Since we know that no other artist painted on that wall before Vasari sealed it up, those pigments are likely related to mural painting and most likely to da Vinci. If so, we have found one of the most highly praised works of art ever—by far Leonardo's most important commission and the one that made him the top artistic influence of his time.

WHY STUDY HISTORY ❓

❝ What we are doing is rediscovering the spirit of the Renaissance; we are blending art and science. As long as we live a life of *curiosity and passion*, there is a bit of Leonardo in all of us. ❞ —Maurizio Seracini

NATIONAL GEOGRAPHIC

Brunelleschi's Dome

BY TOM MUELLER

Adapted from "Brunelleschi's Dome,"
by Tom Mueller, in *National Geographic*, February 2014

In 1418, the town fathers of Florence finally addressed a problem they'd been ignoring for decades: the enormous hole in the roof of their cathedral. They announced a contest to design the ideal dome, which would be the cathedral's crowning glory. Leading architects flocked to Florence and presented their ideas. One candidate named Filippo Brunelleschi promised to build not one but two domes, one nested inside the other. He refused to explain how he'd do this because he was afraid that a competitor would steal his ideas. Nevertheless, in 1420 the town fathers agreed to put Brunelleschi in charge of the dome project.

After he assembled the necessary tool kit, Brunelleschi began work on the dome, which he shaped with a series of stunning technical innovations. His double-shell design produced a structure that was far lighter than a solid dome of such size would have been. He also wove regular courses of herringbone brickwork, little known before his time, into the texture of the dome.

Throughout the years of construction, Brunelleschi oversaw the production of bricks of various dimensions and attended to the supply of choice stone and marble. He led an army of masons and stonecutters, carpenters, blacksmiths, and other craftsmen. When they were puzzled by some tricky construction detail, he'd shape a model out of wax or clay or carve up a turnip to illustrate what he wanted.

Brunelleschi and his workmen eventually did their victory dance. On March 25, 1436, the pope blessed the finished cathedral to the tolling of bells and cheering of proud Florentines. A decade later, workmen laid the cornerstone of the lantern, the decorative marble structure that Brunelleschi designed to top his masterpiece.

On April 15, 1446, the great architect died. He was buried in the crypt of the cathedral. A memorial plaque nearby celebrated his "divine intellect." These were high honors but fitting for the architect who had paved the way for the cultural and social revolutions of the Renaissance.

For more from National Geographic
Check out "Lady with a Secret" at NGLSync.Cengage.com

UNIT INQUIRY: MAP THE NEW WORLDVIEW

In this unit, you learned about medieval and early modern Europe. Based on your understanding of the text, what new ideas emerged during the Renaissance? How did these new ideas transform, or change, European culture?

ASSIGNMENT Create an idea map of the new worldview that emerged during the Renaissance because of humanism, an intellectual movement that emphasized the individual. The idea map should illustrate how humanism transformed medieval ideas about religion, philosophy, science, art, literature, and education. Be prepared to present your idea map and explain the overall impact of humanism to the class.

Plan As you create your idea map, think about European culture during the Middle Ages. Then think about how Renaissance humanism shifted the focus of European culture from divine matters to human beings and their needs. You might want to use a graphic organizer to help organize your thoughts. ▶

Produce Use your notes to produce detailed descriptions of how humanism transformed European culture. You might want to write the descriptions in outline or paragraph form.

Present Choose a creative way to present your idea map to the class. Consider one of these options:

- Create a multimedia presentation using paintings from the Middle Ages and Renaissance to illustrate how humanism transformed ideas about art.

- Write a monologue for a "Renaissance Man" that describes a day in his/her life.

- Design a brochure for a school that describes all the "new thinking" that will be taught to students.

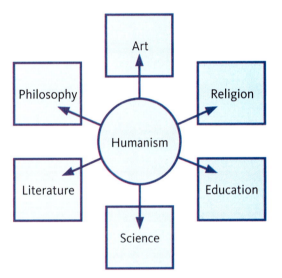

1. The collapse of the Roman Empire began a 1,000-year-long period called the Middle Ages in western Europe.
2. Humanism led to a rebirth in classical learning, stimulating a period of great creativity known as the Renaissance.
3. Johann Gutenberg developed the printing press.
4. Martin Luther wrote the 95 Theses, which criticized church practices and launched the Reformation.
5. Europeans explored and colonized much of Africa, Asia, and the Americas, which prompted the exchange of goods, ideas, people, plants, animals, and diseases.

6-10. **NOW IT'S YOUR TURN** Complete the list with five more things to remember about medieval and early modern Europe.

TO IDENTIFY INNOVATIONS AND TECHNOLOGIES THAT SET THE STAGE FOR THE MODERN WORLD

New inventions and technologies are finding their way around the globe, and new trade relationships are beginning to make the world, as shown in Units 4 and 5, more recognizable for us. Understanding the events and developments that laid the groundwork for our society will help you, as global citizens, understand its complexity, promise, and challenges.

Fred Hiebert
▶ Watch the Why Study History video

KEY TAKEAWAYS UNITS 4–5

PATTERNS IN HISTORY: SIMILAR DEVELOPMENTS ACROSS LOCATIONS

- Changes in religion, the arts, government, and economics begin to leapfrog each other—a change in one area brings change in others.
- The world economy begins to globalize as communication expands and trade patterns develop.
- With new economic relationships comes increasing conflict between countries and political groups.

GOVERNMENT

- New empires, including the Mongol in East Asia and the Khmer in Southeast Asia, rise to power.
- In Europe, modern nation-states emerge and extend their power.
- Enlightenment ideas inspire revolutions and major changes in governments.

MOVEMENT OF PEOPLE AND IDEAS

- Trade develops along the Silk Roads during the Mongol Empire.

- The Columbian Exchange is established among Europe, Africa, and the Americas.
- Writers, poets, and artists help spread enlightened ideas from Europe to Russia and the Americas.

ARTISTIC EXPRESSION

- Art reflects changing ideas of human identity.
- Renaissance artists revive classical ideals and depict their subjects more realistically, reflecting the humanist ideal of the individual.

TECHNOLOGY & INNOVATION

- Chinese inventions, including movable type, the compass, and gunpowder, lay the groundwork for European innovations.
- As a result, the invention of the printing press enables widespread communication, while new sailing ships put more explorers on the high seas.
- New weapons like cannons and longbows make conflict more deadly.

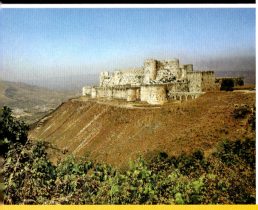

History is a living thing, and you are part of it.

You've just read about centuries and centuries of events that may seem like they have little connection to your life—but you might be surprised. Those long-gone people and dramatic occurrences have brought us to where we are today, and the things happening all over the world while you sit in class each day will shape your life for years to come. If you don't keep an eye on the issues that will someday become the history of your generation, who will?

As this *World History* book went to the printer, important new National Geographic stories were just hitting the news. So we narrowed them down to the five stories that follow. Remember: These are just a few of the many intriguing stories surfacing around the world, and they're still developing. As a global citizen, it's up to you to ask yourself: What happened next? How did this turn out? **Go find out!**

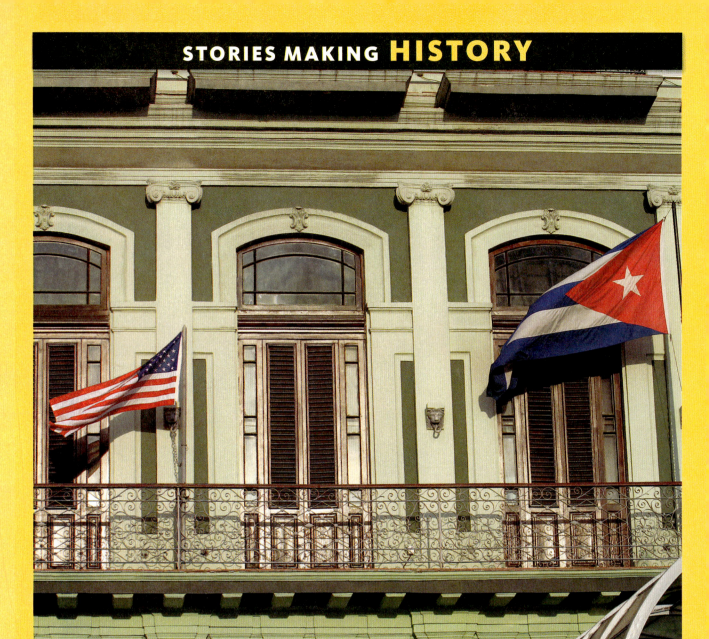

Renewing Relationships: Cuba and the United States

Serving as The Geographer for National Geographic's Maps Division is an epic job. On any given day, Juan José Valdés and his team have the monumental task of creating and updating maps in a world where borders change frequently and sometimes without much notice. In 2011, Valdés stood expectantly outside a house in Havana, Cuba; but he wasn't in the country to make a map. He was visiting the place where he was born in 1953, and attempting to reconnect to a country he hadn't entered in 50 years.

∧
The national flags of the United States and Cuba fly outside the Cuban hotel where the first U.S. congressional delegation to Cuba stayed in 2015.

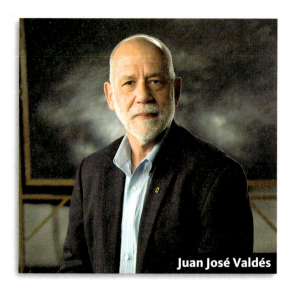

Juan José Valdés

A year later, Juan visited Cuba again and reunited with his remaining family. A cousin approached him saying, "You are Cuban."

"Yes, I am Cuban," Juan answered, his voice trembling with emotion.

Like so many Cuban-Americans, Juan's life has been marked by enormous changes. When he was a child in Havana during the 1950s, a dictator named Fulgencio Batista ruled the country with an iron hand. A young law student and activist named Fidel Castro led rebels who waged a war to end Batista's rule. In 1959, Castro and his forces overthrew Batista.

Castro had promised free elections and other reforms. Yet once he took power, he quickly established a Communist government, in which the state owns or controls factories and other businesses. Castro refused to hold free elections, and he denied Cuban citizens freedom of speech and other rights most Americans take for granted. Castro also formed an alliance with the Soviet Union, in spite of the fact that the United States was in the middle of a Cold War with the Soviets. The U.S. response was swift and severe: diplomatic relations and trade with Cuba ended, and no one could travel between Cuba and the United States.

Hundreds of thousands of Cubans desperately wanted to leave Cuba for other countries like the United States. They didn't want to live in a Communist country. Juan's family could not leave right away, but they managed to get an airline ticket for Juan in 1961. At the age of seven, he traveled alone on an airplane to Miami, Florida. He lived with an elderly couple in Miami, until several months later, when his parents were able to leave Cuba and join him. Their family was reunited and built a life together in the United States.

Meanwhile, Cuba and the United States remained locked in tension. In April 1961, President John F. Kennedy authorized a group of American-trained Cuban exiles to attack Cuba at the Bay of Pigs and try to overthrow Castro. The invasion was a disaster for the United States. The Cuban exiles were outnumbered and many were captured. In October 1962, the Soviet Union tried to set up missiles with nuclear warheads in Cuba. This dangerous situation, known as the Cuban Missile Crisis, ended only when President Kennedy confronted the Soviets and forced them to remove the missiles.

But the world changes daily. On December 17, 2014, President Barack Obama announced that the United States would work to restore diplomatic and trade relations with Cuba and move to open an embassy in Havana, with Congressional approval. On April 11, 2015, President Obama met with Cuban President Raúl Castro in Panama in the first face-to-face discussion between the leaders of the two countries in more than 50 years. Both leaders expressed hope that the two countries will be able to interact without the tension and restrictions of the past.

This change is important for both nations, but it's also important for people like Juan Valdés who have roots in Cuba. As tensions between the countries continue to subside, Cuban-Americans will be able to travel more easily to Cuba and reconnect with relatives they left behind long ago. Yet change is never without complication. Cubans will have to adjust to the impact the lifted trade embargo has on the local economy they are used to. Others may find it unusual to welcome American tourists to their country after so many decades without them. It's likely that the Cuban people will find themselves and their country in a period of transition and adjustment for years to come. ▪

Into the Okavango Delta: A Live-Data Expedition

Located on the continent of Africa in the northwestern part of Botswana, the Okavango Delta is one of the richest wildlife areas on Earth. Unlike most deltas, it doesn't flow into an ocean or sea—it's an inland delta made up of flat, grassy savannas that are flooded by the Okavango River during the winter. This miraculous ecosystem was declared the 1000th UNESCO World Heritage Site in 2015, in part because its unique, seasonal wetlands give many endangered large mammals salvation after their long migration across the Kalahari Desert.

^
National Geographic Emerging Explorers Steve Boyes and Shah Selbe and their team document and share their experiences with the species of the Okavango Delta.

Visible from space, the Okavango Delta is huge—the size of the state of Texas. It's one of Africa's last truly wild landscapes, like the Sahara, the Serengeti, and the Congo. 100,000 elephants roam free across the land. Lions, leopards, hyenas, rhino, cheetahs, crocodiles, and wild dogs also thrive here, as well as nearly 500 bird species and over 1,000 plants.

Since 2011, an expedition team made up of Ba Yei river bushmen and National Geographic Emerging Explorers Steve Boyes and Shah Selbe and their team has been making annual visits to the remote land of the delta in one of the first "live-data" expeditions. That means the team constantly uploads data from the field to their website—intotheokavango.org—via satellite. This data is also available through a public API, or application program interface, which allows anyone to analyze and examine the collected information. "We're connecting society with the wilderness," explains conservation biologist, and Into the Okavango expedition leader, Steve Boyes.

Every ten seconds, state-of-the-art sensors record personal data about expedition members, including heart rate, the amount of energy they are using, and GPS positional data. Cameras automatically take pictures of the team's current location and record sound clips every ten minutes. Team members also post water quality data, and document their animal and bird sightings. They tweet progress updates constantly for people who are tracking their movements online and analyzing the expedition's data.

This mobile computer station allows sensors to be programmed and data to be posted from the field.

Team members also respond to questions and suggestions from their followers.

The team has crossed the Okavango Delta five times so far in dug-out canoes, the traditional mode of transportation for Ba Yei river bushmen. Their goal is to continue conducting in-depth biodiversity surveys in this delicate ecosystem so that any major changes can be noted and addressed.

"We have unprecedented opportunities to improve the world. But only if we act in time." –Shah Selbe

In 2015, the team's two-month "Source to Sand" expedition includes plans to cover the entire Okavango River system. They'll start at the river's source in Angola and travel 1,000 miles down the river through Namibia's Caprivi Strip, into untouched wilderness in the heart of the Okavango Delta in Botswana.

The team gathers in Okavango after a long trek in 2014.

This Okavango Delta exploration team has made an exciting step forward into expedition technology. For the first time, National Geographic explorers can share their movements, findings, and the sights and sounds of their surroundings, as well as their personal data, thoughts, and emotions in real-time while exploring one of the world's richest wilderness areas. This ground-breaking expedition gives people everywhere the chance to experience— and hopefully support—one of the world's most vibrant and important ecosystems. ■

Peacemaking Through Photography

The shifting nature of national boundaries is a theme throughout history as well as in current news stories. The world's newest nation is one of those stories. In July 2011, South Sudan became an independent country after citizens voted to break away from Sudan. Why did one country become two?

Photos taken by the students of National Geographic's South Sudan Photo Camp capture friends, family members, and daily life.

412

For the first half of the 20th century, Sudan was a British colony. During British rule, English-speaking Christians and members of many different tribes lived in the southern part of the country. Arabic-speaking Muslims lived in the northern part. When the British left in 1956, two civil wars took place: one in the 1960s and another in the 1980s. War finally ended, but old wounds and animosities did not disappear. A 2005 peace agreement included an option for independence. In January 2011, southern Sudanese people voted to split from Sudan. South Sudan became the world's newest country in July 2011, with the city of Juba as its capital.

Immediately, the new country faced a number of problems, including border disputes with Sudan. Then, in December 2013, widespread violence broke out between rival political groups. Since then, more than 10,000 South Sudanese have been killed, and 2 million have been internally displaced, or forced to leave their homes. Tens of thousands of South Sudanese have fled the country altogether, and many now live in neighboring Ethiopia as refugees. Both sides are responsible for violence committed against others based on their ethnic and tribal background. The fighting in South Sudan also disrupted farming, and now 11 million people face a serious food crisis.

In September 2014, National Geographic responded to the situation in South Sudan with an outreach program called Photo Camp. This program empowers young people to tell their own stories about their life and community through photography, guided by the mentorship of National Geographic photographers. Over a period of five days, 20 University of Juba students from different ethnic backgrounds learned photography from National Geographic photographers and photo editors. This lively group took nearly 32,000 images, including the ones you see on the left. They also engaged in cross-tribal peace-building activities.

Why photography? National Geographic photographers Ed Kashi, Matt Moyer, and Amy Toensing explain. According to Toensing, the students at Photo Camp are eager to learn about cameras and photography.

Moyer observes, "To see the students take the cameras and go into their communities, document positive things, and see their world with new eyes is just really inspiring."

National Geographic Photo Camp teaches photography skills, but it also encourages storytelling. Ed Kashi says, "I believe in the power of storytelling. And I believe in the importance of bridging these gaps of misunderstanding. Photo Camp represents that spirit, that desire to bring people together to share stories and to try to make the world a better place."

Participants in National Geographic's South Sudan Photo Camp examine the photos they took.

"We are the same—we are all South Sudanese."

–Mabil Dau Mabil, student

South Sudan participants responded to Photo Camp in a number of ways. For Catherine Koro, the benefits reached far beyond photography. She said, "It's about how you can look into something differently." Students saw their communities and each other with new eyes. Mabil Dau Mabil said they purposely avoided identifying themselves as belonging to the Dinka, Bari, Kuku, or Madi tribes.

These budding photographers understand that the story of South Sudan is just beginning. Even in the midst of the country's current turmoil, they remain hopeful. Akuot Chol Mayak predicts, "The world's eyes are on this nation, not because it's special, but because it is the newest. We are still on the move, but we shall reach there."

Think It Through

The articles in this section focus on history-making events and issues that have a profound effect on people and cultures across the globe. Consider and discuss the questions below to further your understanding of these important topics.

1 Choose one article that connects to your own life and experiences in some way and explain why. How does this article relate to your own personal history?

2 Which of the five articles would be most likely to motivate you to take action as a global citizen? How might you get involved?

3 Which topic are you most interested in finding out more about, and why? How might you seek additional information or updates?

Inquiry Project: Roundtable

Consider each of the newsworthy issues discussed in this section and select the one you feel is the most important or impactful within the world today. Why do you feel your chosen global issue is the most important one?

Assignment Become an expert on the issue you have chosen alongside others who have also chosen that issue. Participate in a roundtable discussion. Articulate why you feel your chosen issue is the most important one, and support your argument.

Plan Connect with other students in your class who share your opinion and discuss what you already know about this issue and what questions you still have. Develop a solid understanding of the topic by gathering information from multiple print and digital sources. Be sure to note your sources and summarize ideas in your own words.

Produce From your research, develop a list of reasons and arguments to support the notion that your chosen topic has the most impact on the world.

Present Participate in a classroom-wide roundtable discussion. Along with others who share your opinion about the topic you have chosen, work to explain why your topic has the most world impact. Use evidence from your research to support your argument. Listen respectfully as others present their viewpoints.

REP 1 Students frame questions that can be answered by historical study and research.

STUDENT REFERENCES

AVAILABLE ONLINE

Skills Handbook
Primary Source Handbook
Geography Handbook
World Religions Handbook
Economics and Government Handbook

GLOSSARY

A

absolute monarch *n.* a ruler who has unlimited authority

adapt *v.* to change

adobe *n.* a kind of clay that when dried is used as a building material

aqueduct *n.* a long stone channel that carries clean water

arabesque *n.* an abstract design made up of patterns or flowers, leaves, vines, or geometric shapes

arch *n.* a curved structure over an opening

archipelago *n.* a collection of islands

aristocracy *n.* an upper class that is richer and more powerful than the rest of society

B

barbarian *n.* in this context, a person who lived outside the Roman Empire

bas-relief *n.* a realistic sculpture with figures raised against a flat background

bodhisattva *n.* an enlightened being who is worshipped as a god in Buddhism

bourgeoisie *n.* the middle class

bubonic plague *n.* a disease that killed more than a third of Europe's population during the Middle Ages

bureaucracy *n.* a system of government in which appointed officials in specialized departments run the various offices

burgher *n.* a wealthy, town-dwelling merchant during the Middle Ages

bushido *n.* a strict code of behavior followed by the samurai in feudal Japan

C

cacao *n.* a bean used to make chocolate

caliph *n.* the title of the chief Muslim leader who was regarded as a successor of Muhammad from A.D. 632 to 1924

calligraphy *n.* a form of elegant writing

caravan *n.* a group of people that travels together

caravel *n.* a small, fast ship used by Spanish and Portuguese explorers

cartography *n.* the study of maps and mapmaking

catacomb *n.* a hidden underground chamber where people are buried

cathedral *n.* a towering church built during the Middle Ages; often the place from which a bishop ruled

celadon *n.* a type of Chinese pottery with a unique blue-green color

chinampa *n.* a floating field that supported agriculture

chivalry *n.* a code of conduct for knights

city-state *n.* a self-governing unit made up of a city and its surrounding lands and settlements; a city that controls the surrounding villages and towns

clan *n.* a group of families that shares a common ancestor

classical *adj.* relating to ancient Greek and Roman culture

clergy *n.* the religious leaders who oversee ceremonies and deliver teachings of the Christian Church

codex *n.* a folded book made of tree bark paper

colony *n.* a group of people that settles in a new land but keeps ties to its native country

commerce *n.* the buying and selling of goods

commodity *n.* a trade good

common law *n.* a system of law established in England to make sure people received equal treatment

conquistador *n.* a Spanish conqueror who sought gold and other riches in the Americas

contract *n.* an agreement between two or more people

convert *v.* to change one's religion

cosmopolitan *adj.* worldly

cottage industry *n.* a system of making and selling goods in which people work in their own homes

creation story *n.* an account that explains how the world began and how people came to exist

creed *n.* a statement of belief

crossroads *n.* the place where two roads meet

cultivate *v.* to grow a crop

D

daimyo *n.* a class of large landowning families in medieval Japan

denomination *n.* a branch of one type of religion

deplete *v.* to use something up, such as a resource

desertification *n.* the process by which once fertile land is transformed into a desert

dhow *n.* a ship with a long, thin hull and triangular sails

diversity *n.* a range of different things; a variety

divine *adj.* having the nature of a god

divine right *n.* a right to rule believed to be given by God to a king or queen

GLOSSARY

E

elliptical *adj.* oval

embassy *n.* a group of people who represent their nation in a foreign country

emperor *n.* the supreme ruler of an empire

enlightened despot *n.* an absolute ruler who applied Enlightenment principles to his or her reign

epistle *n.* a letter

excommunicate *v.* to officially exclude a member of a church from its rituals and membership

exploit *v.* to mistreat

F

feudalism *n.* a political and social system in which a vassal receives protection from a lord in exchange for obedience and service

free enterprise *n.* an economic system in which people buying and selling products determine what products are needed and what price should be paid for them

fresco *n.* a picture painted directly onto a wall

G

geocentric theory *n.* a theory that places Earth at the center of the universe

geoglyph *n.* a large, geometric design or shape drawn on the ground

glyph *n.* a symbolic picture used to represent a word, syllable, or sound

golden age *n.* a period of great cultural achievement

griot *n.* a West African storyteller who relates stories through the oral tradition

guild *n.* a group of craftspeople that helped protect and improve the working conditions of its members

H

haiku *n.* a form of Japanese poetry that has 17 syllables in three unrhymed lines of 5, 7, and 5 syllables

hanbok *n.* a traditional Korean jacket and skirt or pant combination

heliocentric theory *n.* a theory that places the sun at the center of the universe

heresy *n.* beliefs contrary to Church teachings; opposition to Church policy

highland *n.* a type of land that is high above the sea

hub *n.* a center

humanism *n.* a movement that focused on the importance of the individual

hypothesis *n.* an explanation that can be tested

I

icon *n.* an image of Jesus or a saint

imam *n.* a Muslim religious leader

impose *v.* to force someone to do something

indulgence *n.* the release from punishment for sins, sold by papal officials

iron *n.* a metal that is found in rock

isolationism *n.* a rejection of foreign contact and outside influences

J

janissary *n.* a highly trained and disciplined soldier in the Ottoman army

K

kabuki *n.* a form of Japanese drama that involves luxurious costumes and elaborate makeup

karma *n.* in Hinduism, a state of being influenced by a person's actions and conduct; determines the kind of life into which a person will be reborn

khanate *n.* a region of the Mongol empire

kimchi *n.* a spicy pickled vegetable mix that serves as Korea's national dish

kiva *n.* a circular-shaped chamber built in the ground by the ancient Pueblo

knight *n.* a warrior in medieval Europe

L

laissez-faire *n.* a policy that calls for less government involvement in economic affairs

lingua franca *n.* a language commonly used by many different groups of people

longbow *n.* a weapon that allowed archers to fire arrows

lord *n.* a nobleman who received land from a king in medieval feudal society

lowland *n.* a type of land that is low and level

M

maize *n.* a type of corn first domesticated by early Mesoamericans

manor *n.* a self-contained world located on land belonging to a lord

mansa *n.* a West African king

mariner *n.* a sailor

medieval *adj.* a period in history that spanned from the A.D. 500s to the 1500s; from the Latin *medieum* (middle) and *aevum* (age)

meditation *n.* the act of achieving inner peace and an enlightened realization of the divine aspect in each person

mercantilism *n.* an economic theory that a nation's wealth and power depends on the possession of precious metals, such as gold and silver

mercenary *n.* a hired soldier

migration *n.* the movement from one place to another

minaret *n.* a tall, slender tower that is part of a mosque

missionary *n.* a person who goes to another country to do religious work; a person who tries to spread Christianity to others

monastery *n.* a Christian religious community

monsoon *n.* a strong seasonal wind in South and Southeast Asia

mosaic *n.* a grouping of tiny colored stone cubes set in mortar to create a picture or design

mosque *n.* a Muslim place of worship

mother culture *n.* a civilization that greatly influences other civilizations

mound builder *n.* a Native American culture that built mounds and cities in the Mississippi River Valley region between 1000 B.C. and A.D. 500

movable type *n.* the individual clay tablets that could be arranged on a board to form text

N

nation-state *n.* a country with an independent government and a population united by a shared culture, language, and national pride; a political unit in which people have a common culture and identity

natural right *n.* a right, such as life or liberty, that a person is born with

nirvana *n.* in Buddhism, a state of bliss or the end of suffering caused by the cycle of rebirth

noble *n.* a member of a high class in society who inherits his or her status

noh *n.* a form of drama that grew out of Japanese Shinto rituals and often retells well-known folktales

O

oasis *n.* a fertile place with water in a desert

ondol *n.* a Korean system of heating in which an outside fire heats thick stones set into a floor

oral history *n.* an unwritten account of events, often passed down through the generations as stories or songs

oral tradition *n.* the passage of spoken histories and stories from one generation to the next

oratory *n.* the art of public speaking

P

parable *n.* in the Bible, a simple story to illustrate a moral or spiritual lesson

parliament *n.* a group of representatives who shared power with the English monarch

patriarch *n.* the leader of the Eastern Orthodox Church

patron *n.* a wealthy person who financially supports and encourages an artist

perspective *n.* an artistic technique that produces an impression of depth and distance

philosophe *n.* an Enlightenment thinker

pilgrimage *n.* a journey to a holy place

plantation *n.* a large farm where slaves worked to grow and harvest crops

pope *n.* the leader of the Roman Catholic Church

porcelain *n.* a strong, light, and translucent ceramic

potlach *n.* a gift-giving ceremony practiced by the Kwakiutl and Haida Native American tribes

primary source *n.* an artifact or piece of writing that was created by someone who witnessed or lived through a historical event

printing press *n.* an invention that used movable metal type to print pages

prophet *n.* a teacher believed to be inspired by God

Q

quarry *v.* to extract stone from the earth

quinine *n.* a substance from the bark of a tree that is an effective remedy for malaria

quinoa *n.* a high-protein grain native to the Andes Mountains in South America

R

racism *n.* the belief that one race is better than others

reason *n.* the power of the human mind to think and understand in a logical way

regent *n.* a person who rules when a monarch or emperor is unable to do so

reincarnation *n.* in Hinduism, the rebirth of a person's soul into another body after death

Renaissance man *n.* a person who has a wide variety of skills and knowledge

reunify *v.* to join together again

ritual *n.* a formal series of acts always performed in the same way; a religious ceremony

rivalry *n.* a competition

S

samurai *n.* a hired warrior in medieval Japan

savanna *n.* an area of lush tropical grasslands

scarcity *n.* a small supply of something

schism *n.* a separation

scientific method *n.* a logical procedure for developing and testing ideas

scientific rationalism *n.* a school of thought in which observation, experimentation, and mathematical reasoning replace ancient wisdom and church teachings as the source of scientific truth

secondary source *n.* an artifact or writing created after an event by someone who did not see it or live during the time when it occurred

secular *adj.* nonreligious

serf *n.* a person who lived and worked on the private land of a noble or medieval lord

shah *n.* a ruler of the Safavid Empire; the Persian title for "king"

shaman *n.* a medicine healer in Native American cultures

shari'a *n.* an Islamic system of law that covers all aspects of human behavior

shogun *n.* the military ruler of medieval Japan

shogunate *n.* the rule by a shogun

slash-and-burn agriculture *n.* a method of clearing fields for planting

smallpox *n.* a deadly virus that causes a high fever and small blisters on the skin

staple *n.* a main crop produced in a specific place

steppe *n.* a vast, grassy plain

sultan *n.* a ruler of the Ottoman Empire

T

terrace *n.* a stepped platform built into a mountainside

terrace farming *n.* a type of farming in which flat steps are cut into a mountain to provide farmland

terra cotta *n.* a fire-baked clay

tetrarchy *n.* a system of rule by four emperors

theory *n.* a proposed explanation for a set of facts

tolerance *n.* the sympathy for the beliefs and practices of others

totem pole *n.* a tall, elaborately carved and painted tree trunk common in Northwest Coast native cultures

trans-Saharan *adj.* across the Sahara

triangular trade *n.* a transatlantic trade network formed by Europe, West Africa, and the Americas

tribute *n.* a tax paid or goods and services rendered in return for protection

V

vassal *n.* a person, usually a lesser nobleman, who received land and protection from a feudal lord in exchange for obedience and service

vernacular *n.* a person's native language

W

wigwam *n.* a domed tent used as housing by the Algonquin in North America

woodcut *n.* an image carved on a block of wood

A

absolute *adj.* complete (page 50)

accuracy *n.* the freedom from errors (page 360)

accurate *adj.* without mistakes or errors (page 162)

ambitious *adj.* having a desire for fame or success (page 220)

appoint *v.* to give someone a particular job or duty (page 44)

B

benefit *v.* to be helpful to someone or something (page 371)

C

coexist *v.* to live peacefully together (page 130)

commit *v.* to promise to do something (page 14)

communal *adj.* used or shared by a group of people (page 180)

constant *adj.* happening all the time (page 112)

creation *n.* the act of making something that did not exist before (page 386)

crucial *adj.* extremely important or necessary (page 80)

D

decline *v.* to worsen in terms of condition or quality (page 124)

depose *v.* to remove someone from power (page 263)

distinct *adj.* noticeably different or unique (page 186)

E

elaborate *adj.* made with great detail and effort (page 246)

emphasis *n.* the additional importance given to something (page 70)

ensure *v.* to make something certain (page 76)

eternal *adj.* existing at all times; lasting forever (page 272)

ethical *adj.* following accepted rules or behaviors (page 212)

excel *v.* to be or do better than others (page 325)

F

fortified *adj.* strong, strengthened (page 301)

I

interact *v.* to do things with others (page 383)

interval *n.* the period of time between events (page 16)

intricate *adj.* having many parts or details (page 278)

L

luxury *adj.* expensive and unnecessary (page 124)

O

observation *n.* the written descriptions based on something you have watched or seen (page 333)

P

predict *v.* to say that something will happen in the future (page 157)

profit *n.* the money that is made through doing business (page 106)

R

radical *adj.* different from what is typical or ordinary (page 337)

retain *v.* to keep or continue to have (page 295)

revolve *v.* to move or turn around something (page 358)

U

undermine *v.* to make someone or something weaker (page 256)

A

acueducto *s.* canal largo de piedra que transporta agua limpia

adaptar *v.* cambiar

adobe *s.* tipo de arcilla que cuando se seca se usa como material de construcción

agotar *v.* consumir algo por completo, por ejemplo, un recurso

agricultura de tala y quema *s.* método de limpiar los campos para sembrar cultivos

aislacionismo *s.* rechazo al contacto extranjero y a las influencias externas

alminar *s.* torre alta y angosta que es parte de una mezquita

arabesco *s.* diseño abstracto que consiste en patrones o flores, hojas, enredaderas o figuras geométricas

archipiélago *s.* conjunto de islas

arco largo *s.* arma que permitía que los arqueros dispararan sus flechas

arco *s.* estructura curva colocada sobre una abertura

aristocracia *s.* clase alta que es más adinerada y más poderosa que el resto de la sociedad

B

bajorrelieve *s.* escultura realista que contiene figuras realzadas sobre un fondo plano

bancales *s.* tipo de agricultura en que se cortan escalones planos en una montaña para brindar terrenos de cultivo

bárbaro *s.* en este contexto, una persona que vivía fuera del Imperio Romano

burgués *s.* comerciante rico, citadino, durante la Edad Media; miembro de la clase media

burocracia *s.* sistema de gobierno en que funcionarios designados en departamentos especializados están a cargo de distintas oficinas

bushido *s.* estricto código de comportamiento seguido por los samurái en el Japón feudal

C

caballero *s.* guerrero de la Europa medieval

cacao *s.* grano que se usa para hacer chocolate

califa *s.* título del líder musulmán que era considerado sucesor de Mohammed, desde 632 a 1924 D.C.

caligrafía *s.* forma de escritura elegante

carabela *s.* nave pequeña y rápida usada por los exploradores españoles y portugueses

caravana *s.* grupo de personas que viajan juntas

cartografía *s.* estudio de los mapas y de la creación de mapas

catacumba *s.* cámara escondida bajo la superficie en donde se entierra a los muertos

catedral *s.* iglesia alta construida durante la Edad Media; a menudo el lugar en donde gobernaba un obispo

celadón *s.* tipo de cerámica china con un peculiar color verdeazulado

centro de comercio *s.* núcleo comercial

chamán *s.* curandero de las culturas nativo-americanas

chinampa *s.* campo flotante que sustenta la agricultura

cisma *s.* separación

ciudad-estado *s.* unidad que se gobierna a sí misma, formada por una ciudad y sus territorios y asentamientos circundantes; ciudad que controla las aldeas y pueblos circundantes

clan *s.* grupo de familias que comparten un ancestro en común

clásico *adj.* relacionado con la cultura griega y romana antiguas

clero *s.* grupo de líderes religiosos que dirigen las ceremonias e imparten las enseñanzas de la iglesia

códice *s.* libro plegado hecho de papel de corteza de árbol

colonia *s.* grupo de personas que se asientan en un nuevo territorio, pero que mantienen sus lazos con su país nativo

comercio *s.* intercambio de productos; compra y venta de bienes

comercio triangular *s.* red de comercio transatlántico formado por Europa, África Occidental y las Américas

comunal *adj.* compartido

conquistador *s.* explorador español que buscaba oro y otras riquezas en Centroamérica y América del Sur

constructores de montículos *s.* cultura nativo-americana que construyó montículos y ciudades en la región del valle del río Mississippi entre los años 1000 A.C. y 500 D.C.

contrato *s.* acuerdo entre dos o más personas

convertirse *v.* cambiar la propia religión

credo *s.* declaración de creencia

cultivar *v.* sembrar cultivos

cultivo básico *s.* cultivo principal producido en un lugar específico

cultura madre *s.* civilización que tiene una gran influencia sobre otras civilizaciones

D

daimio *s.* clase de familias terratenientes grandes del Japón medieval

denominación *s.* rama de una religión determinada

derecho consuetudinario *s.* sistema legal establecido en Inglaterra para asegurarse de que todas las personas fueran tratadas con igualdad

derecho divino *s.* derecho a gobernar que se creía que Dios daba a un rey o reina

derecho natural *s.* derecho, tal como la vida o la libertad, con los que nace una persona

desertificación *s.* proceso mediante el cual las tierras fértiles se convierten en un desierto

déspota ilustrado *s.* gobernante absolutista que aplicó los principios de la Ilustración a su propio reino

dhow *s.* nave con un casco largo y delgado y velas triangulares

diversidad *s.* rango de cosas diferentes; variedad

divino *adj.* tener la naturaleza de un dios

E

edad de oro *s.* período de grandes logros culturales

elíptico *adj.* ovalado

embajada *s.* grupo de personas que representa a su nación en un país extranjero

emperador *s.* gobernante supremo de un imperio

epístola *s.* carta

escasez *s.* suministro pequeño de algo

estepa *s.* planicie vasta y cubierta de hierbas

excomulgar *s.* excluir oficialmente a un miembro de una iglesia de sus rituales y membresía

explotar *v.* maltratar

extraer *v.* sacar piedras de la tierra

F

feudalismo *s.* sistema político y social en que el vasallo recibe protección de un señor a cambio de obediencia y servicio

filósofo *s.* pensador de la Ilustración

fresco *s.* arte que se pinta directamente sobre una muralla

fuente primaria *s.* artefacto o texto escrito creado por alguien que presenció o vivió un acontecimiento histórico

fuente secundaria *s.* artefacto o texto escrito creado después de un acontecimiento por alguien que no lo vio o presenció durante el tiempo en que ocurrió

G

geoglifo *s.* diseño o forma geométrica grande dibujado sobre el suelo

glifo *s.* dibujo simbólico usado para representar una palabra, sílaba o sonido

gremio *s.* grupo de artesanos que ayudaron a proteger y a mejorar las condiciones laborales de sus miembros

griot *s.* cuentacuentos del África Occidental que cuenta historias a través de la tradición oral

H

haikú *s.* forma de poesía japonesa que consiste en 17 sílabas organizadas en tres versos no rimados de 5, 7 y 5 sílabas respectivamente

hanbok *s.* combinación coreana de vestimenta tradicional que consiste en una chaqueta con falda o pantalón

herejía *s.* creencias contrarias a las enseñanzas de la iglesia; oposición a las políticas de la iglesia

hidalguía *s.* código de comportamiento de los caballeros

hierro *s.* metal que se encuentra en la roca

hipótesis *s.* explicación que puede ponerse a prueba

historia de la creación *s.* narración que explica cómo comenzó el mundo y cómo nacieron las personas

historia oral *s.* registro no escrito de acontecimientos, que a menudo se transmite de una generación a otra a través de historias o canciones

hombre renacentista *s.* persona con una amplia variedad de destrezas y conocimientos

humanismo *s.* movimiento que se enfoca en la importancia del individuo

I

ícono *s.* imagen de Jesús o de un santo

imán *s.* líder religioso musulmán

imponer *v.* forzar a alguien a hacer algo

imprenta *s.* invento que usaba tipos móviles de metal para imprimir páginas

indulgencia *s.* liberación de los castigos causados por los pecados, vendida por funcionarios papales

intersección *s.* lugar en donde se juntan dos caminos

J

jenízaro *s.* soldado altamente entrenado y disciplinado del ejército otomano

K

kabuki *s.* forma de obra teatral japonesa que incluye disfraces lujosos y maquillaje elaborado

kanato *s.* región del Imperio Mongol

karma *s.* en el hinduismo, estado de estar influenciado por las acciones y el comportamiento; determina el tipo de vida en que una persona volverá a nacer

kimchi *s.* plato nacional de Corea, que consiste en una mezcla de verduras bien condimentadas

kiva *s.* cámara de forma circular construida en el suelo por los indígenas pueblo del pasado

L

laissez-faire *s.* política que exige menos participación del estado en asuntos económicos

lengua franca *s.* idioma que se usa comúnmente entre distintos grupos de personas

libre empresa *s.* sistema económico en que la compra y venta de productos determina qué productos se necesitan y qué precio deben tener

M

maíz *s.* tipo de elote que fue domesticado por los primeros mesoamericanos

mansa *s.* rey de África Occidental

marinero *s.* marino

mecenas *s.* persona adinerada que apoya financieramente y promueve a un artista

medieval *adj.* período de la historia que se expandió desde el siglo VI al siglo XVI; del latín *medieum* (medio) y *aevum* (edad)

meditación *s.* acto de alcanzar la paz interior y el entendimiento del aspecto divino en cada persona

mercancía *s.* producto de comercio

mercantilismo *s.* teoría económica que considera que la riqueza y el poder de una nación dependen de la posesión de metales preciosos, como el oro y la plata

mercenario *s.* soldado asalariado

método científico *s.* procedimiento lógico para desarrollar y poner a prueba las ideas

mezquita *s.* lugar musulmán de adoración

migración *s.* mudarse de un lugar a otro

misionero *s.* persona que va a otro país para realizar labores religiosas; persona que trata de divulgar la cristiandad a otros

monarca absoluto *s.* gobernante con autoridad ilimitada

monasterio *s.* comunidad religiosa cristiana

monzón *s.* vientos estacionales fuertes en el Sudeste Asiático

mosaico *s.* agrupación de cubitos de piedra coloridos que se colocan sobre argamasa para crear un dibujo o diseño

N

nación-estado *s.* país con un gobierno independiente y una población unida por una cultura compartida, un idioma común y orgullo nacional; unidad política en que las personas tienen una cultura e identidad en común

nirvana *s.* en el budismo, un estado de dicha o del final del sufrimiento causado por el ciclo del renacer

noble *s.* miembro de la clase alta de la sociedad que hereda su estatus de sus antepasados

noh *s.* forma de obra teatral que surgió a partir de los rituales japoneses Shinto y que a menudo relata cuentos folclóricos conocidos

O

oasis *s.* lugar fértil con agua en un desierto

ondol *s.* sistema coreano de calefacción en que una fogata al exterior calienta piedras gruesas que se colocan en el suelo

oratoria *s.* arte del discurso público

P

papa *s.* líder de la Iglesia Católica Romana

parábola *s.* en la Biblia, un relato sencillo que ilustra una moraleja o una lección espiritual

parlamento *s.* grupo de representantes que comparten el poder con el rey inglés

patriarca *s.* líder de la Iglesia Ortodoxa oriental

peregrinación *s.* viaje a un lugar sagrado

perspectiva *s.* técnica artística que produce una impresión de profundidad y distancia

peste bubónica *s.* enfermedad que mató a más de un tercio de la población de Europa durante la Edad Media

plantación *s.* granja grande en donde trabajan esclavos para producir y cultivar las siembras

poema épico *s.* historia larga escrita como un poema narrativo

porcelana *s.* cerámica resistente, liviana y translúcida

potlach *s.* ceremonia de entrega de obsequios practicada por las tribus nativo-americanas kwakiutl y haida

profeta *s.* maestro que se cree es inspirado por Dios

Q

quinina *s.* sustancia de la corteza de un árbol que es un antídoto efectivo para la malaria

quínoa *s.* grano alto en proteínas originario de las montañas de los Andes en América del Sur

R

racionalismo científico *s.* escuela de pensamiento en que la observación, experimentación y razonamiento matemático reemplazan el conocimiento ancestral y las enseñanzas de la iglesia como fuente de la verdad científica

racismo *s.* creencia de que una raza es mejor que las otras

razón *s.* poder de la mente humana para pensar y comprender de una manera lógica

reencarnación *s.* en el hinduismo, el renacer del alma de una persona en otro cuerpo después de la muerte

regente *s.* persona que gobierna cuando un monarca o emperador no puede hacerlo

reunificar *v.* volver a unir

ritual *s.* serie de actos formales que siempre se realizan de la misma manera; ceremonia religiosa

rivalidad *s.* competencia

S

sabana *s.* área de praderas tropicales exuberantes

samurái *s.* guerrero asalariado del Japón medieval

secular *adj.* no religioso

señor *s.* miembro de la nobleza que recibía tierras de un rey en la sociedad feudal medieval

señorío *s.* mundo autosuficiente ubicado en las tierras que pertenecían a un señor

shah *s.* gobernante del Imperio Safávida; título persa para "rey"

shari'a *s.* sistema islámico de leyes que cubre todos los aspectos del comportamiento humano

siervo *s.* persona que vivía y trabajaba en los terrenos privados de un noble o de un señor medieval

sogún *s.* gobernante militar del Japón medieval

sogunato *s.* gobierno de un sogún

sultán *s.* gobernante del Imperio Otomano

T

teoría *s.* explicación propuesta para un conjunto de hechos

teoría geocéntrica *s.* teoría que posiciona a la Tierra en el centro del universo

teoría heliocéntrica *s.* teoría que posiciona al Sol como el centro del universo

terracota *s.* arcilla cocida al fuego

terrazas *s.* plataformas de estepa construidas en la ladera de una montaña

tetrarquía *s.* sistema de gobierno de cuatro emperadores

tierras altas *s.* terrenos que están sobre el mar

tierras bajas *s.* tipo de terrenos nivelados de poca altura

tipos móviles *s.* tablas de arcilla individuales que podían organizarse sobre un tablero para formar un texto

tolerancia *s.* respeto por las creencias y las prácticas de otros

tótem *s.* tronco de árbol alto y elaboradamente tallado y pintado, común en las culturas nativas de la costa noroeste

tradición oral *s.* transmisión verbal de historias y relatos de una generación a la siguiente

transahariano *adj.* que va a través del Sahara

tributo *s.* impuesto pagado o bienes y servicios proporcionados a cambio de protección

V

vasallo *s.* persona, usualmente un hombre noble menor, que recibía tierras y protección de un señor feudal a cambio de obediencia y servicio

vernáculo *s.* idioma nativo de una persona

viruela *s.* virus mortal que causa una fiebre alta y ampollas pequeñas en la piel

W

wigwam *s.* tipo de choza con techo en forma de cúpula usada como vivienda por los indígenas algonquinos de América del Norte

X

xilografía *s.* imagen tallada en un bloque de madera

A

absoluto *adj.* completo (pág. 50)

ambicioso *adj.* que desea la fama o el éxito (pág. 220)

asegurar *v.* garantizar algo (pág. 76)

B

beneficiar *v.* ayudar a alguien o a algo (pág. 371)

C

coexistir *v.* vivir en paz en conjunto (pág. 130)

comprometerse *v.* prometer hacer algo (pág. 14)

comunal *adj.* usado o compartido por un grupo de personas (pág. 180)

constante *adj.* que ocurre todo el tiempo (pág. 112)

creación *s.* acción de hacer algo que no existía antes (pág. 386)

crucial *adj.* extremadamente importante o necesario (pág. 80)

D

decaer *v.* empeorar en términos de condición o de calidad (pág. 124)

designar *v.* dar a alguien un trabajo o responsabilidad determinado (pág. 44)

destituir *v.* remover a alguien del poder (pág. 263)

distintivo *adj.* notoriamente diferente o único (pág. 186)

E

elaborado *adj.* hecho con mucho detalle y esfuerzo (pág. 246)

énfasis *s.* importancia adicional que se otorga a algo (pág. 70)

ético *adj.* que sigue las reglas o comportamientos aceptados (pág. 212)

F

fortificado *adj.* fuerte, resistente (pág. 301)

G

ganancia *s.* dinero que se gana al hacer negocios (pág. 106)

girar *v.* moverse o rotar alrededor de algo (pág. 358)

I

interaccionar *v.* hacer cosas con otros (pág. 383)

intervalo *s.* período de tiempo entre los acontecimientos (pág. 16)

intricado *adj.* que contiene muchas partes o detalles (pág. 278)

L

lujoso *adj.* costoso e innecesario (pág. 124)

O

observación *s.* descripción escrita con base en lo observado o visto (pág. 333)

P

precisión *adj.* sin faltas ni errores (pág. 162)

preciso *s.* libre de errores (pág. 360)

predecir *v.* decir qué sucederá en el futuro (pág. 157)

R

radical *adj.* diferente de lo que es típico u ordinario (pág. 337)

retener *v.* mantener o seguir teniendo (pág. 295)

S

sobresalir *v.* ser o desempeñarse mejor que el resto (pág. 325)

socavar *v.* debilitar a alguien o a algo (pág. 256)

INDEX

A

Analyze Cause and Effect, 17, 33, 38, 40, 43, 55, 56, 61, 63, 69, 88, 103, 111, 120, 122, 129, 136, 167, 172, 181, 191, 196, 217, 219, 223, 227, 234, 239, 241, 257, 258, 267, 269, 277, 280, 309, 315, 319, 320, 331, 335, 341, 351, 357, 365, 371, 375, 378, 383, 387, 395

Analyze Language Use, 100, 109, 117, 120, 129, 161, 307, 322, 325, 339, 352

Analyze Sources, 13, 39, 57, 89, 121, 137, 173, 197, 235, 259, 281, 321, 353, 379, 399

Analyze Visuals, 45, 193, 377

Ask Questions, 13, 163

C

Categorize, 267

Compare and Contrast, 13, 23, 79, 83, 113, 131, 151, 157, 169, 172, 177, 189, 191, 195, 196, 215, 221, 231, 233, 245, 247, 251, 258 275, 280, 295, 320, 337, 343, 352, 373, 378, 385, 391, 398

Compare Time Lines, 7, 97, 145, 207, 289

Critical Viewing, 5, 19, 36, 55, 61, 65, 85, 95, 107, 109, 117, 129, 143, 153, 154, 169, 177, 183, 187, 189, 191, 205, 215, 217, 241, 247, 251, 253, 267, 269, 279, 287, 307, 315, 325, 337, 339, 373, 383, 387, 389, 391, 395

D

Describe, 31, 241

Describe Geographic Information, 133, 135

Determine Word Meanings, 51, 155, 260, 269, 280, 351, 357, 380, 398

Distinguish Fact and Opinion, 83

Document-Based Question, 28–29, 66–67, 118–119, 164–165, 224–225, 248–249, 310–311, 346–347, 368–369, 396–397

Draw Conclusions, 31, 33, 37, 56, 73, 85, 88, 111, 115, 117, 120, 136, 153, 161, 169, 171, 172, 183, 187, 189, 193, 210, 219, 234, 258, 280, 292, 299, 307, 320, 349, 352, 359, 375, 378, 398

E

Evaluate, 38, 71, 85, 187, 196, 234, 320, 361, 395

I

Identify Details, 63

Identify Main Ideas, 345

Identify Main Ideas and Details, 15, 45, 58, 71, 88, 103, 107, 127, 133, 136, 148, 163, 172, 233, 277, 279, 299, 325, 363, 383, 398

Identify Problems and Solutions, 35, 79, 253, 377, 391

Integrate Visuals, 159, 231, 341

Interpret Charts, 259, 321

Interpret Diagrams, 57

Interpret Maps, 17, 27, 35, 39, 43, 51, 61, 77, 89, 105, 113, 121, 125, 127, 131, 137, 151, 157, 167, 181, 213, 221, 229, 239, 263, 275, 281, 295, 313, 345, 363, 371, 399

Interpret Visuals, 49, 153, 173, 197, 227, 325, 301, 305, 327, 333, 353, 365, 379

M

Make Connections, 21, 23, 38, 81, 343, 361, 387

Make Generalizations, 56, 65, 69, 81, 229, 247, 258

Make Inferences, 15, 19, 21, 25, 27, 49, 77, 88, 109, 125, 136, 155, 159, 171, 183, 195, 196, 213, 217, 223, 234, 236, 243, 245, 251, 253, 258, 280, 297, 301, 305, 309, 315, 319, 320, 327, 331, 333, 339, 349, 352, 354, 359, 373, 378, 385, 389, 398

Make Predictions, 352

O

Organize Ideas, 10, 38, 40, 56, 122, 136, 174, 196

S

Sequence Events, 10, 25, 37, 38, 55, 73, 107, 115, 120, 136, 174, 196, 215, 234, 279, 297, 313, 352

Summarize, 19, 177

Synthesize, 38, 65, 120, 263, 337, 389, 398

Synthesize and Write, 29, 119, 165, 225, 249, 311, 347, 369, 397

U

Unit Inquiry
Create a Local Trade Exchange, 141
Design an Adaptation Strategy, 201
Leave a Legacy of Innovation, 285
Make an Idea Map, 93
Map the New Worldview, 403

W

Write About History, 39, 57, 89, 121, 137, 173, 197, 235, 259, 281, 321, 353, 379, 399

ACKNOWLEDGMENTS

Text Acknowledgments

235 Li Po, "Zazen on Ching-t'ing Mountain" from Crossing the Yellow River: Three Hundred Poems from the Chinese, translated by Sam Hamill. Copyright ©2000 by Sam Hamill. Reprinted with the permission of The Permissions Company, Inc., on behalf of Tiger Bark Press, www.tigerbarkpress.com.

249 Matsuo Basho, "The Quiet Pond…" from The Classic Tradition of Haiku: An Anthology by Faubion Bowers (editor). Dover Publications, Inc., 1996. (Poem translated by Edward G. Seidensticker)

259 Shuson Kato, "I kill and Ant…" from Haiku Mind: 108 Poems to Cultivate and Open Your Heart, by Patricia Donegan, ©2008 by Patricia Donegan. Reprinted by arrangement with The Permissions Company, Inc., on behalf of Shambhala Publications Inc., Boston, MA. www.shambhala.com.

National Geographic Learning gratefully acknowledges the contributions of the following National Geographic Explorers and affiliates to our program and to our planet:

Salam Al Kuntar, Archaeologist, National Geographic Emerging Explorer
Caroline Alexander, National Geographic Writer/Journalist
Nicole Boivin, Archaeologist, National Geographic Grantee
Steve Boyes, Conservation Biologist, National Geographic Emerging Explorer
Nina Burleigh, Journalist/Author
Michael Cosmopoulos, Archaeologist, National Geographic Grantee
Christopher DeCorse, Archaeologist, National Geographic Grantee
Steven Ellis, Archaeologist, National Geographic Grantee
Francisco Estrada-Belli, Archaeologist, National Geographic Grantee
Beverly Goodman, Geo-Archaeologist, National Geographic Emerging Explorer
Jeff Gusky, National Geographic Photographer
Fredrik Hiebert, Archaeologist, National Geographic Fellow
Patrick Hunt, Archaeologist, National Geographic Grantee
Louise Leakey, Paleontologist, National Geographic Explorer-in-Residence
Christine Lee, Bio-Archaeologist, National Geographic Emerging Explorer
Albert Lin, Research Scientist/Engineer, National Geographic Emerging Explorer
Jodi Magness, Archaeologist, National Geographic Grantee
Sarah Parcak, Archaeologist, National Geographic Fellow
Thomas Parker, Archaeologist, National Geographic Grantee
William Parkinson, Archaeologist, National Geographic Grantee
Matt Piscitelli, Archaeologist, National Geographic Grantee
Jeffrey Rose, Archaeologist, National Geographic Emerging Explorer
Max Salomon, National Geographic Producer
Aziz Abu Sarah, Cultural Educator, National Geographic Emerging Explorer
William Saturno, Archaeologist, National Geographic Grantee
Anna Secor, Political Geographer, National Geographic Grantee
Shah Selbe, Conservation Technologist, National Geographic Emerging Explorer
Maurizio Seracini, Cultural Heritage Engineer, National Geographic Fellow
Hayat Sindi, Science Entrepreneur, National Geographic Emerging Explorer
Christopher Thornton, Archaeologist, National Geographic Lead Program Officer of Research, Conservation, and Exploration
Soultana Maria Valamoti, Archaeologist, National Geographic Grantee
Juan José Valdés, National Geographic Geographer
Simon Worrall, National Geographic Writer
Xiaobai Angela Yao, Geographer, National Geographic Grantee
Dave Yoder, Photojournalist, National Geographic Grantee

Photographic Credits

Source/Aurora Photos. **12** ©The Thorburn Group/National Geographic Learning. **14** ©The Thorburn Group/National Geographic Learning. **13** ©Roger Ressmeyer/Eureka Premium/Corbis. **15** ©Araldo de Luca/Fine Art/Corbis. **16** ©The Thorburn Group/National Geographic Learning. **17** ©Mapping Specialists/National Geographic Learning. **18** ©The Thorburn Group/National Geographic Learning. **19** ©Guido Baviera/Terra/Corbis. **20** ©The Thorburn Group/National Geographic Learning. **21** (tr) ©Ensuper/Shutterstock.com. (cl) ©Ifong/Shutterstock.com. (br) ©Zoonar/A Maltsev/Age Fotostock. **22** ©The Thorburn Group/National Geographic Learning. **22–23** ©Araldo de Luca/Corbis art/Corbis. **24** ©The Thorburn Group/National Geographic Learning. **25** ©Scala/Ministero per i Beni e le Attività culturali/Art Resource, NY. **26** ©The Thorburn Group/National Geographic Learning. **26–27** ©Mapping Specialists/National Geographic Learning. **28** ©Alfredo Dagli Orti/The Art Archive at Art Resource, NY. **29** ©akg-images/Superstock, Inc. **30** (t) ©The Thorburn Group/National Geographic Learning. (b) ©Image Source/Corbis. **31** ©Raimund Kutter/imageBROKER/age fotostock. **32** ©The Thorburn Group/National Geographic Learning. **33** (tl) ©Dea/G. Dagli Orti/De Agostini Picture Library/Getty Images. (tr) ©Stefano Bianchetti/Fine Art/Corbis. (cl) ©Dea/G. Dagli Orti/De Agostini/Getty Images. (cr) ©akg-images. **35** ©Mapping Specialists/National Geographic Learning. **34** ©The Thorburn Group/National Geographic Learning. **36** ©Look and Learn/Bridgeman Images. **39** (b) ©Mapping Specialists/National Geographic Learning. (t) ©Image Source/Aurora Photos. **40–41** ©Rabouan Jean-Baptiste/Latitude/Corbis. **42** ©The Thorburn Group/National Geographic Learning. **43** ©Mapping Specialists/National Geographic Learning. **44** ©The Thorburn Group/National Geographic Learning. **45** (t) ©Erich Lessing/Art Resource, NY. (b) ©The Thorburn Group/National Geographic Learning. **47** ©Michele Burgess/Alamy Stock Photo. **48** ©Precision Graphics/National Geographic Learning. **49** ©The Thorburn Group/National Geographic Learning. **50** ©The Thorburn Group/National Geographic Learning. **51** (t) ©Mapping Specialists/National Geographic Learning. (b) ©The Metropolitan Museum of Art. Image source: Art Resource, NY. **52–53** ©AGF Srl/Alamy Stock Photo. **53** (tc) ©Saint Apollinare in Classe Ravenna/Dagli Orti/The Art Archive/Picture Desk. (tr) ©Erich Lessing/Art Resource, NY. (c) ©Gina Martin/National Geographic Creative. (bc) ©James L.Stanfield/National Geographic Creative. (br) ©Cubo Images/Superstock. **54** (t) (b) ©The Thorburn Group/National Geographic Learning. **55** ©SuperStock. **57** ©Rabouan Jean-Baptiste/Latitude/Corbis. **58–59** ©Tino Soriano/National Geographic Learning. **60** ©The Thorburn Group/National Geographic Learning. **61** ©John Warburton Lee/SuperStock. (tr) ©Mapping Specialists/National Geographic Learning. **62** ©The Thorburn Group/National Geographic Learning. **63** ©Kazuyoshi Nomachi/Latitude/Corbis. **64** ©The Thorburn Group/National Geographic Learning. **65** © Bruno Zanzottera/Parallelozero/Aurora Photos. **66** ©Roland and Sabrina Michaud/Akg-Images. **68** ©Suhaib Salem SJS/GB/Reuters. **69** ©The Thorburn Group/National Geographic Learning. **70** ©The Thorburn Group/National Geographic Learning. **71** ©Roland and Sabrina Michaud/Akg-Images. **72** ©The Thorburn Group/National Geographic Learning. **72–73** ©José Antonio Moreno/Age Fotostock. **74–75** ©Sylvain Grandadam/Age Fotostock. **76** (t) ©The Thorburn Group/National Geographic Learning. (c) ©UniversalImagesGroup/Getty Images. **77** ©Mapping Specialists/National Geographic Learning. **78** ©The Thorburn Group/National Geographic Learning. **79** ©Ivan Vdovin/Age Fotostock. **80** ©The Thorburn Group/National Geographic Learning. **81** ©Sheila Terry/Science Source. **82** ©Jonathan Torgovnik/Getty Images. **83** ©Todd Heisler/The New York Times/Redux. **84** ©The Thorburn Group/National Geographic Learning. **85** ©Glenn Beanland/ Lonely Planet Images/Getty Images. **86–87** (t) ©Dea/G.Dagli Orti/De Agostini Picture Library/Getty Images. (b) ©The Metropolitan Museum of Art/Art Resource, NY. (br) ©Bonhams, London, UK /Bridgeman Images. (t) ©RMN-Grand Palais/Art Resource, NY. (c) ©Michael Weber/Image Broker/Alamy Stock Photo. (cr) ©bpk, Berlin/Museum fuer Islamische Kunst/Staatliche Museen/German/Art Resource, NY. **89** (t) ©Tino Soriano/National Geographic Learning. (c) ©Mapping Specialists/National Geographic Learning. **90** ©Jim Haberman. **91** ©Jim Haberman. **92** ©Michael Melford/National Geographic Creative. **94–95** ©Scott Carr/500Prime. **95** ©Christopher DeCorse. **96** (tl) ©De Agostini Picture Lib./G. Dagli Orti/Akg-Images. (tr) ©Douglas Pearson/The Image Bank/Getty Images. (b) ©Universal History Archive/Universal Images Group/Getty Images. **97** (tl) ©Ulrich Doering/Alamy Stock Photo. (tr) ©Bridgeman Giraudon/Art Resource, NY. (b) ©bpk, Berlin/Art Resource, NY. **98** (bl) ©Hoberman Collection/Encyclopedia/Corbis. (br) ©Bill Stormont/Comet/Corbis. **99** ©Mapping Specialists/National Geographic Learning. **100–101** ©Joe Penney/Reuters. **102** ©The Thorburn Group/National Geographic Learning. **103** ©Frans Lemmens/The Image Bank/Getty Images. **104** ©The Thorburn Group/National Geographic Learning. **105** (t) ©Mapping Specialists/National Geographic Learning. (b) ©Fadel Senna/Getty Images. **106** (t) (b) ©The Thorburn Group/National Geographic Learning. **106–107** ©Johnny Haglund/Lonely Planet Images/Getty Images. **108** (t) ©The Thorburn Group/National Geographic Learning. (b) ©Mali: 16th century musical treatise from Timbuktu/Pictures From History / Bridgeman Images. **109** ©Ivern Photo/Age Fotostock. **110** (t) ©CDA/Guillemot/akg-images. (cr) ©Head, 600 BC-AD 250 (terracotta), Nigerian /Cleveland Museum of Art, OH, USA / Andrew R. and Martha Holden Jennings Fund / Bridgeman Images. (br) ©Andrea Jemolo/akg-images. (bl) ©Andrea Jemolo/akg-images. (cl) ©Werner Forman/akg-images. **111** ©The Thorburn Group/National Geographic Learning. **112** ©The Thorburn Group/National Geographic Learning. **113** ©Mapping Specialists/National Geographic Learning. **114** ©The Thorburn Group/National Geographic Learning. **114–115** ©Precision Graphics/National Geographic Learning. **116** (t) (b) ©The Thorburn Group/National Geographic Learning. **117** ©Daniel Lainé/Cosmos/Redux. (bl) ©F.Jimenez Meca/Shutterstock.com. (br) ©Two-stringed instrument, Hausa people (Nigeria), collected between 1960–73 (wood, hide & leather), African, (20th century) /Collection of the Lowe Art Museum, University of Miami / Gift of Professor and Mrs. Robert R. Ferens / Bridgeman Images. (bc) ©Fortune Fish/Alamy Stock Photo. **118** ©Bibliotheque Nationale de France/National Geographic Creative. **119** ©Detail from the Catalan Atlas, 1375 (vellum) (detail of 151844), Cresques, Abraham (1325–87) / Bibliotheque Nationale, Paris, France / Bridgeman Images. **121** (t) ©Joe Penney/Reuters. (b) ©Mapping Specialists/National Geographic Learning. **122–123** ©Jorgen Schytte/StillPictures/Aurora Photos. **124** (t) ©The Thorburn Group/National Geographic Learning. (b) ©Werner Forman/Universal Images Group/Getty Images. **125** ©David Else/Getty Images. (tr) ©Mapping Specialists/National Geographic Learning. **126** ©The Thorburn Group/National Geographic Learning. **127** ©Mapping Specialists/National Geographic Learning. (b) ©John Warburton-Lee/DanitaDelimont.com. **128** ©The Thorburn Group/National Geographic Learning. **129** ©John Warburton Lee/SuperStock. **130** ©The Thorburn Group/National Geographic Learning. **131** ©Mapping Specialists/National Geographic Learning. **132** ©The Thorburn Group/National Geographic Learning. **132–133** ©Stefano Gulmanelli/Marka/Age Fotostock. **133** (b) ©Simon Colmer/Alamy Stock Photo. **134** ©DEA PICTURE LIBRARY/Getty Images. **135** ©The Thorburn Group/National Geographic Learning. **137** (cl) ©National Geographic Learning. (cr) ©Gavin Hellier/AWL Images Ltd. (t) ©Jorgen Schytte/StillPictures/Aurora Photos. **138** ©Christopher DeCorse. **139** ©Christopher DeCorse. **140** ©Jordi Cami/Cover/Getty Images. **142–143** ©Kenneth Garret/National Geographic Creative. **143** (tr) ©Kenneth Garret/National Geographic Creative. **144** (t) ©Album/Art Resource, NY. (b) ©Apic/Hulton Archive/Getty Images. **145** (tl) ©Michel Zabe /AZA/INAH/Bridgeman Images. (tr) ©Gonzalo Azumendi/Age Fotostock. (b) ©Andrea Fremiotti/Gallery Stock/Galeries/Corbis. **146 147** ©Mapping Specialists/National Geographic Learning. **148–149** ©Simon Norfolk/Institute. **150** ©The Thorburn Group/National Geographic Learning. **151** (t) ©Mapping Specialists/National Geographic Learning. (b) ©National Geographic Learning. **152** (b) ©Werner Forman/Universal Images Group/Getty Images. **152** ©The Thorburn Group/National Geographic Learning. **153** ©Kenneth Garrett. **154** ©Gianni Dagli Orti/The Art Archive/Art Resource, NY. **155** ©The Thorburn Group/National Geographic Learning. **156** ©The Thorburn Group/National Geographic Learning. **157** (r) ©Mapping Specialists/National Geographic Learning. (l) ©The Trustees of the British Museum / Art Resource, NY. **158** ©The Thorburn Group/National Geographic Learning. **159** ©Precision Graphics/National Geographic Learning. **160** ©Tyrone Turner/EPA/Alamy Stock Photo. **161** ©Kenneth Garrett/National

Geographic Creative. **162** ©The Thorburn Group/National Geographic Learning. **162–163** ©Egmont Strigl/imagebroker/Age Fotostock. **164** ©Ethnologisches Museum, Staatliche Museen, Berlin, Germany/Art Resource, NY. **166** ©The Thorburn Group/National Geographic Learning. **167** (t) ©Mapping Specialists/National Geographic Learning. (b) ©Quetzacoatl, depicted in a turquoise mosaic mask(15th-16th century). Mixtec-Aztec deity/Universal History Archive/UIG/The Bridgeman Art Library. **168** ©The Thorburn Group/National Geographic Learning. **168–169** ©Kenneth Garret/National Geographic Creative. **169** (b) ©Gianni Dagli Orti/The Art Archive/Art Resource, NY. **170** ©The Thorburn Group/National Geographic Learning. **171** ©Portrait of Montezuma II (oil on canvas), European School, (16th century)/Palazzo Pitti, Florence, Italy/Bridgeman Images. **173** (t) ©Simon Norfolk/Institute. (cl) ©Rahmo/Shutterstock.com. (cr) ©f9photos/Shutterstock.com. (bl) ©Werner Forman/Universal Images Group/Getty Images. **174–175** ©Kenneth Garrett/National Geographic Society/Museos del Banco Central de Costa Rica. **176** ©The Thorburn Group/National Geographic Learning. **177** ©ROBERT CLARK/National Geographic. **178** (t) ©Kenneth Garrett/National Geographic Society/Museos del Banco Central de Costa Rica. (b) ©MUSEO LARCO, LIMA – PERÚ. **178–179** ©Y. Yoshii/PAS. **179** (bl) ©Kenneth Garrett/National Geographic Learning. (br) ©Kenneth Garrett/National Geographic Society/Museos del Banco Central de Costa Rica. **180** ©The Thorburn Group/National Geographic Learning. **181** ©Mapping Specialists/National Geographic Learning. **182** ©The Thorburn Group/National Geographic Learning. **182–183** ©Image Source/Getty Images. **184–185** ©Mireille Vautier/Alamy Stock Photo. **186** ©The Thorburn Group/National Geographic Learning. **187** ©Stuart Dee/Getty Images. **188** ©The Thorburn Group/National Geographic Learning. **189** (t) ©National Geographic Learning. (b) ©Jason Langley/AGE Fotostock. **190** ©The Thorburn Group/National Geographic Learning. **191** ©Joel Sartore/National Geographic Creative. **192** ©The Thorburn Group/National Geographic Learning. **193** (t) ©Wood Ronsaville Harlin Inc/National Geographic Creative. (b) ©Ira Block/National Geographic Creative. **194** ©The Thorburn Group/National Geographic Learning. **195** ©CharlineXia Ontario Canada Collection / Alamy Stock Photo. **197** (t) ©Kenneth Garrett/National Geographic Society/Museos del Banco Central de Costa Rica. (b) ©MIKE THEISS/National Geographic. **198** ©Bruce Smith/National Geographic Creative. **199** ©Kenneth Garrett/National Geographic Creative. **200** ©Kenneth Garrett/National Geographic Creative. **202–203** ©David Santiago Garcia/Aurora Photos. **202** (t) ©Winn Brewer/National Geogrpahic Learning. (bl) ©Hakbong Kwon/Alamy Stock Photo. (br) ©Terence Kong/500Prime. **204–205** ©Hakbong Kwon/Alamy Stock Photo. **205** (tr) ©Erik Jepsen. **206** (t) ©DeA Picture Library/Art Resource, NY. (c) ©DeA Picture Library/Akg-Images. (b) ©British Library/Akg-Images. (b) ©Fine Art Images/Heritage Images/Hulton Fine Art Collection/Getty Images. **207** (t) ©Rabatti - Dominge/Akg-Images. (b) ©Interfoto/Alamy Stock Photo. **208** ©Werner Forman/Universal Images Group/Getty Images. **208–209** ©Mapping Specialists/National Geographic Learning. **210–211** ©Sean Pavone/Alamy Stock photo. **212** ©The Thorburn Group/National Geographic Learning. **213** ©National Geographic Learning. **214** ©The Thorburn Group/National Geographic Learning. **215** ©Vidler Steve/Travelpix/Age Fotostock. **216** ©The Thorburn Group/National Geographic Learning. **217** ©Two camels, Tang Dynasty (618–907) (glazed earthenware), Chinese School / Private Collection / Paul Freeman / Bridgeman Images. **218** ©The Thorburn Group/National Geographic Learning. **219** (cl) ©Science Source. (tr) ©RMN-Grand Palais / Art Resource, NY. (tl) ©hjochen/Shutterstock.com. (cr) ©iBird/Shutterstock.com. **220** ©GL Archive/Alamy Stock Photo. **221** ©National Geographic Learning. **222** ©The Thorburn Group/National Geographic Learning. **223** ©Robert Harding Picture Library/SuperStock. **224** ©Dea/J e Bulloz/AGE Fotostock. **225** ©Erik S. Lesser/epa/Corbis Wire/Corbis. **226** ©The Thorburn Group/National Geographic Learning. **227** ©Precision Graphics/National Geographic Learning. **228** ©The Thorburn Group/National Geographic Learning. **228–229** ©National Geographic Maps. **230** ©The Thorburn Group/National Geographic Learning. **231** ©Precision Graphics/National Geographic Learning. **232** ©O. Louis Mazzatenta/National Geographic Creative. **233** ©Courtesy of Christine Lee. **235** (t) ©Sean Pavone/Alamy Stock photo. (b) ©Ma Xiaoliang/TAO Images Limited/Alamy Stock Photo.

236–237 ©Masterfile. **238** ©The Thorburn Group/National Geographic Learning. **239** ©Mapping Specialists/National Geographic Learning. **240** ©The Thorburn Group/National Geographic Learning. **240–241** ©Deco/Alamy Stock Photo. **242** ©Vanni Archive/ Art Resource, NY. **243** ©The Thorburn Group/National Geographic Learning. **244** ©The Thorburn Group/National Geographic Learning. **245** ©Kazuhiro Nogi/Staff/Getty Images. **246** (t) ©The Thorburn Group/National Geographic Learning. (b) ©rodho/Shutterstock.com. **247** ©Quim Llenas/Cover/Getty Images. **248** ©Illustration from 'The Tale of Genji' (colour woodblock print), Kunisada, Utagawa (1786–1864) / Private Collection / Bridgeman Images. **250** ©The Thorburn Group/National Geographic Learning. **251** ©Catherine Karnow/Corbis. **252** (tl) ©The Thorburn Group/National Geographic Learning. (b) ©Asian Art & Archaeology, Inc./Corbis. **252–253** ©Warner Brothers/Everett Collection. **254–255** ©The Ann & Gabriel Barbier-Mueller Museum: The Samurai Collection, Dallas, Texas.Photograph by Brad Flowers. **256** ©The Thorburn Group/National Geographic Learning. **257** ©Newark Museum/Art Resource, NY. **259** ©Masterfile. (b) ©Precision Graphics/National Geographic Learning. **260–261** ©TOPIC PHOTO AGENCY IN/Topic Photo Agency/AGE Fotostock. **262** ©The Thorburn Group/National Geographic Learning. **263** ©Mapping Specialists/National Geographic Learning. **264** (t) ©DeA Picture Library/Art Resource, NY. (cr) ©The Metropolitan Museum of Art. Image source/Art Resource, NY. (c) Jade teardrop-shapes set in gold, from tomb of King ©Muryong, Kyongju, South Korea, Goldsmith's art, Korean Civilisation, Kingdom of Baekje, Three Kingdoms period, 5th-6th century / De Agostini Picture Library/Bridgeman Images. (b) ©Erich Lessing/Art Resource, NY. (tr) ©DeA Picture Library/Art Resource, NY. **265** (cl) ©DeAgostini/Superstock. (b) ©Avalokitesvara, bodhisattva of great compassion, gilded bronze statue, Korea, Korean Civilisation, Three Kingdoms period, 6th-7th century / De Agostini Picture Library / Bridgeman Images. (tl) ©Vase with figurines, From tomb of King Michu / De Agostini Picture Library / Bridgeman Images. **266** ©The Thorburn Group/National Geographic Learning. **267** ©Chorus of women, detail from Amrita-Raja banner, 1755, color on silk, ambrosia painting, 18th century, Korean Civilization, Joseon dynasty / De Agostini Picture Library / G. Dagli Orti / Bridgeman Images. **268** ©The Thorburn Group/National Geographic Learning. **268–269** ©Eye Ubiquitous/Eye biquitous/Superstock. **270** Moustafellou/IML/ Icarus/Age Fotostock. (tr) ©Mapping Specialists/National Geographic Learning. **271** ©The Thorburn Group/National Geographic Learning. **273** (t) ©Danish Siddiqui/REUTERS. (bl) © The Metropolitan Museum of Art. Image source: Art Resource, NY. (bc) ©V&A Images, London/Art Resource, NY. (br) © Smart-foto/Shutterstock.com. (t) ©Vivek Prakash/Reuters. **274** ©The Thorburn Group/National Geographic Learning. **275** ©Mapping Specialists/National Geographic Learning. **276** ©The Thorburn Group/National Geographic Learning. **277** ©BODY Philippe/hemis.fr/Getty Images. **278** ©The Thorburn Group/National Geographic Learning. **278–279** ©W.E. GARRETT/National Geographic Creative. **281** (t) ©TOPIC PHOTO AGENCY IN/Topic Photo Agency/AGE Fotostock. (b) ©Mapping Specialists/National Geographic Learning. **282** ©Ben Horton. **283** ©Erik Jepsen. **284** ©Robert Clark/National Geographic Creative. **286–287** ©Terence Kong/500Prime. **287** (tr) ©Rocco Rorandelli/TerraProject/Contrasto/Redux. **288** (t) Dea/A. DagliI Orti/De Agostini/Getty Images. (c) ©Gianni Dagli Orti/Fine Art Premium/Corbis. (b) Ronaldo Schemidt/AFP/Getty Images. **289** (t) ©Science & Society Picture Library/Getty Images. (b) JTB Photo/JTB Media Creation/Alamy stock Photo. **290–291** ©Mapping Specialists/National Geographic Learning. **290** (bl) ©Universal History Archive/Universal Images Group/Getty Images. (br) ©National Gallery, London/Art Resource, NY. **291**(bl) Alinari Archives/Fine Art/Corbis. (bc) ©The Metropolitan Museum of Art. Image source: Art Resource, NY. (br) Dea/G. Nimatallah/De Agostini Picture Library/Getty Images. **292–293** ©Slawek Staszczuk/500px. **294** ©The Thorburn Group/National Geographic Learning. **295** ©Mapping Specialists/National Geographic Learning. **296** ©Dea/A.Dagli Orti/De Agostini/Getty Images. **297** ©Stefano Baldini/Age Fotostock. **298** ©Robert Clark/National Geographic Creative. **299** ©Mapping Specialists/National Geographic Learning. **300** ©Precision Graphics/National Geographic Learning. **301** ©The Thorburn Group/National

Geographic Learning. ©The Thorburn Group/National Geographic Learning. **302–303** (t) ©The Board of Trustees of the Armouries/Heritage-Images/The Image Works. (b) ©Nikreates/Alamy Stock Photo. (c) ©Ivan Smuk/Alamy Stock Photo. **303** (br) ©Dea/A.Dagli Orti/De Agostini Picture Library/Getty Images. **304** ©The Thorburn Group/National Geographic Learning. **305** ©Precision Graphics/National Geographic Learning. **306** ©The Thorburn Group/National Geographic Learning. **307** ©Xavier Arnau Serrat/Photographer's Choice/Getty Images. **308** ©The Thorburn Group/National Geographic Learning. **308–309** ©Sebastian Wasek/Age Fotostock. **310** ©Stapleton Collection/Corbis. **312** ©The Thorburn Group/National Geographic Learning. **313** (t) ©Mapping Specialists/National Geographic Learning. (b) ©Scala/Art Resource, NY. **314** ©The Thorburn Group/National Geographic Learning. **315** (t) ©British Library Board/Robana/Art Resource, NY. (b) Historiated Initial depicting Joan of Arc (1412–31), 15th century (vellum), French School, (15th century) / Centre Historique des Archives Nationales, Paris, France / Archives Charmet / Bridgeman Images. **316–317** ©Scala/Art Resource, NY. **318** ©The Thorburn Group/National Geographic Learning. **318–319** ©Jon Bower/Loop Images/Age Fotostock. **321** (t) ©Slawek Staszczuk/500px. **322–323** ©Francesco Riccardo Iacomino/500px. **324** ©The Thorburn Group/National Geographic Learning. **325** ©Sistine Chapel (Cappella Sistina), by Michelangelo Buonarroti, 16th Century, fresco (post restoration), Buonarroti, Michelangelo (1475–1564)/Musei e Gallerie Pontificie, Musei Vaticani, Vatican City / Mondadori Portfolio / Bridgeman Images. **326** (t) ©The Thorburn Group/National Geographic Learning. (b) ©Scala/Art Resource, NY. **327** ©Fernando G. Baptista/National Geographic Creative. **328–329** ©Image Asset Management/World History Archive/age fotostock. **330** ©The Thorburn Group/National Geographic Learning. **331** Alinari/Art Resource, NY. **332** ©SuperStock. **333** ©Mona Lisa, c.1503–6 (oil on panel), Vinci, Leonardo da (1452–1519) / Louvre, Paris, France/Bridgeman Images. **334** ©David Yoder/National Geographic Creative. **335** ©Eric Kruszewski/National Geographic Creative. **336** ©The Thorburn Group/National Geographic Learning. **337** ©Imagno/Getty Images. **338** ©Portrait of William Shakespeare (oil on canvas), Taylor, John (d.1651) (after)/Private Collection / Photo ©Philip Mould Ltd, London / Bridgeman Images. **339** ©20th Century Fox/The Kobal Collection/Morton, Merrick/Picture-Desk. **340** ©The Thorburn Group/National Geographic Learning. **341** (bl) ©Lebrecht Music & Arts/Fine Art/Corbis. (t) ©Precision Graphics/National Geographic Learning. **342** ©The Thorburn Group/National Geographic Learning. **343** (tl) ©Charles Kogod/National Geographic Creative. (tr) GraphicaArtis/Fine Art/Corbis. (bl) ©Brian Jannsen/age fotostock/Getty Images. (br) ©Konstantin L/Shutterstock.com. (bc) ©Itsmejust/Shutterstock.com. (cr) ©Details Michelangelo Buonarroti (1475–1564) David, detail of head in profile. Location: Accademia, Florence, Italy Photo Credit: Scala / Art Resource, NY. **344** Portrait of King Henry VIII (1491–1547),c.1575 (oil on panel), English School, (16th century) / Private Collection/ Photo ©Philip Mould Ltd, London / Bridgeman Images. **344** ©The Thorburn Group/National Geographic Learning. **345** ©Mapping Specialists/National Geographic Learning. **346** ©Fine Art Photographic Library/Fine Art/Corbis. **347** ©Mansell/Getty Images. **348** ©The Thorburn Group/National Geographic Learning. **349** ©Mapping Specialists/National Geographic Learning. **350** ©The Thorburn Group/National Geographic Learning. **351** ©Wojtek Buss/age fotostock. **353** ©Francesco Riccardo Iacomino/500px. (cl) ©Scala/Art Resource, NY. (cr) ©Nimatallah/Art Resource, NY. **354–355** ©Dave Yoder/National Geographic Creative. **356** ©The Thorburn Group/National Geographic Learning. **357** ©Scenographia Systematis Mundani/British Library, London, UK/British Library Board. All Rights Reserved/Bridgeman Images. **358** ©The Thorburn Group/National Geographic Learning. **359** (tr) ©Science & Society Picture Library/Getty Images. (tc) ©Replica of Newton's colour wheel, 17th century/Dorling Kindersley/UIG/Bridgeman Images. (tl) ©Clive Streeter/Dorling Kindersley/Science Museum, London/Science Source. **360** ©The Thorburn Group/National Geographic Learning. **361** ©De Agostini Picture Library/G. Costa/Bridgeman Images. **362** ©Mapping Specialists/National Geographic Learning. **363** ©The Thorburn Group/National Geographic Learning. **364** ©The Thorburn Group/National Geographic Learning. **365** ©National Geographic Learning.

366–367 ©James L. Stanfield/National Geographic Creative. **368** ©Reuters. **369** ©Ullstein Bild/akg-images. **370** (t) (b) ©The Thorburn Group/National Geographic Learning. **371** ©National Geographic Learning. **372** ©The Thorburn Group/National Geographic Learning. **373** ©Diego Rivera/akg-images. **374** ©The Thorburn Group/National Geographic Learning. **375** ©Robert Clark/National Geographic. **376** ©The Thorburn Group/National Geographic Learning. **377** ©Precision Graphics/National Geographic Learning. **379** (t) ©Dave Yoder/National Geographic Creative. (b) ©Mapping Specialists/National Geographic Learning. **380–381** Rick Lacoume/500Prime. **382** ©The Thorburn Group/National Geographic Learning. **383** (b) ©DEA/G.Dagli Orti/Getty Images. (t) ©Leemage/Corbis. **384** ©The Thorburn Group/National Geographic Learning. **385** (tl) ©After Nicholas de Largilliere/Getty Images. (cl) ©Fine Art Images/Heritage Images/Getty Images. (tr) ©De Agostini Editore/Age Fotostock. (cr) ©bpk, Berlin/Art Resource, NY. **386** ©The Thorburn Group/National Geographic Learning. **387** (t) ©Charles Platiau/Reuters. (c) ©Active Museum/Alamy Stock Photo. **388** ©The Thorburn Group/National Geographic Learning. **389** ©H. Mark Weidman Photography/Alamy Stock Photo. **390** ©The Thorburn Group/National Geographic Learning. **391** ©The Gallery Collection/Corbis. **392–393** ©RMN-Grand Palais/Art Resource, NY. **394** (t) (b) ©The Thorburn Group/National Geographic Learning. **395** Alfredo Dagli Orti / The Art Archive at Art Resource, NY. **396** ©Capitol Collection, Washington, USA/Bridgeman Images. **399** (t) ©Rick Lacoume/500Prime. (b) ©Mapping Specialists/National Geographic Learning. **400** ©Dave Yoder/Aurora Photos/Alamy Stock Photo. **401** Dave Yoder/National Geographic Creative. **402** ©Dave Yoder/National Geographic Creative. **404–405** ©O. Louis Mazzatenta/National Geographic Creative. **404** (c) ©Winn Brewer/National Geogrpahic Learning. **406** (tr) ©2014 Dotjang Agany Awer/National Geographic Photo Camp South Sudan. (cl) ©ed nazarko/500px. (c) ©2014 Emmanuela Henry Andrew Kenyi/National Geographic Photo Camp South Sudan. (cr) ©Bobby Haas/National Geographic Creative. (bl) ©David Doubilet/National Geographic Creative. (br 2) ©Jose Luis Gonzalez/Reuters. (br 1) ©Mahmoud Hebbo/REUTERS. **407** (tl) ©Alexandre Meneghini/Reuters. (cl) ©David Doubilet/National Geographic Creative. (bl) ©AP Images/Richard Drew. (bl) ©JD Dallet/arabianEye/Getty Images. (tr©2014 Dotjang Agany Awer/National Geographic Photo Camp South Sudan. **408** ©Stringer/Reuters. **409** ©Erin West Kephart/National Geographic Learning. **410** (t) ©Bobby Haas/National Geographic Creative. (cr) (cl) (bl) ©Shah Selbe. **411** (cr) (bl) ©Shah Selbe. **412** (tl) ©2014 Simon Odhol/National Geographic Photo Camp South Sudan. (tc) ©2014 Catherine Simon Arona Samuel/National Geographic Photo Camp South Sudan. (tr) ©2014 Dotjang Agany Awer/National Geographic Photo Camp South Sudan. (cl) ©2014 Holly Moses Edward/National Geographic Photo Camp South Sudan. (c) ©2014 Simon Odhol/National Geographic Photo Camp South Sudan. (cr) ©2014 Duku Stephen Savio/National Geographic Photo Camp South Sudan. (bl) ©2014 Duku Stephen Savio/National Geographic Photo Camp South Sudan. (bc) ©2014 Lisok James Moses/National Geographic Photo Camp South Sudan. (br) ©2014 Samuel Oyet Faustino/National Geographic Photo Camp South Sudan. **413** ©2014 Lisok James Moses/National Geographic Photo Camp South Sudan. **414** ©Beverly Joubert/National Geographic Creative. **R1** ©Kenneth Garrett/ National Geographic Creative.

Map Credits

Unless otherwise indicated, all maps were created by Mapping Specialists.

Illustrator Credits

Unless otherwise indicated, all illustrations were created by Precision Graphics.

Terra cotta statues surround Chinese emperor Shi Huangdi's tomb and are thought to have helped guide him into the afterlife.

IT'S ABOUT BEING A GLOBAL CITIZEN.

As a global citizen, you are empowered to act responsibly in the 21st century by showing empathy and respect for others, making informed decisions and finding your own voice, and actively participating in a rich and diverse environment. Go for it!

NATIONAL GEOGRAPHIC

STORIES MAKING
HISTORY